# Hubley Toy Catalogs
## 1946-1965

Steve Butler

4880 Lower Valley Road, Atglen, PA 19310 USA

Library of Congress Control Number: 2001099723



The Author welcomes comments concerning the information in this book as well as Hubley toy vehicles that may be purchased to expand his collection. Please address these matters to:

Steve Butler
2696 Brookmar Dr.
York, PA 17404

Additional copies of this book and of ***Hubley Toy Vehicles 1946-1965*** signed by the author may be ordered for $29.95 plus $3.00 for postage and handling for each from the Author at the above address.

Designed by Bonnie M. Hensley
Cover design by Bruce M. Waters
Type set in Korinna BT

ISBN: 0-7643-1563-3
Printed in China
1 2 3 4

Published by Schiffer Publishing Ltd.
4880 Lower Valley Road
Atglen, PA 19310
Phone: (610) 593-1777; Fax: (610) 593-2002
E-mail: Schifferbk@aol.com
Please visit our web site catalog at **www.schifferbooks.com**
We are always looking for people to write books on new and related subjects.
If you have an idea for a book please contact us at the above address.

This book may be purchased from the publisher.
Include $3.95 for shipping.
Please try your bookstore first.
You may write for a free catalog.

In Europe, Schiffer books are distributed by
Bushwood Books
6 Marksbury Ave.
Kew Gardens
Surrey TW9 4JF England
Phone: 44 (0) 20 8392-8585; Fax: 44 (0) 20 8392-9876
E-mail: Bushwd@aol.com
Free postage in the U.K., Europe; air mail at cost.

# CONTENTS

# PROLOGUE

*I have been collecting Hubley toy vehicles for many years, possibly because I was the proud owner of several in my earlier years. A little over a year ago that avocation, supplemented by the support of my wife and my publisher, provided the inspiration for my book titled* **Hubley Toy Vehicles 1946-1965**.

*Occasionally I would have the unusual opportunity to acquire an original Hubley factory catalog. Those catalogs became my most useful and most frequented reference source regarding the post-World War II Hubley toy vehicles I was and am collecting. However, I'd often have to look through multiple catalogs to obtain information I was seeking. To avoid further deterioration of my catalogs, which themselves are of significant value, and to facilitate the reference process, I began to enter all of the information related to toy vehicles from the catalogs into a computer file and printed out that file for my use.*

*Twenty-one of these Hubley factory catalogs covering primarily toy vehicles from 1946 through 1965 have been essential in my collecting efforts. They are the same catalogs used to create my computer files which subsequently became the detail listings included in my book* **Hubley Toy Vehicles 1946-1965**. *After all, it seemed there was no better reference source regarding the toys I owned or still hoped to own than the information published by the manufacturer. All twenty-one catalogs are duplicated herein. Perhaps you'll find them as interesting and useful as I have.*

Steve Butler
January, 2002

# INTRODUCTION

Essentially, three types of catalogs have been used to move products from the inventories of toy manufacturers into the hands of owners. These are retailer, distributor and factory catalogs.

Retailer catalogs are the most common of the three types and, thereby, usually the least valuable. Sears' catalogs are very common and serve as good examples. Other national retailers issued catalogs as did a myriad of local businesses such as department stores and hardware stores. These types of catalogs are often colorful although sometimes issued on inexpensive paper stock. Retailer catalogs cover only the toys offered by the issuer and reflect the prices sought by that seller. Further, the catalogs may contain overstock and obsolete items from prior periods. For that reason and because of their otherwise limited scope and variances in pricing, retailer catalogs tend to be of marginal use to toy collectors.

Distributors (or wholesalers) ordered toys from manufacturers for resale to primarily local retailers. Distributors thus tended to operate on a more regional basis. They include companies like the Edw. K. Tryon Co. of Philadelphia, and Ohio firms such as Williams Wholesale Distributors, John J. Getreu & Sons, and Bostwick-Braun Company. Distributor catalogs cover a much wider range of toys than retailer catalogs and tend to be printed on better paper stock but often in black-and-white. The prices shown in distributor catalogs are typically suggested list prices and thus more consistent than prices in retailer catalogs. A separate "confidential" price list is usually provided as a supplement. Obsolete items can be found in distributor catalogs, but much less frequently. That, combined with their wider scope and more consistent pricing, makes distributor catalogs of more use to collectors.

Factory catalogs are limited to the products of the manufacturer (in this case Hubley). They are intended for distribution to distributors and retailers alike. Thus, the prices included in the catalogs or provided as supplements are virtually always wholesale prices and may include suggested retail prices as well. Illustrations are typically in full color and accompanied by descriptive and packaging information as well. The paper stock used is often of improved quality as compared to retailer and distributor catalogs. The type of information and the level of detail presented make them of optimum use to collectors and thus the most valuable of the three types of catalogs.

However, it should be noted that factory catalogs must be prepared much more in advance than distributor and retailer catalogs in order to determine potential sales and to plan production accordingly. For that reason factory catalogs often reflect preproduction planning as opposed to actual production. Very infrequently factory catalogs will include toys never produced. The 1941 Tootsietoy issue is an example. (This situation has not been observed in Hubley catalogs used for this book.) More often, factory catalogs will list or depict a toy in a color other than issued or with features or accessories that never made it into production. (This situation does occur infrequently in the Hubley catalogs.)

# FACTORY CATALOGS

Reproduced in this section are twenty-one original factory catalogs issued by the Hubley Manufacturing Company from 1946 until their acquisition by Gabriel Industries in 1966. The catalogs cover primarily toy vehicles, but do include numerous toy guns and several other Hubley products such as banks and craft items. The 424 pages are presented as found in those original catalogs except for the reduction from their original 8.5" by 11" size and in full color as applicable which is primarily the case.

Some of the pages have annotations made by their original (i.e., business or buyer) owners. These annotations may include pricing, intended order items, out-of-stock items and the like, and can be of interest as well. Some of the toys are depicted via photos but most are via excellent factory artwork. For some toys the actual packaging is shown as well.

Hubley assigned a model name and model number to virtually all of its products. That information accompanies the depiction of each toy as well as other information such as size, color(s), accessories, and the like. Note that the lengths provided are usually correct but may vary depending upon any overhang for the likes of truck ladders and booms. The colors listed are typically correct as well, but very infrequently do not agree with the artwork shown. In addition there are a few examples of colors listed but not issued and omissions of colors known to have been issued. (Refer to *Hubley Toy Vehicles 1946-1965* for these and other variances between catalogs and actual production.)

The catalogs are presented in order by year from 1946 through 1965. Most of the catalogs have the year printed on their cover page. Others such as the 1949 issues do not which indicates they were intended for multi-year use.

# CATALOGS 1946 - 1965

# 1946

# HUBLEY

# METAL TOYS

It's A HUBLEY TOY

## *Spring Line 1946*

*Export Sales Representative*

GUITERMAN COMPANY, INC.

35 South William Street, New York 4, N. Y.

Cable Address - Guiterman New York

PRINTED IN U. S. A.

DECEMBER 1, 1945

THE HUBLEY MANUFACTURING COMPANY

LANCASTER, PENNSYLVANIA

# HUBLEY TOYS

Here is the Hubley Toy Line for the Spring of 1946—only a few numbers, but the kind of toys for which children have been looking and longing, during four long years of war.

Since 1942 The Hubley Manufacturing Company has been devoting all its efforts to the production of vital war materials but, now that Victory has been won, can once again turn to the business of making children happy.

Each item, here pictured, is reproduced in accurate detail, painted in attractive colors, and will find a ready market in any toy department.

* * * * * *

# HUBLEY *CAST IRON* BANKS

No. 818 Mammy Bank

[illegible]

No. 820 Kitty Bank

[illegible]

No. 823 Fido Bank

[illegible]

# HUBLEY METAL *KIDDIE* TOYS

## (DIE CAST)

**No. 441 U. S. Army Plane**

[illegible]

**No. 452 Deluxe Sedan**

[illegible]

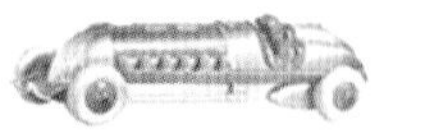

**No. 456 Racer**

[illegible]

**No. 455 U. S. Army Plane**

[illegible]

**No. 473 Hook & Ladder**

[illegible]

1946

# HUBLEY "*HUBOID*" TOYS

**No. 100 Scotty**

Length 5 inches; height $4\frac{1}{4}$ inches.
Packed 1 in a box; 3 dozen to a carton. Weight per carton 20 lbs. gross; 18 lbs. net.
Black with Red Collar and Red Wheels. Furnished with Pull Cord and Ball.
Dimensions: $14\frac{1}{2}$" x $11\frac{1}{2}$" x $13\frac{3}{4}$".

**No. 120 Ducky-Wucky**

Length $4\frac{3}{4}$ inches; height $4\frac{3}{4}$ inches.
Packed 1 in a box; 3 dozen to a carton. Weight per carton 20 lbs. gross; 18 lbs. net.
White with Yellow Hat, Blue Ribbon, Blue Base and Red Wheels. Furnished with Pull Cord and Ball.
Dimensions: $14\frac{1}{4}$" x $10\frac{3}{4}$" x $15\frac{3}{4}$".

**No. 105 Mary's Lamb**

Length $4\frac{3}{4}$ inches; height $4\frac{1}{2}$ inches.
Packed 1 in a box; 3 dozen to a carton. Weight per carton 19 lbs. gross; 17 lbs. net.
White with Blue Ribbon and Red Wheels. Furnished with Pull Cord and Ball.
Dimensions: $14\frac{1}{2}$" x $11\frac{1}{2}$" x $13\frac{3}{4}$".

**No. 125 Tractor**

Length $5\frac{3}{4}$ inches; height $3\frac{3}{4}$ inches.
Packed 1 in a box; 3 dozen to a carton. Weight per carton 25 lbs. gross; 21 lbs. net.
Red with Black Rubber Wheels.
Dimensions: 14" x $11\frac{3}{4}$" x $17\frac{5}{8}$".

# 1947

# HUBLEY

# TOY LINE

It's A HUBLEY TOY

*Spring Line 1947*

Printed in U. S. A.

January 1, 1947

THE HUBLEY MANUFACTURING COMPANY

LANCASTER, PENNSYLVANIA

## HUBLEY "*HUBOID*" TOYS

**No. 100 Scotty**

Length 5 inches; height 4¾ inches.
Packed 1 in a box; 3 dozen to a carton. Weight per carton 18 lbs.
Black with Red Collar and Red Wheels.

**No. 120 Ducky-Wucky**

Length 4¾ inches; height 4¼ inches.
Packed 1 in a box; 3 dozen to a carton. Weight per carton 19 lbs.
White with Yellow Hat, Blue Ribbon, Blue Base and Red Wheels.

**No. 105 Mary's Lamb**

Length 4¾ inches; height 4½ inches.
Packed 1 in a box; 3 dozen to a carton. Weight per carton 17 lbs.
White with Blue Ribbon and Red Wheels.

**No. 125 Tractor**

Length 5¾ inches; height 3¾ inches.
Packed 1 in a box; 3 dozen to a carton. Weight per carton 24 lbs.
Red with Black Rubber Wheels.

## HUBLEY "*HUBOID*" TOYS

TWO NEW SPRING ITEMS

**No. 110 Panda**

Length 5 inches; height 3¾ inches.
Packed 1 in a box; 3 dozen to a carton. Weight per carton 22 lbs.
Black and White with Red Rubber Wheels.

**No. 115 Elephant**

Length 5 inches; height 4 inches.
Packed 1 in a box; 3 dozen to a carton. Weight per carton 21 lbs.
Grey with Red Blanket and Red Rubber Wheels.

## HUBLEY *CAST IRON* BANKS

**No. 818 Mammy Bank**

Height 5½ inches.
Packed 1 in box, 1 doz. to carton; weight per carton, 13 lbs.
Painted in Natural Colors.

**No. 820 Kitty Bank**

Height 5¼ inches.
Packed 1 in a designed box; 1 dozen to carton. Weight per carton 20 lbs.
Painted White with Pink or Blue Ribbons.

**No. 823 Fido Bank**

Height 5 inches.
Packed 1 in box; 1 dozen to carton. Weight per carton 23 lbs.
Painted White with Black Ears.

# HUBLEY METAL *KIDDIE* TOYS

## (DIE CAST)

No. 452 Deluxe Sedan

Length 7 inches.
Packed 6 in a box; 3 dozen to a carton. Weight per carton 20 lbs.
Assorted Colors. Rubber Tired Wheels.

No. 455 U. S. Army Plane

Length 6 inches.
Packed 6 in a box; 3 dozen to a carton. Weight per carton 20 lbs.
Painted Red and Aluminum. Furnished with Retractable Landing Gear and Rubber Tired Wheels.

It's A HUBLEY TOY

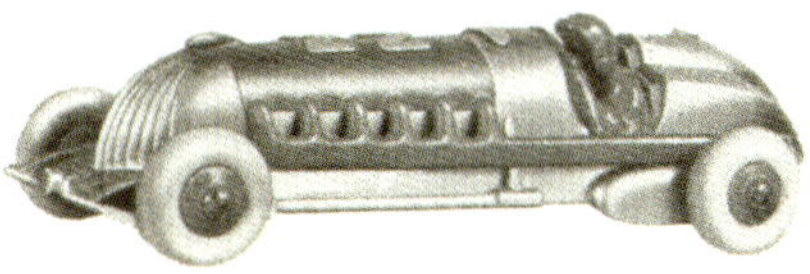

No. 456 Racer

Length 7½ inches.
Packed 6 in a box; 3 dozen to a carton. Weight per carton 24 lbs.
Painted Red and Aluminum. Rubber Tired Wheels.

No. 473 Hook & Ladder

Length 10 inches.
Packed 1 in a box; 1 dozen to a carton. Weight per carton 14 lbs.
Painted Red with Nickel Trimming and Ladders. Rubber Tired Wheels.

# 1948

# KIDDIE TOYS CREATED BY

# HUBLEY

MEMBER OF TOY MFRS. U.S.A.
TRADE MARK AMERICAN TOYS

## HUBLEY "KIDDIE" TOYS

*"They look just like real ones"*

The toy-buyer finds in any catalog a bewildering assortment of items from which to make the selection of those numbers which his experience tells him will win the hearts of the children and the dollars of the grown-ups. To successfully select those toys which will fill both demands requires a shrewd judgment coupled with some experience.

Every toy in this catalog has a definite appeal to some group of prospective customers.

### Made to Sell

Hubley Toys are made to sell. They are produced in large quantities in a modern factory and can therefore be "priced right." But most important of all, they are designed and finished with the appeal to both children and parents in mind. Their accurate details, bright and permanent finish, novel "play" features, and sturdy strength assure them a prominent place on the counters of any toy store or toy department.

THE HUBLEY MANUFACTURING CO.

LANCASTER, PENNSYLVANIA

Catalog 25

No. 462 Tow Truck

Scale model.
Length, 7 inches.
Packed 1 in a box; 3 dozen to a carton.
Weight per carton, 25 lbs.
Four assorted colors, aluminum sides, and movable boom.
Rubber wheels.

No. 458 Convert-ible

Scale model.
Length, 7¼ inches.
Packed 1 in a box; 3 dozen to a carton.
Weight per carton, 22 lbs.
Assorted colors with nickel windshield.
Rubber wheels.

No. 457 Racer

Scale model.
Length, 7 inches.
Packed 1 in a box; 3 dozen to a carton.
Weight per carton, 21 lbs.
Assorted colors with nickel man.
Rubber wheels.

No. 459 Taxi Cab

Scale model.
Length, 7 inches.
Packed 1 in a box; 3 dozen to a carton.
Weight per carton, 21 lbs.
Orange and black combination.
Rubber wheels.



1948



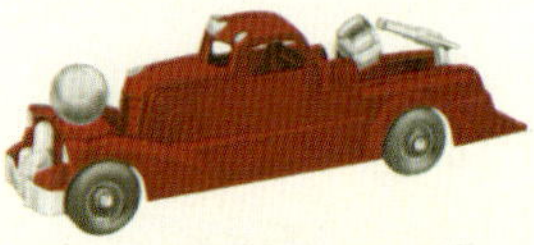

No. 453 Fire Engine

Scale model.
Length, 7¼ inches.
Packed 1 in a box; 3 dozen to a carton.
Weight per carton, 24 lbs.
Red, with aluminum ball, nickel searchlight and nozzle.
Rubber wheels.

No. 454 Hook and Ladder

Scale model.
Length, 7¼ inches.
Packed 1 in a box; 3 dozen to a carton.
Weight per carton, 23 lbs.
Red with aluminum trimming, two nickel ladders.
Rubber wheels.

No. 461 Pick-up Truck

Scale model.
Length, 7 inches.
Packed 1 in a box; 3 dozen to a carton.
Weight per carton, 25 lbs.
Four assorted colors, aluminum sides and drop end gate.
Rubber wheels.

No. 460 Stake Truck

Scale model.
Length, 7 inches.
Packed 1 in a box; 3 dozen to a carton.
Weight per carton, 24 lbs.
Four assorted colors, aluminum sides and drop end gate.
Rubber wheels.

No. 475 Tractor

Scale model.
Length, 6¾ inches.
Packed 1 in a box; 1 dozen to a carton.
Weight per carton, 15 lbs.
Red with blue man.
Black rubber wheels with painted disc.

No. 470
Stake
Truck

Scale model.
Length, 9½ inches.
Packed 1 in a box; 1 dozen to a carton.
Weight per carton, 18 lbs.
Orange chassis, black body, aluminum trimming and nickel sides.
Rubber wheels.

No. 471
Lumber
Truck

Scale model.
Length, 9½ inches.
Packed 1 in a box; 1 dozen to a carton.
Weight per carton, 17 lbs.
Red chassis, black body, aluminum trimming.
Complete with load of 12 pieces lumber.
Rubber wheels.

No. 472
Hook and
Ladder

Scale model.
Length, 10¼ inches.
Packed 1 in a box; 1 dozen to a carton.
Weight per carton, 19 lbs.
Red with aluminum trimming, three nickel ladders and revolving ladder turret and two nickel axes.
Rubber wheels.

No. 474
Tow
Truck

Scale model.
Length, 9¾ inches.
Packed 1 in a box; 1 dozen to a carton.
Weight per carton, 14 lbs.
Red with nickel searchlight, winch and boom.
Rubber wheels.



1948

No. 10 Taxi Cab Set

Box dimensions, 11¼ x 8 inches.
Packed 1 set of three taxicabs to a box; 1 dozen sets to a carton.
Weight per carton, 24 lbs.
Two-tone finish, three assorted colors to set. Beautiful display box.
All toys equipped with rubber wheels.

No. 20 Midget Racer Set

Box dimensions, 11¼ x 8 inches.
Packed 1 set of three racers to a box; 1 dozen sets to a carton.
Weight per carton, 24 lbs.
Three assorted colors to set.
All toys equipped with nickel man and rubber wheels. Beautiful display box.

## HUBLEY "KIDDIE" TOYS ★

**No. 30 Fire Department**

Box dimensions, 14½ x 11 inches.
Packed 1 set to a box; 1 dozen sets to a carton.
Weight per carton, 33 lbs.
Set consists of Fire Engine, Hook and Ladder, Fire Chief's car, Motorcycle, two nickel ladders and two nickel axes.
All toys painted red with aluminum trimming and rubber wheels. Beautiful display box.



## HUBLEY "KIDDIE" TOYS ★

**No. 500 Tractor Trailer Truck**

**"Three in One" Toy**

Length, 17½ inches.
Packed 1 in a box; ½ dozen to a carton.
Weight per carton, 35 lbs.
Red with aluminum trimming.
Furnished with removable aluminum sides; also load of logs and chains to make a lumber truck. Knee action rear wheels; 14 black rubber tires and retractable trailer support with two red rubber wheels.
Attractive individual box.

From this attractive all die cast toy can be made three separate and distinct vehicles. By removing the metal stakes, the toy is transformed into a flat bottom truck. The logs, chains and springs furnished can be put into place, making a lumber truck, as illustrated.

IT'S A HUBLEY TOY

PRINTED IN U. S. A.

# 1949
# METAL

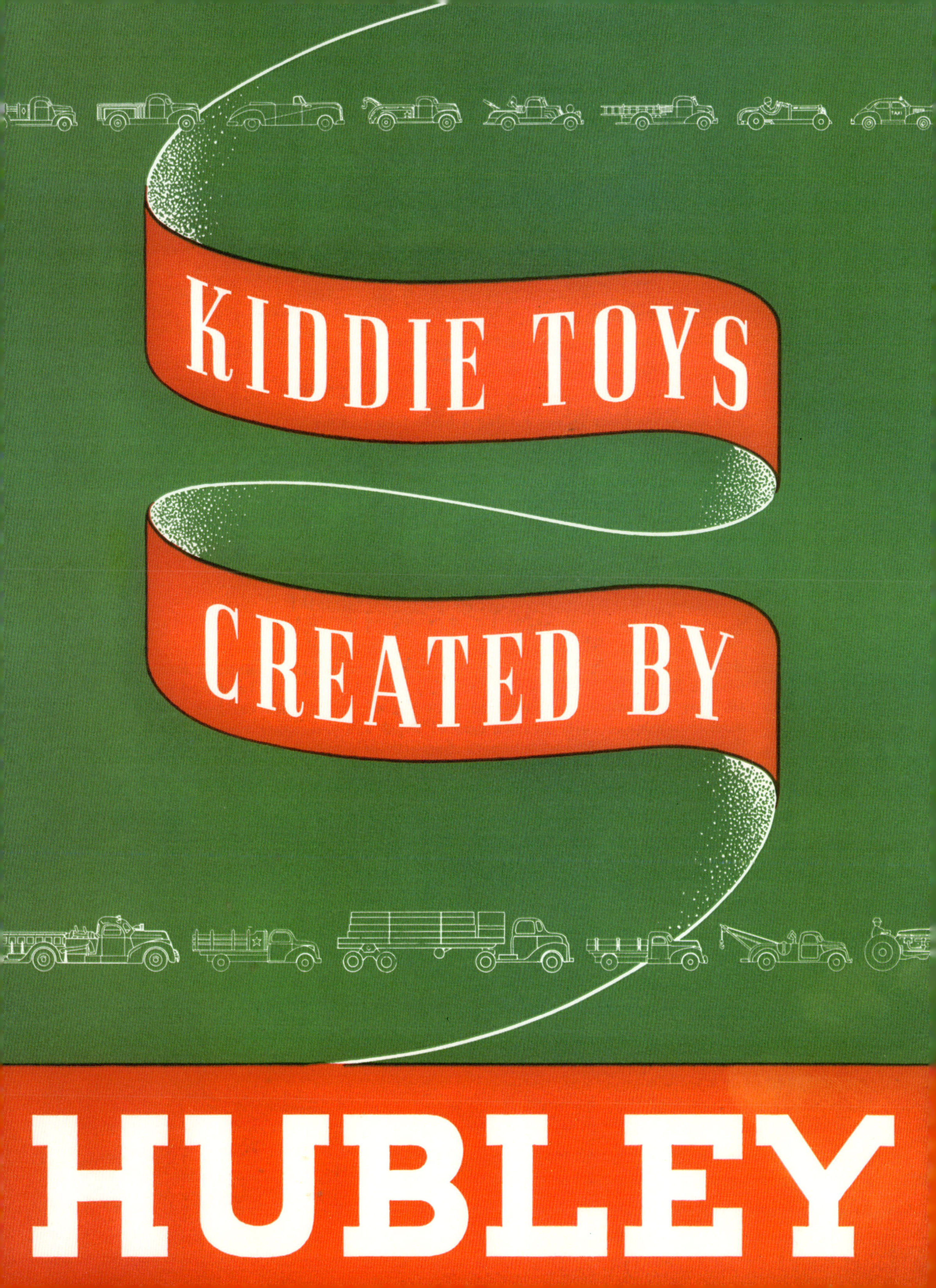
KIDDIE TOYS
CREATED BY
HUBLEY

# HUBLEY "KIDDIE" TOYS

*"They look just like real ones"*

The toy-buyer finds in any catalog a bewildering assortment of items from which to make the selection of those numbers which his experience tells him will win the hearts of the children and the dollars of the grown-ups. To successfully select those toys which will fill both demands requires a shrewd judgment coupled with some experience.

Every toy in this catalog has a definite appeal to some group of prospective customers.

## Made to Sell

Hubley Toys are made to sell. They are produced in large quantities in a modern factory and can therefore be "priced right." But most important of all, they are designed and finished with the appeal to both children and parents in mind. Their accurate details, bright and permanent finish, novel "play" features, and sturdy strength assure them a prominent place on the counters of any toy store or toy department.

THE HUBLEY MANUFACTURING CO.

LANCASTER, PENNSYLVANIA

Catalog 26

**No. 457 Racer**

Scale model.
Length, 7 inches.
Packed 1 in a box; 3 dozen to a carton.
Weight per carton, 21 lbs.
Assorted colors with nickel man.
Rubber wheels.

**No. 459 Taxi Cab**

Scale model.
Length, 7 inches.
Packed 1 in a box; 3 dozen to a carton.
Weight per carton, 21 lbs.
Orange and black combination.
Rubber wheels.

**No. 461 Pick-up Truck**

Scale model.
Length, 7 inches.
Packed 1 in a box; 3 dozen to a carton.
Weight per carton, 25 lbs.
Four assorted colors, nickel sides and drop end gate.
Rubber wheels.

**No. 460 Stake Truck**

Scale model.
Length, 7 inches.
Packed 1 in a box; 3 dozen to a carton.
Weight per carton, 25 lbs.
Four assorted colors, nickel sides and drop end gate.
Rubber wheels.

**No. 464 Fire Engine**

Length, 7½ inches.
Packed 1 in a box; 3 dozen to a carton.
Weight per carton, 25 lbs.
Red with nickel pumper top and windshield.
Rubber wheels.

**No. 463 Hook and Ladder**

Length of truck, 7½ inches.
Packed 1 in a box; 3 dozen to a carton.
Weight per carton, 23 lbs.
Red with nickel windshield.
Revolving ladder turret and plastic ladder.
Rubber wheels.



1949

**No. 462 Tow Truck**

Scale model.
Length, 7 inches.
Packed 1 in a box; 3 dozen to a carton.
Weight per carton, 25 lbs.
Four assorted colors, nickel sides, and movable boom.
Rubber wheels.

**No. 465 Convertible**

Length, 7 inches.
Packed 1 in a box; 3 dozen to a carton.
Weight per carton, 24 lbs.
Assorted colors with nickel windshield.
Movable nickel top.
Rubber wheels.

**No. 475 Tractor**

Scale model.
Length, 6¾ inches.
Packed 1 in a box; 1 dozen to a carton.
Weight per carton, 15 lbs.
Red with nickel man.
Black rubber wheels with painted disc.

**No. 470 Stake Truck**

Scale model.
Length, 9½ inches.
Packed 1 in a box; 1 dozen to a carton.
Weight per carton, 18 lbs.
Orange chassis, black body, aluminum trimming and nickel sides.
Rubber wheels.

**No. 471 Lumber Truck**

Scale model.
Length, 9½ inches.
Packed 1 in a box; 1 dozen to a carton.
Weight per carton, 16 lbs.
Red chassis, black body, nickel trimming.
Complete with load of 12 pieces lumber.
Rubber wheels.

**No. 472 Hook and Ladder**

Scale model.
Length, 10¼ inches.
Packed 1 in a box; 1 dozen to a carton.
Weight per carton, 16 lbs.
Red with aluminum trimming, three nickel ladders and revolving ladder turret and two nickel axes.
Rubber wheels.

**No. 474 Tow Truck**

Scale model.
Length, 9¾ inches.
Packed 1 in a box; 1 dozen to a carton.
Weight per carton, 14 lbs.
Red with nickel searchlight, winch and boom.
Rubber wheels.

## HUBLEY "KIDDIE" TOYS ★

**No. 476 Dump Truck**

Length, 9½ inches.
Packed 1 in a box; 1 dozen to a carton.
Weight per carton, 19 lbs.
Green chassis; red movable dump.
Rubber wheels.

**No. 477 Cement Mixer**

Length, 10 inches.
Packed 1 in a box; 1 dozen to a carton.
Weight per carton, 20 lbs.
Red chassis, green body, revolving aluminum mixer.
Rubber wheels.

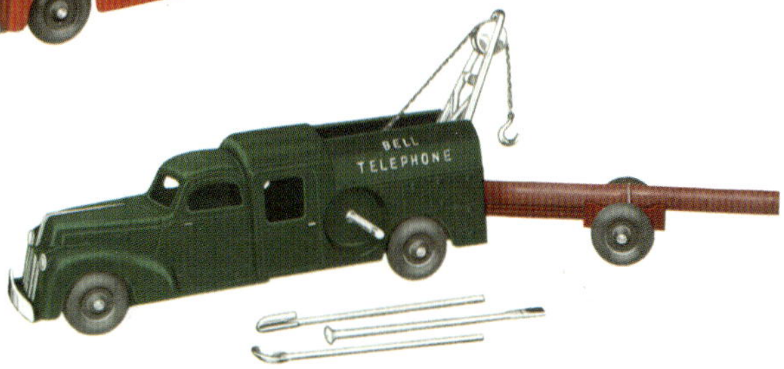


**No. 478 Bell Telephone Truck**

Length of truck, 10½ inches.
Packed 1 in a box; 1 dozen to a carton.
Weight per carton, 24 lbs.
Olive green with aluminum trimming.
Equipped with red trailer and telegraph pole; nickel winch and boom; three digging tools.
Rubber wheels.



## HUBLEY "KIDDIE" TOYS ★

**No. 10 Taxi Cab Set**

Box dimensions, 11¼ x 8 inches.
Packed 1 set of three taxicabs to a box; 1 dozen sets to a carton.
Weight per carton, 26 lbs.
Two-tone finish, three assorted colors to set. Beautiful display box.
All toys equipped with rubber wheels.

**No. 20 Midget Racer Set**

Box dimensions, 11¼ x 8 inches.
Packed 1 set of three racers to a box; 1 dozen sets to a carton.
Weight per carton, 25 lbs.
Three assorted colors to set.
All toys equipped with nickel man and rubber wheels. Beautiful display box.



1949

## HUBLEY "KIDDIE" TOYS ★

**No. 30 Fire Department**

Box dimensions, 14½ x 11 inches.
Packed 1 set to a box; 1 dozen sets to a carton.
Weight per carton, 35 lbs.
Set consists of Fire Engine, Hook and Ladder, Fire Chief's Car, Motorcycle, plastic ladder and two nickel axes.
All toys painted red with aluminum trimming and rubber wheels.
Beautiful display box.



## HUBLEY "KIDDIE" TOYS ★

**No. 40 Truck Assortment**

Box dimensions, 11½ x 8¼ inches.
Packed 1 set of three trucks to a box; 1 dozen sets to a carton.
Weight per carton, 34 lbs.
Three assorted trucks to a box—each a different color.
All toys equipped with rubber wheels.
Beautiful display box.

## HUBLEY "KIDDIE" TOYS ★

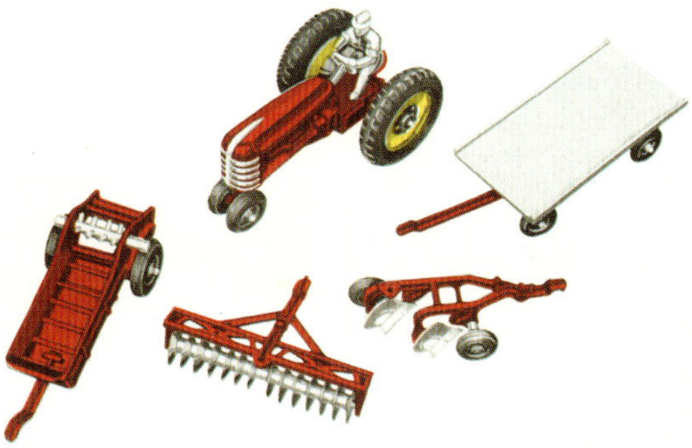

**No. 50 Farm Set**

Five assorted farm toys to a set—tractor, plow, disc, spreader and farm wagon.

Packed 1 set in an attractive box; ½ dozen sets to a carton.

Weight per carton, 24 lbs.

Toys painted red with aluminum and nickel trimming.

Rubber wheels.

[ Page Ten ]

## HUBLEY "KIDDIE" TOYS ★

**No. 500 Tractor Trailer Truck**

**"Three in One" Toy**

Length, 17½ inches.

Packed 1 in a box; ½ dozen to a carton.

Weight per carton, 36 lbs.

Red with aluminum trimming.

Furnished with removable aluminum sides; also load of logs and chains to make a lumber truck. Knee action rear wheels; 14 black rubber tires and retractable trailer support with two red rubber wheels.

Attractive individual box.

From this attractive all die cast toy can be made three separate and distinct vehicles. By removing the metal stakes, the toy is transformed into a flat bottom truck. The logs, chains and springs furnished can be put into place, making a lumber truck, as illustrated.

[ Page Eleven ]

IT'S A HUBLEY TOY

PRINTED IN U. S. A.

# 1949
# PLASTIC

PLASTIC
Kiddie Toys
Created by
HUBLEY

## HUBLEY "KIDDIE" TOYS ★

**No. 305 Fire Chief Car**

Length, 6 inches.
Packed 12 in a box; 3 dozen to a carton.
Weight per carton, 5 lbs.
Red and black with aluminum trimming.
Rubber wheels.

**No. 308 Taxi Cab**

Length, 6 inches.
Packed 12 in a box; 3 dozen to a carton.
Weight per carton, 5 lbs.
Three assorted colors in two-toned finish.
Rubber wheels.

**No. 327 Auto Set**

Box dimensions, 8¼ x 12 inches.
Packed 1 set to a box; 1 dozen sets to a carton.
Weight per carton, 12 lbs.
Set consists of Sedan, Taxi Cab, Fire Engine and Hook & Ladder in assorted colors.
All toys equipped with rubber wheels.

( Page Two )

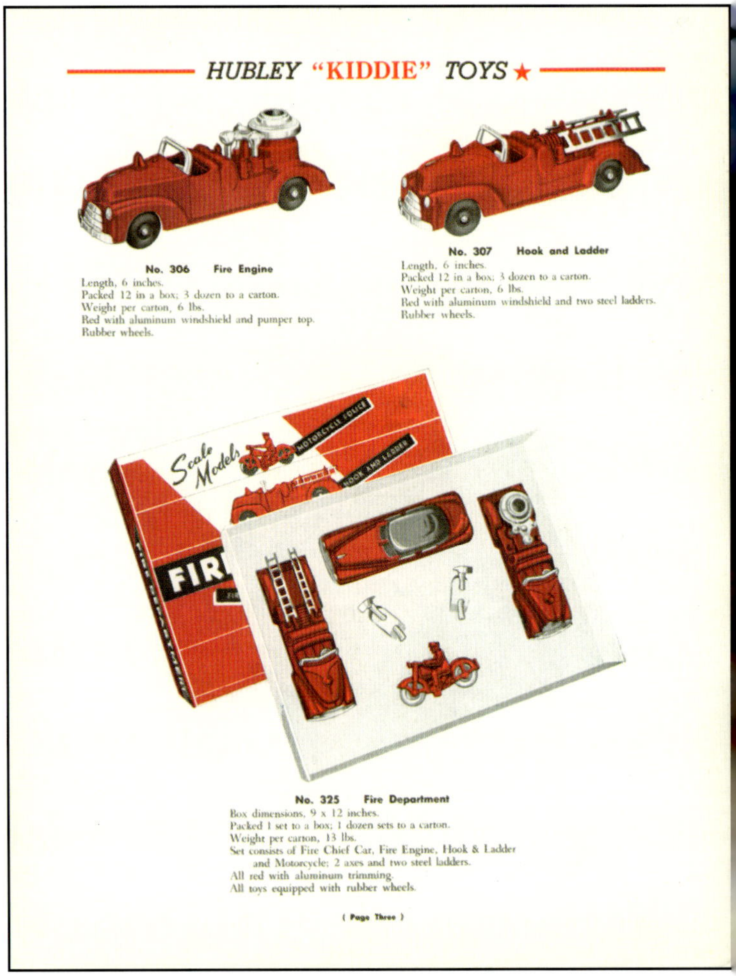

## HUBLEY "KIDDIE" TOYS ★

**No. 306 Fire Engine**

Length, 6 inches.
Packed 12 in a box; 3 dozen to a carton.
Weight per carton, 6 lbs.
Red with aluminum windshield and pumper top.
Rubber wheels.

**No. 307 Hook and Ladder**

Length, 6 inches.
Packed 12 in a box; 3 dozen to a carton.
Weight per carton, 6 lbs.
Red with aluminum windshield and two steel ladders.
Rubber wheels.

**No. 325 Fire Department**

Box dimensions, 9 x 12 inches.
Packed 1 set to a box; 1 dozen sets to a carton.
Weight per carton, 13 lbs.
Set consists of Fire Chief Car, Fire Engine, Hook & Ladder and Motorcycle; 2 axes and two steel ladders.
All red with aluminum trimming.
All toys equipped with rubber wheels.

( Page Three )

**No. 326 Taxi Cab Set**

Box dimensions, 8¼ x 11¾ inches.
Packed 1 set to a box, 1 dozen sets to a carton.
Weight per carton, 10 lbs.
Set consists of three assorted color taxi cabs, taxi stand, bus stop and parking meter.
All toys beautiful two-toned finish with rubber wheels.

THE HUBLEY MANUFACTURING COMPANY, LANCASTER, PA.

# 1950

# Hubley

## KIDDIE TOYS

THE HUBLEY MANUFACTURING COMPANY • • • LANCASTER • PA •

# HUBLEY "KIDDIE" TOYS

*"They look just like real ones"*

The toy-buyer finds in any catalog a bewildering assortment of items from which to make the selection of those numbers which his experience tells him will win the hearts of the children and the dollars of the grown-ups. To successfully select those toys which will fill both demands requires a shrewd judgment coupled with some experience.

Every toy in this catalog has a definite appeal to some group of prospective customers.

## Made to Sell

Hubley Toys are made to sell. They are produced in large quantities in a modern factory and can therefore be "priced right." But most important of all, they are designed and finished with the appeal to both children and parents in mind. Their accurate details, bright and permanent finish, novel "play" features, and sturdy strength assure them a prominent place on the counters of any toy store or toy department.

THE HUBLEY MANUFACTURING CO.

LANCASTER, PENNSYLVANIA

Catalog 27

**No. 456 Racer**

Scale model.
Length, 7 inches.
Packed 1 in a box; 3 dozen to a carton.
Weight per carton, 21 lbs.
Nickel plated with red man and red radiator. Rubber wheels.

**No. 459 Taxi Cab**

Scale model.
Length, 7 inches.
Packed 1 in a box; 3 dozen to a carton.
Weight per carton, 21 lbs.
Orange and black combination.
Rubber wheels.

**No. 461 Pick-up Truck**

Scale model.
Length, 7 inches.
Packed 1 in a box; 3 dozen to a carton.
Weight per carton, 25 lbs.
Four assorted colors, nickel sides and drop end gate.
Rubber wheels.

**No. 460 Stake Truck**

Scale model.
Length, 7 inches.
Packed 1 in a box; 3 dozen to a carton.
Weight per carton, 25 lbs.
Four assorted colors, nickel sides and drop end gate.
Rubber wheels.

**No. 464 Fire Engine**

Length, 7½ inches.
Packed 1 in a box; 3 dozen to a carton.
Weight per carton, 25 lbs.
Red with nickel pumper top and windshield.
Rubber wheels.

**No. 463 Hook and Ladder**

Length of truck, 7½ inches.
Packed 1 in a box; 3 dozen to a carton.
Weight per carton, 23 lbs.
Red with nickel windshield.
Revolving ladder turret and plastic ladder.
Rubber wheels.



1950

**No. 462 Tow Truck**

Scale model.
Length, 7 inches.
Packed 1 in a box; 3 dozen to a carton.
Weight per carton, 25 lbs.
Four assorted colors, nickel sides, and movable boom.
Rubber wheels.

**No. 465 Convertible**

Length, 7 inches.
Packed 1 in a box; 3 dozen to a carton.
Weight per carton, 24 lbs.
Assorted colors with nickel windshield.
Movable nickel top.
Rubber wheels.

**No. 473 Tractor**

Scale model.
Length, 7¾ inches.
Packed 1 in a box; 1 dozen to a carton.
Weight per carton, 17 lbs.
Red with aluminum trimming, nickel man, treaded rubber tires with yellow plastic hub.

**No. 470 Stake Truck**

Scale model.
Length, 9½ inches.
Packed 1 in a box; 1 dozen to a carton.
Weight per carton, 18 lbs.
Orange chassis, black body, aluminum trimming and nickel sides.
Rubber wheels.

**No. 472 Hook and Ladder**

Scale model.
Length, 10¼ inches.
Packed 1 in a box; 1 dozen to a carton.
Weight per carton, 16 lbs.
Red with aluminum trimming, three nickel ladders and revolving ladder turret and two nickel axes.
Rubber wheels.

**No. 471 Lumber Truck**

Scale model.
Length, 9½ inches.
Packed 1 in a box; 1 dozen to a carton.
Weight per carton, 16 lbs.
Red chassis, black body, nickel trimming.
Complete with load of 12 pieces lumber.
Rubber wheels.

**No. 474 Tow Truck**

Scale model.
Length, 9¼ inches.
Packed 1 in a box; 1 dozen to a carton.
Weight per carton, 14 lbs.
Red with nickel searchlight, winch and boom.
Rubber wheels.

**No. 476 Dump Truck**

Length, 9½ inches.
Packed 1 in a box; 1 dozen to a carton.
Weight per carton, 19 lbs.
Green chassis; red movable dump.
Rubber wheels.

**No. 477 Cement Mixer**

Length, 10 inches.
Packed 1 in a box; 1 dozen to a carton.
Weight per carton, 20 lbs.
Red chassis, green body, revolving aluminum mixer.
Rubber wheels.

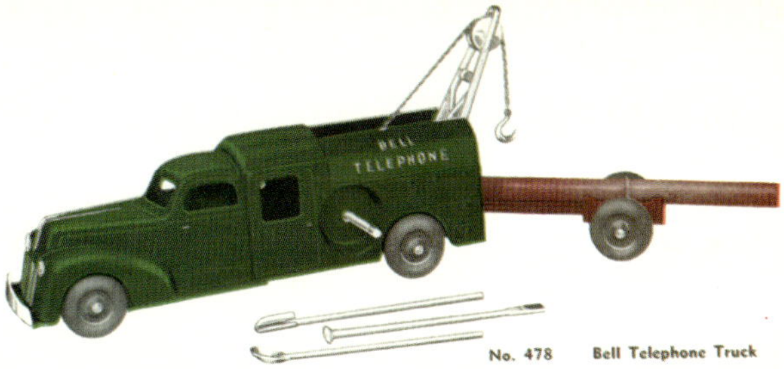


**No. 478 Bell Telephone Truck**

Length of truck, 10½ inches.
Packed 1 in a box; 1 dozen to a carton.
Weight per carton, 24 lbs.
Olive green with aluminum trimming.
Equipped with red trailer and telegraph pole; nickel winch and boom; three digging tools.
Rubber wheels.

**No. 480 Road Roller**

Length, 10¼ inches.
Packed 1 in a box; 1 dozen to a carton.
Weight per carton, 19 lbs.
Orange with aluminum trimming, nickel wheels. Front wheels operated by steering lever.

**No. 481 Road Scraper**

Length, 10¾ inches.
Packed 1 in a box; 1 dozen to a carton.
Weight per carton, 19 lbs.
Yellow with aluminum trimming, nickel scraper. Front wheels operated by steering wheel.
Rubber wheels.

**No. 479 Motorcycle**

Length, 8½ inches.
Packed 1 in a box; 1 dozen to a carton.
Weight per carton, 20 lbs.
Red with aluminum trimming.
Black removable cop.
Rubber wheels.

**No. 501 Auto Transport**

Length, 18 inches.
Packed 1 in a box; ½ dozen to a carton.
Weight per carton, 20 lbs.
Red tractor and trailer with aluminum trimming.
Equipped with four assorted color plastic cars; also runway to be used for running cars on the trailer.
Transport and cars all furnished with black rubber wheels.



1950

**No. 502 Lumber Truck**

Length, 17½ inches.
Packed 1 in a box; ½ dozen to a carton.
Weight per carton, 32 lbs.
Red with aluminum trimming; knee action rear wheels; load of logs with chains and springs to hold them in place.
Retractable trailer support.
Rubber wheels.

**No. 503 Stake Truck**

Length, 17½ inches.
Packed 1 in a box; ½ dozen to a carton.
Weight per carton, 26 lbs.
Orange with aluminum trimming; nickel sides; knee action rear wheels; retractable trailer support. Sides can be removed to make flat bottom truck.
Rubber wheels.

**No. 25 Big 3 Assortment**

Dimensions, 11½ x 8½ inches.
Packed 1 set to a box; 1 dozen sets to a carton.
Weight per carton, 25 lbs.
Set consists of Taxi Cab, Racer and Tow Truck.
Assorted colors.
Toys equipped with rubber wheels.

## HUBLEY "KIDDIE" TOYS ★

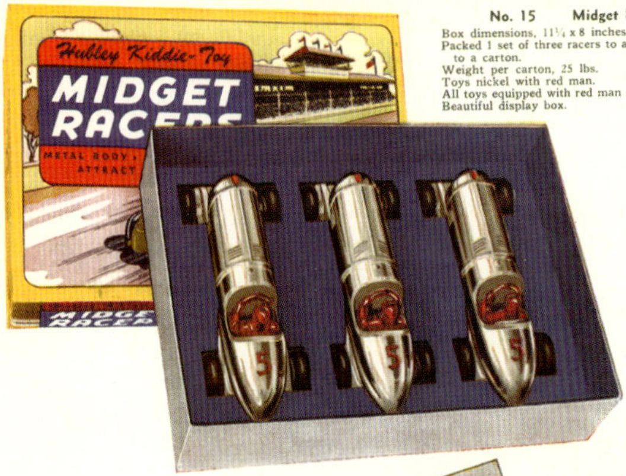


**No. 15 Midget Racer Set**

Box dimensions, 11¼ x 8 inches.
Packed 1 set of three racers to a box; 1 dozen sets to a carton.
Weight per carton, 25 lbs.
Toys nickel with red man.
All toys equipped with red man and rubber wheels.
Beautiful display box.

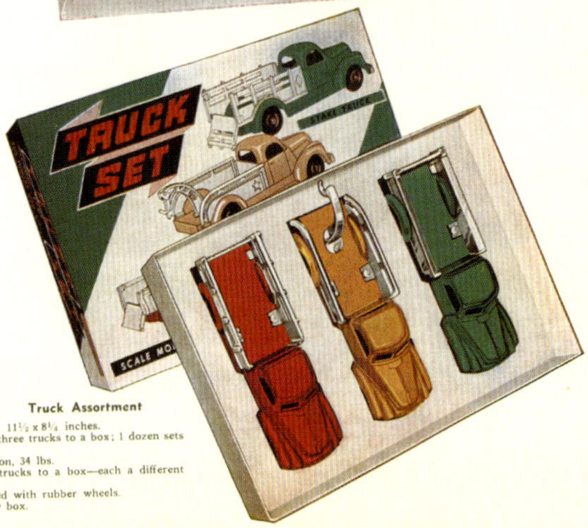


**No. 40 Truck Assortment**

Box dimensions, 11½ x 8¼ inches.
Packed 1 set of three trucks to a box; 1 dozen sets to a carton.
Weight per carton, 34 lbs.
Three assorted trucks to a box—each a different color.
All toys equipped with rubber wheels.
Beautiful display box.

## HUBLEY "KIDDIE" TOYS ★

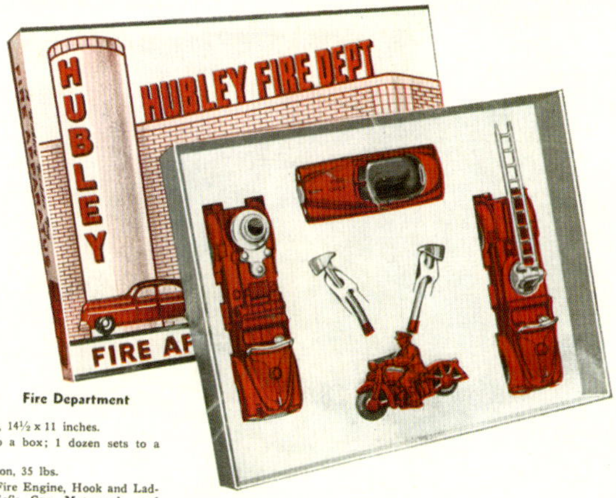


**No. 30 Fire Department**

Box dimensions, 14½ x 11 inches.

Packed 1 set to a box; 1 dozen sets to a carton.

Weight per carton, 35 lbs.

Set consists of Fire Engine, Hook and Ladder, Fire Chief's Car, Motorcycle, and plastic ladder.

All toys painted red with aluminum trimming and rubber wheels.

Beautiful display box.

**No. 50**
**Farm Set**

Five assorted farm toys to a set—tractor, plow, disc, spreader and farm wagon.

Packed 1 set in an attractive box; ½ dozen sets to a carton.

Weight per carton, 24 lbs.

Toys painted red with aluminum and nickel trimming.

Rubber wheels.

[ Page Eleven ]

IT'S A HUBLEY TOY

PRINTED IN U. S. A.

# 1951

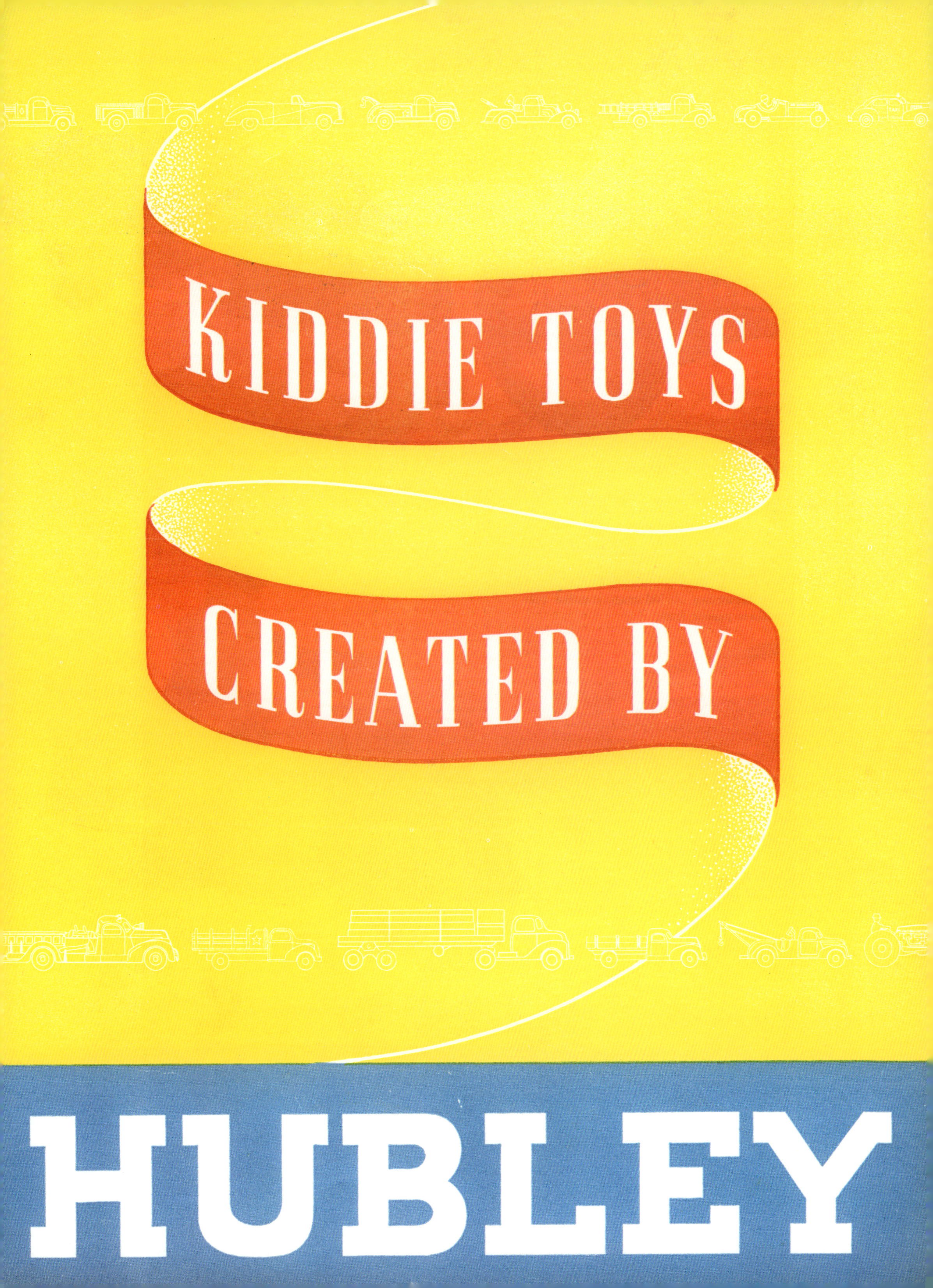
KIDDIE TOYS
CREATED BY
HUBLEY

## HUBLEY "KIDDIE" TOYS ★

**No. 475 Dump Truck**

(Metal)

Length, 8½ inches.

Packed 1 in a box; 1 dozen to a carton.

Weight per carton, 12 lbs.

Green plastic cab, red metal dump; metal chassis; movable dump. Rubber wheels.

**No. 473 Tractor**

(Metal)

Scale model.

Length, 7¼ inches.

Packed 1 in a box; 1 dozen to a carton.

Weight per carton, 17 lbs.

Red with aluminum trimming, nickel man, treaded rubber tires with yellow plastic hub.

**No. 479 Motorcycle**

(Metal)

Length, 8½ inches.

Packed 1 in a box; 1 dozen to a carton.

Weight per carton, 13 lbs.

Red metal motorcycle with aluminum trimming.

Removable black, plastic cop.

Rubber wheels.

**No. 481**
**Road Scraper**

(Metal)

Length, 10¾ inches.

Packed 1 in a box; 1 dozen to a carton.

Weight per carton, 15 lbs.

Yellow with aluminum trimming, nickel scraper. Front wheels operated by steering wheel.

Rubber wheels.

## HUBLEY "KIDDIE" TOYS ★

**No. 482**
**Telephone Truck**

(Metal)

Length of truck, 8½ in.

Packed 1 in a box; 1 dozen to a carton.

Weight per carton, 18 lbs.

Plastic cab; metal body, chassis and trailer. Olive green with aluminum trimming. Red trailer with telephone pole, nickel winch and boom; three digging tools. Rubber wheels.

**No. 350 Hook and Ladder**

(Metal and Plastic)

Length, 12½ inches.

Packed 1 in a box; 1 dozen to a carton.

Weight per carton, 17 lbs.

Plastic cab and trailer; metal chassis. Red with aluminum trimming; two revolving searchlights. Revolving ladder turret with four plastic ladders. Metal axe. Rubber wheels.

**No. 351 Log Truck**

(Plastic and Metal)

Length, 12 inches.
Packed 1 in a box; 1 dozen to a carton.

Weight per carton, 18 lbs.

Plastic cab and trailer; metal chassis. Orange with aluminum trimming. Retractable trailer support. Load of logs. Rubber wheels.

**No. 310 Motorcycle**

(Plastic)

Length, 5 inches.

Packed 12 in a box; 3 dozen to a carton.

Weight per carton, 8 lbs.

Red and green motorcycle; blue man.

Rubber wheels.

**No. 309 Tractor**

(Plastic)

Length, 4¾ inches.

Packed 12 in a box; 3 dozen to a carton.

Weight per carton, 11 lbs.

Red, green and orange with aluminum trimming. Rubber wheels.

**No. 311 Airplane**

(Plastic)

Length, 5 inches.

Packed 12 in a box; 3 dozen to a carton.

Weight per carton, 6 lbs.

Red and aluminum combination.

Aluminum propeller; retractable landing gear. Rubber wheels.

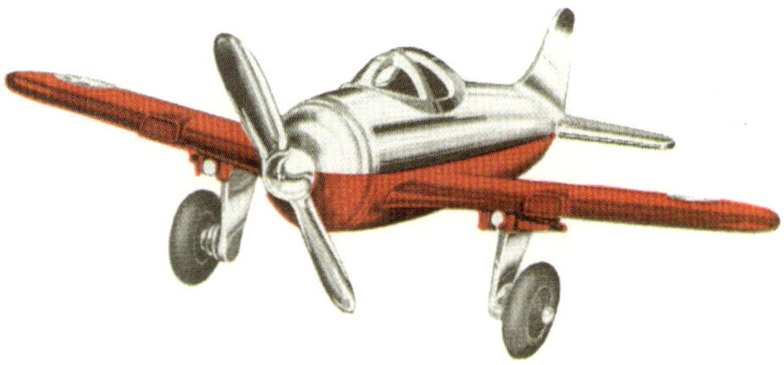

**No. 320 Dump Truck**

(Plastic)

Length, 7 inches.

Packed 6 in a box; 3 dozen to a carton.

Weight per carton, 10 lbs.

Green and red or green and yellow.

Aluminum trimming; movable dump.

Rubber wheels.

**No. 321 Tow Truck**

(Plastic)

Length, 7 inches.

Packed 6 in a box; 3 dozen to a carton.

Weight per carton, 10 lbs.

Red and green or red and cream; aluminum trimming.

Rubber wheels.

# 1952

Oh boy!
Lift the hood and see the motor.
Hubley
MANUFACTURING CO. • LANCASTER • PA.
KIDDIE TOYS for 1952
with added play features

# Packing and Weights

## HUBLEY "KIDDIE TOYS"

| No. | Name | | Pieces in Box | Case Packing | Weight per Carton | Catalog Page |
|---|---|---|---|---|---|---|
| 305 | Fire Chief Car | *(Plastic)* | 12 | 3 doz. | 4 lbs. | 3 |
| 306 | Fire Engine | *(Plastic)* | 12 | 3 doz. | 6 lbs. | 3 |
| 307 | Hook & Ladder | *(Plastic)* | 12 | 3 doz. | 5 lbs. | 3 |
| 308 | Taxi Cab | *(Plastic)* | 12 | 3 doz. | 4 lbs. | 3 |
| 309 | Tractor | *(Plastic)* | 12 | 3 doz. | 11 lbs. | 4 |
| 310 | Motorcycle | *(Plastic)* | 12 | 3 doz. | 8 lbs. | 4 |
| 311 | Airplane | *(Plastic)* | 12 | 3 doz. | 6 lbs. | 4 |
| 315 | Road Roller | *(Plastic)* | 1 | 3 doz. | 9 lbs. | 5 |
| 316 | Road Scraper | *(Plastic)* | 1 | 3 doz. | 13 lbs. | 5 |
| 322 | Dump Truck | *(Plastic)* | 1 | 3 doz. | 10 lbs. | 6 |
| 323 | Wrecker | *(Plastic)* | 1 | 3 doz. | 11 lbs. | 6 |
| 324 | Hook & Ladder | *(Plastic)* | 1 | 3 doz. | 11 lbs. | 7 |
| 325 | Racer | *(Plastic)* | 1 | 3 doz. | 10 lbs. | 8 |
| 326 | Airplane | *(Plastic)* | 1 | 3 doz. | 7 lbs. | 8 |
| 327 | Telephone Truck | *(Plastic)* | 1 | 3 doz. | 11 lbs. | 7 |
| 328 | Tractor | *(Plastic)* | 1 | 3 doz. | 16 lbs. | 9 |
| 472 | Tractor | *(Metal)* | 1 | 1 doz. | 14 lbs. | 10 |
| 475 | Dump Truck | *(Metal)* | 1 | 1 doz. | 13 lbs. | 11 |
| 355 | Hook & Ladder | *(Plastic)* | 1 | 1 doz. | 11 lbs. | 12 |
| 354 | Earth Mover | *(Plastic)* | 1 | 1 doz. | 15 lbs. | 13 |
| 356 | Log Truck | *(Plastic)* | 1 | 1 doz. | 18 lbs. | 14 |
| 480 | Road Roller | *(Metal)* | 1 | 1 doz. | 21 lbs. | 15 |
| 481 | Road Scraper | *(Metal)* | 1 | 1 doz. | 15 lbs. | 16 |
| 482 | Telephone Truck | *(Metal)* | 1 | 1 doz. | 19 lbs. | 17 |
| 352 | Motor Express | *(Plastic)* | 1 | 1 doz. | 16 lbs. | 18 |
| 353 | Auto Transport | *(Plastic)* | 1 | 1 doz. | 13 lbs. | 19 |
| 504 | Large Telephone Truck | *(Metal)* | 1 | ½ doz. | 21 lbs. | 20 |
| 505 | Large Log Truck | *(Metal)* | 1 | ½ doz. | 22 lbs. | 21 |

### BOXED ASSORTMENTS

| No. | Name | | Pieces in Box | Case Packing | Weight per Carton | Catalog Page |
|---|---|---|---|---|---|---|
| 3 | Fire Department | *(Plastic)* | 1 | 1 doz. | 12 lbs. | 22 |
| 4 | Farm Set | *(Plastic)* | 1 | 1 doz. | 11 lbs. | 23 |
| 55 | Highway Set | *(Plastic)* | 1 | 1 doz. | 18 lbs. | 24 |
| 60 | Road Building Set | *(Plastic)* | 1 | 1 doz. | 22 lbs. | 26 |
| 65 | Truck Set | *(Plastic)* | 1 | 1 doz. | 16 lbs. | 25 |
| 50 | Farm Set (Large) | *(Metal)* | 1 | ½ doz. | 17 lbs. | 27 |

**No. 305 Fire Chief Car**
(Plastic)

Length 6 inches. Packed 12 in a box; 3 dozen to a carton. Red and black with aluminum trimming. Rubber wheels.

**No. 306 Fire Engine**
(Plastic)

Length 6 inches. Packed 12 in a box; 3 dozen to a carton. Red with aluminum windshield and pumper top. Rubber wheels.

**No. 307 Hook and Ladder**
(Plastic)

Length 6 inches. Packed 12 in a box; 3 dozen to a carton. Red with aluminum windshield and two steel ladders. Rubber wheels.

**No. 308 Taxi Cab**
(Plastic)

Length 6 inches. Packed 12 in a box; 3 dozen to a carton. Three assorted colors in two-toned finish. Rubber wheels.



1952

**No. 311 Airplane**
(Plastic)

Length 5 inches. Packed 12 in a box; 3 dozen to a carton. Red and bright metallic combination. Retractable landing gear. Rubber wheels.

**No. 309 Tractor**
(Plastic)

Length 4¾ inches. Packed 12 in a box; 3 dozen to a carton. Red, green and orange with aluminum trimming. Rubber wheels.

**No. 310 Motorcycle**
(Plastic)

Length 5 inches. Packed 12 in a box; 3 dozen to a carton. Red and green motorcycle; blue man. Rubber wheels.

**No. 315 Road Roller**
(Plastic)

Length 5¾ inches. Packed one in a box; 3 dozen to a carton. Shown actual size. Bright green plastic body. Heavy red wooden wheels and roller. Accurately detailed after the real thing down to the small rivets.

**No. 316 Road Scraper**
(Plastic)

Length 6¼ inches. Packed one in a box; 3 dozen to a carton. Shown actual size. Bright yellow plastic body, completely and accurately detailed, even to controls in the driver's seat. Aluminum finished scraper bar can be adjusted over a 90 degree angle. Black rubber wheels.

# LIFT THE HOOD · · SEE THE MOTOR

**No. 322 Dump Truck**
(Plastic)

Length 6½ inches. Packed one in a box; 3 dozen to a carton. Plastic cab and dump body in assorted colors, red and green, aluminum trimming. Spring clip holds dump body down. Tail gate swings open automatically when dump raised. Hood lifts up exposing realistic 6 cylinder motor. Chassis enclosed with realistic chassis details. Black rubber wheels.

*"Lift the hood...."*

**No. 323 Wrecker**
(Plastic)

Length 6¼ inches. Packed one in a box; 3 dozen to a carton. Red plastic cab and body in assorted colors, green and ivory. Aluminum trimming. Turning crank raises or lowers metal hook. Realistic 6 cylinder motor underneath hood. Hood lifts up. Chassis enclosed underneath with realistic details. Black rubber wheels.



**No. 324 Fire Truck**
(Plastic)

Length 7¾ inches. Packed one in a box; 3 dozen to a carton. Bright red plastic cab and body. Aluminum trimming. Two ivory plastic ladders can be removed and joined together. Ladders engage on truck body "to reach a fire". Hood lifts up exposing realistic 6 cylinder motor. Chassis enclosed underneath with realistic details. Black rubber wheels.

*Detailed, enclosed chassis*

**No. 327 Telephone Truck**
(Plastic)

Length 6½ inches. Packed one in a box; 3 dozen to a carton. Plastic cab and body. Realistic olive green color with bright trimming. 6 cylinder motor under hood. Hood lifts up to "work on motor". Chassis enclosed underneath with realistic chassis details. Two plastic digging tools. Black rubber wheels.

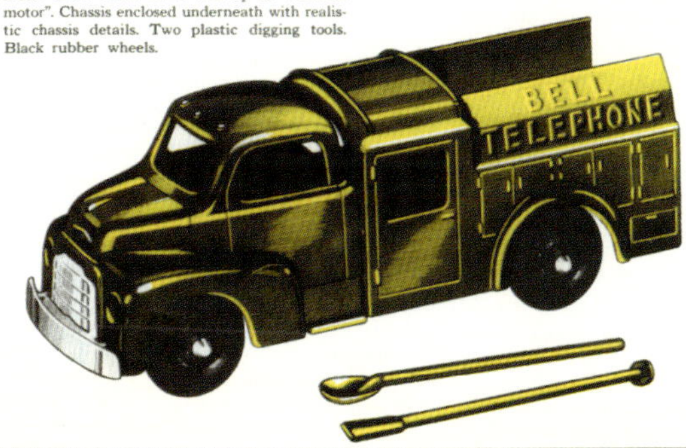




1952

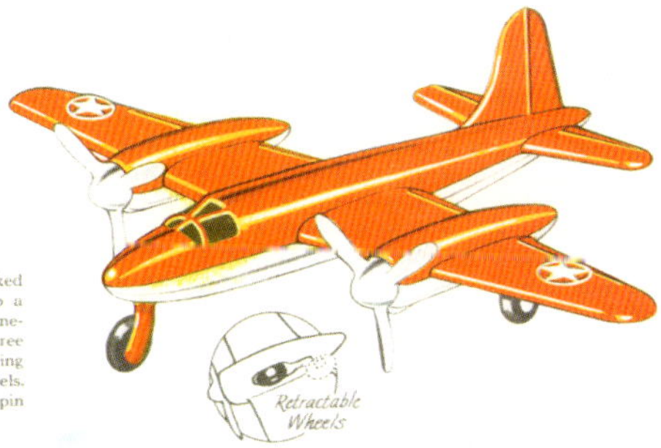


**No. 326 Attack Bomber**
(Plastic)

Length 6¼ inches. Packed one in a box; 3 dozen to a carton. Red and bright metallic combination. Three wheeled retractable landing gear, black rubber wheels. Three bladed propellers spin freely.

**No. 325 Racer**
(Plastic)

Length 6¾ inches. Packed one in a box; 3 dozen to a carton. Yellow with red trim or red with yellow trim. Driver stationary. Hood lifts up exposing realistic 4 cylinder racing motor. Bottom enclosed with realistic chassis details. Rubber wheels.

**No. 328 Tractor**
(Plastic)

Length 5½ inches. Packed one in a box; 3 dozen to a carton. Green plastic with aluminum finish steering wheel. Fine, realistic detailing of engine, chassis, hood, and seat. Trailer hitch on rear. Black rubber wheels. Rear tires are treaded, front tires grooved like the real tractor.

**Craftsmanship**

To Hubley, craftsmanship implies many things. Not only expertness in design but good modeling and competence in production.

First of all, Hubley Toys are planned, designed, and modeled by artisans with many years of experience in the toy business.

They must be attractive to children and must have a maximum of real life details.

They must "play" well and must have realistic, educational play features with careful thought to the safety of the child.

They must be well made to provide long, hard play in normal use.

They must sell well and this is our pledge to you: Hubley craftsmanship at attractive prices will be our continuing aim.

**The Hubley Manufacturing Company, Lancaster, Pa.**

# HUBLEY TRACTOR

**No. 472 Tractor**
(Metal)

Length 7 inches. Packed one in a box; 1 dozen to a carton. Red chassis with realistic die cast engine details visible from both sides. Bright aluminum trimming, radiator grille and die cast steering wheel. Yellow wheels, black rubber tires. Note rear tires are treaded, front tires are grooved in true-to-life detail.

# HUBLEY DUMP TRUCK

**No. 475 Dump Truck**
(Metal & Plastic)

Length 8½ inches. Packed one in a box; 1 dozen to a carton. Green plastic cab with bright aluminum trimming. Red metal dump body. Bright metal chassis, tail gate and latch mechanism. Pressing down latch handle allows dump to raise. Tailgate opens automatically. Black rubber wheels, dual in rear.

1952

# HUBLEY HOOK and LADDER

**No. 355 Hook and Ladder**
(Plastic)

Length 12¾ inches. Packed one in a box; 1 dozen to a carton. Red plastic cab and trailer. Bright metallic plastic chassis, radiator grille and bumper. Metal ladder turret. Cab is removable so you can see and "work on" the accurately detailed V-8 motor. Chassis is closed underneath with realistic details. Trailer carries four removable, ivory plastic ladders plus a bright metal fireman's axe. Ladders each 5 inches long, easily joined together to make an extension. Placed on the revolving turret, they can be raised and lowered over a 180 degree arc. The turret itself can be turned in a complete circle. Aluminum finished searchlights also swivel in a complete circle. Trailer can be unhitched. Black rubber wheels.

*Remove the cab and see the motor* — *Four sectional ladders mount on revolving turret. Searchligts turn* — *Ladders join together with simple pin and socket*



# HUBLEY EARTH MOVER

**No. 354 Earth Mover**
(Plastic)

Length 14 inches. Packed one in a box; one dozen to a carton. Yellow and red combination. Dump body can be unhitched. Throwing lever at rear opens bottom boards, emptying load. Black rubber wheels, spare behind driver's seat.

*Realistic cab and hitch detail.* — *Lever drops bottom boards.*

# HUBLEY LOG TRUCK

**No. 356 Log Truck**
(Plastic)

Length 12¼ inches. Packed one in a box; 1 dozen to a carton. Tractor chassis bright metallic plastic. Cab lifts off revealing detailed V-8 engine. Bottom enclosed with realistic detail. Trailer hitch for quick, easy removal of trailer. Cab and trailer bright orange plastic. 12 smooth dowel logs loaded on the trailer. Chain opens to remove the logs. Dolly wheels swing down and lock in position when trailer unhitched. Rear wheels have their own independent wheel suspension. Black rubber wheels. Dual wheels on rear of tractor and trailer.

# HUBLEY ROAD ROLLER

**No. 480 Road Roller**
(Metal)

Length 10 inches. Packed one in a box; one dozen to a carton. Rugged orange body and front roller mounting, aluminum trimming. Solid metal wheels, bright aluminum finish. Accurate modeling and detailing. Front roller consists of two wheels mounted together, just like the real thing. Roller steers by lever in driver's compartment.

1952

# HUBLEY ROAD SCRAPER

**No. 481 Road Scraper**
(Metal)

Length 10¾ inches. Packed one in a box; one dozen to a carton. Yellow with bright scraper and trimming. Front wheels operated by steering wheel. Black rubber wheels. The rear wheels are mounted independently to roll over stones or obstacles. Spring and notch construction holds scraper firmly in place, also permits adjustment over a 90 degree angle.

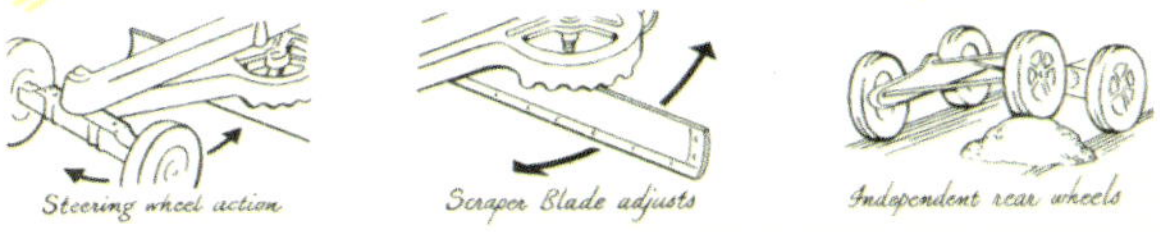




# HUBLEY TELEPHONE TRUCK

**No. 482 Bell Telephone Truck**
(Metal and Plastic)

Length of truck 8½ inches. Trailer 4¾ inches; pole 6 inches. Packed one in a box; one dozen to a carton. Plastic cab, metal body, chassis and trailer. Realistic olive green color with bright aluminum trimming. Equipped with detachable red trailer and telephone pole. Bright finish metal winch and boom operated by turning crank on side of truck. Boom lifts out. Three digging tools. Black rubber wheels.

# HUBLEY MOTOR EXPRESS

**No. 352 Motor Express**

Length 12½ inches. Packed 1 in a box; 12 to a carton. Tractor chassis bright metal finish with red cab. Cab lifts off revealing detailed V-8 engine. Bottom enclosed with realistic chassis details. Trailer hitch on rear of tractor permits easy removal of trailer.

Trailer has bright green body with red chassis. Side door slides open; rear doors swing out. Dolly wheels swing down and lock in position when trailer is unhitched. Rear wheels have their own independent wheel suspension. Black rubber tires. Dual wheels on rear of tractor and trailer.

# HUBLEY MOTOR TRANSPORT

**No. 353 Motor Transport**
(Plastic)

Length 13½ inches. Packed one in a box; 1 dozen to a carton. Red plastic cab and trailer with bright trimming. Cab lifts off completely, exposing an accurately detailed V-8 engine. Bright metallic plastic chassis, radiator grille and gas tanks. Trailer hitch on rear. Chassis enclosed with realistic detail. Detachable trailer 9¼ inches long. Carries four plastic toy Cadillac cars which can be driven off or on the trailer over the removable plastic ramp. Ramp hooks into trailer. When not in use it is carried out of sight underneath. Toy Cadillac cars are yellow, green, blue, tan, with bright aluminum trim. Each over 4 inches long. Black rubber wheels.

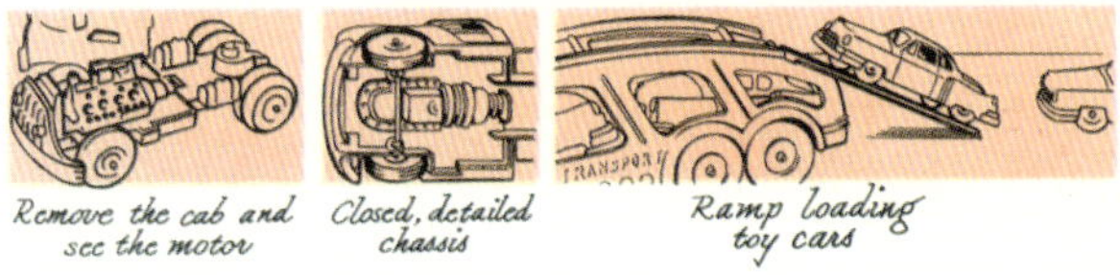




1952

# HUBLEY TELEPHONE TRUCK

**No. 504 Telephone Truck**
(Metal)

Length of truck 12½ inches. Packed one in a box; ½ dozen to a carton. Olive green metal cab and body. Bright lettering and trim. Removable boom in rear. Turning crank handle raises or lowers rope and hook. Top of truck slides back to cover open half in rear. Ivory colored plastic ladder. Three bright metal digging tools fit inside truck. Red metal two wheeled pole trailer hooks on rear of truck. 11 inch pole removable. Black rubber wheels, dual in rear.

# HUBLEY LOG TRUCK

**No. 505 Log Truck**
(Metal)

Length 18 inches. Packed one in a box; ½ dozen to a carton. Orange cab and trailer with bright trim. Bright metal chassis, chains, and springs on trailer. Chassis enclosed underneath with realistic detail. Trailer carries 5 smooth logs (one with red flag) each 12 inches long. Wheels are independently mounted to roll over stones or obstacles. Black rubber wheels.

# No. 3 Fire Department Set

One set to a box; one dozen boxes to a carton. Set consists of: No. 305 Fire Chief, No. 307 Hook & Ladder; No. 310 Motorcycle.



# No. 4 Farm Set

One set to a box; one dozen to a carton. Set consists of: No. 328 Tractor, Cultipacker, plastic Farm Wagon.

# No. 55 Highway Set

One set to a box; one dozen boxes to a carton. Set consists of: No. 315 Road Roller, No. 316 Road Scraper, No. 322 Dump Truck, No. 309 Tractor.



# No. 65 Lift The Hood Toy Set

One set to a box; one dozen boxes to a carton. Set consists of: No. 322 Dump Truck, No. 323 Wrecker, No. 324 Fire Truck, No. 327 Telephone Truck.

## No. 60 Road Building Set

One set to a box; one dozen boxes to a carton. Set consists of: No. 315 Road Roller, No. 316 Road Scraper, and plastic Flat Bed Truck.

26

## No. 50 Farm Set

One set to a box; ½ dozen boxes to a carton. Metal and plastic.

27

IT'S A HUBLEY TOY

*Catalog design and production by Andes · Design and Advertising · Lancaster · Pa · Printed United States of America*

# 1953

# HUBLEY Kiddie Toys

·· Spring 1953 ··

# Packing, Weights and Index

## HUBLEY "KIDDIE TOYS"

| No. | Name | | Pieces in Box | Case Packing | Weight per Carton | Catalog Page |
|---|---|---|---|---|---|---|
| 306 | Fire Engine | (Plastic) | 12 | 3 doz. | 6 lbs. | 4 |
| 307 | Hook and Ladder | (Plastic) | 12 | 3 doz. | 5 lbs. | 4 |
| 309 | Tractor | (Plastic) | 12 | 3 doz. | 11 lbs. | 5 |
| 310 | Motorcycle | (Plastic) | 12 | 3 doz. | 8 lbs. | 4 |
| 311 | Airplane | (Plastic) | 12 | 3 doz. | 6 lbs. | 4 |
| 315 | Road Roller | (Plastic) | 1 | 3 doz. | 9 lbs. | 5 |
| 316 | Road Scraper | (Plastic) | 1 | 3 doz. | 12 lbs. | 5 |
| 322 | Dump Truck | (Plastic) | 1 | 3 doz. | 10 lbs. | 7 |
| 323 | Wrecker | (Plastic) | 1 | 3 doz. | 11 lbs. | 6 |
| 324 | Hook and Ladder | (Plastic) | 1 | 3 doz. | 11 lbs. | 6 |
| 325 | Racer | (Plastic) | 1 | 3 doz. | 10 lbs. | 8 |
| 326 | Airplane | (Plastic) | 1 | 3 doz. | 7 lbs. | 8 |
| 327 | Telephone Truck | (Plastic) | 1 | 3 doz. | 11 lbs. | 6 |
| 328 | Tractor | (Plastic) | 1 | 3 doz. | 16 lbs. | 8 |
| 329 | Gas Truck | (Plastic) | 1 | 3 doz. | 12 lbs. | 7 |
| 330 | Motor Express | (Plastic) | 1 | 3 doz. | 12 lbs. | 7 |
| 352 | Motor Express | (Plastic) | 1 | 1 doz. | 16 lbs. | 10 |
| 353 | Auto Transport | (Plastic) | 1 | 1 doz. | 13 lbs. | 11 |
| 354 | Earth Mover | (Plastic) | 1 | 1 doz. | 13 lbs. | 9 |
| 355 | Hook and Ladder | (Plastic) | 1 | 1 doz. | 10 lbs. | 9 |
| 356 | Log Truck | (Plastic) | 1 | 1 doz. | 17 lbs. | 10 |
| 357 | Cattle Truck | (Plastic) | 1 | 1 doz. | 14 lbs. | 11 |
| 457 | Racer | (Metal) | 1 | 3 doz. | 20 lbs. | 12 |
| 460 | Stake Truck | (Metal) | 1 | 3 doz. | 25 lbs. | 12 |
| 462 | Tow Truck | (Metal) | 1 | 3 doz. | 28 lbs. | 12 |
| 463 | Hook and Ladder | (Metal) | 1 | 3 doz. | 23 lbs. | 13 |
| 464 | Fire Engine | (Metal) | 1 | 3 doz. | 25 lbs. | 13 |
| 467 | Navy Plane | (Metal) | 1 | 1 doz. | 8 lbs. | 13 |
| 470 | Lumber Truck | (Metal) | 1 | 1 doz. | 16 lbs. | 14 |
| 472 | Tractor | (Metal) | 1 | 1 doz. | 13 lbs. | 14 |
| 474 | Tow Truck | (Metal) | 1 | 1 doz. | 14 lbs. | 15 |
| 476 | Dump Truck | (Metal) | 1 | 1 doz. | 15 lbs. | 15 |
| 477 | Cement Mixer | (Metal) | 1 | 1 doz. | 17 lbs. | 16 |
| 478 | Telephone Truck | (Metal) | 1 | 1 doz. | 22 lbs. | 16 |
| 480 | Road Roller | (Metal) | 1 | 1 doz. | 21 lbs. | 17 |
| 481 | Road Scraper | (Metal) | 1 | 1 doz. | 15 lbs. | 17 |
| 490 | Tractor | (Metal) | 1 | 1 doz. | 21 lbs. | 18 |
| 504 | Telephone Truck | (Metal) | 1 | ½ doz. | 20 lbs. | 19 |
| 505 | Log Truck | (Metal) | 1 | ½ doz. | 21 lbs. | 20 |
| 506 | Carryall | (Metal) | 1 | ½ doz. | 24 lbs. | 21 |
| 507 | Motor Express | (Metal) | 1 | ½ doz. | 32 lbs. | 22 |

### BOXED ASSORTMENTS

| No. | Name | | Pieces in Box | Case Packing | Weight per Carton | Catalog Page |
|---|---|---|---|---|---|---|
| 4 | Farm Set | (Plastic) | 1 | 1 doz. | 11 lbs. | 24 |
| 50 | Farm Set | (Metal) | 1 | ½ doz. | 17 lbs. | 23 |
| 60 | Road Building Set | (Plastic) | 1 | 1 doz. | 22 lbs. | 26 |
| 65 | Truck Set | (Plastic) | 1 | 1 doz. | 18 lbs. | 25 |



1953



**No. 311 Airplane**
Length 5 inches. Packed 12 in a box; 3 dozen to a carton. Weight per carton 6 lbs. Red and bright metallic combination. Retractable landing gear. Rubber wheels.

**No. 307 Hook and Ladder**
Length 6 inches. Packed 12 in a box; 3 dozen to a carton. Weight per carton 5 lbs. Red with aluminum windshield and two steel ladders. Rubber wheels.

**No. 306 Fire Engine**
Length 6 inches. Packed 12 in a box; 3 dozen to a carton. Weight per carton 6 lbs. Red with aluminum windshield and pumper top. Rubber wheels.

**No. 310 Motorcycle**
Length 5 inches. Packed 12 in a box; 3 dozen to a carton. Weight per carton 8 lbs. Red and green motorcycle; blue man. Rubber wheels.





**No. 309 Tractor**
Length 4¾ inches. Packed 12 in a box; 3 dozen to a carton. Weight per carton 11 lbs. Red, green and orange with aluminum trimming. Rubber wheels.

**No. 316 Road Scraper**
Length 6¼ inches. Packed 1 in a box; 3 dozen to a carton. Weight per carton 12 lbs. Shown actual size. Yellow plastic body with adjustable aluminum finished scraper. Rubber wheels.

**No. 315 Road Roller**
Length 5¾ inches. Packed 1 in a box; 3 dozen to a carton. Weight per carton 9 lbs. Shown actual size. Green plastic body with red wooden wheels and roller.

## LIFT THE HOOD AND SEE THE MOTOR.

All six toys on these pages possess the "lift the hood" feature. By pressing the release under the cab the hood lifts up exposing a 6 cylinder motor to work on. Each chassis enclosed underneath with realistic details. Black rubber wheels throughout. See each toy for colors and packing. All plastic.

**No. 323 Wrecker**
Length 6¼ inches. Packed 1 in a box; 3 dozen to a carton. Weight per carton 11 lbs. Red plastic cab; body in assorted colors, green and ivory. Aluminum trimming. Crank operates metal hook.

**No. 327 Telephone Truck**
Length 6½ inches. Packed 1 in a box; 3 dozen to a carton. Weight per carton 11 lbs. Olive green color with bright trimming. Two plastic digging tools.

**No. 324 Hook and Ladder**
Length 7¾ inches. Packed 1 in a box; 3 dozen to a carton. Weight per carton 11 lbs. Red with aluminum trimming; two ivory plastic ladders which can be removed and joined together.





**No. 322 Dump Truck**
Length 6½ inches. Packed 1 in a box; 3 dozen to a carton. Weight per carton 10 lbs. Cab and dump body in assorted colors, red and green; also green and yellow, with aluminum trimming. Spring clip holds dump body down. Tail gate swings open when dump is raised.

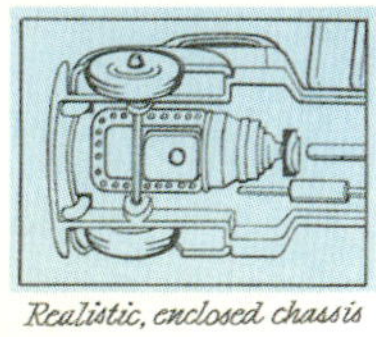

**No. 330 Motor Express**
Length 6½ inches. Packed 1 in a box; 3 dozen to a carton. Weight per carton 12 lbs. Red and green combination, with aluminum trimming. Rear tail gate opens.

**No. 329 Gas Truck**
Length 6½ inches. Packed 1 in a box; 3 dozen to a carton. Weight per carton 12 lbs. Red and bright metallic combination, with aluminum trimming.



1953

**No. 326 Airplane**
Length 6¼ inches. Packed 1 in a box; 3 dozen to a carton. Weight per carton 7 lbs. Red and bright metallic combination. Three wheeled retractable landing gear. Rubber wheels.

**No. 325 Racer**
Length 6¾ inches. Packed 1 in a box; 3 dozen to a carton. Weight per carton 10 lbs. Yellow with red trimming and red with yellow trimming. Hood lifts up exposing realistic motor. Rubber wheels.

**No. 328 Tractor**
Length 5½ inches. Packed 1 in a box; 3 dozen to a carton. Weight per carton 16 lbs. Red, green and orange with aluminum finish steering wheel. Realistic detailing of engine, chassis, hood and seat. Black rubber wheels, treaded on rear, grooved on front like real tractor.





**No. 354 Earth Mover**
Length 14 inches. Packed 1 in a box; 1 dozen to a carton. Weight per carton 13 lbs. Yellow and red combination. Bottom opens when lever at rear is thrown. Black rubber wheels with spare behind driver's seat.

**No. 355 Hook and Ladder**
Length 12¾ inches. Packed 1 in a box; 1 dozen to a carton. Weight per carton 10 lbs. Red cab and trailer with aluminum trimming. Four removable plastic ladders which can be attached to revolving turret. Aluminum finished searchlights and metal axe. Rubber wheels.

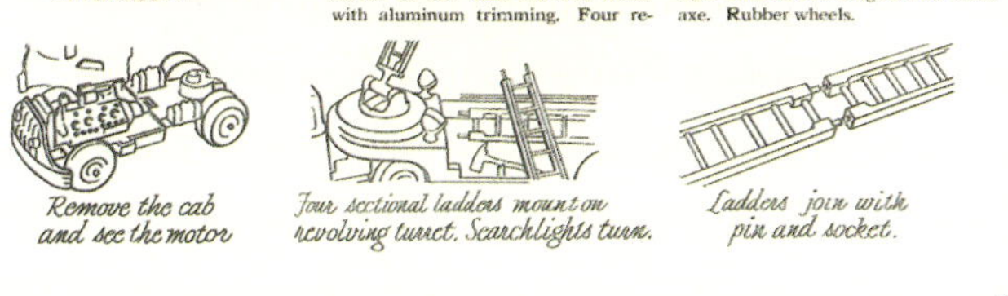

**No. 356 Log Truck**

Length 12¼ inches. Packed 1 in a box; 1 dozen to a carton. Weight per carton 17 lbs. Orange cab and trailer with aluminum trimming. Cab lifts off revealing detailed V-8 engine. Realistic chassis details. Twelve logs with chain to hold them in place. Retractable trailer support. Black rubber wheels, dual on rear of tractor. Rear wheels on trailer have knee action.

**No. 352 Motor Express**

Length 12½ inches. Packed 1 in a box; 1 dozen to a carton. Weight per carton 16 lbs. Red and green combination with aluminum trimming. Cab lifts off revealing detailed V-8 engine. Realistic chassis details. Side door slides open. Rear doors swing out. Retractable trailer support. Black rubber wheels, dual on rear of tractor. Rear wheels on trailer have knee action.

**No. 353 Auto Transport**

Length 13½ inches. Packed 1 in a box; 1 dozen to a carton. Weight per carton 13 lbs. Red with aluminum trimming. Cab lifts off revealing detailed V-8 engine. Realistic chassis details. Four plastic cars in assorted colors, which can be driven on or off trailer over removable ramp which hooks under trailer. Black rubber wheels, dual on rear of tractor.

**No. 357 Cattle Truck**

Length 12½ inches. Packed 1 in a box; 1 dozen to a carton. Weight per carton 14 lbs. Red and yellow combination with aluminum trimming. Cab lifts off exposing detailed V-8 engine. Realistic chassis details. Rear doors swing out. Retractable trailer support. Black rubber wheels, dual on rear of tractor. Rear wheels on trailer have knee action.

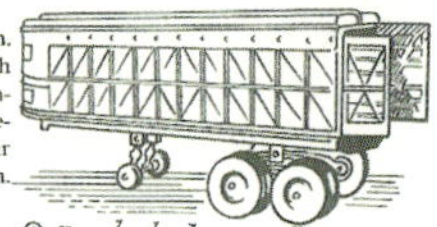




1953

**No. 460 Stake Truck**

Length 7 inches. Packed 1 in a box; 3 dozen to a carton. Weight per carton 25 lbs. Assorted colors with aluminum sides and drop end gate. Rubber wheels.

**No. 462 Tow Truck**

Length 7 inches. Packed 1 in a box; 3 dozen to a carton. Weight per carton 25 lbs. Assorted colors with aluminum finished sides and movable boom. Rubber wheels.

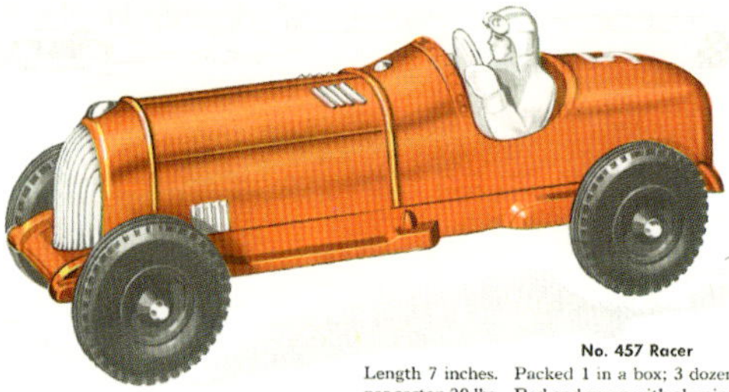

**No. 457 Racer**

Length 7 inches. Packed 1 in a box; 3 dozen to a carton. Weight per carton 20 lbs. Red and green with aluminum man and trimming. Rubber wheels.





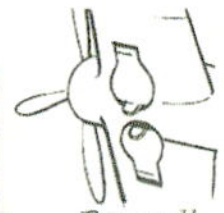


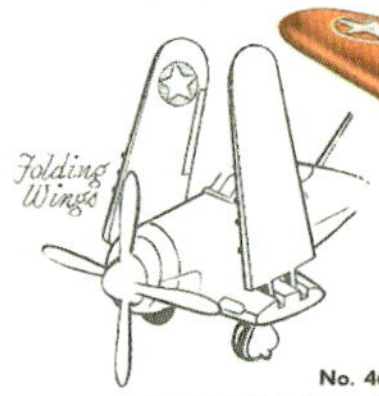


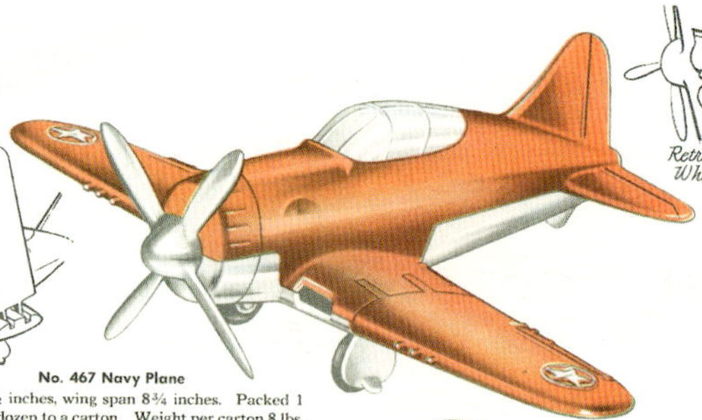

**No. 467 Navy Plane**

Length 6½ inches, wing span 8¾ inches. Packed 1 in a box; 1 dozen to a carton. Weight per carton 8 lbs. Red and aluminum trimming. Cockpit enclosed with transparent plastic bubble. Wings fold. Retractable landing gear. Rubber wheels. Revolving propeller.

**No. 464 Fire Engine**

Length 7½ inches. Packed 1 in a box; 3 dozen to a carton. Weight per carton 25 lbs. Red with aluminum finished pumper top and windshield. Rubber wheels.

**No. 463 Hook and Ladder**

Length 7½ inches. Packed 1 in a box; 3 dozen to a carton. Weight per carton 23 lbs. Red with aluminum finished windshield. Revolving ladder turret and plastic ladder. Rubber wheels.

**No. 470 Lumber Truck**

Length 10 inches. Packed 1 in a box; 1 dozen to a carton. Weight per carton 16 lbs. Orange with aluminum trimming. Five removable logs with chain to hold them in place. Rubber wheels.

**No. 472 Tractor**

Length 7 inches. Packed 1 in a box; 1 dozen to a carton. Weight per carton 13 lbs. Red with realistic engine details. Bright aluminum trimming. Yellow plastic wheels with black rubber tires.

**No. 474 Tow Truck**

Length 9¾ inches. Packed 1 in a box; 1 dozen to a carton. Weight per carton 14 lbs. Red with aluminum finished winch and boom. Rubber wheels.

**No. 476 Dump Truck**

Length 9½ inches. Packed 1 in a box; 1 dozen to a carton. Weight per carton 15 lbs. Green chassis, red movable dump. Aluminum trimming. Rubber wheels.



1953

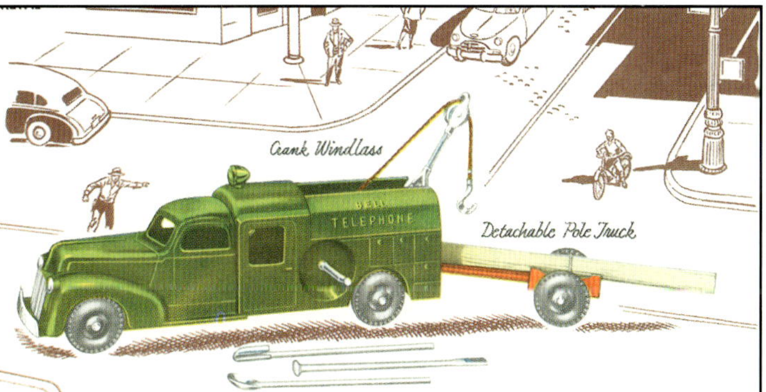


**No. 478 Telephone Truck**

Length of truck 10½ inches. Packed 1 in a box; 1 dozen to a carton. Weight per carton 22 lbs. Olive green with aluminum trimming. Equipped with red trailer and telegraph pole; aluminum finished winch and red boom; three digging tools. Rubber wheels.

**No. 477 Cement Mixer**

Length 10 inches. Packed 1 in a box; 1 dozen to a carton. Weight per carton 17 lbs. Red chassis, green body, revolving aluminum finished mixer. Rubber wheels.

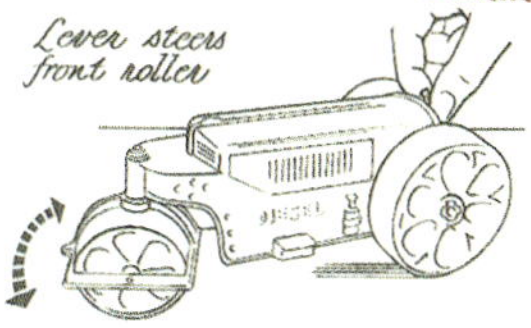


**No. 480 Road Roller**

Length 10 inches. Packed 1 in a box; 1 dozen to a carton. Weight per carton 21 lbs. Orange body with aluminum trimming and metal wheels. Steers by lever in driver's compartment.

**No. 481 Road Scraper**

Length 10¾ inches. Packed 1 in a box; 1 dozen to a carton. Weight per carton 15 lbs. Yellow with bright scraper and trimming. The rear wheels are mounted independently to roll over stones and obstacles. Adjustable scraper. Front wheels operated by steering wheel. Rubber wheels.

# HUBLEY TRACTOR

**No. 490 Tractor**

Length 9½ inches. Packed 1 in a box; 1 dozen to a carton. Weight per carton 21 lbs. Red with aluminum trimming. Realistic engine details visible on both sides. Spring action driver's seat. Front wheels operated by steering wheel. All metal wheels with black, treaded, rubber tires.

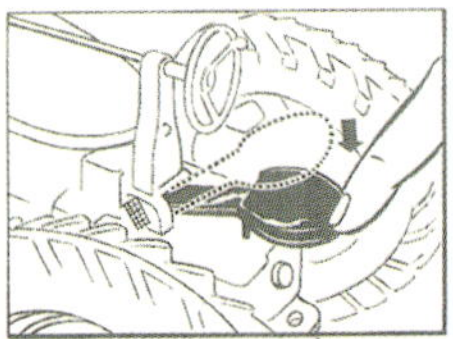

*Spring Mounted Seat*

*Front wheels steer*





# HUBLEY TELEPHONE TRUCK

**No. 504 Telephone Truck**

Length 12½ inches. Packed 1 in a box; ½ dozen to a carton. Weight per carton 20 lbs. Olive green with aluminum trimming. Removable boom in rear. Crank raises or lowers rope and hook. Top of truck slides back to cover open half in rear. Plastic ladder. Three metal digging tools. Red trailer hooks on rear. 11 inch telegraph pole. Black rubber wheels, dual in rear.

*Sliding top cover.* *Pole trailer in travelling position.* *Winch in operation.*



1953



# HUBLEY LOG TRUCK

**No. 505 Log Truck**

Length 18 inches. Packed 1 in a box; ½ dozen to a carton. Weight por carton 21 lbs. Orange with aluminum trimming. Cab lifts off revealing motor. Realistic chassis details. Trailer carries 5 logs each 12 inches long. Wheels are independently mounted to roll over stones or obstacles. Two chains to hold logs in place. Black rubber wheels.

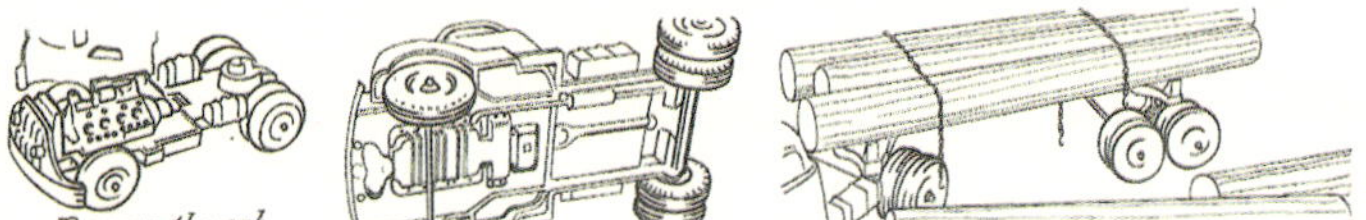

*Remove the cab and see the motor* *Closed chassis, realistic detail.* *Logs unload.* *Note also-independent rear wheels.*





# HUBLEY CARRYALL

**No. 506 Carryall**

Length 19½ inches. Packed 1 in a box; ½ dozen to a carton. Weight per carton 24 lbs. Orange flat bed machinery carrier. Cab lifts off revealing realistic motor. Seven wheels realistically mounted on rear of trailer. Complete with 10¾ inch metal road scraper. Black rubber wheels.

For details of Road Scraper only. See Page 17.

*Remove the cab and see the motor*

# HUBLEY MOTOR EXPRESS

**No. 507 Motor Express**

Length 18 inches. Packed 1 in a box; ½ dozen to a carton. Weight per carton 32 lbs. Red and green combination with aluminum trimming. Cab lifts off revealing realistic motor. Side door slides open. Rear door swings out. Independently mounted rear wheels to roll over stones and obstacles. Retractable trailer support. Black rubber wheels, dual in rear.

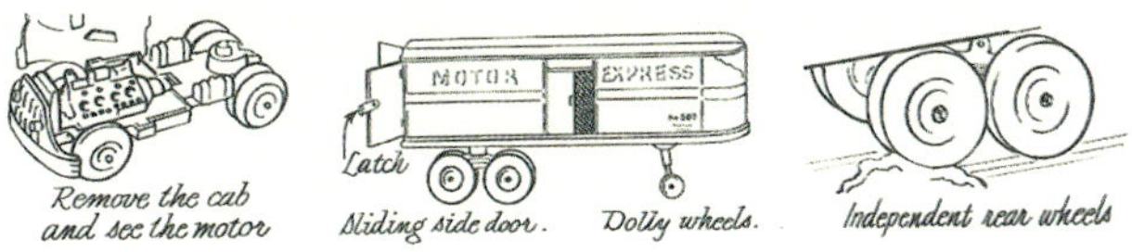






# No. 50 Farm Set

One set to a box; ½ dozen boxes to a carton. Metal and plastic.

# No. 4 Farm Set

One set to a box; one dozen to a carton. Set consists of: No. 328 Tractor, Cultipacker, plastic Farm Wagon.

# No. 65 Lift The Hood Toy Set

One set to a box; one dozen boxes to a carton. Set consists of: No. 322 Dump Truck, No. 323 Wrecker, No. 324 Fire Truck, No. 327 Telephone Truck.

1953



## No. 60 Road Building Set

One set to a box; one dozen boxes to a carton. Set consists of: No. 315 Road Roller, No. 316 Road Scraper, and plastic Flat Bed Truck.

**Craftsmanship**

To Hubley, craftsmanship implies many things. Not only expertness in design but good modeling and competence in production.

First of all, Hubley Toys are planned, designed, and modeled by artisans with many years of experience in the toy business.

They must be attractive to children and must have a maximum of real life details.

They must "play" well and must have realistic, educational play features with careful thought to the safety of the child.

They must be well made to provide long, hard play in normal use.

They must sell well and this is our pledge to you: Hubley craftsmanship at attractive prices will be our continuing aim.

**The Hubley Manufacturing Company, Lancaster, Pa.**

HUBLEY

*nted in the United States of America, 1953*
*gned and Produced by Andes, Lancaster, Pa.*

# 1954

# HUBLEY

## Kiddie Toys

for 1954

## Packing, Weights and Index — HUBLEY "KIDDIE TOYS"

| No. | Name | | Pieces in Box | Case Packing | Weight Per Carton | Catalog Page |
|---|---|---|---|---|---|---|
| 306 | Fire Engine | (Plastic) | 12 | 3 doz. | 6 lbs. | 3 |
| 307 | Hook and Ladder | (Plastic) | 12 | 3 doz. | 5 lbs. | 3 |
| 309 | Tractor | (Plastic) | 12 | 3 doz. | 11 lbs. | 4 |
| 310 | Motorcycle | (Plastic) | 12 | 3 doz. | 8 lbs. | 3 |
| 311 | Airplane | (Plastic) | 12 | 3 doz. | 6 lbs. | 3 |
| 315 | Road Roller | (Plastic) | 6 | 3 doz. | 9 lbs. | 4 |
| 316 | Road Scraper | (Plastic) | 6 | 3 doz. | 12 lbs. | 4 |
| 322 | Dump Truck | (Plastic) | 6 | 3 doz. | 10 lbs. | 4 |
| 323 | Tow Truck | (Plastic) | 6 | 3 doz. | 11 lbs. | 5 |
| 324 | Hook and Ladder | (Plastic) | 6 | 3 doz. | 11 lbs. | 5 |
| 325 | Racer | (Plastic) | 6 | 3 doz. | 10 lbs. | 5 |
| 326 | Airplane | (Plastic) | 6 | 3 doz. | 7 lbs. | 5 |
| 327 | Telephone Truck | (Plastic) | 6 | 3 doz. | 11 lbs. | 6 |
| 328 | Tractor | (Plastic) | 6 | 3 doz. | 16 lbs. | 6 |
| 329 | Gas Truck | (Plastic) | 6 | 3 doz. | 12 lbs. | 6 |
| 330 | Motor Express | (Plastic) | 6 | 3 doz. | 12 lbs. | 6 |
| 351 | Lumber Truck | (Plastic) | 1 | 1 doz. | 17 lbs. | 7 |
| 352 | Motor Express | (Plastic) | 1 | 1 doz. | 16 lbs. | 8 |
| 353 | Auto Transport | (Plastic) | 1 | 1 doz. | 13 lbs. | 8 |
| 354 | Earth Mover | (Plastic) | 1 | 1 doz. | 13 lbs. | 7 |
| 355 | Hook and Ladder | (Plastic) | 1 | 1 doz. | 10 lbs. | 7 |
| 357 | Cattle Truck | (Plastic) | 1 | 1 doz. | 15 lbs. | 9 |
| 358 | Hubley Tanker | (Plastic) | 1 | 1 doz. | 13 lbs. | 9 |
| 452 | Stake Truck | (Metal) | 1 | 3 doz. | 20 lbs. | 10 |
| 453 | Tow Truck | (Metal) | 1 | 3 doz. | 20 lbs. | 10 |
| 454 | Log Truck | (Metal) | 1 | 3 doz. | 20 lbs. | 10 |
| 455 | Sport Car | (Metal) | 1 | 3 doz. | 20 lbs. | 10 |
| 456 | Tractor | (Metal) | 1 | 3 doz. | 24 lbs. | 11 |
| 463 | Hook and Ladder | (Metal) | 1 | 3 doz. | 21 lbs. | 11 |
| 464 | Fire Engine | (Metal) | 1 | 3 doz. | 24 lbs. | 11 |
| 467 | Navy Plane | (Metal) | 1 | 1 doz. | 9 lbs. | 11 |
| 469 | Log Truck | (Metal) | 1 | 1 doz. | 15 lbs. | 12 |
| 471 | Dump Truck | (Metal) | 1 | 1 doz. | 13 lbs. | 12 |
| 473 | Tractor | (Metal) | 1 | 1 doz. | 15 lbs. | 12 |
| 474 | Tow Truck | (Metal) | 1 | 1 doz. | 12 lbs. | 13 |
| 480 | Road Roller | (Metal) | 1 | 1 doz. | 21 lbs. | 14 |
| 481 | Road Scraper | (Metal) | 1 | 1 doz. | 15 lbs. | 14 |
| 483 | Cement Mixer | (Metal) | 1 | 1 doz. | 16 lbs. | 14 |
| 484 | Telephone Truck | (Metal) | 1 | 1 doz. | 20 lbs. | 13 |
| 485 | Sport Car | (Metal) | 1 | 1 doz. | 17 lbs. | 13 |
| 490 | Tractor | (Metal) | 1 | 1 doz. | 29 lbs. | 15 |
| 500 | Tractor-Loader | (Metal) | 1 | ½ doz. | 17 lbs. | 22 |
| 504 | Telephone Truck | (Metal) | 1 | ½ doz. | 20 lbs. | 23 |
| 505 | Log Truck | (Metal) | 1 | ½ doz. | 22 lbs. | 24 |
| 506 | Carryall | (Metal) | 1 | ½ doz. | 25 lbs. | 25 |
| 507 | Motor Express | (Metal) | 1 | ½ doz. | 34 lbs. | 26 |
| 508 | Dump Truck | (Metal) | 1 | ½ doz. | 20 lbs. | 27 |

### BOXED ASSORTMENTS

| No. | Name | | Pieces in Box | Case Packing | Weight Per Carton | Catalog Page |
|---|---|---|---|---|---|---|
| 4 | Farm Set | (Plastic) | 1 | 1 doz. | 11 lbs. | 16 |
| 25 | Assortment | (Plastic) | 1 | 1 doz. | 16 lbs. | 17 |
| 35 | Fire Department | (Plastic) | 1 | 1 doz. | 18 lbs. | 18 |
| 45 | Assortment | (Metal) | 1 | 1 doz. | 30 lbs. | 20 |
| 50 | Farm Set | (Metal) | 1 | ½ doz. | 16 lbs. | 21 |
| 60 | Road Building Set | (Plastic) | 1 | 1 doz. | 22 lbs. | 19 |

### PLASTIC

306

**No. 306 Fire Engine**

Length 6 inches. Packed 12 in a box; 3 dozen to a carton. Weight per carton 6 lbs. Red with aluminum trimming. Rubber wheels.

307

**No. 307 Hook and Ladder**

Length 6 inches. Packed 12 in a box; 3 dozen to a carton. Weight per carton 5 lbs. Red with aluminum trimming. Two steel ladders. Rubber wheels.

310

**No. 310 Motorcycle**

Length 5 inches. Packed 12 in a box; 3 dozen to a carton. Weight per carton 8 lbs. Red and green motorcycle, blue man. Rubber wheels.

311

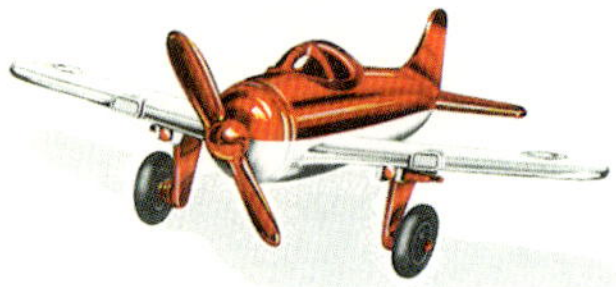

**No. 311 Airplane**

Length 5 inches, wingspread 6¼ inches. Packed 12 in a box; 3 dozen to a carton. Weight per carton 6 lbs. Red and silver combination. Retractable landing gear. Rubber wheels.



1954

### PLASTIC

**No. 309 Tractor**

Length 4¾ inches. Packed 12 in a box; 3 dozen to a carton. Weight per carton 11 lbs. Red, green, and orange with aluminum trimming. Rubber wheels.

309

**No. 316 Road Scraper**

Length 6¼ inches. Packed 6 in a box; 3 dozen to a carton. Weight per carton 12 lbs. Yellow body with adjustable aluminum finished scraper. Rubber wheels.

316

**No. 315 Road Roller**

Length 5¾ inches. Packed 6 in a box; 3 dozen to a carton. Weight per carton 9 lbs. Green body. Red wooden wheels and roller.

315

**No. 322 Dump Truck**

Length 6½ inches. Packed 6 in a box; 3 dozen to a carton. Weight per carton 10 lbs. Cab and dump body in assorted colors—red and green, also green and yellow. Aluminum trimming. Rubber wheels. Spring clip holds dump body down. Tail gate swings open when dump is raised.

*"Lift the hood, see the motor" feature. By pressing release under cab the hood lifts up exposing a 6 cylinder motor to work on. Chassis is enclosed underneath with realistic details.*

322

### PLASTIC

323

**No. 323 Tow Truck**

Length 6½ inches. Packed 6 in a box; 3 dozen to a carton. Weight per carton 11 lbs. Red plastic cab. Body in assorted colors—green and ivory. Aluminum trimming. Rubber wheels. Crank operates metal hook.

*"Lift the hood, see the motor" feature. See No. 322, page 4 for details.*

324

**No. 324 Hook and Ladder**

Length 7¾ inches. Packed 6 in a box; 3 dozen to a carton. Weight per carton 11 lbs. Red with aluminum trimming; two ivory plastic ladders which can be removed and joined together. Rubber wheels.

*"Lift the hood, see the motor" feature. See No. 322, page 4 for details.*

325

**No. 325 Racer**

Length 6¾ inches. Packed 6 in a box; 3 dozen to a carton. Weight per carton 10 lbs. Red and silver combination. Rubber wheels. Hood lifts up exposing realistic motor.

326

**No. 326 Airplane**

Length 6¼ inches, wingspread 8 inches. Packed 6 in a box; 3 dozen to a carton. Weight per carton 7 lbs. Red and silver combination. Three wheeled retractable landing gear. Rubber wheels.

## PLASTIC

**No. 327 Telephone Truck**

ength 6½ inches. Packed 6 in a ox; 3 dozen to a carton. Weight er carton 11 lbs. Olive green color with aluminum trimming. Two lastic digging tools. Rubber wheels.

*"Lift the hood, see the motor" feature. See No. 322, page 4 for details.*

327

**No. 329 Gas Truck**

ength 6½ inches. Packed 6 in a ox; 3 dozen to a carton. Weight er carton 12 lbs. Red and silver ombination with aluminum trimming. Rubber wheels.

*"Lift the hood, see the motor" feature. See No. 322, page 4 for details.*

329

**No. 330 Motor Express**

Length 6½ inches. Packed 6 in a ox; 3 dozen to a carton. Weight per carton 12 lbs. Red and green combination with aluminum trimming. Rubber wheels. Rear tail gate opens.

*"Lift the hood, see the motor" feature. See No. 322, page 4 for details.*

*Tail gate opens*

330

**No. 328 Tractor**

Length 5½ inches. Packed 6 in a box; 3 dozen to a carton. Weight per carton 16 lbs. Red, green, and orange with aluminum trimming. Realistic detailing of engine, chassis, hood and seat. Black rubber wheels, treaded on rear, grooved on front like real tractor.

328



## PLASTIC

**No. 351 Lumber Truck**

Length 14¼ inches. Packed 1 in a box; 1 dozen to a carton. Weight per carton 17 lbs. Green cab and red trailer with aluminum trimming. Nine pieces of lumber with chain to hold them in place. 14 black rubber wheels plus 2 on retractable trailer support. Rear wheels on trailer have knee action.

*"Remove the cab, see the motor" feature. See No. 353 below for details.*

351

*Lumber unloading, dolly wheels down*

**No. 354 Earth Mover**

Length 14 inches. Packed 1 in a box; 1 dozen to a carton. Weight per carton 13 lbs. Orange with aluminum trimming. 6 black rubber wheels plus spare behind driver's seat. Trailer bottom opens when lever at rear is thrown.

354

*Realistic cab and hitch*
*Lever drops bottom boards*

**No. 355 Hook and Ladder**

Length 12¾ inches. Packed 1 in a box; 1 dozen to a carton. Weight per carton 10 lbs. Red cab and trailer with aluminum trimming. Three removable ivory plastic ladders which can be attached to revolving turret. Aluminum finished searchlights. 8 black rubber wheels.

*"Remove the cab, see the motor" feature. Cab lifts off, revealing detailed V-8 engine to work on. Chassis enclosed underneath with realistic details.*

355

*Remove the cab and see the motor.*

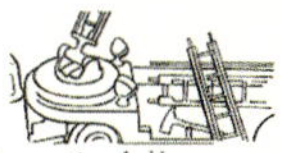

*Three-section ladder mounts on revolving turret. Searchlights turn.*

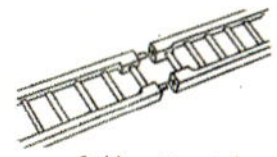

*Ladders join with pin and socket.*



1954

## PLASTIC

**No. 352 Motor Express**

Length 12½ inches. Packed 1 in a box; 1 dozen to a carton. Weight per carton 16 lbs. Red and green combination with aluminum trimming. Side door slides open, rear doors swing out. 14 black rubber wheels plus 2 on retractable trailer support. Rear wheels on trailer have knee action.

*"Remove the cab, see the motor" feature. See No. 353 below.*

352

*Doors open, dolly wheels down*

**No. 353 Auto Transport**

Length 13½ inches. Packed 1 in a box; 1 dozen to a carton. Weight per carton 13 lbs. Red with aluminum trimming. Four plastic cars in assorted colors that can be driven on or off trailer over removable ramp which hooks under trailer. 10 black rubber wheels.

*"Remove the cab, see the motor" feature. Cab lifts off, revealing detailed V-8 engine to work on. Chassis enclosed underneath with realistic details.*

353

*Remove the cab and see the motor*

*Ramp loading cars*



## PLASTIC

**No. 357 Cattle Truck**

Length 12½ inches. Packed 1 in a box; 1 dozen to a carton. Weight per carton 15 lbs. Red and yellow combination with aluminum trimming. Rear doors swing out. 14 black rubber wheels plus 2 on retractable trailer support. Rear wheels on trailer have knee action.

*"Remove the cab, see the motor" feature See No. 353, page 8.*

357

*Trailer unhitches, dolly wheels drop, rear doors open, as in illustration under 352, opposite.*

**No. 358 Hubley Tanker**

Length 12¾ inches. Packed 1 in a box; 1 dozen to a carton. Weight per carton 13 lbs. Red with aluminum trimming. 14 black rubber wheels plus 2 on retractable trailer support. Rear wheels on trailer have knee action.

*"Remove the cab, see the motor" feature. See No. 353, page 8.*

358

*Trailer unhitches, dolly wheels drop.*

## METAL

No. 452 Stake Truck

Length 7 inches. Packed 1 in a box; 3 dozen to a carton. Weight per carton 20 lbs. Assorted colors with bright metal sides, tail gate, bumper and grill. Rubber wheels.

452

No. 453 Tow Truck

Length 7 inches. Packed 1 in a box; 3 dozen to a carton. Weight per carton 20 lbs. Assorted colors with bright metal sides, movable boom, bumper and grill. Rubber wheels.

453

No. 454 Log Truck

Length 7½ inches. Packed 1 in a box; 3 dozen to a carton. Weight per carton 20 lbs. Assorted colors with bright metal bed, bumper and grill. 5 logs. Rubber wheels.

454

No. 455 Sport Car

Length 7½ inches. Packed 1 in a box; 3 dozen to a carton. Weight per carton 20 lbs. Assorted colors—red and yellow. Aluminum trimming. Clear green tinted windshield and interior. Realistic detailing of interior. Black rubber wheels.

455

## METAL

No. 456 Tractor

Length 5½ inches. Packed 1 in a box; 3 dozen to a carton. Weight per carton 24 lbs. Red with aluminum trimming. Realistic detailing of engine, chassis, hood and seat. Black rubber wheels, treaded front and rear like real tractor.

456

No. 464 Fire Engine

Length 7½ inches. Packed 1 in a box; 3 dozen to a carton. Weight per carton 24 lbs. Red with bright metal pumper top and windshield. Black rubber wheels.

464

No. 463 Hook and Ladder

Length 7½ inches. Packed 1 in a box; 3 dozen to a carton. Weight per carton 21 lbs. Red with bright metal windshield. Revolving ladder turret and ivory plastic ladder. Black rubber wheels.

463

No. 467 Navy Plane

Length 6½ inches, wingspread 8¾ inches. Packed 1 in a box; 1 dozen to a carton. Weight per carton 9 lbs. Bright metal with red trim. Cockpit enclosed with transparent bubble. Folding wings, retractable landing gear, revolving propeller. Black rubber wheels.

467

1954

## METAL

No. 469 Log Truck

Length 10 inches. Packed 1 in a box; 1 dozen to a carton. Weight per carton 15 lbs. Orange with bright metal bed, bumper and grill. Five removable logs with chain to hold them in place. 6 black rubber wheels.

469

No. 471 Dump Truck

Length 9½ inches. Packed 1 in a box; 1 dozen to a carton. Weight per carton 13 lbs. Green chassis, red movable dump. Bright metal tail gate, bumper and grill. Tail gate opens automatically when dump is raised. 6 black rubber wheels.

471

No. 473 Tractor

Length 7¼ inches. Packed 1 in a box; 1 dozen to a carton. Weight per carton 15 lbs. Red with aluminum trimming and yellow rear wheels. Realistic engine details. Black rubber tires, treaded front and rear like a real tractor.

473

## METAL

No. 474 Tow Truck

Length 9¾ inches. Packed 1 in a box; 1 dozen to a carton. Weight per carton 12 lbs. Red with aluminum trimming. Bright metal movable winch and boom. Black rubber wheels.

474

No. 484 Telephone Truck

Length of truck 10½ inches. Packed 1 in a box; 1 dozen to a carton. Weight per carton 20 lbs. Olive green with bright metal winch and boom, bumper and grill. Equipped with red trailer, telephone pole, and three bright metal digging tools. 6 black rubber wheels plus 2 on trailer.

*Crank windlass as on No. 474 above.*

484

No. 485 Sport Car

Length 9 inches. Packed 1 in a box; 1 dozen to a carton. Weight per carton 17 lbs. Red with bright metal bumpers, grill, headlights, windshield and interior. Interior realistically detailed. Chassis enclosed on bottom with realistic details. 4 black rubber wheels, plus spare mounted "continental fashion" on rear.

485

**METAL**

### No. 480 Road Roller

Length 10 inches. Packed 1 in a box; 1 dozen to a carton. Weight per carton 21 lbs. Orange body with aluminum trimming. Bright metal wheels. Steers by lever in driver's compartment.

480

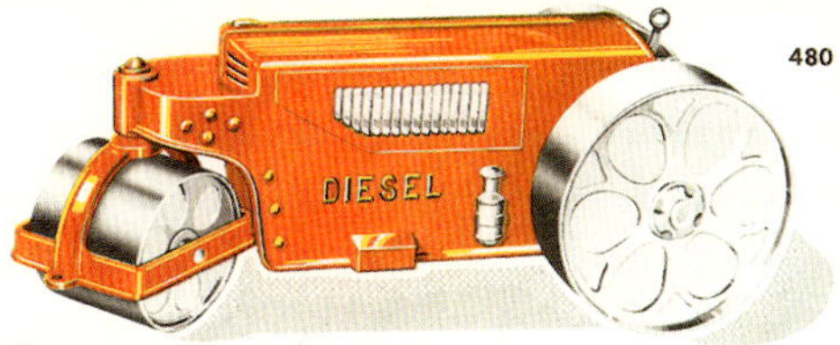

### No. 483 Cement Mixer

Length 10 inches. Packed 1 in a box; 1 dozen to a carton. Weight per carton 16 lbs. Red chassis, green body. Bright metal bumper, grill and revolving mixer. 6 black rubber wheels.

483

### No. 481 Road Scraper

Length 10¾ inches. Packed 1 in a box; 1 dozen to a carton. Weight per carton 15 lbs. Yellow with bright metal adjustable scraper. Aluminum trimming. The rear wheels are mounted independently to roll over stones and obstacles. The front wheels are operated by the steering wheel. 6 black rubber wheels.

481

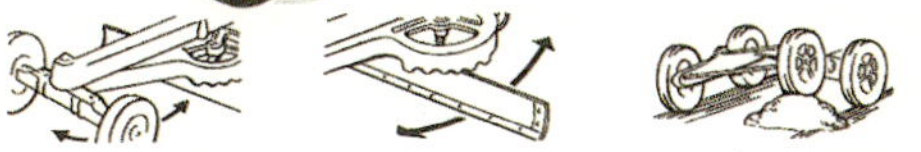

Steering Wheel action — Scraper Blade adjustable — Independent rear wheels



**METAL**

490

### No. 490 Tractor

Length 9½ inches. Packed 1 in a box; 1 dozen to a carton. Weight per carton 29 lbs. Red with aluminum trimming. Realistic engine details visible on both sides. Spring action driver's seat. Front wheels turned by steering wheel. All metal rear wheels. Black rubber tires treaded front and rear like a real tractor.

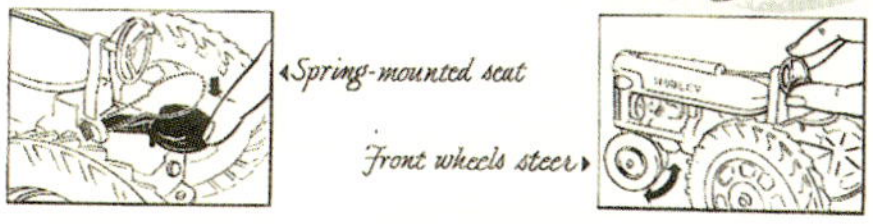


## *Craftsmanship*

This is a good word to describe the thought and competent production behind Hubley Toys.

It covers expert design and good modeling by Hubley artisans, practiced by many years of experience in the toy business. It means the ability to build toys attractive to children, with lots of real life details. These toys must provide genuine educational play features, yet be safe, and "play" well for many long hours.

Craftsmanship helps Hubley Toys sell well, and that is where it enters our pledge to you: Hubley craftsmanship at attractive prices will be our continuing aim.

**The Hubley Manufacturing Company, Lancaster, Pa.**



1954

## No. 4 Farm Set (Plastic)

*328 Tractor*
*5½ inches long*

*Wagon*

*Cultipacker*

**PLASTIC**

Set consists of No. 328 Tractor, Cultipacker and Wagon. Packed 1 set in a box; 1 dozen sets to a carton. Weight per carton 11 lbs. Toys red with aluminum trimming. Black rubber wheels.

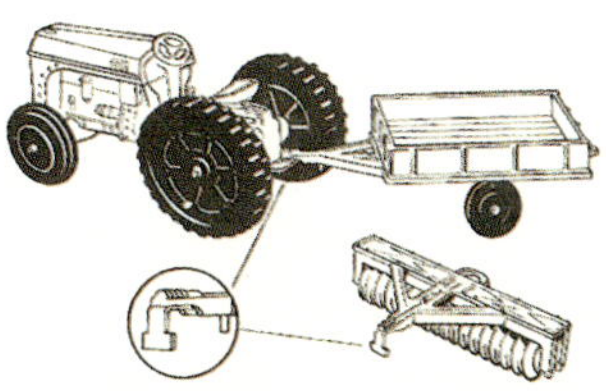

*Metal hitch for strength*

*Attractive red, yellow, blue and green carton. Die cut lid folds to form self display.*



## No. 25 Assortment (Plastic)

*328 Tractor*

*316 Road Scraper*
*6¼ inches long*

*325 Racer*

**PLASTIC**

Set consists of green No. 328 Tractor, yellow No. 316 Road Scraper, red and yellow No. 325 Racer, red and silver No. 326 Airplane. Packed 1 set in a box; 1 dozen sets to a carton. Weight per carton 16 lbs. Black rubber wheels.

*326 Airplane*
*8 inch wing span*

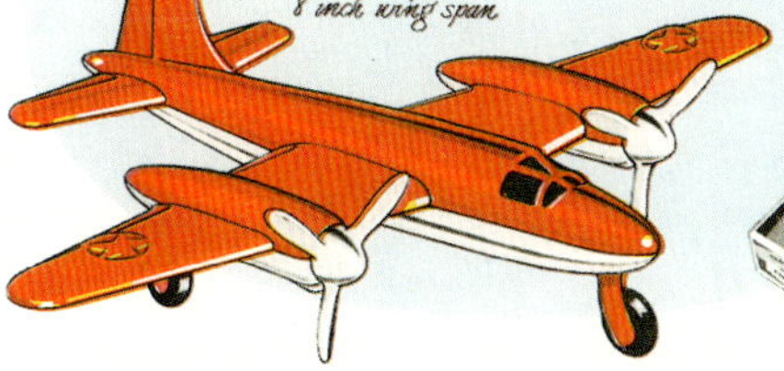

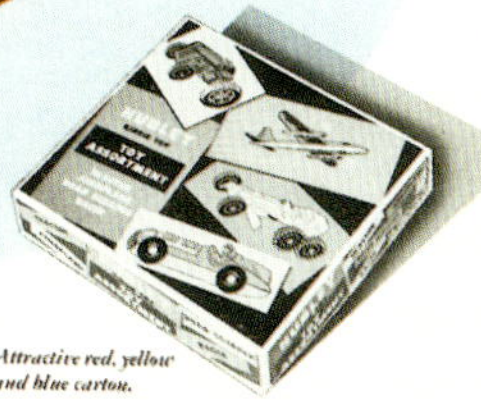

*Attractive red, yellow and blue carton.*

## No. 35 Fire Department (Plastic)

*355 Hook and Ladder*
*12 3/4 inches long*

*305 Fire Chief Car*

*311 Airplane*

*310 Motorcycle*

**PLASTIC**

Set consists of red No. 355 Hook and Ladder with 3 ivory ladders, red No. 305 Fire Chief Car, red and silver No. 311 Airplane, red No. 310 Motorcycle with black Cop. Packed 1 set in a box; 1 dozen sets to a carton. Weight per carton 18 lbs. Black rubber wheels.

*Attractive carton printed in red, yellow, blue and black.*

18

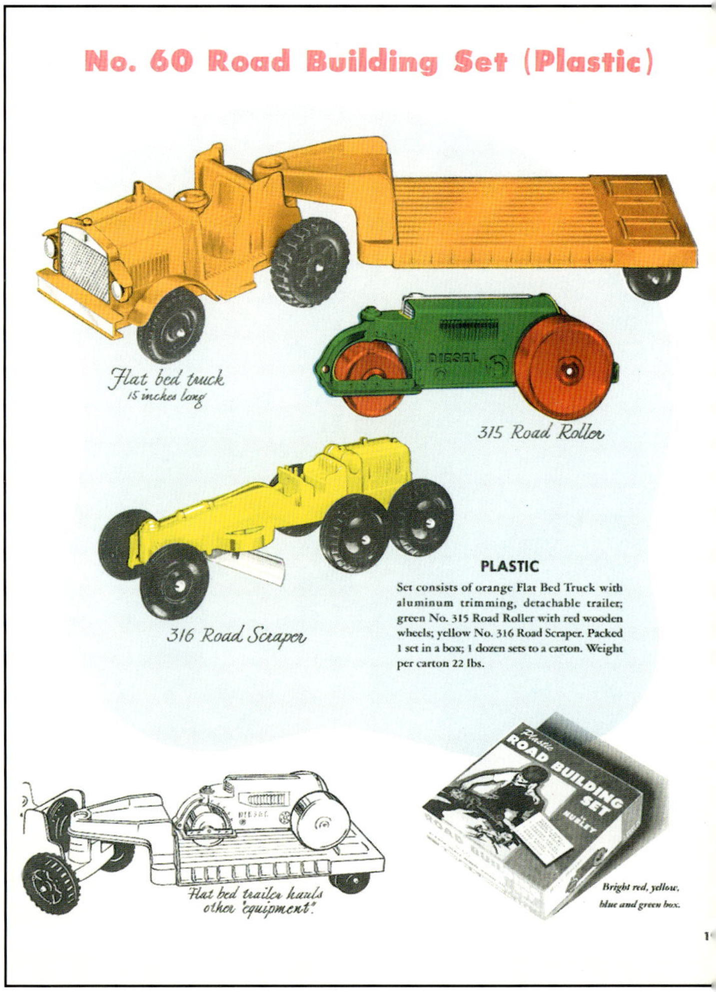

## No. 60 Road Building Set (Plastic)

*Flat bed truck*
*15 inches long*

*315 Road Roller*

*316 Road Scraper*

**PLASTIC**

Set consists of orange Flat Bed Truck with aluminum trimming, detachable trailer; green No. 315 Road Roller with red wooden wheels; yellow No. 316 Road Scraper. Packed 1 set in a box; 1 dozen sets to a carton. Weight per carton 22 lbs.

*Flat bed trailer hauls other "equipment".*

*Bright red, yellow, blue and green box.*

1954

## No. 45 Assortment (Metal)

*467 Navy Plane*
*Wing span 8 3/4 inches*

*452 Stake Truck*
*6 3/4 inches long*

*455 Sport Car*

*456 Tractor*

**METAL**

Set consists of bright metal No. 467 Navy Plane with red trimming, yellow No. 455 Sport Car, green No. 452 Stake Truck with bright metal sides, red No. 456 Tractor. Packed 1 set in a box; 1 dozen sets to a carton. Weight per carton 30 lbs.

*Eye catching box printed in red, yellow, blue, green and black.*

20

## No. 50 Farm Set (Metal)

*Flat bed wagon*

*472 Tractor*
*7 inches long*

*Cultipacker*

*Manure spreader*

*Plow*

**METAL**

Set consists of No. 472 Tractor, Plow, Cultipacker, Spreader and Farm Wagon, all interlocking. Packed 1 set in a box; ½ dozen sets to a carton. Weight per carton 16 lbs. Toys red with aluminum trimming. Black rubber wheels.

*Attractive red, yellow, blue and green box.*

*All pieces hitch together*

21

# HUBLEY TRACTOR-LOADER

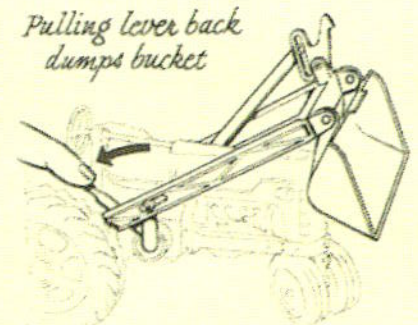

*Pulling lever back dumps bucket*

**METAL**

**No. 500 Tractor-Loader**

Length 13 inches. Packed 1 in a box; ½ dozen to a carton. Weight per carton 17 lbs. Red with bright metal loader mechanism and steering wheel. Aluminum trimming on radiator. Engine details, spring seat, steering, and wheels same as No. 490 Tractor, page 15. Side lever raises, lowers and dumps loader.

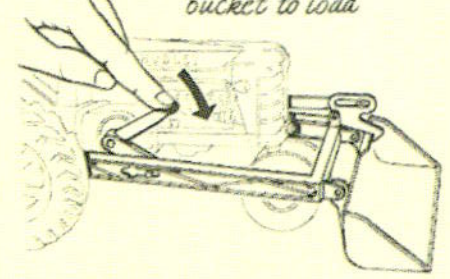

*Pushing Lever forward lowers bucket to load*

# HUBLEY TELEPHONE TRUCK

*Sliding Top Cover*

*Pole Trailer in travelling position*

**METAL**

**No. 504 Telephone Truck**

Length 12½ inches. Packed 1 in a box; ½ dozen to a carton. Weight per carton 20 lbs. Olive green with aluminum trimming. Bright metal bumper, grill, and removable boom. Crank raises or lowers rope and hook. Top of truck slides back to cover open half in rear. Equipped with red trailer and 11 inch pole, 3 bright metal digging tools, and ivory plastic ladder. Trailer hooks on rear. 6 black rubber wheels, plus 2 on trailer.

*Winch in operation*





# HUBLEY LOG TRUCK

*Remove the cab and see the motor*

**METAL**

**No. 505 Log Truck**

Length 18 inches. Packed 1 in a box; ½ dozen to a carton. Weight per carton 22 lbs. Orange with bright metal chassis, bumper and grill. "Remove the cab, see the motor" feature, plus enclosed chassis with realistic details. Trailer carries 5 logs, each 12 inches long. Two chains hold logs in place. 14 black rubber wheels. Rear wheels on trailer have knee action.

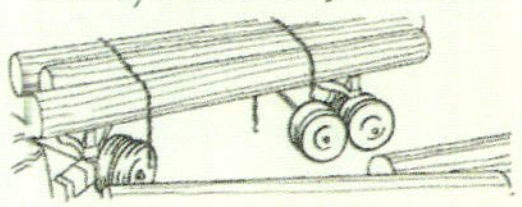

*Logs unload*
*Note independent action of rear wheels*

# HUBLEY CARRYALL

*Steering Wheel action*

**METAL**

**No. 506 Carryall**

Length 19½ inches. Packed 1 in a box; ½ dozen to a carton. Weight per carton 25 lbs. Orange flat bed machinery carrier. Bright metal bumper and grill. Aluminum trimming. Complete with No. 481 metal Road Scraper 10¾ inches long (see page 14). 6 black rubber wheels on cab, 7 realistically mounted on rear of carrier.

*"Remove the cab, see the motor" feature like No. 505, page 24.*

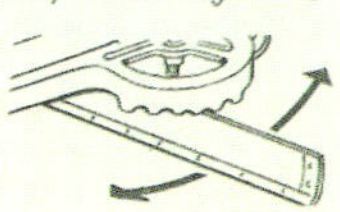

*Scraper Blade adjustable*



1954

26

# HUBLEY MOTOR EXPRESS

**METAL**

**No. 507 Motor Express**

Length 18 inches. Packed 1 in a box; ½ dozen to a carton. Weight per carton 34 lbs. Red and green combination with aluminum trimming. Bright metal chassis, bumper and grill. Side door on trailer slides open, rear doors swing out. 14 black rubber wheels plus 2 on retractable trailer support. Rear wheels on trailer have knee action.

*Remove the cab feature as on 505 - see page 24*

*Independent action, rear wheels of trailer*

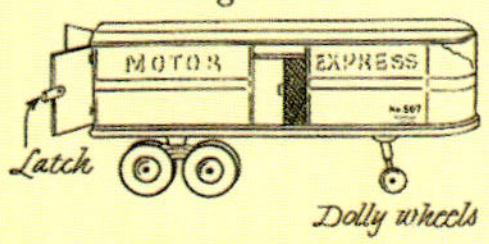


# HUBLEY DUMP TRUCK

**METAL**

**No. 508 Dump Truck**

Length 17 inches. Packed 1 in a box; ½ dozen to a carton. Weight per carton 20 lbs. Green cab with aluminum trimming. Bright metal chassis, bumper and grill. Movable red dump with aluminum trimming. Pushing lever on side raises dump, tail gate opens automatically. 14 black rubber wheels. Rear wheels on trailer have knee action.

*Remove the cab feature as on 505 -- see page 24.*

*Independent action, rear wheels of trailer.*

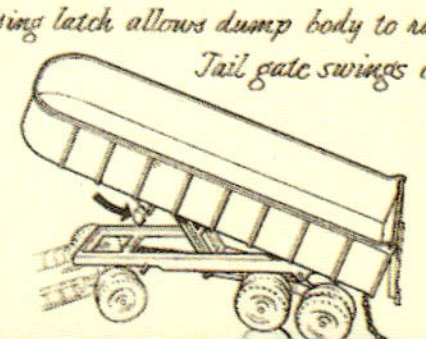

nted in the United States of America

Wm. D. Andes, Design and Advertising, Lancaster, P

# 1955

# Hubley

## Kiddie Toys

Kids love 'em!

HUBLEY MANUFACTURING COMPANY, LANCASTER, PA. ☆ SPRING 1955

## Packing, Weights and Index — HUBLEY "KIDDIE TOYS"

| No. | Name | | | Pieces in Box | Case Packing | Weight Per Carton | Catalog Page |
|---|---|---|---|---|---|---|---|
| 309 | Tractor | .15 | (Plastic) | 12 | 3 doz. | 11 lbs. | 3 |
| 310 | Motorcycle | .15 | (Plastic) | 12 | 3 doz. | 8 lbs. | 3 |
| 311 | Airplane | .15 | (Plastic) | 12 | 3 doz. | 5 lbs. | 3 |
| 316 | Road Scraper | .20 | (Plastic) | 6 | 3 doz. | 12 lbs. | 3 |
| 325 | Racer | .20 | (Plastic) | 6 | 3 doz. | 10 lbs. | 4 |
| 328 | Tractor | .20 | (Plastic) | 6 | 3 doz. | 16 lbs. | 4 |
| 331 | Diesel Dump Truck | .25 | (Plastic) | 6 | 3 doz. | 10 lbs. | 4 |
| 332 | Diesel Tow Truck | .25 | (Plastic) | 6 | 3 doz. | 11 lbs. | 4 |
| 333 | Diesel Hook & Ladder | .25 | (Plastic) | 6 | 3 doz. | 11 lbs. | 5 |
| 334 | Diesel Telephone Truck | .25 | (Plastic) | 6 | 3 doz. | 11 lbs. | 5 |
| 335 | Diesel Gas Truck | .25 | (Plastic) | 6 | 3 doz. | 12 lbs. | 5 |
| 336 | Diesel Motor Express | .25 | (Plastic) | 6 | 3 doz. | 12 lbs. | 5 |
| 352 | Motor Express | .85 | (Plastic) | 1 | 1 doz. | 16 lbs. | 6 |
| 357 | Cattle Truck | .85 | (Plastic) | 1 | 1 doz. | 15 lbs. | 6 |
| 359 | Milk Tanker | .75 | (Plastic) | 1 | 1 doz. | 13 lbs. | 6 |
| 430 | Airplane | .25 | (Metal) | 6 | 3 doz. | 17 lbs. | 7 |
| 431 | Dump Truck | .25 | (Metal) | 6 | 3 doz. | 17 lbs. | 7 |
| 432 | Sport Car | .25 | (Metal) | 6 | 3 doz. | 17 lbs. | 7 |
| 452 | Stake Truck | .30 | (Metal) | 1 | 3 doz. | 21 lbs. | 8 |
| 453 | Tow Truck | .30 | (Metal) | 1 | 3 doz. | 20 lbs. | 8 |
| 454 | Log Truck | .30 | (Metal) | 1 | 3 doz. | 20 lbs. | 8 |
| 455 | Sport Car | .30 | (Metal) | 1 | 3 doz. | 17 lbs. | 8 |
| 456 | Tractor | .30 | (Metal) | 1 | 3 doz. | 23 lbs. | 9 |
| 464 | Fire Engine | .30 | (Metal) | 1 | 3 doz. | 24 lbs. | 9 |
| 465 | Hook & Ladder | .30 | (Metal) | 1 | 3 doz. | 21 lbs. | 9 |
| 466 | Air Compressor | .30 | (Metal) | 1 | 3 doz. | 24 lbs. | 9 |
| 467 | Navy Plane | .50 | (Metal) | 1 | 1 doz. | 9 lbs. | 10 |
| 468 | Hook & Ladder | .50 | (Metal) | 1 | 1 doz. | 16 lbs. | 10 |
| 469 | Log Truck | .50 | (Metal) | 1 | 1 doz. | 15 lbs. | 10 |
| 471 | Dump Truck | .50 | (Metal) | 1 | 1 doz. | 14 lbs. | 11 |
| 473 | Hubley Jr. Tractor | .50 | (Metal) | 1 | 1 doz. | 14 lbs. | 11 |
| 474 | Tow Truck | .50 | (Metal) | 1 | 1 doz. | 12 lbs. | 11 |
| 480 | Road Roller | .75 | (Metal) | 1 | 1 doz. | 23 lbs. | 12 |
| 481 | Road Scraper | .75 | (Metal) | 1 | 1 doz. | 14 lbs. | 12 |
| 483 | Cement Mixer | .75 | (Metal) | 1 | 1 doz. | 16 lbs. | 12 |
| 484 | Telephone Truck | .75 | (Metal) | 1 | 1 doz. | 21 lbs. | 13 |
| 485 | Sport Car | .75 | (Metal) | 1 | 1 doz. | 18 lbs. | 13 |
| 486 | Deluxe Sport Car | .75 | (Metal) | 1 | 1 doz. | 20 lbs. | 13 |
| 490 | Tractor | 1.00 | (Metal) | 1 | 1 doz. | 29 lbs. | 14 |
| 491 | Shovel Truck | 1.00 | (Metal) | 1 | 1 doz. | 25 lbs. | 14 |
| 492 | Auto Transport | 1.25 | (Metal) | 1 | 1 doz. | 20 lbs. | 15 |
| 493 | Lumber Truck | 1.00 | (Metal) | 1 | 1 doz. | 22 lbs. | 15 |
| 500 | Tractor-Loader | 1.50 | (Metal) | 1 | ½ doz. | 19 lbs. | 24 |
| 504 | Telephone Truck | 2.00 | (Metal) | 1 | ½ doz. | 21 lbs. | 25 |
| 505 | Log Truck | 2.00 | (Metal) | 1 | ½ doz. | 22 lbs. | 26 |
| 506 | Carryall | 2.00 | (Metal) | 1 | ½ doz. | 25 lbs. | 27 |
| 507 | Motor Express | 2.00 | (Metal) | 1 | ½ doz. | 34 lbs. | 28 |
| 508 | Dump Truck | 2.00 | (Metal) | 1 | ½ doz. | 22 lbs. | 29 |
| 509 | Custom Sport Car | 2.00 | (Metal) | 1 | ½ doz. | 28 lbs. | 30 |

### BOXED ASSORTMENTS

| No. | Name | | | Pieces in Box | Case Packing | Weight Per Carton | Catalog Page |
|---|---|---|---|---|---|---|---|
| 5 | Farm Set | .50 | (Metal) | 1 | 1 doz. | 11 lbs. | 18 |
| 10 | Assortment | .75 | (Metal) | 1 | 1 doz. | 20 lbs. | 19 |
| 40 | Assortment | 1.25 | (Metal) | 1 | 1 doz. | 30 lbs. | 20 |
| 45 | Assortment | 1.50 | (Metal) | 1 | 1 doz. | 30 lbs. | 21 |
| 50 | Farm Set | 1.50 | (Metal) | 1 | ½ doz. | 18 lbs. | 22 |
| 60 | Road Building Set | 1.00 | (Plastic) | 1 | 1 doz. | 22 lbs. | 16 |
| 70 | Assortment of Six Diesel Trucks | 1.50 | (Plastic) | 1 | ½ doz. | 16 lbs. | 17 |
| 85 | Deluxe Assortment | 4.25 | (Metal) | 1 | ¼ doz. | 35 lbs. | 23 |

### 309 TRACTOR

Length 4¾ inches. Packed 12 in a box; 3 dozen to a carton. Weight per carton 11 lbs. Red, green and orange with aluminum trimming. Rubber wheels.

### 310 MOTORCYCLE

Length 5 inches. Packed 12 in a box; 3 dozen to a carton. Weight per carton 8 lbs. Red and green motorcycle, blue man. Rubber wheels.

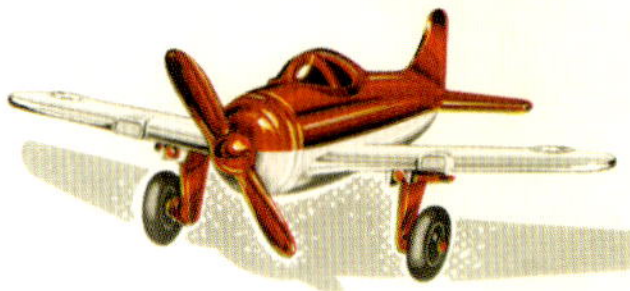

### 311 AIRPLANE

Length 5 inches. Packed 12 in a box; 3 dozen to a carton. Weight per carton 5 lbs. Red and bright metallic combination. Retractable landing gear. Rubber wheels.

### 316 ROAD SCRAPER

Length 6¼ inches. Packed 6 in a box; 3 dozen to a carton. Weight per carton 12 lbs. Yellow body with adjustable aluminum finished scraper. Rubber wheels.





### RACER 325

th 6¾ inches. Packed 6 in a 3 dozen to a carton. Weight arton 10 lbs. Aluminum with imming and red with alumi- trimming. Hood lifts up ex- g realistic motor. Rubber ls.

### TRACTOR 328

h 5½ inches. Packed 6 in a 3 dozen to a carton. Weight arton 16 lbs. Red, green and e with aluminum finish steer- heel. Realistic detailing of e, chassis, hood and seat. rubber wheels, treaded on grooved on front like real r.

### IESEL DUMP TRUCK 331

h 6⅜ inches. Packed 6 in a dozen to a carton. Weight rton 10 lbs. Cab and dump in assorted colors, red and also green and yellow, with num trimming. Spring clip dump body down. Tail gate open when dump is raised. tic chassis details. Rubber .

### IESEL TOW TRUCK 332

h 6⅜ inches. Packed 6 in a dozen to a carton. Weight ton 11 lbs. Red plastic cab, n assorted colors, green and Aluminum trimming. Real- assis details. Rubber wheels.

### 333 DIESEL HOOK & LADDER

Length 8¼ inches. Packed 6 in a box; 3 dozen to a carton. Weight per carton 11 lbs. Red with aluminum trimming; two aluminum plastic ladders which can be removed and joined together. Realistic chassis details. Rubber wheels.

### 334 DIESEL TELEPHONE TRUCK

Length 6¾ inches. Packed 6 in a box; 3 dozen to a carton. Weight per carton 11 lbs. Olive green color with bright trimming. Realistic chassis details. Two plastic digging tools. Rubber wheels.

### 335 DIESEL GAS TRUCK

Length 7 inches. Packed 6 in a box; 3 dozen to a carton. Weight per carton 12 lbs. Red and bright metallic combination with aluminum trimming. Realistic chassis details. Rubber wheels.

### 336 DIESEL MOTOR EXPRESS

Length 7 inches. Packed 6 in a box; 3 dozen to a carton. Weight per carton 12 lbs. Red and green combination with aluminum trimming. Realistic chassis details. Rear tail gate opens. Rubber wheels.

## PLASTIC

### MOTOR EXPRESS 352

Length 12½ inches. Packed 1 in a box; 1 dozen to a carton. Weight per carton 16 lbs. Red and green combination with aluminum trimming. Realistic chassis details. Side door slides open. Rear doors swing out. Retractable trailer support. Black rubber wheels, dual on rear of tractor. Rear wheels on trailer have knee action.

*"Remove the cab, see the motor" feature. See below.*

*Doors open, dolly wheels down*

### CATTLE TRUCK 357

Length 12½ inches. Packed 1 in a box; 1 dozen to a carton. Weight per carton 15 lbs. Red and yellow combination with aluminum trimming. Rear doors swing out. Retractable trailer support. Black rubber wheels, dual on rear of tractor. Rear wheels on trailer have knee action.

*"Remove the cab, see the motor" feature. See below.*

*Trailer unhitches, dolly wheels drop, rear doors open, as in illustration under 352, above*

### MILK TANKER 359

Length 12¾ inches. Packed 1 in a box; 1 dozen to a carton. Weight per carton 13 lbs. Red cab with aluminum trimming and white trailer. 14 black rubber wheels plus 2 on retractable trailer support. Rear wheels on trailer have knee action.

*Remove the cab and see the motor*

*Trailer unhitches, dolly wheels drop.*



## METAL

### 430 AIRPLANE

Length 6 inches, wingspread 6¼ inches. Packed 6 in a box; 3 dozen to a carton. Weight per carton 17 lbs. Red with aluminum wings. Folding wings, retractable landing gear, rubber wheels.

*Folding wings*

*Tailgate opens automatically when body is raised*

### 431 DUMP TRUCK

Length 5⅝ inches. Packed 6 in a box; 3 dozen to a carton. Weight per carton 17 lbs. Green chassis, and red movable dump, bright metal trim. Tail gate opens when dump is raised. Rubber wheels.

### 432 SPORT CAR

Length 5⅞ inches. Packed 6 in a box; 3 dozen to a carton. Weight per carton 17 lbs. Assorted colors, red, green, and yellow with aluminum trim. Rubber wheels, including spare mounted continental fashion on rear.

*Fine interior details*

1955

## METAL

*Tail gate opens*

### STAKE TRUCK 452

Length 7 inches. Packed 1 in a box; 3 dozen to a carton. Weight per carton 21 lbs. Assorted colors with bright metal sides, tail gate, bumper and grill. Rubber wheels.

### LOG TRUCK 454

Length 7½ inches. Packed 1 in a box; 3 dozen to a carton. Weight per carton 20 lbs. Assorted colors with bright trimming. 5 logs. Rubber wheels.

### TOW TRUCK 453

Length 7 inches. Packed 1 in a box; 3 dozen to a carton. Weight per carton 20 lbs. Assorted colors with bright metal sides, stationary boom. Rubber wheels.

### SPORT CAR 455

Length 7½ inches. Packed 1 in a box; 3 dozen to a carton. Weight per carton 17 lbs. Yellow with transparent green windshield. Aluminum trimming. Realistic details. Rubber wheels.

*View into "cockpit"*



## METAL

### 456 TRACTOR

Length 5½ inches. Packed 1 in a box; 3 dozen to a carton. Weight per carton 23 lbs. Red with aluminum trim. Realistic detailing of engine, chassis. Black rubber wheels treaded front and rear like real tractor.

### 466 AIR COMPRESSOR

Length 6¾ inches. Packed 1 in a box; 3 dozen to a carton. Weight per carton 24 lbs. Assorted colors, red, green, and orange, with aluminum compressor. Rubber wheels.

### 464 FIRE ENGINE

Length 7½ inches. Packed 1 in a box; 3 dozen to a carton. Weight per carton 24 lbs. Red with aluminum finished pumper top and windshield. Rubber wheels.

*Ladders mount in holes*

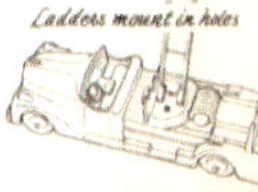

### 465 HOOK & LADDER

Length 8½ inches. Packed 1 in a box; 3 dozen to a carton. Weight per carton 21 lbs. Red with aluminum finished windshield and ladders. Rubber wheels.

## NAVY PLANE 467

Length 6½ inches, wingspread 8¾ inches. Packed 1 in a box; 1 dozen to a carton. Weight per carton 9 lbs. Bright metal with red trim. Cockpit enclosed with transparent green plastic bubble. Rubber wheels, revolving propeller, folding wings, retractable landing gear.

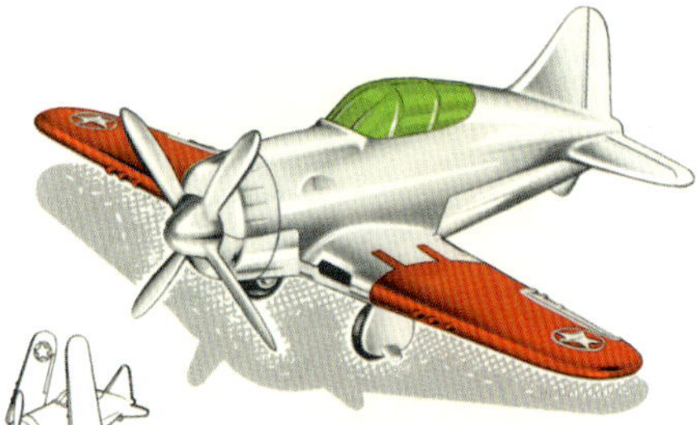

## LOG TRUCK 469

Length 10 inches. Packed 1 in a box; 1 dozen to a carton. Weight per carton 15 lbs. Orange with bright metal bed, bright trim. 5 removable logs, with chain to hold them in place. Rubber wheels.

## HOOK & LADDER 468

Length 11¼ inches. Packed 1 in a box; 1 dozen to a carton. Weight per carton 16 lbs. Red with aluminum trimming. Revolving ladder turret with aluminum ladders. Rubber wheels.





## 473 HUBLEY JR. TRACTOR

Length 7½ inches. Packed 1 in a box; 1 dozen to a carton. Weight per carton 14 lbs. Red with aluminum trim. Yellow rear wheels. Realistic engine details. Rubber tires treaded front and rear like a real tractor.

## 471 DUMP TRUCK

Length 9½ inches. Packed 1 in a box; 1 dozen to a carton. Weight per carton 14 lbs. Green chassis, red movable dump, bright metal trim. Tail gate opens when dump is raised. Rubber wheels.

## 474 TOW TRUCK

Length 9¾ inches. Packed 1 in a box; 1 dozen to a carton. Weight per carton 12 lbs. Red with aluminum finished movable winch and boom. Rubber wheels.



1955



## ROAD ROLLER 480

Length 10 inches. Packed 1 in a box; 1 dozen to a carton. Weight per carton 23 lbs. Orange body with aluminum trimming and metal wheels. Steers by lever in driver's compartment.

## CEMENT MIXER 483

Length 10 inches. Packed 1 in a box; 1 dozen to a carton. Weight per carton 16 lbs. Red cab, green body, bright metal revolving mixer and trim. Rubber wheels.

## ROAD SCRAPER 481

Length 10¾ inches. Packed 1 in a box; 1 dozen to a carton. Weight per carton 14 lbs. Yellow with bright scraper and trimming. The rear wheels are mounted independently to roll over stones and obstacles. Adjustable scraper. Front wheels operated by steering wheel. Rubber wheels.

## 484 TELEPHONE TRUCK

Length 10½ inches. Packed 1 in a box; 1 dozen to a carton. Weight per carton 21 lbs. Olive green with bright metal movable winch and boom. Equipped with red trailer and telephone pole. Three bright metal digging tools. Crank windlass as on No. 474. Rubber wheels.

## 485 SPORT CAR

Length 9 inches. Packed 1 in a box; 1 dozen to a carton. Weight per carton 18 lbs. Assorted colors – red, green and yellow, with aluminum trim. Chassis enclosed on bottom with realistic details. Rubber wheels including spare mounted "continental fashion" on rear.

## 486 DELUXE SPORT CAR

Length 9¼ inches. Packed 1 in a box; 1 dozen to a carton. Weight per carton 20 lbs. Color red with removable black top. Realistic wrap-around transparent windshield. Realistic dashboard and steering wheel. Aluminum trim and rubber wheels.

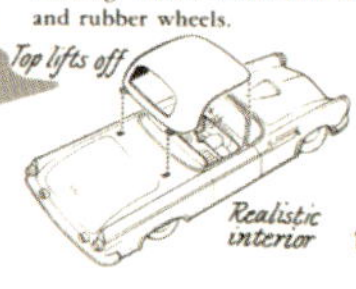

## TRACTOR 490

Length 9½ inches. Packed 1 in a box; 1 dozen to a carton. Weight per carton 29 lbs. Red with aluminum trimming. Realistic engine details visible on both sides. Spring action driver's seat. Front wheels operated by steering wheel. All metal wheels with black rubber tires, treaded front and rear like real tractor.

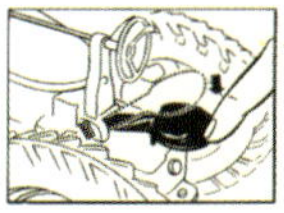

Spring-mounted seat

Front wheels steer

## SHOVEL TRUCK 491

Length 13¼ inches. Packed 1 in a box; 1 dozen to a carton. Weight per carton 25 lbs. Green cab and chassis with red operator's cab which turns on swivel. Shovel and working mechanism aluminum. Bucket opens to release load. Rubber wheels.

Bucket dumps when boom is raised to full height

Shovel cab swings to either side

Bucket is closed when boom is down





## 492 AUTO TRANSPORT

Ramp loading toy cars

Length 14 inches. Packed 1 in a box; 1 dozen to a carton. Weight per carton 20 lbs. Red with aluminum trimming. Realistic chassis details. Four plastic cars in assorted colors, which can be driven on or off trailer over removable ramp, which hooks under trailer. Black rubber wheels, dual on rear of tractor.

## 493 LUMBER TRUCK

Unloading lumber

Length 13¾ inches. Packed 1 in a box; 1 dozen to a carton. Weight per carton 22 lbs. Orange cab and trailer with aluminum trimming. Realistic chassis details. Twelve pieces of lumber with double chain to hold them in place. Black rubber wheels, dual on rear of tractor. Rear wheels on trailer have knee action.



1955

# No. 60 Road Building Set (Plastic)

Flat bed truck
15 inches long

315 Road Roller

316 Road Scraper

### PLASTIC

Set consists of Flat Bed Truck, Road Roller and Road Scraper. Packed 1 set in a box; 1 dozen sets to a carton. Weight per carton 22 lbs. Orange flat bed truck, green road roller with red wheels, yellow scraper. All toys have aluminum trimming.

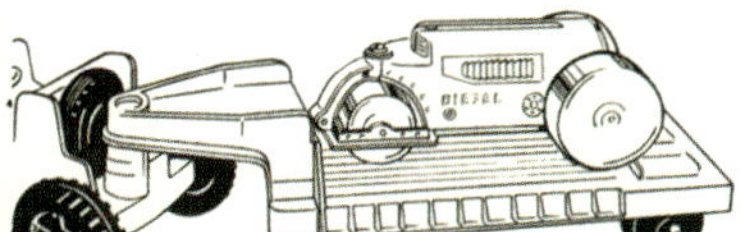

Flat bed trailer hauls other equipment.

Bright red, yellow, blue and green box.



# No. 70 Assortment (Plastic)

331 Dump

332 Tow

333 Hook & Ladder

334 Telephone

335 Gas

### PLASTIC

No. 70 Assortment of Six Diesel Trucks. Set consists of No. 331 Dump Truck, 332 Tow Truck, 333 Hook & Ladder, 334 Telephone Truck, 335 Gas Truck and 336 Motor Express. Packed 1 set in a box; ½ dozen sets to a carton. Weight per carton 16 lbs. All toys have aluminum trimming and rubber wheels.

336 Motor Express

Colorful yellow, blue, red, green and black box. Die cut lid folds back to form self display.

# No. 5 Farm Set (Metal)

456 Tractor
5½ inches long

Wagon

Cultipacker

**METAL**

Set consists of Tractor, Cultipacker and Wagon. Packed 1 set in a box; 1 dozen sets to a carton. Weight per carton 11 lbs. Toys red with aluminum trimming. Black rubber wheels.

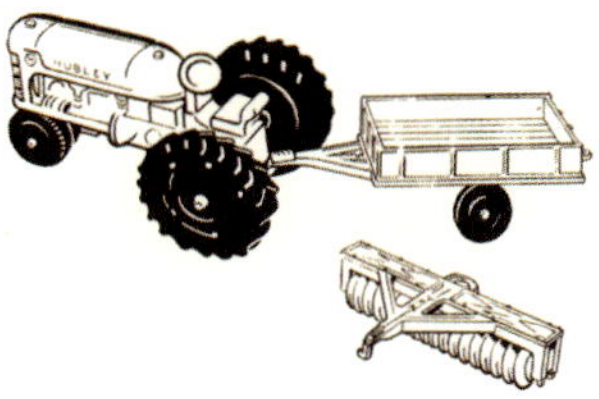

*Red, yellow, green and black box.*

*All pieces hitch together*



# No. 10 Assortment (Metal)

430 Airplane

432 Sport Car

431 Dump Truck

**METAL**

Set consists of No. 430 Airplane, 431 Dump Truck and 432 Sport Car. Packed 1 set in a box; 1 dozen sets to a carton. Weight per carton 20 lbs. All toys have rubber wheels.

*Attractive yellow, red, blue, green and black box. Die cut lid folds to form self display.*



1955

# No. 40 Assortment (Metal)

454 Log Truck

453 Tow Truck

456 Tractor

**METAL**

Set consists of No. 454 Log Truck, 453 Tow Truck, 456 Tractor and 455 Sport Car. Packed 1 set in a box; 1 dozen sets to a carton. Weight per carton 30 lbs. All toys have rubber wheels.

455 Sport Car

*Colorful red, green, orange and black box. Die cut lid folds back to form self display.*



# No. 45 Assortment (Metal)

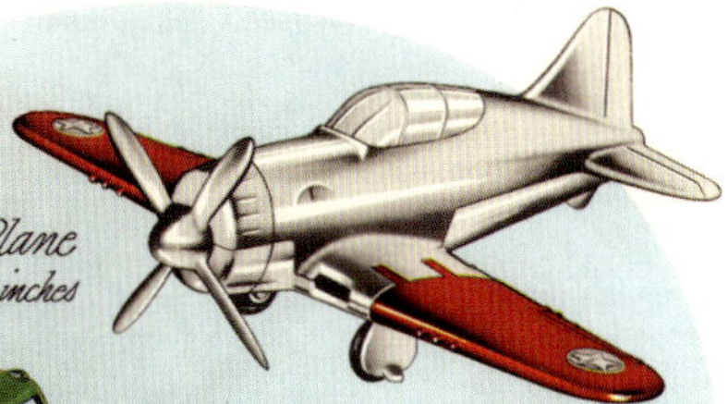

467 Navy Plane
Wing span 8¾ inches

452 Stake Truck
6¾ inches long

**METAL**

Set consists of 467 Navy Airplane, 455 Sport Car, 452 Stake Truck, 456 Tractor. Packed 1 set in a box; 1 dozen sets to a carton. Weight per carton 30 lbs. All toys have rubber wheels.

455 Sport Car

456 Tractor

*Eye catching box printed in red, yellow, blue, green and black.*

# No. 50 Farm Set (Metal)

**METAL**

Set consists of Hubley Jr. Tractor, Plow, Cultipacker, Spreader and Farm Wagon, all interlocking. Packed 1 set in a box; ½ dozen sets to a carton. Weight per carton 18 lbs. Toys red with aluminum trimming. Black rubber wheels.

*Eye catching red, yellow, blue, green and black box.*

# No. 85 Deluxe Assortment (Metal)

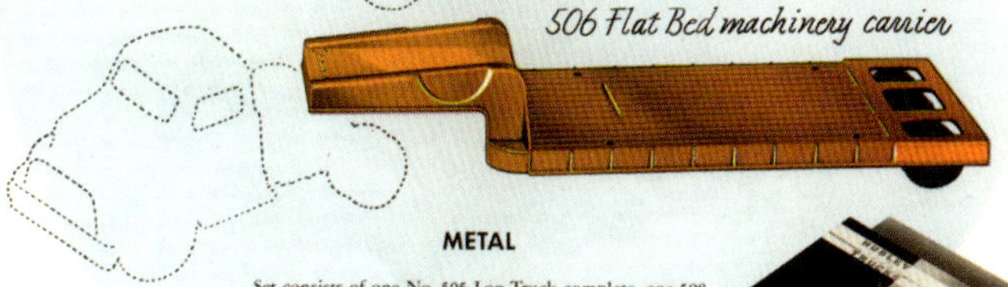


**METAL**

Set consists of one No. 505 Log Truck complete, one 508 Dump Truck complete and one Carryall trailer bed. Packed 1 set in a box; ¼ dozen sets to a carton. Weight per carton 35 lbs. All toys have numerous play features, aluminum trimming and rubber wheels.

*Attractive red, blue and silver box.*



1955

# HUBLEY TRACTOR-LOADER

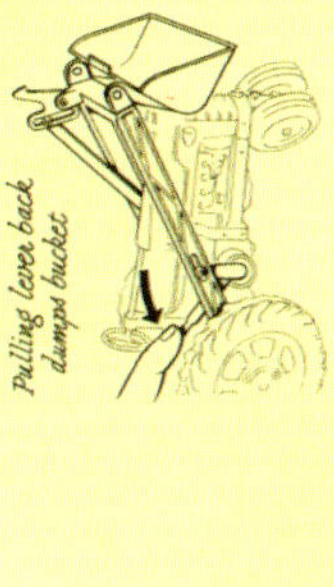


**METAL**

**No. 500 Tractor-Loader**

Length 13 inches. Packed 1 in a box; ½ dozen to a carton. Weight per carton 19 lbs. Red with bright metal loader mechanism and steering wheel. Aluminum trimming. Realistic engine details, spring seat. Steering wheel operates front wheels. Side lever raises, lowers, and dumps loader.

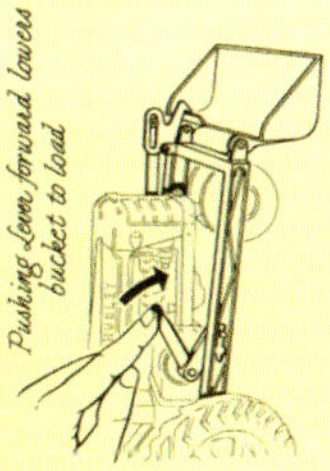




# HUBLEY TELEPHONE TRUCK

**METAL**

**No. 504 Telephone Truck**

Length 12½ inches. Packed 1 in a box; ½ dozen to a carton. Weight per carton 21 lbs. Olive green with aluminum trimming. Removable boom in rear. Crank raises or lowers rope and hook. Top of truck slides back to cover open half in rear. Plastic ladder, three bright metal digging tools. Red trailer hooks on rear. 11 inch pole. Black rubber wheels, dual in rear.

# HUBLEY LOG TRUCK

*Remove the cab and see the motor*

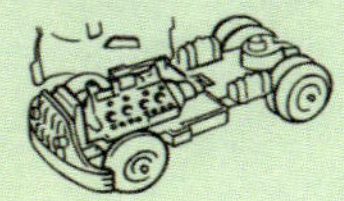

**METAL**

**No. 505 Log Truck**

Length 18 inches. Packed 1 in a box; ½ dozen to a carton. Weight per carton 22 lbs. Orange with aluminum trimming. "Remove the cab, see the motor" feature, realistic chassis details. Trailer carries 5 logs each 12 inches long. Wheels are independently mounted to roll over stones or obstacles. Two chains to hold logs in place. Black rubber wheels.

*Logs unload. Note independent action of rear wheels*

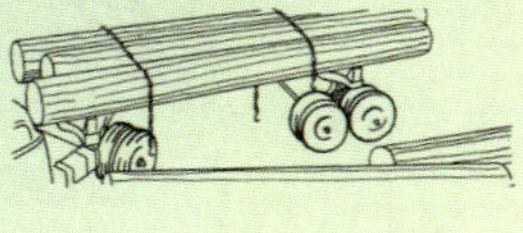

# HUBLEY CARRYALL

*Steering Wheel action*

**METAL**

**No. 506 Carryall**

Length 19½ inches. Packed 1 in a box; ½ dozen to a carton. Weight per carton 25 lbs. Orange flat bed machinery carrier. Seven wheels realistically mounted on rear of carrier. Complete with 10¾ inch metal road scraper. (See No. 481, page 12.) Black rubber wheels.

*Scraper Blade adjustable*

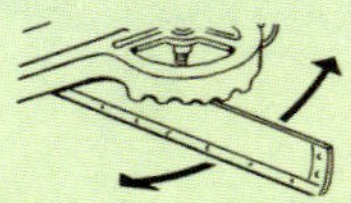

"Remove the cab, see the motor" feature like No. 505, opposite.





# HUBLEY MOTOR EXPRESS

*Remove the cab feature as on 505 - see page 26*

*Independent action, rear wheels of trailer*

**METAL**

**No. 507 Motor Express**

Length 18 inches. Packed 1 in a box; ½ dozen to a carton. Weight per carton 34 lbs. Red and green combination with aluminum trimming. Side door slides open. Rear doors swing out. Independently mounted rear wheels to roll over stones and obstacles. Retractable trailer support. Black rubber wheels, dual in rear.

*Sliding side door*

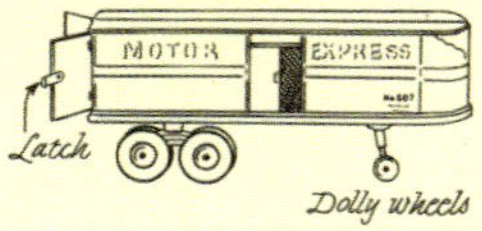


# HUBLEY DUMP TRUCK

*Remove the cab feature as on 505 -- see page 26.*

*Independent action, rear wheels of trailer.*

**METAL**

**No. 508 Dump Truck**

Length 17 inches. Packed 1 in a box; ½ dozen to a carton. Weight per carton 22 lbs. Green cab, bright metal chassis. Movable red dump, aluminum trimming. Pushing lever on side raises dump, tail gate opens automatically. Rear wheels on trailer have knee action. Black rubber wheels.

*Releasing latch allows dump body to raise. Tail gate swings open.*

# HUBLEY CUSTOM SPORT CAR

METAL

**No. 509 Custom Sport Car**

Length 12¾ inches. Packed 1 in a box; ½ dozen to a carton. Weight per carton 28 lbs. Red with aluminum trim. Realistic wrap-around transparent windshield. Realistic chassis and dashboard details. Working steering mechanism. Front hood opens revealing finely detailed motor. Rear trunk opens for removal of spare tire. Black rubber wheels.

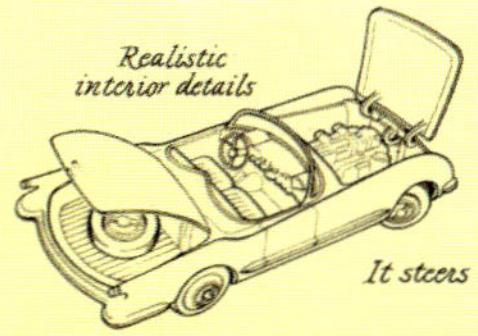


## Craftsmanship

This is a good word to describe the thought and competent production behind Hubley Toys.

It covers expert design and good modeling by Hubley artisans, practiced by many years of experience in the toy business. It means the ability to build toys attractive to children, with lots of real life details. These toys must provide genuine educational play features, yet be safe, and "play" well for many long hours.

Craftsmanship helps Hubley Toys sell well, and that is where it enters our pledge to you: Hubley craftsmanship at attractive prices will be our continuing aim.

**The Hubley Manufacturing Company, Lancaster, Pa.**



1955

Printed in the United States of America
Wm. D. Andes, Design and Advertising, Lancaster, Pa

# 1956

1956

# HUBLEY Kiddie Toys

THE HUBLEY MANUFACTURING COMPANY,
LANCASTER, PA., U. S. A.

# Acetate No. 100 "Small Stuff" Animals

**100 ANIMALS Acetate**
Length 3 inches. Packed individually in color-printed polyethylene bags; 3 dozen to a carton. Weight per carton 4 lbs. 1 each Scottie, Lamb, Panda and Elephant. Non-toxic finish. Red rubber wheels.

**150 ANIMAL ASSORTMENT Acetate**
Boxed assortment of four animals—Scottie, Lamb, Panda and Elephant. Supplied with non-toxic finish and red rubber wheels. Packed 1 set to a box; 1 dozen sets to a carton. Weight per carton 6 lbs.

*Attractive blue, red, pink and black box. Die cut lid folds back to form self display.*

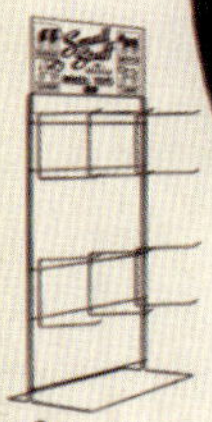

Sturdy metal display stand available with orders of one gross or more, at slight additional cost. Packs flat in corrugated carton. Shipping weight about 2 lbs.



## Polystyrene

**309 TRACTOR**
Length 4 3/4 inches. Packed 12 in a box; 3 dozen to a carton. Weight per carton 11 lbs. Red, green and orange with aluminum trimming. Rubber wheels.

**311 AIRPLANE**
Length 5 inches. Packed 12 in a box; 3 dozen to a carton. Weight per carton 5 lbs. Red and bright metallic combination. Retractable landing gear. Rubber wheels.

**310 MOTORCYCLE**
Length 5 inches. Packed 12 in a box; 3 dozen to a carton. Weight per carton 8 lbs. Red and green motorcycle, blue man. Rubber wheels.



1956

**306 FIRE ENGINE**
**Polyethylene**
Length 6 inches. Packed 12 in a box; 3 dozen to a carton. Weight per carton 6 lbs. Red with aluminum trimming. Rubber wheels.

Made of unbreakable polyethylene

**307 HOOK & LADDER**
**Polyethylene**
Length 6 inches. Packed 12 in a box; 3 dozen to a carton. Weight per carton 5 lbs. Red with aluminum trimming and two steel ladders. Rubber wheels.

Made of unbreakable polyethylene

**316 ROAD SCRAPER**
**Polyethylene**
Length 6 1/4 inches. Packed 6 in a box; 3 dozen to a carton. Weight per carton 11 lbs. Yellow body with adjustable aluminum finished scraper. Rubber wheels.

Made of unbreakable polyethylene

*Scraper Blade adjustable*

## Polystyrene

**325 RACER**
Length 6 1/4 inches. Packed 6 in a box; 3 dozen to a carton. Weight per carton 10 lbs. White with red trimming and red with white trimming. Hood lifts up exposing realistic motor. Rubber wheels.

*Lift the hood, see the motor.*

## Polystyrene

**331 DIESEL DUMP TRUCK**
Length 6 5/8 inches. Packed 6 in a box; 3 dozen to a carton. Weight per carton 11 lbs. Cab and dump body in assorted colors, red and green, also green and yellow, with aluminum trimming. Spring clip holds dump body down. Tail gate swings open when dump is raised. Realistic chassis details. Rubber wheels.

**332 DIESEL WRECKER**
Length 6 5/8 inches. Packed 6 in a box; 3 dozen to a carton. Weight per carton 11 lbs. Red plastic cab and body in assorted colors, green and ivory. Aluminum trimming. Realistic chassis details. Rubber wheels.

**333 DIESEL HOOK & LADDER**
Length 8 1/4 inches. Packed 6 in a box; 3 dozen to a carton. Weight per carton 11 lbs. Red with aluminum trimming; two aluminum plastic ladders which can be removed and joined together. Realistic chassis details. Rubber wheels.

**334 DIESEL TELEPHONE TRUCK**
Length 6 3/4 inches. Packed 6 in a box; 3 dozen to a carton. Weight per carton 11 lbs. Olive green color with bright trimming. Realistic chassis details. Two plastic digging tools. Rubber wheels.

## Polystyrene

**335 DIESEL GAS TRUCK**
Length 7 inches. Packed 6 in a box; 3 dozen to a carton. Weight per carton 11 lbs. Red and bright metallic combination with aluminum trimming. Realistic chassis details. Rubber wheels.

**336 DIESEL MOTOR EXPRESS**
Length 7 inches. Packed 6 in a box; 3 dozen to a carton. Weight per carton 13 lbs. Red and green combination with aluminum trimming. Realistic chassis details. Rear tail gate opens. Rubber wheels.

**337 TRACTOR**
Length 5½ inches. Packed 6 in a box; 3 dozen to a carton. Weight per carton 18 lbs. Red, green and orange with aluminum finish steering wheel. Realistic detailing of engine, chassis, hood and seat. Yellow rear wheels with rubber tires, treaded on rear, grooved on front like real tractor.

## Metal

**429 LOG TRUCK**
Length 5¾ inches. Packed 6 in a box; 1 dozen to a carton. Weight per carton 4 lbs. Orange with bright trimming. 5 logs. Rubber wheels.

**430 AIRPLANE**
Length 6 inches. Packed 6 in a box; 1 dozen to a carton. Weight per carton 5 lbs. Red with aluminum wings, folding wings, retractable landing gear. Rubber wheels.

**431 DUMP TRUCK**
Length 5⅝ inches. Packed 6 in a box; 1 dozen to a carton. Weight per carton 5 lbs. Green chassis, red movable dump, bright metal trim. Tail gate opens when dump is raised. Rubber wheels.

**432 M.G.**
Length 5⅞ inches. Packed 6 in a box; 1 dozen to a carton. Weight per carton 6 lbs. Colors assorted red, green and yellow with aluminum trim. Rubber wheels (including spare mounted Continental fashion) on rear.

1956

## Metal

**451 TRACTOR**
Length 5½ inches. Packed 1 in a box; 1 dozen to a carton. Weight per carton 8 lbs. Colors assorted, red and orange with aluminum trim. Realistic detailing of engine and chassis. Wheels yellow, rubber tires treaded on rear, grooved on front like real tractor.

**455 JAGUAR**
Length 7½ inches. Packed 1 in a box; 1 dozen to a carton. Weight per carton 6 lbs. Colors assorted, red and cream, green and cream. Transparent windshield. Aluminum trimming. Realistic details. Rubber wheels.

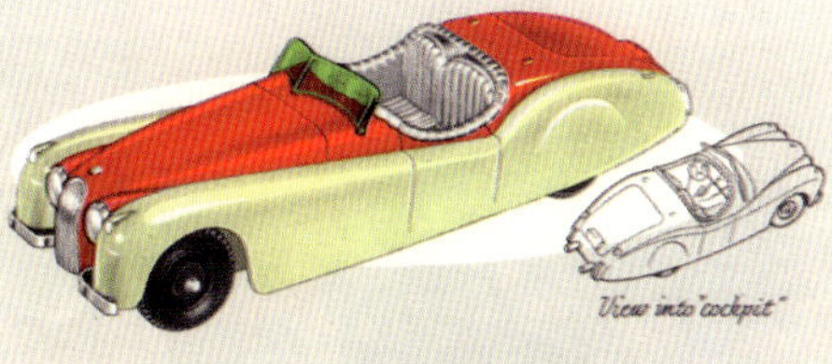


**458 DUMP TRUCK**
Length 7 5/16 inches. Packed 1 in a box; 1 dozen to a carton. Weight per carton 8 lbs. Green chassis, orange dump, bright metal trim. Rubber wheels.

## Metal

**459 LOG TRUCK**
Length 7⅜ inches. Packed 1 in a box; 1 dozen to a carton. Weight per carton 7 lbs. Orange with bright trim. 5 logs. Rubber wheels.

**465 HOOK & LADDER**
Length 8½ inches. Packed 1 in a box; 1 dozen to a carton. Weight per carton 7 lbs. Red with aluminum finished windshield and ladders. Rubber wheels.

**466 AIR COMPRESSOR**
Length 6¾ inches. Packed 1 in a box; 3 dozen to a carton. Weight per carton 22 lbs. Colors assorted with aluminum compressor. Rubber wheels.

**473 HUBLEY JR. TRACTOR**
Length 7¼ inches. Packed 1 in a box; 1 dozen to a carton. Weight per carton 14 lbs. Colors assorted red and orange with aluminum trim. Yellow rear wheels with treaded rubber tires. Realistic engine details.

**467 NAVY PLANE**
Length 6½ inches, wing span 8¾ inches. Packed 1 in a box; 1 dozen to a carton. Weight per carton 9 lbs. Colors assorted red and blue with bright metal folding wings. Cockpit enclosed with transparent bubble. Rubber wheels, revolving propeller. Retractable landing gear.

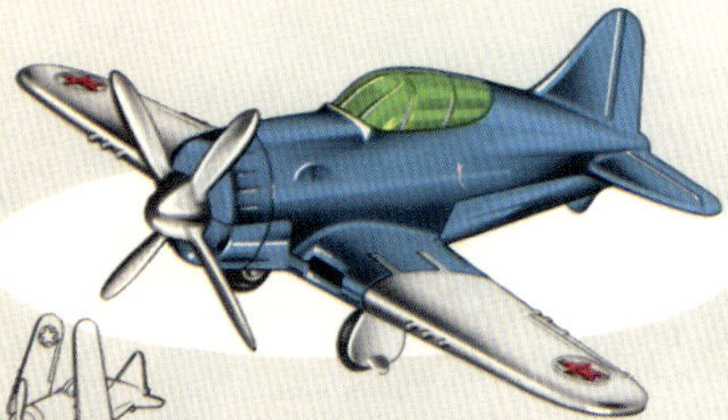

Folding wings

**468 HOOK & LADDER**
Length 11¼ inches. Packed 1 in a box; 1 dozen to a carton. Weight per carton 13 lbs. Colors red with aluminum trimming. Revolving ladder turret with aluminum ladders. Rubber wheels.

Ladders mount in revolving turret

Crank Windlass

**474 TOW TRUCK**
Length 9¾ inches. Packed 1 in a box; 1 dozen to a carton. Weight per carton 12 lbs. Red with aluminum finished winch and boom. Rubber wheels.

**481 ROAD SCRAPER**
Length 10¾ inches. Packed 1 in a box; 1 dozen to a carton. Weight per carton 14 lbs. Colors assorted red, orange and green with bright scraper and trimming. The rear wheels are mounted independently to roll over stones and obstacles. Adjustable scraper. Front wheels operated by steering wheel. Rubber wheels.

Steering Wheel action

Scraper Blade adjustable

Independent rear wheels

**486 THUNDERBIRD**
Length 9¼ inches. Packed 1 in a box; 1 dozen to a carton. Weight per carton 12 lbs. Color red with removable metallic top. Realistic wrap-around transparent windshield. Realistic dashboard and steering wheel. Aluminum trim and rubber wheels.

Realistic interior

Top lifts off



1956



**479 LOG TRUCK**
Length 11 inches. Packed 1 in a box; 1 dozen to a carton. Weight per carton 17 lbs. Orange with bright metal trim. 5 removable logs with chain. Rubber wheels.

**480 ROAD ROLLER**
Length 10 inches. Packed 1 in a box; 1 dozen to a carton. Weight per carton 25 lbs. Orange body with aluminum trimming and metal wheels. Steers by lever in driver's compartment.

Lever steers front roller.

**478 DUMP TRUCK**
Length 10 inches. Packed 1 in a box; 1 dozen to a carton. Weight per carton 19 lbs. Red chassis, cream cab, green dump with bright metal trim. Tail gate opens when dump is raised. Rubber wheels.

Dump body raises when lever is thrown forward

Tail gate swings open

Mixer drum rotates when truck moves

**487 CEMENT MIXER**
Length 10⅝ inches. Packed 1 in a box; 1 dozen to a carton. Weight per carton 18 lbs. Grey chassis, red cab, green body, with bright metal revolving mixer and trim. Rubber wheels.

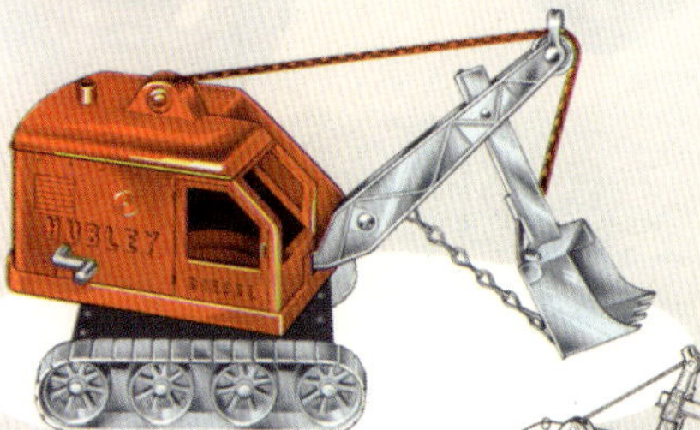

**488 POWER SHOVEL**
Length 8 inches. Packed 1 in a box; 1 dozen to a carton. Weight per carton 20 lbs. Orange with black striping. Shovel and working mechanism bright metal.

Shovel cab swings to either side

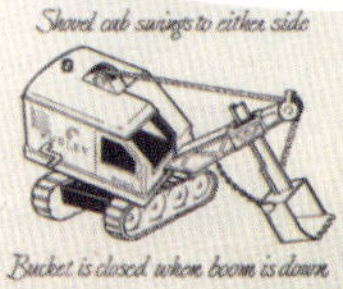
Bucket is closed when boom is down

Bucket dumps when boom is raised to full height

**485 M.G.**
Length 9 inches. Packed 1 in a box; 1 dozen to a carton. Weight per carton 18 lbs. Colors assorted, red, green and yellow with aluminum trim. Chassis enclosed on bottom with realistic details. Rubber wheels, including spare mounted (Continental Fashion) on rear.

Rear view

### 490 TRACTOR

Length 9½ inches. Packed 1 in a box; 1 dozen to a carton. Weight per carton 29 lbs. Red with aluminum trimming. Realistic engine details visible on both sides. Spring action driver's seat. Front wheels operated by steering wheel. All metal wheels with black, treaded rubber tires.

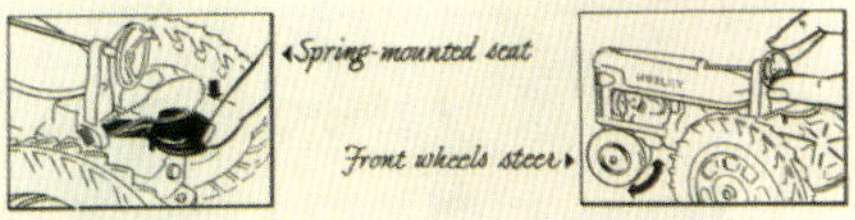


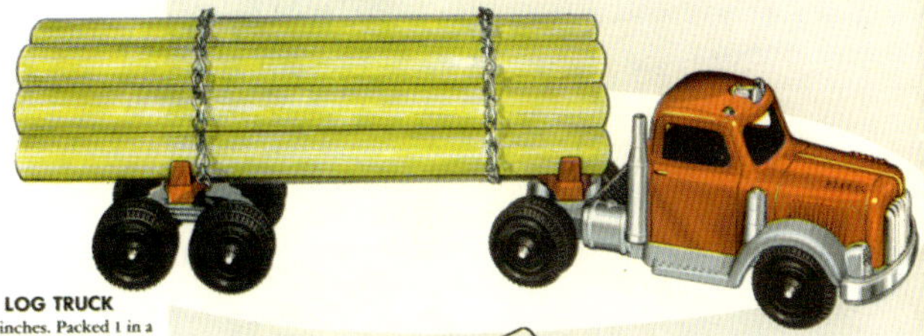

### 493 LOG TRUCK

Length 13¾ inches. Packed 1 in a box; 1 dozen to a carton. Weight per carton 27 lbs. Orange cab and trailer with aluminum trimming. Realistic chassis details. Nine logs with double chain to hold logs in place. Black rubber wheels, dual on rear of tractor. Rear wheels on trailer have knee action.

### 494 SHOVEL TRUCK

Length 13 inches. Packed 1 in a box; 1 dozen to a carton. Weight per carton 22 lbs. Grey chassis, red cab, and green operator's cab which turns on swivel. Shovel and working mechanism bright metal. Bucket opens to release load. Rubber wheels.

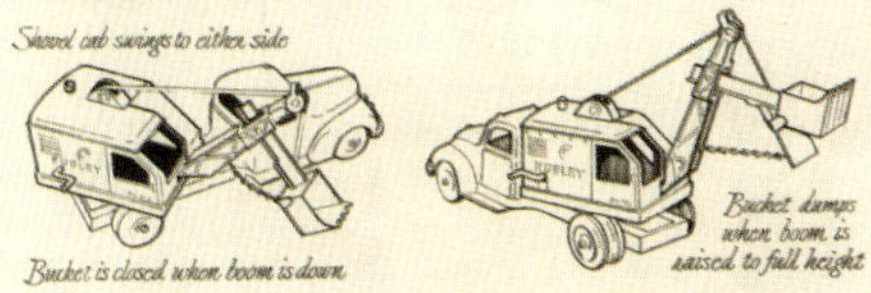


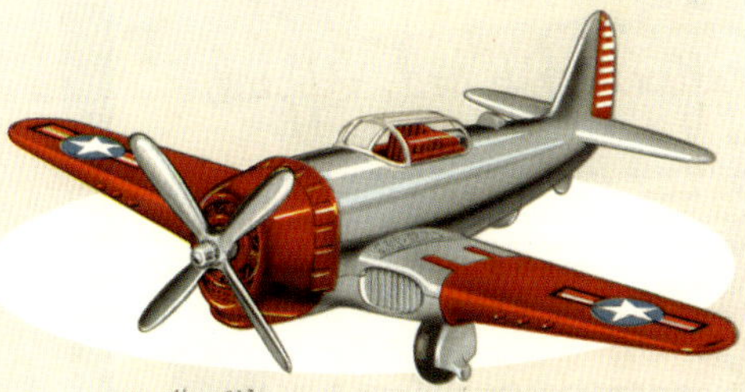

### 495 Navy Fighter Bomber

Length 10 inches. Packed 1 in a box; 1 dozen to a carton. Weight per carton 29 lbs. Colors: red wings, aluminum body with red, white and blue trim. Cockpit enclosed with transparent sliding bubble. Revolving propeller, folding wings, retractable landing gear and rubber wheels.

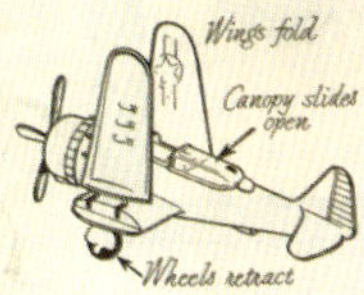




1956

### 492 AUTO TRANSPORT

Length 14 inches. Packed 1 in a box; 1 dozen to a carton. Weight per carton 27 lbs. Red chassis with ivory cab and red trailer with aluminum trimming. Realistic chassis details. Four plastic cars in assorted colors, which can be driven on or off trailer over removable ramp, which hooks under trailer. Black rubber wheels, dual on rear of tractor.

## Craftsmanship and Appeal

The two go hand in hand with Hubley Kiddie Toys. First of all, realistic detail is brought to life in miniature by skillful American designers. Then sturdy, durable construction and safe, educational, play features are added. Attractive packaging completes the formula. The result: the finest big line of toys in America today—52 individual items and 10 boxed assortments!

Continuing design, good craftsmanship and more play features—all at competitive prices—is Hubley's pledge to you.

**The Hubley Manufacturing Company, Lancaster, Pa., U.S.A.**

*American-made Toys for American girls and boys.*



## No. 6 Farm Set (Metal)

451 Tractor
5½ inches long

Cultipacker

Wagon

**METAL**

Set consists of Tractor, Cultipacker and Wagon. Packed 1 set in a box; 1 dozen sets to a carton. Weight per carton 15 lbs. Toys red with aluminum trimming. Black rubber wheels.

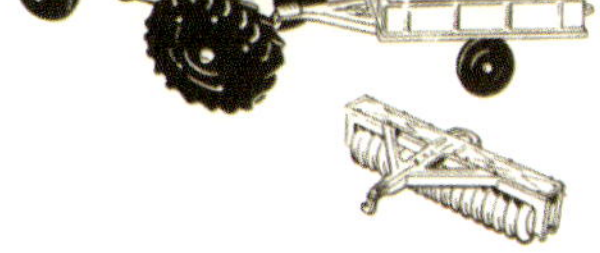

*Colorful red, yellow, green, and black box. Die cut lid folds back to form self display.*

*All pieces hitch together*

# No. 11 Assortment (Metal)

429 Log Truck

430 Airplane

432 Sport Car

**METAL**

Set consists of #429 Log Truck, 430 Airplane, 431 Dump Truck and 432 Sports Car. Packed 1 set in a box; 1 dozen sets to a carton. Weight per carton 20 lbs. All toys have rubber wheels.

431 Dump Truck

*Red, yellow, blue, and black box. Die cut lid folds back to form self display.*



# No. 46 Assortment (Metal)

458 Dump Truck

467 Navy Plane

**METAL**

Set consists of 467 Navy Airplane, 458 Dump Truck and 459 Log Truck. Packed 1 set in a box; 1 dozen sets to a carton. Weight per carton 24 lbs. All toys have rubber wheels.

459 Log Truck

*Red, pink, green and black box. Die cut lid folds back to form self display.*



1956

# No. 50 Farm Set (Metal)

Flat bed wagon

473 Tractor
7¼ inches long

Cultipacker

Manure spreader

Plow

**METAL**

Set consists of Hubley Jr. Tractor, Plow, Cultipacker, Spreader and Farm Wagon, all interlocking. Packed 1 set in a box; ½ dozen sets to a carton. Weight per carton 19 lbs. Toys red with aluminum trimming. Black rubber wheels.

*Eye catching red, yellow, blue, green and black box.*

All pieces hitch together



# No. 55 Assortment (Metal)

468 Hook and Ladder

467 Navy Plane

**METAL**

Set consists of 467 Navy Airplane, 468 Hook & Ladder and 486 Thunderbird. Packed 1 set in a box; ½ dozen sets to a carton. Weight per carton 19 lbs. All toys have rubber wheels.

486 Thunderbird

*Bright red, yellow, blue and black box.*

# No. 75 Road Building Set (Metal)

473 Tractor

487 Cement Mixer

488 Power Shovel

478 Dump Truck

**METAL**

Set consists of 473 Hubley Jr. Tractor, #481 Road Scraper, #478 Dump Truck, #487 Cement Mixer and #488 Power Shovel. Packed 1 set in a box; ¼ dozen sets to a carton. Weight per carton 23 lbs. All toys have rubber wheels and have numerous play features.

481 Road Scraper

*Eye catching red, yellow, brown, blue, green and black box.*



# No. 86 Deluxe Assortment (Metal)

Either of the cabs hitches to any of the bodies shown.

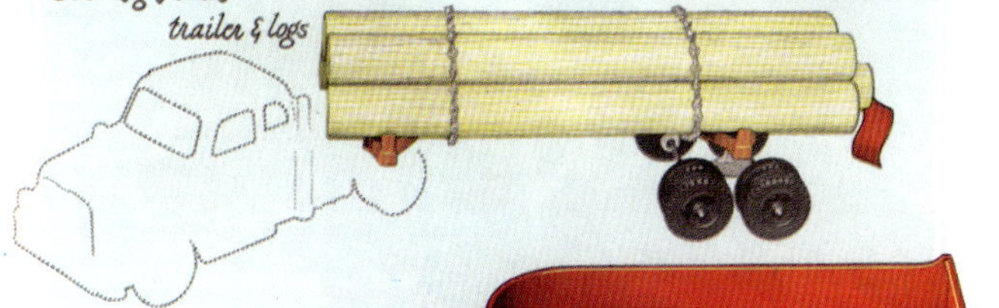

510 Log Truck trailer & logs

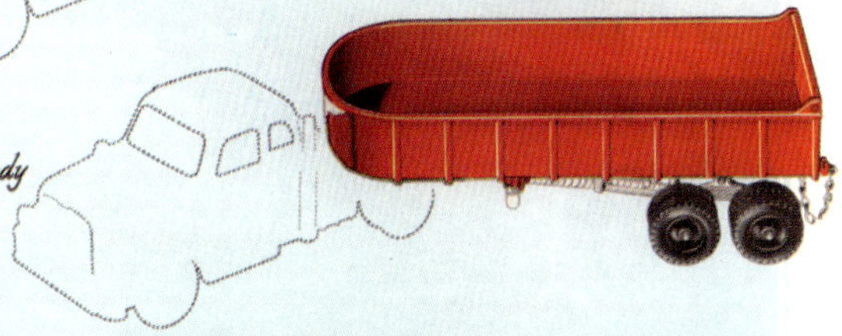

512 Dump Body

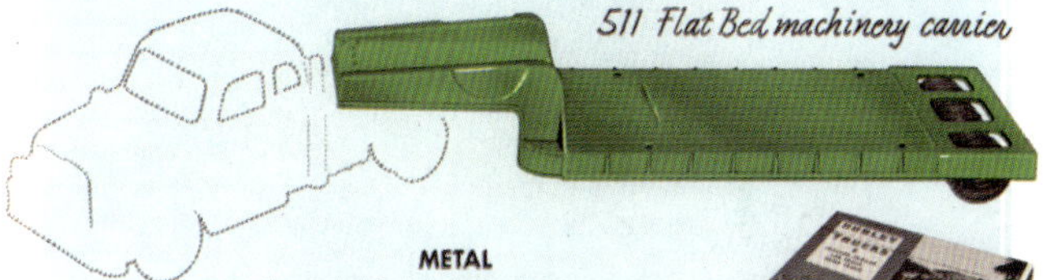

511 Flat Bed machinery carrier

**METAL**

Set consists of one #510 Log Truck complete, one #512 Dump Truck complete and one Carryall trailer bed. Packed 1 set in a box; ¼ dozen sets to a carton. Weight per carton 35 lbs. All toys have numerous play features, aluminum trimming and rubber wheels.

*Attractive red, yellow, blue, green, black box.*



1956

# No. 60 Road Building Set

Flat bed truck
15 inches long

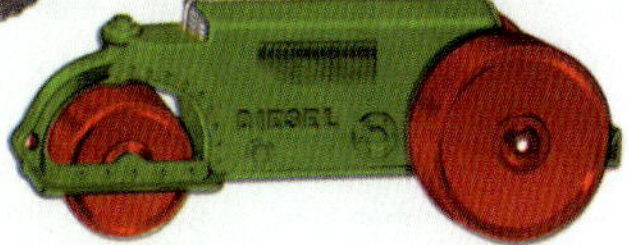

315 Road Roller

316 Road Scraper

**POLYSTYRENE**

Set consists of Flat Bed Truck, Road Roller and Road Scraper. Packed 1 set in a box; 1 dozen sets to a carton. Weight per carton 22 lbs. Orange flat bed truck, green road roller with red wheels, yellow scraper. All toys have aluminum trimming.

"Flat bed trailer hauls other equipment."

*Bright red, yellow, blue, and green box. Die cut lid folds back to form self display.*



# No. 70 Assortment

331 Dump

332 Tow

333 Hook & Ladder

334 Telephone

335 Gas

**POLYSTYRENE**

No. 70 Assortment of Six Diesel Trucks. Set consists of No. 331 Dump Truck, 332 Tow Truck, 333 Hook & Ladder, 334 Telephone Truck, 335 Gas Truck and 336 Motor Express. Packed 1 set in a box; ½ dozen sets to a carton. Weight per carton 12 lbs. All toys have aluminum trimming and rubber wheels.

336 Motor Express

*Colorful yellow, blue, red, green and black box. Die cut lid folds back to form self display.*

## No. 500 Tractor-Loader (Metal)

*Pulling lever back dumps bucket*

**500 Tractor-Loader Metal**

Length 13 inches. Packed 1 in a box; ½ dozen to a carton. Weight per carton 19 lbs. Red with bright metal loader mechanism and steering wheel. Aluminum trimming. Realistic engine details, spring seat, steering wheel operates front wheels. Side lever raises, lowers and dumps loader.

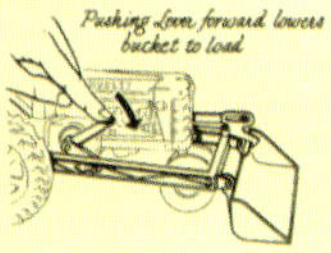

*Pushing lever forward lowers bucket to load*

## No. 504 Telephone Truck (Metal)

*Sliding Top Cover*

*Pole Trailer in travelling position*

**504 Telephone Truck Metal**

Length 12½ inches. Packed 1 in a box; ½ dozen to a carton. Weight per carton 21 lbs. Olive green with aluminum trimming. Removable boom in rear. Crank raises or lowers rope and hook. Top of truck slides back to cover open half in rear. Plastic ladder. Three metal digging tools. Red trailer hooks on rear. 11-inch telephone pole. Black rubber wheels, dual in rear.

*Winch in operation*



## HUBLEY CORVETTE

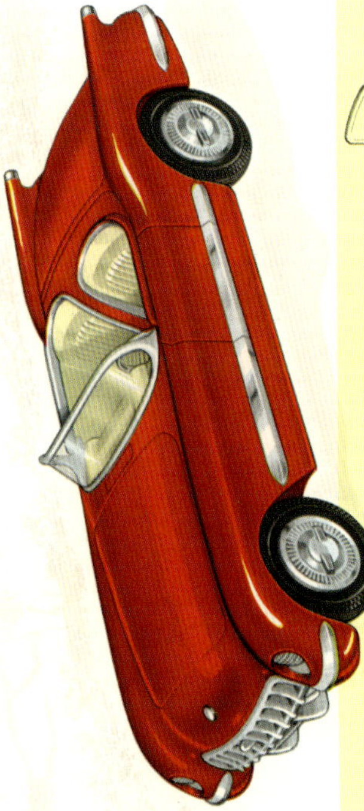

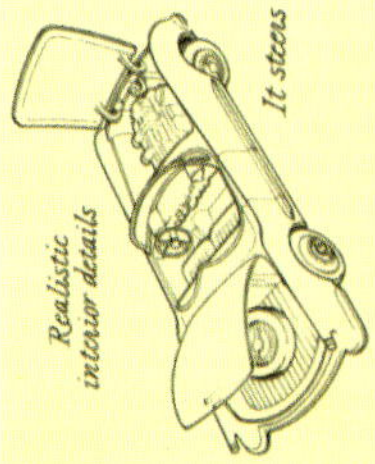

*Realistic interior details*

*It steers!*

**METAL**

**509 Corvette**

Length 12¾ inches. Packed 1 in a box; ½ dozen to a carton. Weight per carton 23 lbs. Colors red with aluminum trim. Realistic wrap-around transparent windshield. Realistic chassis and dashboard details. Working steering mechanism. Front hood opens revealing finely detailed motor. Rear trunk opens for removal of spare tire.



1956

## HUBLEY LOG TRUCK

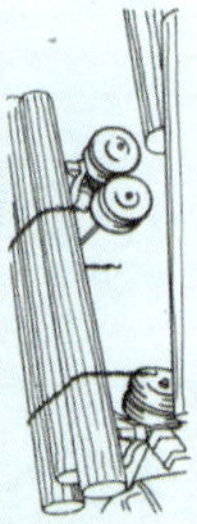

*Logs unload*

*Note independent action of rear wheels*

**METAL**

**510 Log Truck**

Length 20½ inches. Packed 1 in a box; ½ dozen to a carton. Weight per carton 25 lbs. Orange with grey chassis and aluminum trimming. Realistic chassis details. Trailer carries 5 logs, each 14 inches long. Wheels are independently mounted to roll over stones or obstacles. Two chains to hold logs in place. Black rubber wheels.



## HUBLEY CARRYALL

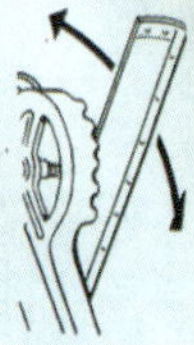

*Scraper Blade adjustable*

**METAL**

**511 Carryall**

Length 20½ inches. Packed 1 in a box; ½ dozen to a carton. Weight per carton 27 lbs. Green chassis and ivory cab with aluminum trim. Green flat bed machinery carrier. Seven wheels realistically mounted on rear of trailer. Complete with 10¾ inch metal road scraper. Black rubber wheels.

*Steering Wheel action*

# HUBLEY DUMP TRUCK

### METAL

**512 Dump Truck**

Length 18 inches. Packed 1 in a box; ½ dozen to a carton. Weight per carton 25 lbs. Red chassis, ivory cab with aluminum trim. Movable red dump, aluminum trim. Pushing lever on side raises dump, tail gate opens automatically. Rear wheels on trailer have knee action. Rubber wheels.

# HUBLEY FIRE TRUCK

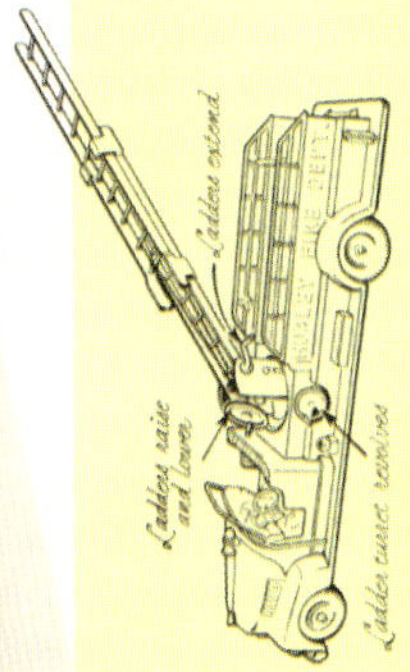

### METAL

**520 Fire Truck**

Length 19 inches. Packed 1 in a box; ½ dozen to a carton. Weight per carton 25 lbs. Red with black seat and bright metal trim. Ladders aluminum and elevate and revolve through 360 degree arc. Rubber wheels.



1956

# INDEX

| No. | Name | | Pieces in Box | Carton Packing | Carton Weight | Catalog Page |
|---|---|---|---|---|---|---|
| 100 | "Small Stuff" Animals | (Acetate) | One per bag | 3 doz. | 4 lbs. | 2 |
| 306 | Fire Engine | (Polyethylene) | 12 | 3 doz. | 6 lbs. | 4 |
| 307 | Hook & Ladder | (Polyethylene) | 12 | 3 doz. | 5 lbs. | 4 |
| 309 | Tractor | (Polystyrene) | 12 | 3 doz. | 11 lbs. | 3 |
| 310 | Motorcycle | (Polystyrene) | 12 | 3 doz. | 8 lbs. | 3 |
| 311 | Airplane | (Polystyrene) | 12 | 3 doz. | 5 lbs. | 3 |
| 316 | Road Scraper | (Polyethylene) | 6 | 3 doz. | 11 lbs. | 4 |
| 325 | Racer | (Polystyrene) | 6 | 3 doz. | 10 lbs. | 4 |
| 331 | Diesel Dump Truck | (Polystyrene) | 6 | 3 doz. | 11 lbs. | 5 |
| 332 | Diesel Tow Truck | (Polystyrene) | 6 | 3 doz. | 11 lbs. | 5 |
| 333 | Diesel Hook & Ladder | (Polystyrene) | 6 | 3 doz. | 11 lbs. | 5 |
| 334 | Diesel Telephone Truck | (Polystyrene) | 6 | 3 doz. | 11 lbs. | 5 |
| 335 | Diesel Gas Truck | (Polystyrene) | 6 | 3 doz. | 11 lbs. | 6 |
| 336 | Diesel Motor Express | (Polystyrene) | 6 | 3 doz. | 13 lbs. | 6 |
| 337 | Tractor | (Polystyrene) | 6 | 3 doz. | 18 lbs. | 6 |
| 429 | Log Truck | (Metal) | 6 | 1 doz. | 4 lbs. | 7 |
| 430 | Airplane | (Metal) | 6 | 1 doz. | 5 lbs. | 7 |
| 431 | Dump Truck | (Metal) | 6 | 1 doz. | 5 lbs. | 7 |
| 432 | M.G. | (Metal) | 6 | 1 doz. | 6 lbs. | 7 |
| 451 | Tractor | (Metal) | 1 | 1 doz. | 8 lbs. | 8 |
| 455 | Jaguar | (Metal) | 1 | 1 doz. | 6 lbs. | 8 |
| 458 | Dump Truck | (Metal) | 1 | 1 doz. | 8 lbs. | 8 |
| 459 | Log Truck | (Metal) | 1 | 1 doz. | 7 lbs. | 9 |
| 465 | Hook & Ladder | (Metal) | 1 | 1 doz. | 7 lbs. | 9 |
| 466 | Air Compressor | (Metal) | 1 | 3 doz. | 22 lbs. | 9 |
| 467 | Navy Plane | (Metal) | 1 | 1 doz. | 9 lbs. | 10 |
| 468 | Hook & Ladder | (Metal) | 1 | 1 doz. | 13 lbs. | 10 |
| 473 | Hubley Jr. Tractor | (Metal) | 1 | 1 doz. | 14 lbs. | 10 |
| 474 | Tow Truck | (Metal) | 1 | 1 doz. | 12 lbs. | 11 |
| 478 | Dump Truck | (Metal) | 1 | 1 doz. | 19 lbs. | 12 |
| 479 | Log Truck | (Metal) | 1 | 1 doz. | 17 lbs. | 12 |
| 480 | Road Roller | (Metal) | 1 | 1 doz. | 23 lbs. | 12 |
| 481 | Road Scraper | (Metal) | 1 | 1 doz. | 14 lbs. | 11 |
| 485 | M.G. | (Metal) | 1 | 1 doz. | 18 lbs. | 13 |
| 486 | Thunderbird | (Metal) | 1 | 1 doz. | 12 lbs. | 11 |
| 487 | Cement Mixer | (Metal) | 1 | 1 doz. | 18 lbs. | 13 |
| 488 | Power Shovel | (Metal) | 1 | 1 doz. | 20 lbs. | 13 |
| 490 | Tractor | (Metal) | 1 | 1 doz. | 29 lbs. | 14 |
| 492 | Auto Transport | (Metal) | 1 | 1 doz. | 27 lbs. | 16 |
| 493 | Log Truck | (Metal) | 1 | 1 doz. | 27 lbs. | 14 |
| 494 | Shovel Truck | (Metal) | 1 | 1 doz. | 22 lbs. | 15 |
| 495 | Navy Fighter Bomber | (Metal) | 1 | 1 doz. | 29 lbs. | 15 |
| 500 | Tractor Loader | (Metal) | 1 | ½ doz. | 19 lbs. | 26 |
| 504 | Telephone Truck | (Metal) | 1 | ½ doz. | 21 lbs. | 26 |
| 509 | Corvette | (Metal) | 1 | ½ doz. | 23 lbs. | 27 |
| 510 | Log Truck | (Metal) | 1 | ½ doz. | 25 lbs. | 28 |
| 511 | Carryall | (Metal) | 1 | ½ doz. | 27 lbs. | 29 |
| 512 | Dump Truck | (Metal) | 1 | ½ doz. | 25 lbs. | 30 |
| 520 | Fire Truck | (Metal) | 1 | ½ doz. | 25 lbs. | 31 |

**BOXED ASSORTMENTS**

| No. | Name | | Pieces in Box | Carton Packing | Carton Weight | Catalog Page |
|---|---|---|---|---|---|---|
| 6 | Farm Set | (Metal) | 1 | 1 doz. | 15 lbs. | 17 |
| 11 | Assortment | (Metal) | 1 | 1 doz. | 20 lbs. | 18 |
| 46 | Assortment | (Metal) | 1 | 1 doz. | 24 lbs. | 19 |
| 50 | Farm Set | (Metal) | 1 | ½ doz. | 19 lbs. | 20 |
| 55 | Assortment | (Metal) | 1 | ½ doz. | 19 lbs. | 21 |
| 60 | Road Building Set | (Polystyrene) | 1 | 1 doz. | 22 lbs. | 24 |
| 70 | Diesel Truck Set | (Polystyrene) | 1 | ½ doz. | 12 lbs. | 25 |
| 75 | Road Building Set | (Metal) | 1 | ¼ doz. | 23 lbs. | 22 |
| 86 | Deluxe Assortment | (Metal) | 1 | ¼ doz. | 35 lbs. | 23 |
| 150 | "Small Stuff" Animal Assortment | (Acetate) | 1 | 1 doz. | 6 lbs. | 2 |

# HUBLEY

THE HUBLEY MANUFACTURING CO.
LANCASTER, PA., U.S.A.

Printed in the United States of America

Andes · Design and Advertising · Lancaster

# 1957

# 1957

# Hubley

## METAL and PLASTIC

## "KIDDIE TOYS"

THE HUBLEY MANUFACTURING CO., LANCASTER, PA., U.S.A.

# Acetate No. 100 "Small Stuff" Animals

**100 ANIMALS Acetate**
Length 3 inches. Packed individually in color-printed polyethylene bags; 3 dozen to a carton. Weight per carton 3 lbs. 1 each Scottie, Lamb, Panda and Elephant. Non-toxic finish. Red rubber wheels.

**150 ANIMAL ASSORTMENT Acetate**
Boxed assortment of four animals—Scottie, Lamb, Panda and Elephant. Supplied with non-toxic finish and red rubber wheels. Packed 1 set to a box; 1 dozen sets to a carton. Weight per carton 6 lbs.

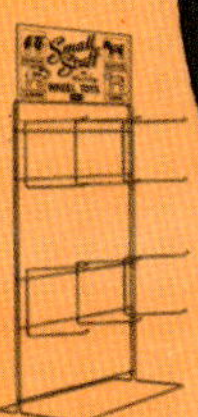

Attractive blue, red, pink and black box. Die cut lid folds back to form self display.

Sturdy metal display stand available with orders of one gross or more, at slight additional cost. Packs flat in corrugated carton. Shipping weight about 2 lbs.

SOFT UNBREAKABLE

## Polyethylene

**306 FIRE ENGINE**
**Soft, unbreakable polyethylene**
Length 6 inches. Red. Packed 12 in a box; 3 dozen to a carton. Weight per carton 5 lbs. Rubber wheels.

SOFT UNBREAKABLE

**307 HOOK & LADDER**
**Soft, unbreakable polyethylene**
Length 6 inches. Packed 12 in a box; 3 dozen to a carton. Weight per carton 5 lbs. Red with two steel ladders. Rubber wheels.

## Polystyrene

**309 TRACTOR**
**Polystyrene**
Length 4¾ inches. Packed 12 in a box; 3 dozen to a carton. Weight per carton 11 lbs. Red, green and orange. Rubber wheels.

**310 MOTORCYCLE**
**Polystyrene**
Length 5 inches. Packed 12 in a box; 3 dozen to a carton. Weight per carton 8 lbs. Red and green motorcycle, blue man. Rubber wheels.

**311 AIRPLANE**
**Polystyrene**
Length 5 inches. Packed 12 in a box; 3 dozen to a carton. Weight per carton 5 lbs. Assorted colors. Retractable landing gear. Rubber wheels.



1957

## Polyethylene

SOFT UNBREAKABLE

Scraper blade adjusts

**316 ROAD SCRAPER**
**Soft, unbreakable polyethylene**
Length 6¼ inches. Packed 6 in a box; 1 dozen to a carton. Weight per carton 4 lbs. Yellow body with aluminum trim and adjustable scraper. Rubber wheels.

Removable ladder

**317 REPAIR TRUCK**
**Soft, unbreakable polyethylene**
Length 7¼ inches. Packed 6 in a box; 1 dozen to a carton. Weight per carton 4 lbs. Green and red with white ladder. Rubber wheels. Removable ladder.

**318 LOG TRUCK**
**Soft, unbreakable polyethylene**
Length 7¾ inches. Packed 6 in a box; 1 dozen to a carton. Weight per carton 4 lbs. Orange with 5 removable logs. Rubber wheels.

**319 GAS TRUCK**
**Soft, unbreakable polyethylene**
Length 7¼ inches. Packed 6 in a box; 1 dozen to a carton. Weight per carton 4 lbs. Assorted color combination. Rubber wheels.



SOFT UNBREAKABLE

## Polyethylene

Tailgate swings open when dump raised.

**320 DUMP TRUCK**
**Soft, unbreakable polyethylene**
Length 6¾ inches. Packed 6 in a box; 1 dozen to a carton. Weight per carton 3 lbs. Green and red, and green and yellow color combinations. Tail gate swings open when dump is raised. Rubber wheels.

Ladders mount in holes.

**322 HOOK & LADDER**
**Soft, unbreakable polyethylene**
Length 8¼ inches. Packed 6 in a box; 1 dozen to a carton. Weight per carton 3 lbs. Red with two ivory ladders, which can be removed and joined together. Rubber wheels.

**321 TOW TRUCK**
**Soft, unbreakable polyethylene**
Length 7 inches. Packed 6 in a box; 1 dozen to a carton. Weight per carton 3 lbs. Two color combinations in red, white and green. Rubber wheels.

## Polystyrene

Lift the hood and see the motor.

**325 RACER**
**Polystyrene**
Length 6¾ inches. Packed 6 in a box; 1 dozen to a carton. Weight per carton 4 lbs. White with red trimming and red with white trimming. Also green and ivory combination. Hood lifts up exposing realistic motor. Rubber wheels.

*Metal*

**429 LOG TRUCK**
Length 5¾ inches. Packed 6 in a box; 1 dozen to a carton. Weight per carton 4 lbs. Orange with bright trimming and cream top. 5 logs. Black wheels.

**430 AIRPLANE**
Length 6 inches. Packed 6 in a box; 1 dozen to a carton. Weight per carton 5 lbs. Assorted red and blue with aluminum wings. Folding wings, retractable landing gear. Black wheels.

Folding wings.

Tailgate swings open.

**431 DUMP TRUCK**
Length 5⅝ inches. Packed 6 in a box; 1 dozen to a carton. Weight per carton 5 lbs. Green chassis with cream top, red movable dump. Tail gate opens when dump is raised. Black wheels.

**432 M.G.**
Length 5⅞ inches. Packed 6 in a box; 1 dozen to a carton. Weight per carton 6 lbs. Colors assorted red with cream seat and yellow with black seat. Black wheels, including spare mounted continental fashion on rear.

Fine interior details.

*Metal*

Movable boom.

**453 TOW TRUCK**
Length 7 inches. Packed 1 in a box; 1 dozen to a carton. Weight per carton 7 lbs. Assorted colors with bright metal sides, boom, bumper and grill. Movable boom. Black wheels.

**455 JAGUAR**
Length 7½ inches. Packed 1 in a box; 1 dozen to a carton. Weight per carton 6 lbs. Colors assorted, red and cream, green and cream. Transparent windshield. Aluminum trimming. Realistic details. Black wheels.

View into "cockpit"

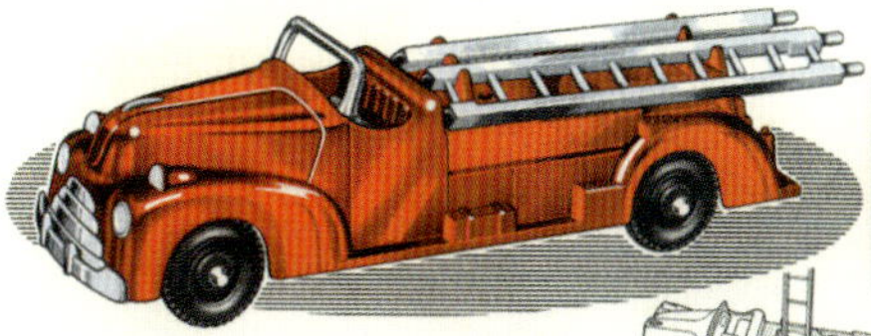

**465 HOOK & LADDER**
Length 8½ inches. Packed 1 in a box; 1 dozen to a carton. Weight per carton 7 lbs. Red with aluminum finished windshield and ladders. Black wheels.

Ladders mount in holes.

**466 AIR COMPRESSOR**
Length 6¾ inches. Packed 1 in a box; 1 dozen to a carton. Weight per carton 8 lbs. Colors assorted with aluminum compressor. Black wheels.



1957

*Metal*

**451 TRACTOR**
Length 5½ inches. Packed 1 in a box; 1 dozen to a carton. Weight per carton 8 lbs. Colors, red and orange with aluminum trim. Realistic detailing of engine and chassis. Yellow hub on rear wheels. Rubber tires treaded on rear, grooved on front like real tractor.

Tailgate swings open.

**458 DUMP TRUCK**
Length 7 5/16 inches. Packed 1 in a box; 1 dozen to a carton. Weight per carton 8 lbs. Green chassis, red dump, bright metal trim. Black wheels.

**459 LOG TRUCK**
Length 7⅜ inches. Packed 1 in a box; 1 dozen to a carton. Weight per carton 7 lbs. Orange with bright trim. 5 logs. Black wheels.

**460 STAKE TRUCK**
ength 7⅜ inches. Packed 1 in a ox; 1 dozen to a carton. Weight er carton 8 lbs. All red with bright rim. Black wheels.



*Metal*

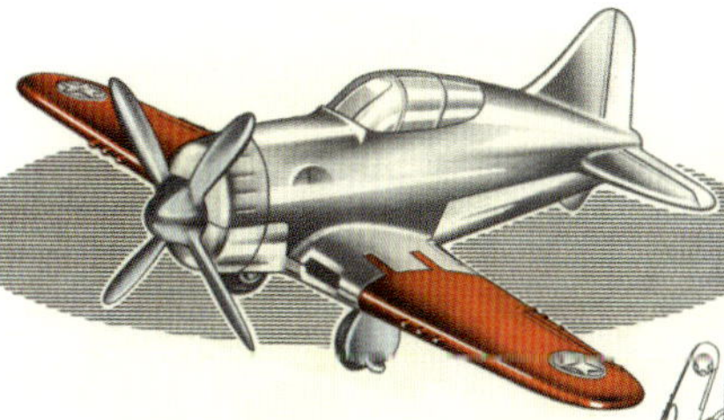

**467 NAVY PLANE**
Length 6½ inches, wing span 8¾ inches. Packed 1 in a box; 1 dozen to a carton. Weight per carton 9 lbs. Colors grey body with assorted red and blue wing tips. Cockpit enclosed with transparent bubble. Black wheels, revolving propeller. Retractable landing gear.

Folding wings.

**472 TRACTOR**
Length 7¼ inches. Packed 1 in a box; 1 dozen to a carton. Weight per carton 14 lbs. Colors assorted red and orange with aluminum trim. Treaded rubber tires. Realistic engine details.

**471 HOOK & LADDER**
Length 11¼ inches. Packed 1 in a box; 1 dozen to a carton. Weight per carton 13 lbs. Red with aluminum trim. Two ladders. Black wheels.

Ladders mount in holes.

**475 THUNDERBIRD**
Length 9¼ inches. Packed 1 in a box; 1 dozen to a carton. Weight per carton 12 lbs. Colors red and yellow. Realistic dashboard, steering wheel and wrap-around transparent windshield. Aluminum trim and black wheels.

**476 STATION WAGON**
Length 8⅞ inches. Packed 1 in a box; 1 dozen to a carton. Weight per carton 13 lbs. Colors red and cream, and green and cream with massive aluminum grill and bumpers. Black wheels.

**477 STAKE TRUCK**
Length 9½ inches. Packed 1 in a box; 1 dozen to a carton. Weight per carton 11 lbs. Green cab with bright metal grill. Cream truck bed with removable red stakes. Black wheels.

Dump body raises when lever is thrown forward.

Tailgate swings open.

**478 DUMP TRUCK**
Length 10 inches. Packed 1 in a box; 1 dozen to a carton. Weight per carton 15 lbs. Cream chassis, green cab, red dump with bright metal trim. Tail gate opens when dump is raised. Black wheels.

**479 LOG TRUCK**
Length 11 inches. Packed 1 in a box; 1 dozen to a carton. Weight per carton 17 lbs. Orange cab and cream chassis with bright metal trim. 5 removable logs and chain. Black wheels.



1957

Crank windlass

**482 TOW TRUCK**
Length 9¾ inches. Packed 1 in a box; 1 dozen to a carton. Weight per carton 15 lbs. Red cab, cream chassis and green body with bright finish winch and boom. Hook on boom raises and lowers to tow "wrecked" cars. Black wheels.

Mixer drum rotates as truck moves.

**487 CEMENT MIXER**
Length 10⅝ inches. Packed 1 in a box; 1 dozen to a carton. Weight per carton 17 lbs. Cream chassis, orange cab and body with bright metal revolving mixer and trim. Black wheels.





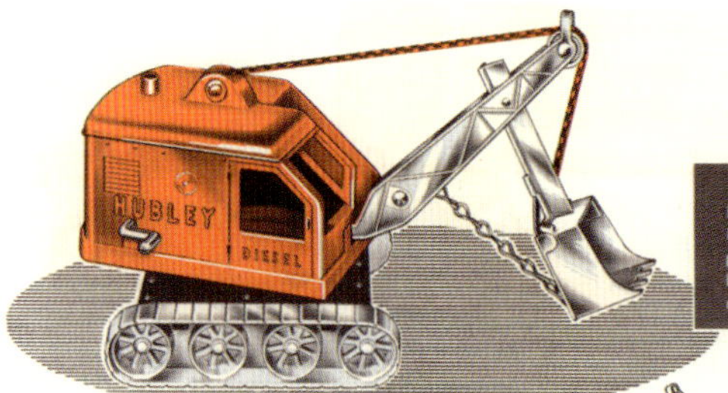


**488 POWER SHOVEL**
Length 8 inches. Packed 1 in a box; 1 dozen to a carton. Weight per carton 18 lbs. Orange with black striping. Shovel and working mechanism bright metal.

Cab swings to either side.

Bucket is closed when boom is down.

Bucket dumps when boom is raised to full height.

Tailgate lowers.

**489 GRAIN TRUCK**
Length 10 inches. Packed 1 in a box; 1 dozen to a carton. Weight per carton 10 lbs. Colors—cream chassis, blue cab and truck bed. Bright metal truck body sides. Tail gate lowers. Black wheels.

*Metal*

**493 LOG TRUCK**
Length 13¾ inches. Packed 1 in a box; 1 dozen to a carton. Weight per carton 27 lbs. Red cab and trailer with aluminum trimming. Realistic chassis details. Nine logs with double chain to hold logs in place. Black wheels, dual on rear of tractor. Rear wheels on trailer have knee action.

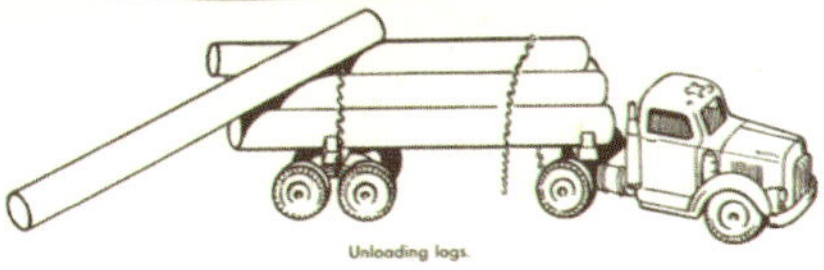

Unloading logs.

**494 SHOVEL TRUCK**
Length 13 inches. Packed 1 in a box; 1 dozen to a carton. Weight per carton 21 lbs. Cream chassis, red cab and green back. Operator's cab turns on a swivel. Shovel and working mechanism bright metal. Bucket opens to release load. Black wheels.

Shovel cab swings to either side.

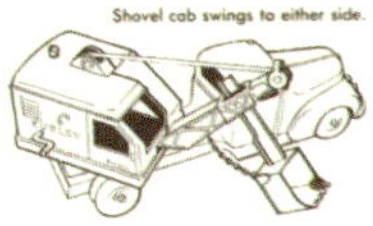

Bucket is closed when boom is down.

Bucket dumps when boom is raised to full height.



*Metal*

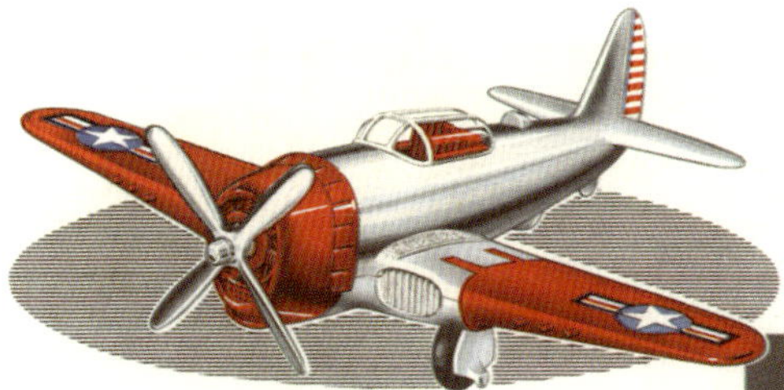

**495 NAVY FIGHTER BOMBER**
Length 10 inches, wingspread 11⅝ inches. Packed 1 in a box; 1 dozen to a carton. Weight per carton 18 lbs. Colors—red wings and cowl, aluminum body with red, white and blue trim. Cockpit enclosed with transparent sliding bubble. Revolving propeller, folding wings, retractable landing gear. Black wheels.

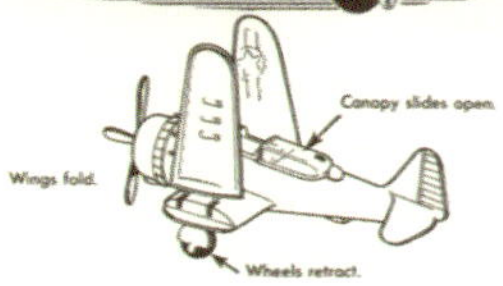

**496 TRACTOR**
Length 9¼ inches. Packed 1 in a box; 1 dozen to a carton. Weight per carton 29 lbs. Red with aluminum trimming. Realistic engine details. Steering wheel operates front wheels. Treaded black tires.

Front wheels steer.

1957

*Metal*

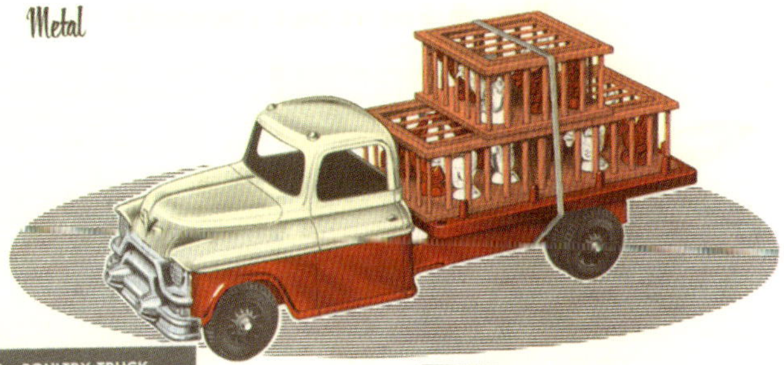

**497 POULTRY TRUCK**
Length 10 inches. Packed 1 in a box; 1 dozen to a carton. Weight per carton 11 lbs. Red chassis and truck bed with cream cab. Complete with three poultry crates with chickens and ducks. Black wheels.

Crates open.

**492 TRANSPORT**
Length 14 inches. Packed 1 in a box; 1 dozen to a carton. Weight per carton 27 lbs. Red chassis with ivory cab and red trailer with aluminum trimming. Realistic chassis details. Four plastic cars in assorted colors, which can be driven on or off trailer over removable ramp, which hooks under trailer. Black wheels, dual on rear of tractor.

Ramp loading toy cars.



## No. 6 Farm Set (Metal)

Set consists of Tractor, Cultipacker and Wagon. Packed 1 set in a box; 1 dozen sets to a carton. Weight per carton 16 lbs. Toys red with aluminum trimming. Black wheels.

**No. 451 Tractor.** 5½ inches long. See description on Page 8.

**Cultipacker.** 3⅝ inches wide. Red frame with grey wood rollers.

**Wagon.** 5½ inches long. Red with rubber wheels.

Colorful red, yellow, green, black box. Die cut lid folds back to form self display.

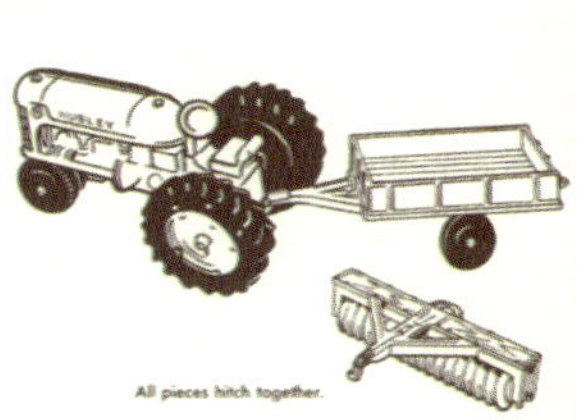

All pieces hitch together.

## No. 12 Boxed Assortment (Metal)

Set consists of 429 Log Truck, 430 Airplane, 431 Dump Truck and 432 Sports Car. Packed 1 set in an attractive box that can be set up as an Airport-Diner-Gas Station; 1 dozen to a carton. Weight per carton 20 lbs. All toys have black wheels.

**No. 429 Log Truck.** See description on Page 6.

**No. 430 Airplane.** See description on Page 6.

**No. 431 Dump Truck.** See description on Page 6.

**No. 432 M.G.** See description on Page 6.

Colorful die cut box sets up to form Airport-Diner-Gas Station as shown above.



## No. 60 Road Building Set

**POLYSTYRENE**

Set consists of Flat Bed Truck, Road Roller and Road Scraper. Packed 1 set in a box; 1 dozen sets to a carton. Weight per carton 22 lbs.

**Flat Bed Truck.** Orange with aluminum trim, 15 inches long. Rubber wheels.

**Road Roller.** Green with aluminum trim, red wheels. 5¾ inches long.

**Road Scraper.** Yellow with adjustable aluminum scraper. 6¼ inches long. Rubber wheels.

Bright red, yellow, blue and green box.

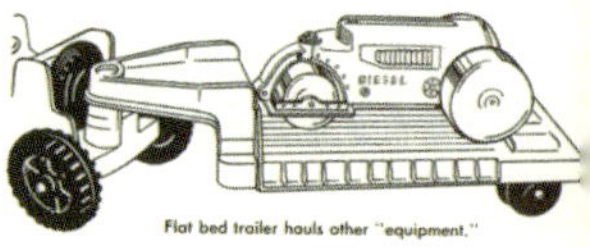

Flat bed trailer hauls other "equipment."



1957

## No. 65 Boxed Assortment

**SOFT, UNBREAKABLE POLYETHYLENE**

Five soft, unbreakable polyethylene trucks in the No. 318–322 Series. Packed 1 set in a box; ½ dozen sets to a carton. Weight per carton 11 lbs. All toys in assorted colors with black rubber wheels. Die cut box sets up to form the Super Highway Maintenance Department.

**No. 318 Log Truck.** Length 7¾ inches. See description on Page 4.

**No. 319 Gas Truck.** Length 7¼ inches. See description on Page 4.

**No. 320 Dump Truck.** Length 6¾ inches. See description on Page 5.

**No. 321 Tow Truck.** Length 7 inches. See description on Page 5.

**No. 322 Hook & Ladder.** Length 8¼ inches. See description on Page 5.

Red, yellow, blue, green and black die cut box.



## No. 50 Farm Set (Metal)

Set consists of Hubley Jr. Tractor, Plow, Cultipacker, Spreader and Farm Wagon, all interlocking. Packed 1 in an attractive box that can be set up as a Barn; ½ dozen to a carton. Weight per carton 19 lbs. Toys red with aluminum trimming. Black wheels.

**Hubley Jr. Tractor.** Length 7¼ inches. Bright red with yellow hub on rear wheels. Black rubber tires and wheels.

**Flat Bed Wagon.** Bed length 6 inches. Bright bed, red hitch.

**Cultipacker.** Width 4¾ inches. Red frame, wood rollers.

**Manure Spreader.** Overall 6¾ inches. Red.

**Plow.** Length 5¼ inches. Red.

All pieces hitch together.

Multi colored, die cut carton sets up as Barn.

## No. 53 Fighter-Bomber Squadron (Metal)

Set consists of one No. 495 Airplane and four No. 430 Airplanes. Packed 1 set in an attractive box, which can be set up as the flight deck of an Aircraft Carrier; ½ dozen to a carton. Weight per carton 24 lbs. Large plane red and aluminum combination; small planes—two red and silver, and two blue and silver. All toys have black wheels.

**No. 495 Airplane.** Length 10 inches, wingspread 11⅜ inches. See description on Page 15.

**No. 430 Airplane.** Length 6 inches, wingspread 6⅛ inches. See description on Page 6.

Bright red, yellow, blue, green, brown and black box. Die cut.

## No. 76 Road Building Set (Metal)

Set consists of a Road Scraper, Dump Truck, Cement Mixer, Power Shovel and Pipe Truck. Packed 1 set in a box; ¼ dozen sets to a carton. Weight per carton 23 lbs. Toys in assorted colors with black wheels and have numerous play features.

**No. 488 Power Shovel.** Length 8 inches. See description Page 13.

**No. 478 Dump Truck.** Length 10 inches. See description Page 11.

**No. 487 Cement Mixer.** Length 10⅜ inches. See description Page 12.

**Pipe Truck.** Length 9½ inches. Orange cab and chassis with bright metal trim. 5 removable black pipes with chain. Black wheels.

**Road Scraper.** Length 10¾ inches. Yellow with bright scraper and trimming. Rear wheels mounted independently to roll over stones and obstacles. Adjustable scraper bar. Front wheels operated by steering wheel. Rubber wheels.

Attractive, bright colored, telescoping lid toy chest.



1957

## No. 87 Super Highway Truck Fleet (Metal)

Set consists of one 510 Log Truck complete, one 512 Dump Truck complete, and one Carryall Trailer Bed with separate Road Scraper. Packed 1 set in a box; ¼ dozen sets to a carton. Weight per carton 35 lbs. All toys have numerous play features, aluminum trimming and black wheels. Either of the cabs hitches to any of the bodies shown.

**No. 510 Log Truck.** Length 20½ inches. See description Page 27.

**No. 512 Dump Truck.** Length 18 inches. See description Page 28.

**Carryall Trailer Bed.** Length 14½ inches. See No. 511 Carryall, Page 28.

**Road Scraper.** Length 10¾ inches. Yellow with bright scraper and trimming. Rear wheels mounted independently to roll over stones and obstacles. Adjustable scraper bar. Front wheels operated by steering wheel. Rubber wheels.

Eye catching red, yellow, blue, and green toy chest with telescoping lid.



## Hubley No. 90 Farm Set (Metal)

Set consists of 525 Tractor, Cultivator, Cultipacker and large Farm Wagon, all interlocking. Cultivator and Cultipacker can be individually attached to Tractor by means of hitch, which permits either to be raised or lowered for operation. Packed 1 set in an attractive corrugated box, which converts into a Play Barn; ¼ dozen to a carton. Weight per carton 27 lbs. Red, grey and aluminum combination with black wheels.

Front wheels steer.

**No. 525 Tractor.** Length 12 inches. See Page 31.

**Cultivator.** 6½″ wide. Red, bright trim.

**Cultipacker.** 6¾″ wide. Red, gray rollers.

**Farm Wagon.** 11″ bed. Red, gray stakes.

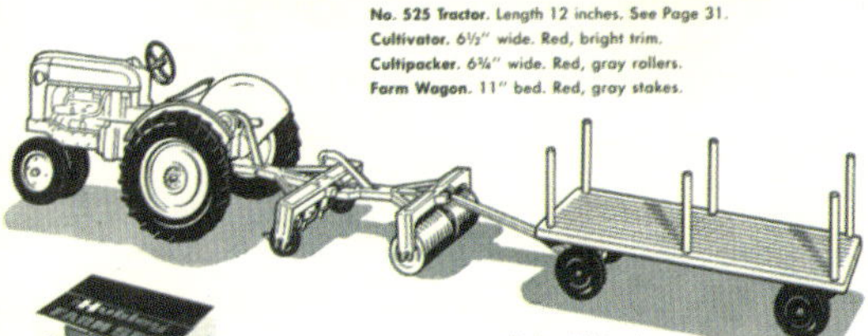

All pieces hitch together.

Hitching to tractor.

Red, white and black corrugated carton, die cut to convert into barn as shown.

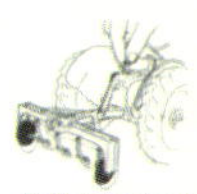

Pushing lever forward raises cultivator

*Metal*

## Hubley Tractor-Loader

**501 TRACTOR-LOADER**
Length 12¾ inches. Packed 1 in a box; ½ dozen to a carton. Weight per carton 19 lbs. Orange with bright metal loader mechanism and steering wheel. Aluminum trimming. Realistic engine details. Steering wheel operates front wheels. Side lever, raises, lowers and dumps loader.

Pulling lever back dumps bucket.

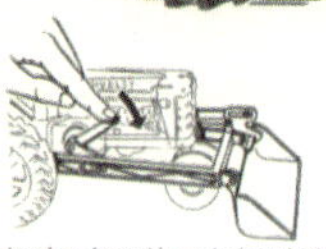

Pushing lever forward lowers bucket to load.

## Hubley Tractor with Cultivator

Front wheels steer.

**502 TRACTOR WITH CULTIVATOR**
Length 9¼ inches. Packed 1 in a box; ½ dozen to a carton. Weight per carton 16 lbs. Red tractor with bright metal cultivator and lowering mechanism. Aluminum trim. Realistic engine details. Steering wheel operates front wheels. Detachable cultivator rake. Side lever raises and lowers rake. Rear wheels metal with black treaded tires.

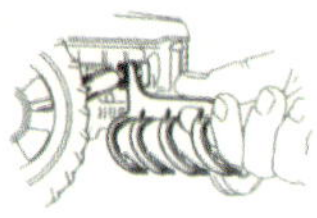

Cultivator blades attached by spring clip.

Lever raises, lowers cultivator blades.



## Hubley Telephone Truck

*Metal*

Sliding top cover.

Pole trailer in travelling position.

**504 TELEPHONE TRUCK**
Length 12½ inches. Packed 1 in a box; ½ dozen to a carton. Weight per carton 21 lbs. Olive green with aluminum trimming. Removable boom in rear. Crank raises and lowers rope and hook. Top of truck slides back to cover open half in rear. One ladder. Three metal digging tools. Red trailer hooks on rear. 11-inch utility pole. Black wheels, dual on rear.

Winch in operation.

## Hubley Log Truck

Logs unload.

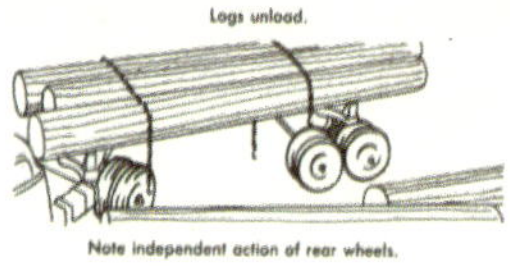

Note independent action of rear wheels.

**510 LOG TRUCK**
Length 20½ inches. Packed 1 in a box; ½ dozen to a carton. Weight per carton 25 lbs. Orange with grey chassis and aluminum trimming. Realistic chassis details. Trailer carries 5 logs, each 14 inches long. Wheels are independently mounted to roll over stones or obstacles. Two chains to hold logs in place. Black wheels.



1957

*Metal*

## Hubley Carryall

**511 CARRYALL**
Length 20½ inches. Packed 1 in a box; ½ dozen to a carton. Weight per carton 23 lbs. Green chassis and ivory cab with aluminum trim. Green flat bed machinery carrier. Seven wheels realistically mounted on rear of trailer. Complete with separate 10¾-inch metal road scraper. Black wheels.

Steering wheel action.

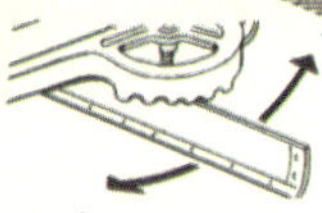

Scraper blade adjustable.

## Hubley Dump Truck

**512 DUMP TRUCK**
Length 18 inches. Packed 1 in a box; ½ dozen to a carton. Weight per carton 23 lbs. Red chassis, ivory cab with aluminum trim. Movable red dump, aluminum trim. Pushing lever on side raises dump, tail gate opens automatically. Rear wheels on trailer have knee action. Black wheels.

Releasing latch allows dump body to raise.

Tailgate swings open.



## HUBLEY FIRE TRUCK

**520 FIRE TRUCK • Metal**
Length 19 inches. Packed 1 in a box; ½ dozen to a carton. Weight per carton 24 lbs. Red with cream seat and bright metal trim. Bright metal ladders elevate and extend with improved gear and rack mechanism, also revolve through 360 degree arc. Black wheels.

Ladders extend.

Ladders raise and lower.

Ladder turret revolves.

# HUBLEY AUTO TRANSPORT

**521 AUTO TRANSPORT • Metal**

Length 19½ inches. Packed 1 in a box; ½ dozen to a carton. Weight per carton 20 lbs. Cream cab, red chassis and trailer with aluminum trimming. Equipped with four assorted color cars of soft unbreakable polyethylene. Equipped with removable ramp to be used for running cars on the trailer. Transport and cars all furnished with black wheels.

# HUBLEY TRACTOR

**525 TRACTOR • Metal**

Length 12 inches. Packed 1 in a box; ½ dozen to a carton. Weight per carton 30 lbs. Grey and red combination with finely detailed, realistic engine details visible from both sides. Red seat and nickel-plated steering wheel. Metal wheels with black treaded tires. "Tricycle" type front wheels operate through steering wheel.

This Tractor combined with other "implements," is shown under No. 90. Farm Set.



1957

# INDEX



## BOXED ASSORTMENTS



**THE HUBLEY MANUFACTURING CO., LANCASTER, PA.**

**Hubley**

★ Hubley Holster Sets ★ Hubley Cap Pistols & Rifles ★ Hubley Kiddie Toys ★

Printed in U. S. America

# 1958

# 1958 Hubley Toys

# Hubley LETTERS

soft, unbreakable
POLYETHYLENE
plastic

**No. 125**

***ALPHABET LETTERS***

Set consists of 50 soft, unbreakable polyethylene letters and numerals in brilliant assorted colors. Colors red, white, and blue. Assortment contains sufficient number of each letter to spell several hundred words.

Assortment is fun to play with, as well as educational.

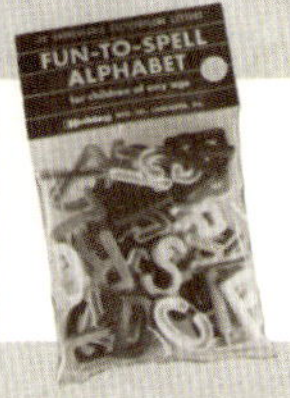


Assorted color letters and numbers packed in transparent polyethylene bag. Attractive header punched for rack hanging. One set per bag, 3 doz. per carton. Wt. 15 lbs.





brilliant, shock-resistant
POLYSTYRENE
plastic

***309 TRACTOR***

Length 4¾ inches. Packed 12 in a box; 3 dozen to a carton. Weight per carton 11 lbs. Red, green and orange with aluminum trimming. Rubber wheels.

***311 AIRPLANE***

Length 5 inches. Packed 12 in a box; 3 dozen to a carton. Weight per carton 5 lbs. Assorted colors. Retractable landing gear. Rubber wheels.

***310 MOTORCYCLE***

Length 5 inches. Packed 12 in a box; 3 dozen to a carton. Weight per carton 8 lbs. Red and green motorcycle, blue man. Rubber wheels.

soft, unbreakable
POLYETHYLENE
plastic

***316 ROAD SCRAPER***

*Soft, unbreakable polyethylene.* Length 6¼ inches. Packed 6 in a box; 3 dozen to a carton. Weight per carton 4 lbs. Yellow body with aluminum trim and adjustable scraper. Rubber wheels.

***317 REPAIR TRUCK***

*Soft, unbreakable polyethylene.* Length 7¼ inches. Packed 6 in a box; 1 dozen to a carton. Weight per carton 4 lbs. Green and red with white ladder. Rubber wheels. Removable ladder.

***319 GAS TRUCK***

*Soft, unbreakable polyethylene.* Length 7¼ inches. Packed 6 in a box; 1 dozen to a carton. Weight per carton 4 lbs. Assorted color combination. Rubber wheels.



soft, unbreakable
POLYETHYLENE
plastic

***320 DUMP TRUCK***

*Soft, unbreakable polyethylene.* Length 6¾ inches. Packed 6 in a box; 1 dozen to a carton. Weight per carton 3 lbs. Green and red, and green and yellow color combinations. Tail gate swings open when dump is raised. Rubber wheels.

***321 TOW TRUCK***

*Soft, unbreakable polyethylene.* Length 7 inches. Packed 6 in a box; 1 dozen to a carton. Weight per carton 3 lbs. Two color combinations in red, white and green. Rubber wheels.

***322 HOOK & LADDER***

*Soft, unbreakable polyethylene.* Length 8¼ inches. Packed 6 in a box; 1 dozen to a carton. Weight per carton 3 lbs. Red with two ivory ladders, which can be removed and joined together. Rubber wheels.

brilliant, shock-resistant
POLYSTYRENE
plastic

***338 HELICOPTER***

*Polystyrene.* Length 5¼ inches. Packed 6 in a box; 1 dozen to a carton. Weight per carton 3 lbs.

***339 DUCK***

*Polystyrene.* Length 5¼ inches. Packed 6 in a box; 1 dozen to a carton. Weight per carton 4 lbs. Black rubber wheels.

***340 BLIMP***

*Polystyrene.* Length 5¼ inches. Packed 6 in a box; 1 dozen to a carton. Weight per carton 4 lbs. Yellow with star insignia. Revolving propeller.



Hubley
METAL TOYS

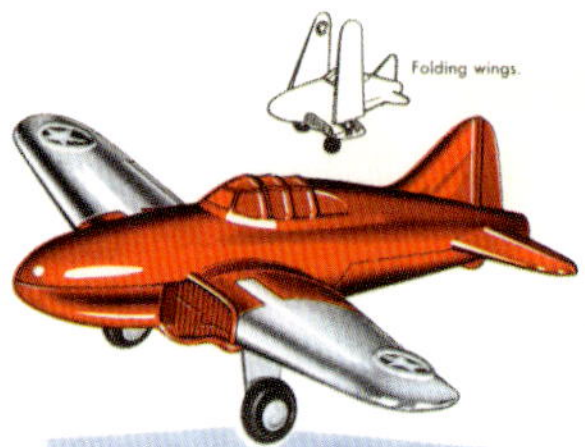


***430 AIRPLANE***

Length 6 inches. Packed 6 in a box; 1 dozen to a carton. Weight per carton 5 lbs. Assorted red and blue with aluminum wings. Folding wings, retractable landing gear. Black wheels.

***429 LOG TRUCK***

Length 5¾ inches. Packed 6 in a box; 1 dozen to a carton. Weight per carton 4 lbs. Orange with bright trimming. 5 logs. Black wheels.

***431 DUMP TRUCK***

Length 5⅝ inches. Packed 6 in a box; 1 dozen to a carton. Weight per carton 5 lbs. Green chassis, red movable dump. Tail gate opens when dump is raised. Black wheels.

***432 M. G.***

Length 5⅞ inches. Packed 6 in a box; 1 dozen to a carton. Weight per carton 6 lbs. Colors assorted red with cream seat and yellow with black seat. Black wheels, including spare mounted (Continental fashion) on rear.

Hubley METAL TOYS

### 451 TRACTOR

Length 5½ inches. Packed 1 in a box; 1 dozen to a carton. Weight per carton 8 lbs. Colors, red and orange with aluminum trim. Realistic detailing of engine and chassis. Rear wheels yellow, rubber tires treaded on rear, grooved on front like real tractor.

### 459 LOG TRUCK

Length 7⅝ inches. Packed 1 in a box; 1 dozen to a carton. Weight per carton 7 lbs. Orange with aluminum trim. 5 logs. Black wheels.

Tailgate swings open.

### 458 DUMP TRUCK

Length 7⁹⁄₁₆ inches. Packed 1 in a box; 1 dozen to a carton. Weight per carton 8 lbs. Green chassis, red dump, bright aluminum trim. Black wheels.

### 466 AIR COMPRESSOR

Length 6¾ inches. Packed 1 in a box; 1 dozen to a carton. Weight per carton 8 lbs. Colors assorted with aluminum compressor. Black wheels.

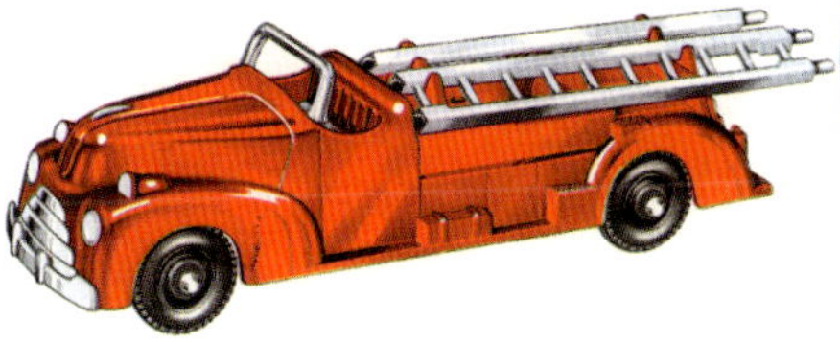

### 465 HOOK & LADDER

Length 8½ inches. Packed 1 in a box; 1 dozen to a carton. Weight per carton 7 lbs. Red with aluminum finished windshield and ladders. Black wheels.

Ladders mount in holes.



Hubley METAL TOYS

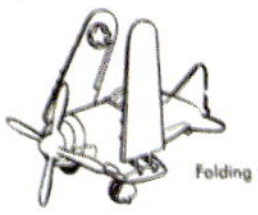

Folding wings.

### 467 NAVY PLANE

Length 6½ inches, wing span 8¾ inches. Packed 1 in a box; 1 dozen to a carton. Weight per carton 9 lbs. Colors: aluminum body with assorted red and blue wing tips. Cockpit enclosed with transparent bubble. Black wheels, revolving propeller. Retractable landing gear.

### 469 LOG TRUCK

Length 10¾ inches. Packed 1 in a box; 1 dozen to a carton. Weight per carton 15 lbs. Yellow with aluminum trimming. Furnished with five 6 inch logs. Four black wheels.

### 470 DUMP TRUCK

Length 9¼ inches. Packed 1 in a box; 1 dozen to carton. Weight per carton 12 lbs. Red cab and chassis; green dump body. Dump operated by side lever. Four black wheels.

Pulling down lever raises dump.



Hubley METAL TOYS

Ladders mount in holes

### 471 HOOK & LADDER

Length 11¼ inches. Packed 1 in a box; 1 dozen to a carton. Weight per carton 13 lbs. Red with aluminum trim. Two ladders. Black wheels.

### 472 TRACTOR

Length 7¼ inches. Packed 1 in a box; 1 dozen to a carton. Weight per carton 14 lbs. Colors assorted red and orange with aluminum trim. Treaded rubber tires. Realistic engine details.

### 476 AMBULANCE

Length 8⅜ inches. Packed 1 in a box; 1 dozen to a carton. Weight per carton 10 lbs. Army olive drab with red cross insignia. Four black wheels.



Hubley METAL TOYS

### 478 DUMP TRUCK

Length 10 inches. Packed 1 in a box; 1 dozen to a carton. Weight per carton 15 lbs. Cream chassis, green cab, red dump with aluminum trim. Tail gate opens when dump is raised. Black wheels.

Dump body raises when lever is thrown forward. Tailgate swings open.

Rotors revolve, also fold for storing in "hangar."

### 483 HELICOPTER

Length 9¼ inches. Packed 1 in a box; 1 dozen to carton. Weight per carton 12 lbs. Dark blue with transparent plastic bubble. Two revolving aluminum finished rotor blades. Two black rubber wheels.

### 482 TOW TRUCK

Length 9⅝ inches. Packed 1 in a box; 1 dozen to a carton. Weight per carton 15 lbs. Red cab, cream chassis and green body with bright finish winch and boom. Hook on boom raises and lowers to tow "wrecked" cars. Black wheels.

Crank windlass.

Pipes join together.

### 485 PIPE TRUCK

Length 11 inches. Packed 1 in a box; 1 dozen to carton. Weight per carton 12 lbs. Orange and cream with aluminum trimming. Five pieces of plastic, interlocking pipe. Black wheels, dual on rear.

### 484 MOTORCYCLE

Length 8½ inches. Packed 1 in a box; 1 dozen to carton. Weight per carton 13 lbs. Red with aluminum trim. Black rubber wheels with sprayed aluminum center. Removable motorcycle policeman in black uniform. Front wheel can be steered by regular handle bar.

Cab swings to either side.

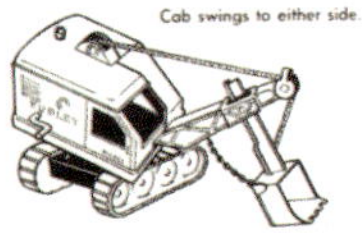
Bucket is closed when boom is down.

Bucket dumps when boom is raised to full height.

### 488 POWER SHOVEL

Length 8 inches. Packed 1 in a box; 1 dozen to a carton. Weight per carton 18 lbs. Orange. Shovel and working mechanism bright metal.



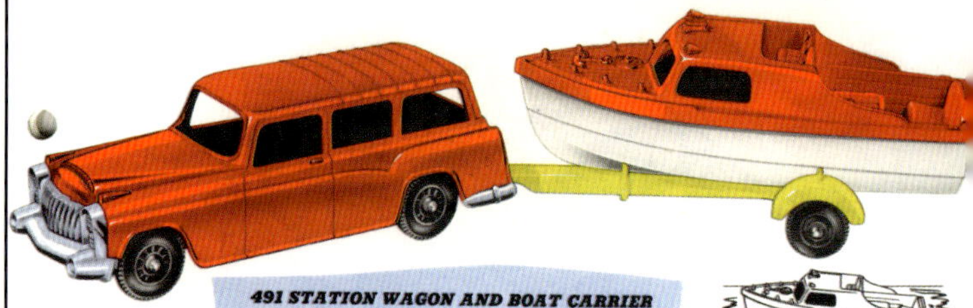

### 491 STATION WAGON AND BOAT CARRIER

Metal and plastic combination. Over-all length 16 inches. Packed 1 in a box; 1 dozen to carton. Weight per carton 14 lbs. Red station wagon with yellow boat trailer; red and white removable polystyrene boat. Black wheels.

Plastic boat floats.

### 495 NAVY FIGHTER BOMBER

Length 10 inches. Packed 1 in a box; 1 dozen to a carton. Weight per carton 18 lbs. Colors: red wings and cowl; aluminum body with red, white and blue trim. Cockpit enclosed with transparent sliding bubble. Revolving propeller, folding wings, retractable landing gear. Black wheels.

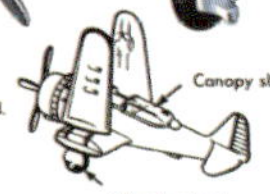
Wings fold.
Canopy slides open.
Wheels retract.

Front wheels steer.

### 496 TRACTOR

Length 9¼ inches. Packed 1 in a box; 1 dozen to a carton. Weight per carton 29 lbs. Red with aluminum trimming. Realistic engine details. Steering wheel operates front wheels. Treaded black tires.

### 497 POULTRY TRUCK

Length 10 inches. Packed 1 in a box; 1 dozen to a carton. Weight per carton 11 lbs. Red chassis and truck bed with cream cab. Complete with three poultry crates containing chickens and ducks. Black wheels.

Crates open.

Fish "swim."

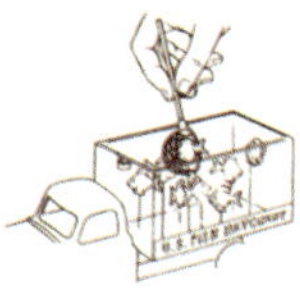

### 498 FISH HATCHERY

Length 10 inches. Packed 1 in a box; 1 dozen to carton. Weight per carton 12 lbs. Red chassis with aluminum trimming. Transparent fish tank complete with "swimming" fish. Polyethylene fish net. Black wheels.

### 499 ROAD ROLLER

Length 10½ inches. Packed 1 in a box; 1 dozen to carton. Weight per carton 19 lbs. Orange with aluminum trimming. Three large black wooden rollers. Front rollers controlled by steering lever.

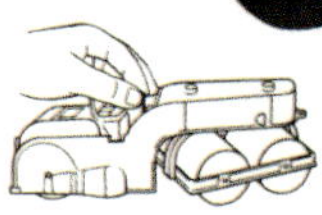
Steering lever action.

### 492 TRANSPORT

Length 14 inches. Packed 1 in a box; 1 dozen to a carton. Weight per carton 27 lbs. Red chassis with ivory cab and red trailer with aluminum trimming. Realistic chassis details. Four plastic cars in assorted colors can be driven on or off trailer over removable ramp, which hooks under trailer. Black wheels, dual on rear of tractor.

Ramp loading toy cars.

## No. 6 FARM SET

Metal. Set consists of toys shown. Packed 1 set per attractive die cut box; 1 doz. per carton. Wt. 16 lbs.

451 TRACTOR 5½ inches long. See description page 6.

WAGON. 5½ inches long. Red with rubber wheels.

All pieces hitch together.

CULTIPACKER. 3⅜ inches wide. Red frame, grey wooden rollers.

Die cut box sets up to form counter display.

## No. 12 BOXED ASSORTMENT

Metal. Consists of 4 toys shown. One set per colorful die cut, set up box; 1 doz. per carton. Wt. 20 lbs.

429 LOG TRUCK See description, page 5.

430 AIRPLANE See description, page 5.

Box sets up to form Airport-Diner-Gas Station.

432 M.G. See description, page 5.

431 DUMP TRUCK See description, page 5.



## No. 65 ASSORTMENT

SOFT UNBREAKABLE POLYETHYLENE. Consists of 5 toys shown. Packed 1 set per multi-colored box; ½ doz. per carton. Wt. 11 lbs. All toys in assorted colors with black wheels.

316 ROAD SCRAPER See description, page 3.

317 REPAIR TRUCK See description, page 3.

Die cut box sets up to form Super Highway Maintenance Department.

319 GAS TRUCK See description, page 3.

320 DUMP TRUCK See description, page 4.

321 TOW TRUCK See description, page 4.

## No. 66 AIR-SEA RESCUE SET

HIGH IMPACT PLASTIC. 5 toys in yellow and olive drab. Full color lithographed box. Packed 1 set per box; ½ doz. per carton. Wt. 10 lbs.

339 DUCK See description, page 4.

311 AIRPLANE See description, page 3.

338 HELICOPTER See description, page 4.

340 BLIMP See description, page 4.

Die cut box forms counter display.

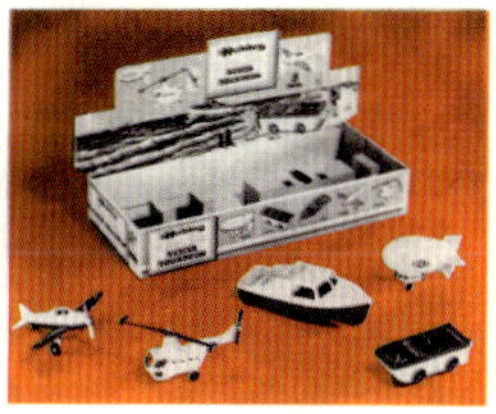

COAST GUARD CUTTER 8". Fine detailing. Floats.



## No. 50 FARM SET

Metal. Consists of Hubley toys shown. All toys are red with aluminum trim. Packed 1 set per die cut box; 1 doz. per carton. Wt. 19 lbs.

CULTIPACKER Width 4⅜ inches. Wood rollers.

FLAT BED WAGON Length 6 inches.

HUBLEY JR. TRACTOR Length 7¼ inches.

MANURE SPREADER. 6⅜ inches overall.

PLOW Length 5¼ inches.

All pieces hitch together.

Multi colored, die cut carton sets up as Barn.

## No. 53 FIGHTER BOMBER SQUADRON

Metal. Consists of the 5 planes shown plus colorful die cut carton which sets up as flight deck of an Aircraft Carrier. No. 495 red and aluminum combination. Nos. 430—two red and silver, two blue and silver. One set per box; ½ doz. per carton. Wt. 21 lbs.

495 AIRPLANE See description, page 11.

Four No. 430 AIRPLANES See description, page 5.

Carton converts into Aircraft Carrier flight deck.



## No. 56 ARMY-AIR COMBAT SET

Metal. 5 toys shown, in yellow and olive drab. One set per attractive die cut, set up box; ½ doz. per carton. Wt. 25 lbs.

No. 495 FIGHTER BOMBER See description, page 11.

Two No. 430 AIRPLANES See description, page 5.

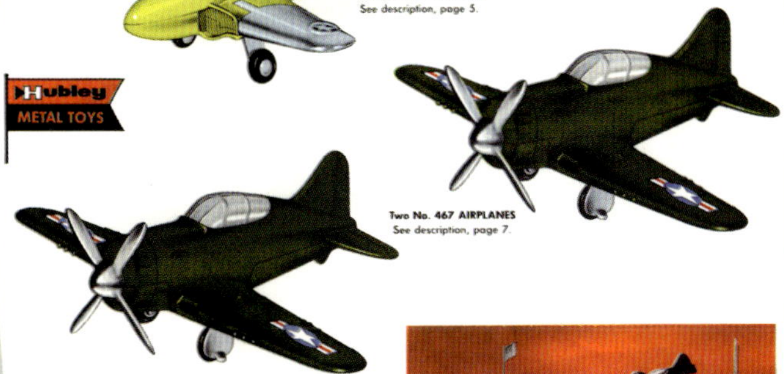

Two No. 467 AIRPLANES See description, page 7.

Colorful lithographed carton converts into "hangar" for additional play features.

## No. 57 FARM SET

Metal. Scale Model Ford Tractor with accessories that hitch. One set per die cut box; ¼ doz. per carton. Wt. 18 lbs.

AUTHORIZED *Ford* REPLICA

Hitching plow. Pushing lever forward raises plow into travelling position. Pulling lever back lowers it into plowing position.

507 FORD TRACTOR
See description, page 25.

Hitching wagon to tractor.

WAGON. 11½". 2 crates with chickens and ducks.

PLOW. 7" wide.

Attractive lithographed box converts into Barn.



## No. 71 ARMY ENGINEERS SET

Metal. 5 toys in olive drab with aluminum trim and U.S. insignia. Packed one set in full color lithographed box; ¼ doz. per carton. Wt. 21 lbs.

470 DUMP TRUCK
See description, page 7.

PIPE TRUCK
10¾". 5 pipes can be joined together.

BULLDOZER. 9". Rubber "doughnut" wheels, seat reversed. Lever operated blade in rear.

481 ROAD SCRAPER. 10¾". Adjustable scraper. Front wheels steer, rear wheels independently mounted.

Attractive box converts into Engineers' headquarters.

499 ROAD ROLLER
See description, page 13.



## No. 80 NAVY AIRFIELD SET

Metal. Toys as illustrated. Packed one set per exceptionally attractive die cut box; ¼ doz. sets per carton. Wt. 24 lbs.

522 AIRFORCE BOMBER TRANSPORTER. See description, page 29.

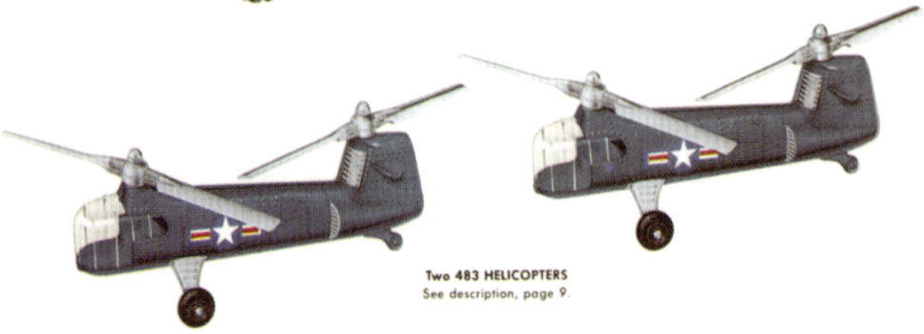

Two 483 HELICOPTERS
See description, page 9.

476 AMBULANCE. White. See description, page 8.

Full color box converts into "hangar."



## No. 90 FARM SET

Metal. No. 525 Tractor and 3 interlocking implements. Packed one set in die cut corrugated box; ¼ doz. per carton. Wt. 24 lbs. Special tractor hitch raises, lowers Cultipacker, Cultivator.

CULTIVATOR
6½ inches wide.

525 TRACTOR
See description, page 30.

FARM WAGON. 11 inches

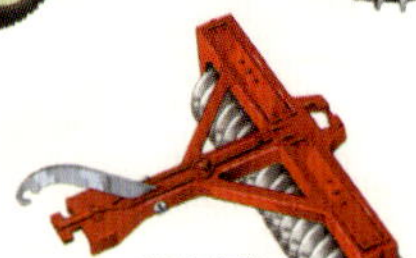

CULTIPACKER
6¾ inches wide.

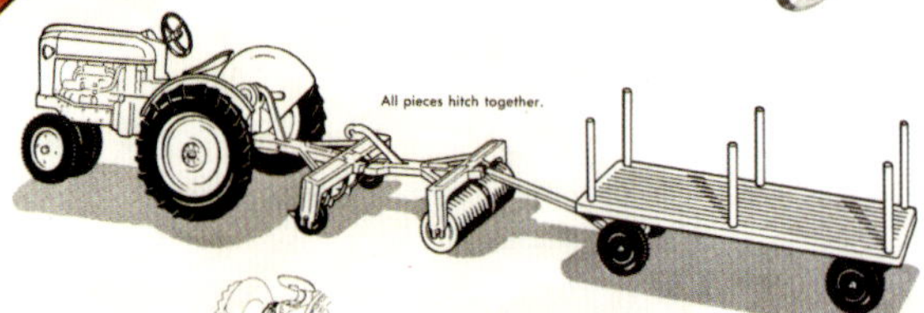

All pieces hitch together.

Hitching to tractor.

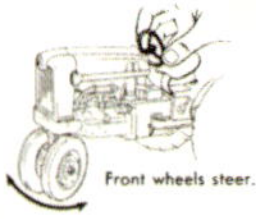

Front wheels steer.

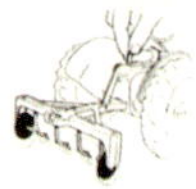

Pushing lever forward raises cultivator

Lithographed box converts into realistic barn.

## 501 TRACTOR LOADER

Length 12¾ inches. Packed 1 in a box; ½ dozen to a carton. Weight per carton 18 lbs. Orange with bright metal loader mechanism and steering wheel. Aluminum trimming. Realistic engine details. Steering wheel operates front wheels. Side lever, raises, lowers and dumps loader.

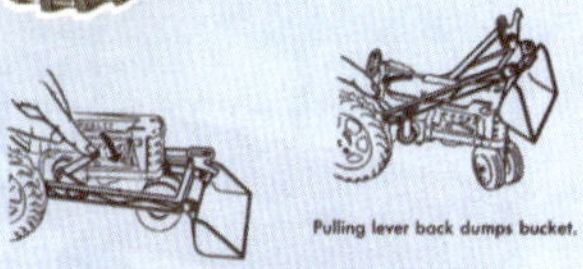

Pushing lever forward lowers bucket to load.

Pulling lever back dumps bucket.

## 502 TRACTOR WITH CULTIVATOR

Cultivator blades attached by spring clip.

Lever raises, lowers cultivator blades.

Length 9¼ inches. Packed 1 in a box; ½ dozen to a carton. Weight per carton 16 lbs. Red tractor with bright metal cultivator and lowering mechanism. Aluminum trim. Realistic engine details. Steering wheel operates front wheels. Detachable cultivator rake. Side lever raises and lowers rake. Metal wheels with black, treaded tires.

Independent rear wheels.

## 503 ROAD GRADER

Length 12¾ inches. Packed 1 in a box; ½ dozen to carton. Weight per carton 13 lbs. Orange with nickel trimming. Movable scraper can be locked in position by adjusting screw. Realistic motor details. Front wheels controlled by steering lever. Rear wheels mounted independently to roll over stones and obstacles.

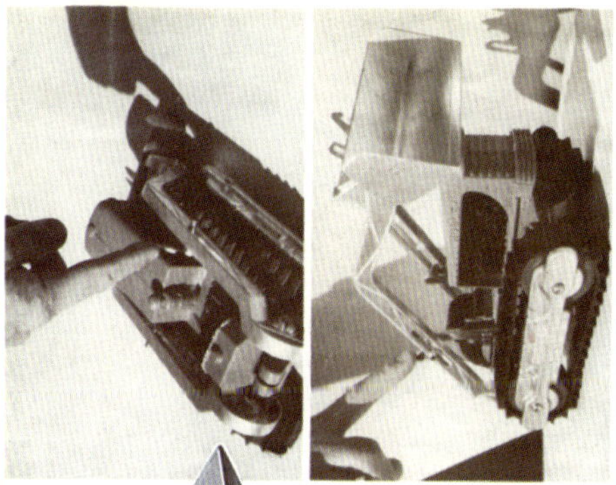

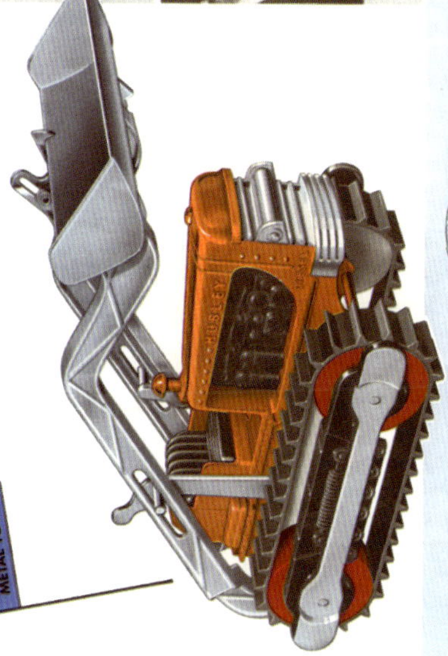

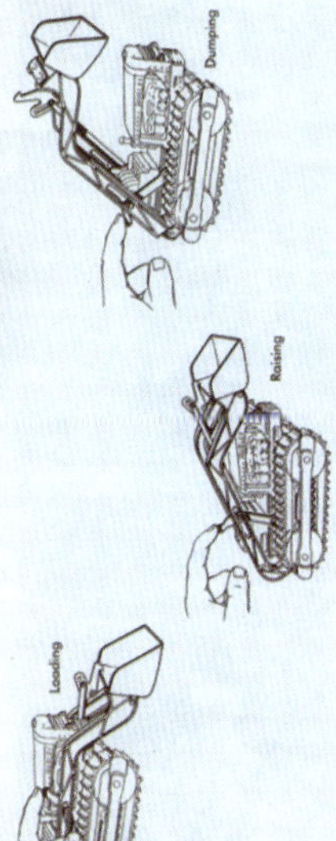


## 505 CAT LOADER

Length 7¾ inches. Packed 1 in a box; ½ dozen to carton. Weight per carton 11 lbs. Orange with black realistic motor details. Aluminum trimming and bright metal loader mechanism. Red wheels with realistic rubber caterpillar tread. Loader operated by lever near driver's seat.

AUTHORIZED *Ford* REPLICA

## 507 FORD TRACTOR

Length 10½ inches. Packed 1 in a box; ½ dozen to carton. Weight per carton 20 lbs. **Scale model** of Ford 961 Powermaster Tractor. Tricycle type wheels. Red and grey with black rubber wheels. Realistic engine details and 3 point hitch for accessories. (See No. 57 Farm Set.)

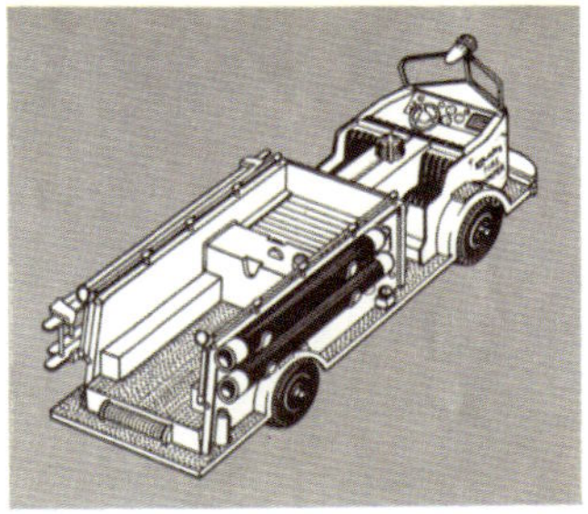

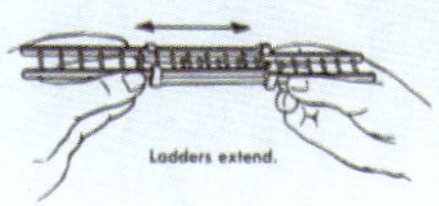


**513 FIRE PUMPER**

Length 14¼ inches. Packed 1 in a box; ½ dozen to carton. Weight per carton 16 lbs. Red with black and aluminum trimming. Black seat and lithographed instrument panel. Supplied with two pieces of black hose and extension ladder. Black wheels.

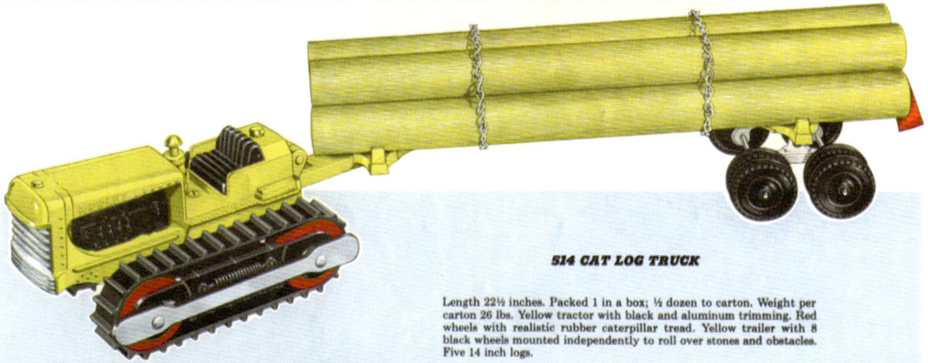

**514 CAT LOG TRUCK**

Length 22½ inches. Packed 1 in a box; ½ dozen to carton. Weight per carton 26 lbs. Yellow tractor with black and aluminum trimming. Red wheels with realistic rubber caterpillar tread. Yellow trailer with 8 black wheels mounted independently to roll over stones and obstacles. Five 14 inch logs.

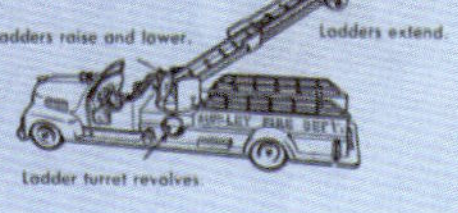


**520 FIRE TRUCK**

Length 19 inches. Packed 1 in a box; ½ dozen to a carton. Weight per carton 24 lbs. Red with cream seat and bright metal trim. Aluminum ladders elevate and revolve through 360 degree arc. Black wheels.

**522 AIR FORCE BOMBER TRANSPORTER**

Length 21¾ inches. Packed 1 in a box; ½ dozen to carton. Weight per carton 26 lbs. Yellow tractor with realistic black motor details and large black rubber "doughnut" wheels. Yellow machinery carrier with six black wheels. No. 495 Navy Fighter Bomber in blue and silver.

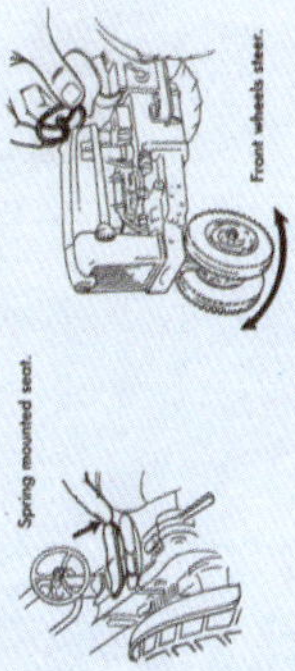


### 525 TRACTOR

Length 12 inches. Packed 1 in a box; ½ dozen to a carton. Weight per carton 29 lbs. Grey and red combination with finely detailed, realistic engine details, visible from both sides. Red seat, nickel plated steering wheel. Metal wheels with black treaded tires. Tricycle type front wheels operate through steering wheel.



# YOUNG AMERICA'S FAVORITES from Hubley

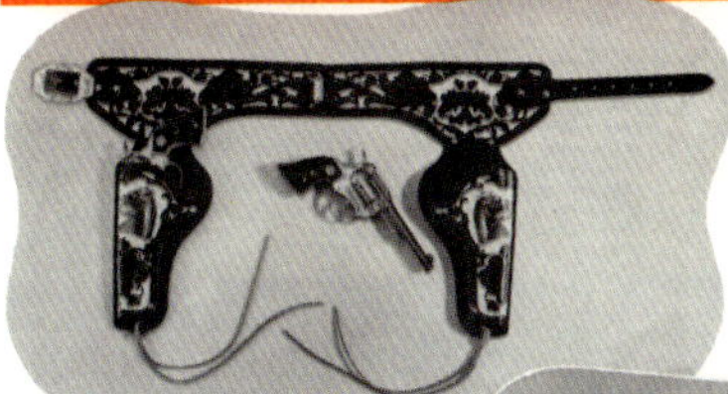

**No. 6055 DOUBLE HOLSTER SET**

Beautiful yellow-in-black inlaid Top Grain Cowhide. Hand colored horse-heads. Hubley Western guns. Exclusive adjusting bar, massive buckle, leather leg ties.

COLT .38

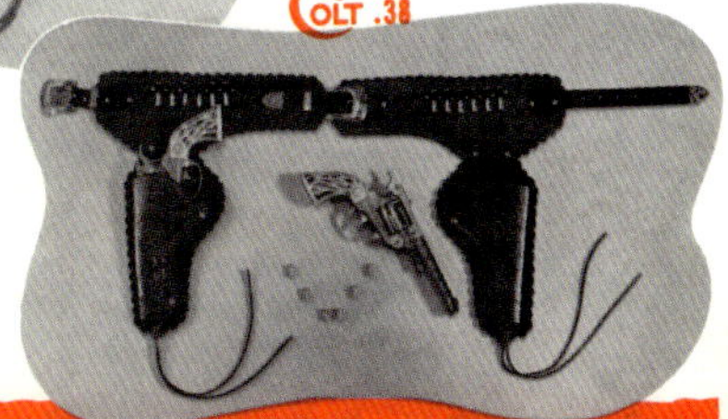

**No. 6087 DOUBLE HOLSTER SET**

Famous Colt .38s in this richly embossed Top Grain Cowhide beauty make it the leader in its class. It's a sight-seller.



**FAMOUS COLT REPRODUCTIONS....**
MADE EXCLUSIVELY BY HUBLEY UNDER LICENSE GRANTED BY COLT

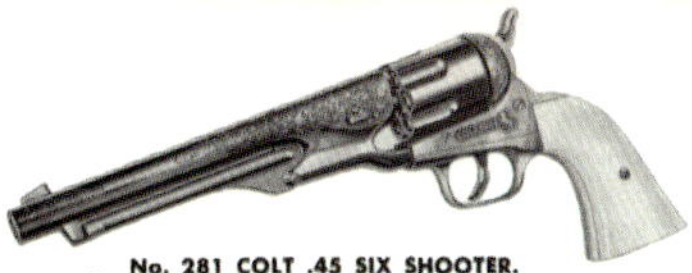

**No. 281 COLT .45 SIX SHOOTER.**
Over 14" long, chromium and gold. Shoots round caps in take-apart metal "cartridges", 6 furnished.

**No. 278 COLT .38 SIX SHOOTER.**
Over 11" long, engraved, new "stag" hand grips. Metal "cartridges" fire round caps.

**COMPANION PLAY ITEM.**
Soft plastic belt Clip No. 178 holds 6 metal "cartridges" and magnetic compass. Sold extra. Kids buy several.

**No. 177 CARTRIDGE CLIP.**
Soft plastic belt clip holds 6 metal "cartridges" for No. 278 gun. One furnished with gun. Kids buy extras.

THE HUBLEY MANUFACTURING COMPANY, LANCASTER, PA., U.S.A.



1958

## 1958 Hubley Toys

| No. | Name | | Pieces in Box | Carton Packing | Carton Weight | Catalog Page |
|---|---|---|---|---|---|---|
| 309 | Tractor | (Polystyrene) | 12 | 3 doz. | 11 lbs. | 3 |
| 310 | Motorcycle | (Polystyrene) | 12 | 3 doz. | 8 lbs. | 3 |
| 311 | Airplane | (Polystyrene) | 12 | 3 doz. | 5 lbs. | 3 |
| 316 | Road Scraper | (Polyethylene) | 6 | 3 doz. | 4 lbs. | 3 |
| 317 | Repair Truck | (Polyethylene) | 6 | 1 doz. | 4 lbs. | 3 |
| 319 | Gas Truck | (Polyethylene) | 6 | 1 doz. | 4 lbs. | 3 |
| 320 | Dump Truck | (Polyethylene) | 6 | 1 doz. | 3 lbs. | 4 |
| 321 | Tow Truck | (Polyethylene) | 6 | 1 doz. | 3 lbs. | 4 |
| 322 | Hook & Ladder | (Polyethylene) | 6 | 1 doz. | 3 lbs. | 4 |
| 338 | Helicopter | (Polystyrene) | 6 | 1 doz. | 4 lbs. | 4 |
| 339 | Duck | (Polystyrene) | 6 | 1 doz. | 4 lbs. | 4 |
| 340 | Blimp | (Polystyrene) | 6 | 1 doz. | 4 lbs. | 4 |
| 429 | Log Truck | (Metal) | 6 | 1 doz. | 4 lbs. | 5 |
| 430 | Airplane | (Metal) | 6 | 1 doz. | 5 lbs. | 5 |
| 431 | Dump Truck | (Metal) | 6 | 1 doz. | 5 lbs. | 5 |
| 432 | M. G. | (Metal) | 6 | 1 doz. | 6 lbs. | 5 |
| 451 | Tractor | (Metal) | 1 | 1 doz. | 8 lbs. | 6 |
| 458 | Dump Truck | (Metal) | 1 | 1 doz. | 8 lbs. | 6 |
| 459 | Log Truck | (Metal) | 1 | 1 doz. | 7 lbs. | 6 |
| 465 | Hook & Ladder | (Metal) | 1 | 1 doz. | 7 lbs. | 6 |
| 466 | Air Compressor | (Metal) | 1 | 1 doz. | 8 lbs. | 6 |
| 467 | Navy Plane | (Metal) | 1 | 1 doz. | 9 lbs. | 7 |
| 469 | Log Truck | (Metal) | 1 | 1 doz. | 15 lbs. | 7 |
| 470 | Dump Truck | (Metal) | 1 | 1 doz. | 12 lbs. | 7 |
| 471 | Hook & Ladder | (Metal) | 1 | 1 doz. | 13 lbs. | 8 |
| 472 | Tractor | (Metal) | 1 | 1 doz. | 14 lbs. | 8 |
| 476 | Ambulance | (Metal) | 1 | 1 doz. | 10 lbs. | 8 |
| 478 | Dump Truck | (Metal) | 1 | 1 doz. | 15 lbs. | 9 |
| 482 | Tow Truck | (Metal) | 1 | 1 doz. | 15 lbs. | 9 |
| 483 | Helicopter | (Metal) | 1 | 1 doz. | 12 lbs. | 9 |
| 484 | Motorcycle | (Metal) | 1 | 1 doz. | 13 lbs. | 10 |
| 485 | Pipe Truck | (Metal) | 1 | 1 doz. | 12 lbs. | 10 |
| 488 | Power Shovel | (Metal) | 1 | 1 doz. | 18 lbs. | 10 |
| 491 | Station Wagon and Boat Carrier | (Metal, Polystyrene) | 1 | 1 doz. | 14 lbs. | 11 |
| 492 | Transport | (Metal) | 1 | 1 doz. | 27 lbs. | 11 |
| 495 | Navy Fighter Bomber | (Metal) | 1 | 1 doz. | 18 lbs. | 11 |
| 496 | Tractor | (Metal) | 1 | 1 doz. | 29 lbs. | 11 |
| 497 | Poultry Truck | (Metal) | 1 | 1 doz. | 11 lbs. | 12 |
| 498 | Fish Hatchery | (Metal) | 1 | 1 doz. | 12 lbs. | 12 |
| 499 | Road Roller | (Metal) | 1 | 1 doz. | 19 lbs. | 13 |
| 501 | Tractor Loader | (Metal) | 1 | ½ doz. | 18 lbs. | 22 |
| 502 | Tractor with Cultivator | (Metal) | 1 | ½ doz. | 16 lbs. | 22 |
| 503 | Road Grader | (Metal) | 1 | ½ doz. | 13 lbs. | 23 |
| 505 | Cat Loader | (Metal) | 1 | ½ doz. | 11 lbs. | 24 |
| 507 | Ford Tractor | (Metal) | 1 | ½ doz. | 20 lbs. | 25 |
| 513 | Fire Pumper | (Metal) | 1 | ½ doz. | 16 lbs. | 26 |
| 514 | Cat Log Truck | (Metal) | 1 | ½ doz. | 26 lbs. | 27 |
| 520 | Fire Truck | (Metal) | 1 | ½ doz. | 24 lbs. | 28 |
| 522 | Air Force Bomber Transporter | (Metal) | 1 | ½ doz. | 26 lbs. | 29 |
| 525 | Tractor | (Metal) | 1 | ½ doz. | 29 lbs. | 30 |

### BOXED ASSORTMENTS

| No. | Name | | Pieces in Box | Carton Packing | Carton Weight | Catalog Page |
|---|---|---|---|---|---|---|
| 6 | Farm Set | (Metal) | 1 set | 1 doz. | 16 lbs. | 14 |
| 12 | Boxed Assortment | (Metal) | 1 set | 1 doz. | 20 lbs. | 14 |
| 50 | Farm Set | (Metal) | 1 set | 1 doz. | 19 lbs. | 16 |
| 53 | Fighter Bomber Squadron | (Metal) | 1 set | ½ doz. | 21 lbs. | 16 |
| 56 | Army-Air Combat Set | (Metal) | 1 set | ½ doz. | 25 lbs. | 17 |
| 57 | Farm Set | (Metal) | 1 set | ¼ doz. | 18 lbs. | 18 |
| 65 | Assortment | (Polyethylene) | 1 set | ½ doz. | 11 lbs. | 15 |
| 66 | Air-Sea Rescue Set | (Polystyrene) | 1 set | ½ doz. | 10 lbs. | 15 |
| 71 | Army Engineers Set | (Metal) | 1 set | ¼ doz. | 21 lbs. | 19 |
| 80 | Navy Airfield Set | (Metal) | 1 set | ¼ doz. | 24 lbs. | 20 |
| 90 | Farm Set | (Metal) | 1 set | ¼ doz. | 24 lbs. | 21 |
| 125 | Alphabet Letters | (Polyethylene) | 1 set | 3 doz. | 15 lbs. | 2 |

THE HUBLEY MANUFACTURING COMPANY, LANCASTER, PENNSYLVANIA, U. S. A.

*Hubley Cap Guns ★★★ Hubley Gun and Holster Sets ★★★ Hubley Toys*

Printed in U. S. of America

# 1959

# TOYS

1959

by Hubley

NEW

## No. 980

## OLD PAL WALKING HOBBY HORSE*

NEW, PATENTED hobby horse that actually walks. Slight rocking motion allows horse to be ridden almost anywhere. Horse can also be led. Heavy gauge steel and plastic. Beautiful enamel finish in contrasting colors. Length 36 inches; height 34 inches. Packed 1 in a corrugated carton; weight per carton 25 lbs.

*TRADEMARK

## No. 203

## FLIP SPECIAL* RIFLE

(OFFICIAL MODEL)

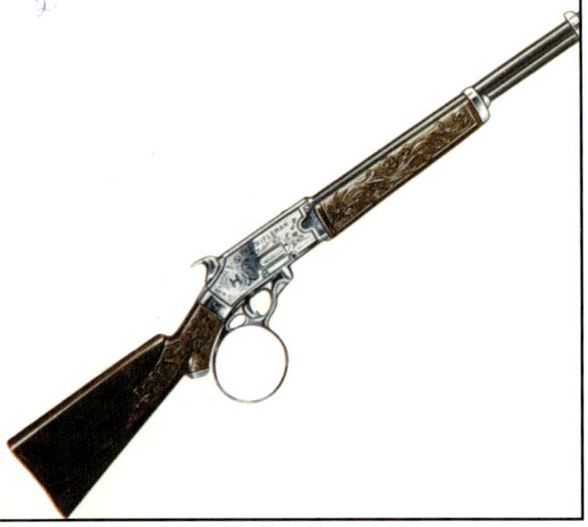

REPLICA OF RIFLE used on "The Rifleman"** TV Program. Shock resistant walnut colored plastic butt and stock, richly engraved. Nickel plated. Beautiful detailed engraving. This unusual gun shoots regular roll caps with an automatic firing action. Packed 1 in a display box; 6 boxes in a carton; weight per carton 19 lbs.

*TRADEMARK
**T.M. FOUR STAR SUSSEX



NEW

## No. 279

## RIC-O-SHAY*

(50-SHOT REPEATER)

REAL RICOCHET NOISE wit each pull of the trigger. Pack aged in deep frame box whic allows counter demonstra tion. Chrome plated wit black smooth finish grips. Re volving cylinder with s brass bullets. Authentic sic action loading. Shoots stan ard roll caps. Length 1 inches. Packed 1 in a box; dozen to a carton; weight p carton 11 lbs.

*TRADEMARK

NEW

## No. 690

## BATTERY POWERED Fighter Bomber PLANE

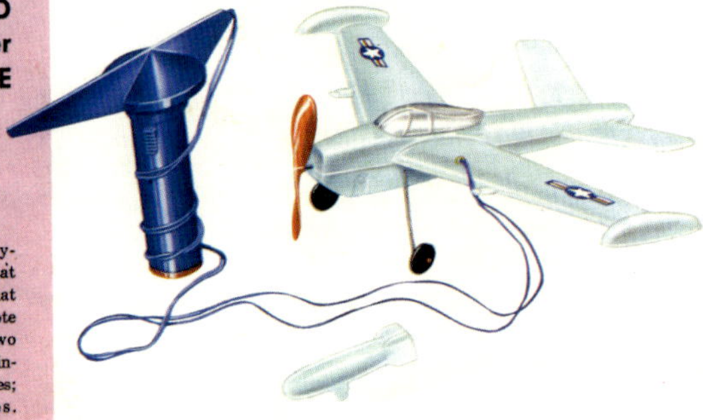

HIGH IMPACT YELLOW styrene plane with rat-tat-tat machine guns and bomb that can be dropped by remote control. Operates on two flashlight batteries (not included). Length 11½ inches; wingspread 15 inches. Packed 1 in a box; ¼ dozen to a carton; weight per carton 7 lbs.

NEW

## No. 675

## HOUSEBOAT

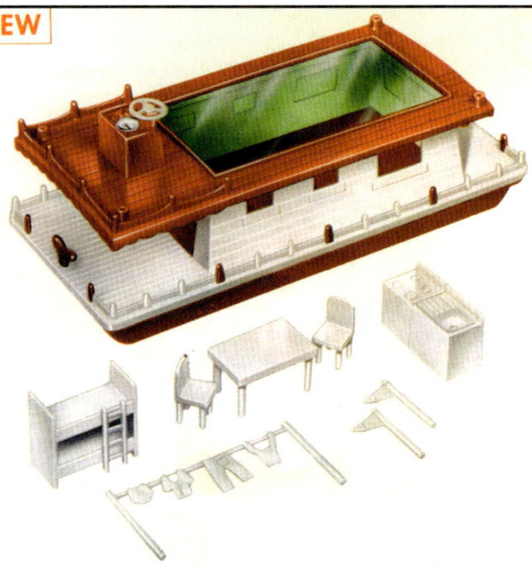

RED AND WHITE polyethylene houseboat. Complete with six pieces of removable furni ture. Real compass on deck Removable laundry lines Floats and pulls. Clear plas tic sun roof. Length 1 inches. Packed 1 in a box; ½ dozen to a carton; weight pe carton 10 lbs.

## No. 691

## TIC TOY CLOCK*

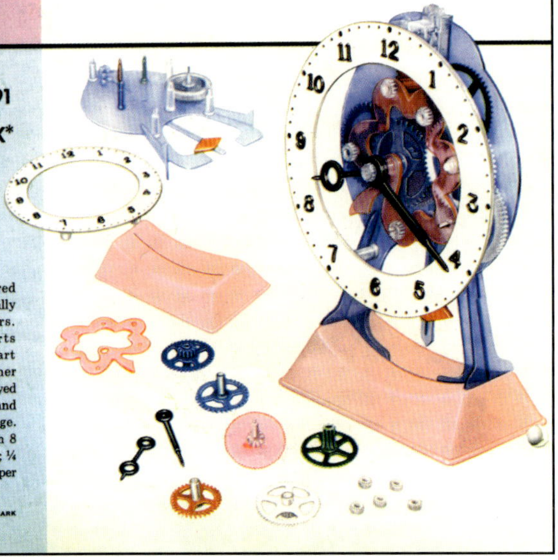

ATTRACTIVE multi-colored plastic clock which actually keeps time for 14 hours. Spring driven, 44 parts which can be taken apart and quickly put together again through color-keyed gear assembly. For boys and girls 5 to 15 years of age. Height 11½ inches; width 8 inches. Packed 1 in a box; ¼ dozen to a carton; weight per carton 10 lbs.

*TRADEMARK



## No. 652

## Howdy, Pardner AUTOGRAPH HAT*

UNBREAKABLE, WASHABL waterproof high impact plas tic. White. Assorted sizes small, medium, large an extra large. Special writin stick included. 15½ inches i diameter; 4 inch brim Packed 1 dozen to a carton weight per 1 dozen carton lbs. Packed 2 dozen to a ca ton; weight per 2 dozen ca ton 11 lbs.

*TRADEMARK · COPYRIGHT 1959

## No. 650 COLOR CAMERA

**NEW**

HIGH IMPACT YELLOW poly-styrene with simulated lens and clicker. Six rolls of "color film" (78 pictures to color). 6 crayons included. Replacement rolls available. Length 5½ inches; height 4 inches. Packed 1 dozen to a carton; weight per carton 9 lbs.

## No. 601 FIREBOAT

**NEW**

"SPRITZY"* the Mystery Water Shooting Fireboat is red and white high impact styrene with black stack. When diaphragm on bottom of boat is squeezed six times, boat pumps two streams of water by itself for approximately 40 seconds. Length 5¼ inches. Packed 1 in a box; 1 dozen to a carton; weight per carton 7 lbs.

*TRADEMARK

**No. 309 TRACTOR**

HIGH IMPACT PLASTIC. Red, yellow and orange with aluminum trimming. Polyethylene wheels. Length 4¾ inches. Packed 12 in a box; 3 dozen to a carton; weight per carton 11 lbs.

**No. 310 MOTORCYCLE**

HIGH IMPACT PLASTIC. Red or green motorcycle, black cop. Rubber wheels. Length 5 inches. Packed 12 in a box; 3 dozen to a carton; weight per carton 8 lbs.

**No. 311 AIRPLANE**

HIGH IMPACT PLASTIC. Red and white colors. Retractable landing gear. Rubber wheels. Length 5 inches. Packed 12 in a box; 3 dozen to a carton; weight per carton 5 lbs.

**No. 340 BLIMP**

HIGH IMPACT PLASTIC. Yellow with star insignia. Revolving propeller. Length 5¼ inches. Packed 6 in a box; 1 dozen to a carton; weight per carton 4 lbs.

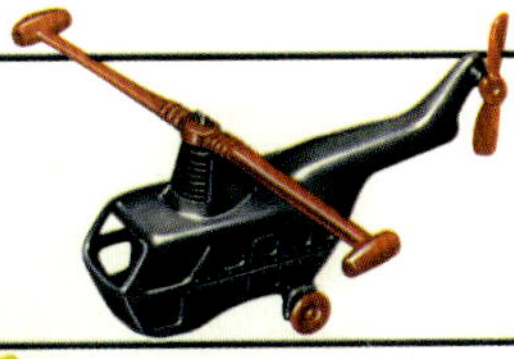

**No. 338 HELICOPTER**

HIGH IMPACT PLASTIC. Red and silver combination. Two rotor blades, revolving horizontally in the front and vertically on the tail. Length 5¼ inches. Packed 6 in a box; 1 dozen to a carton; weight per carton 2 lbs.

**No. 316 ROAD SCRAPER**

SOFT, unbreakable polyethylene. Yellow body. Adjustable scraper. Rubber wheels. Length 6¼ inches. Packed 6 in a box; 1 dozen to a carton; weight per carton 4 lbs.

**No. 339 DUCK**

HIGH IMPACT PLASTIC. Red and white combination. Rubber wheels. Length 5¼ inches. Packed 6 in a box; 1 dozen to a carton; weight per carton 2 lbs.



**No. 360 MILK TRUCK**

**NEW**

SOFT, unbreakable polyethylene. Red, yellow combination. Complete with removable tray of six milk cans. Length 6 inches. Packed 1 in a poly bag; 1 dozen to a carton; weight per carton 4 lbs.

**No. 361 PIG TRUCK**

**NEW**

SOFT, unbreakable polyethylene. Red and yellow truck; two brown removable pigs. Length 6 inches. Packed 1 in a poly bag; 1 dozen to a carton; weight per carton 4 lbs.

**No. 362 TRACTOR TRUCK**

**NEW**

SOFT, unbreakable polyethylene. Color combinations of red and yellow. Removable tractor. Length 6 inches. Packed 1 in a poly bag; 1 dozen to a carton; weight per carton 4 lbs.

**No. 363 CHICKEN TRUCK**

**NEW**

SOFT, unbreakable polyethylene. Red and yellow combination. Complete with crate of 3 ducks and chickens. Length 6 inches. Packed 1 in a poly bag; 1 dozen to a carton; weight per carton 4 lbs.

**No. 430 AIRPLANE**

METAL. Assorted red and blue with aluminum wings. Folding wings, retractable landing gear. Black wheels. Length 6 inches. Packed 6 in a box; 1 dozen to a carton; weight per carton 5 lbs.

**NEW**

## No. 376 SNOW CAT

SOFT, unbreakable polyethylene. Yellow with black caterpillar tread. Real compass on cab. Snow tools furnished. Length 6 inches. Packed 1 in a plastic bag; 1 dozen to a carton; weight per carton 4 lbs.

**NEW**

## No. 377 ROCKET LAUNCHER

SOFT, unbreakable polyethylene. Red and yellow combination with black caterpillar tread. Launcher mounted on revolving turret. Missile can be fired. Length 5¼ inches. Packed 1 in a plastic bag; 1 dozen to a carton; weight per carton 4 lbs.

**NEW**

## No. 378 BULLDOZER

SOFT, unbreakable polyethylene. Red or yellow with black caterpillar tread. Scoop can be raised or lowered by side lever. Length 4½ inches. Packed 1 in a plastic bag; 1 dozen to a carton; weight per carton 4 lbs.

## No. 751
## JET PLANE

NEW

METAL. Red and aluminum combination. Clear plastic bubble on cockpit. Folding wings and retractable landing gear. Black wheels. Length 7 inches; wingspread 6¼ inches. Packed 1 in a box; 1 dozen to a carton; weight per carton 9 lbs.

## No. 469
## LOG TRUCK

METAL. Orange with nickel trimming. Furnished with five 6-inch logs. Four black wheels. Length 10¾ inches. Packed 1 in a box; 1 dozen to a carton; weight per carton 15 lbs.

## No. 470
## DUMP TRUCK

METAL. Red cab and chassis; yellow dump body. Dump operated by side lever. Four black wheels. Length 9¾ inches. Packed 1 in a box; 1 dozen to a carton; weight per carton 12 lbs.



## No. 476
## STATION WAGON

METAL. Red with nickel grill Four black wheels. Length 8⅞ inches. Packed 1 in a box 1 dozen to a carton; weigh per carton 10 lbs.

## No. 471
## HOOK AND LADDER

Ladders mount in holes.

METAL. Red with nickel trim Two white ladders. Black wheels. Length 11¼ inche Packed 1 in a box; 1 dozen t a carton; weight per carto 13 lbs.

## No. 472
## TRACTOR

METAL. Red with aluminum trimming. Treaded rubbe tires. Realistic engine details Length 7¼ inches. Packed in a box; 1 dozen to a carton weight per carton 14 lbs.



## No. 803
## PIPE TRUCK

NEW

METAL. Red truck with aluminum trim. Three large pieces of silver colored pipe. Black treaded wheels. Length 11 inches. Packed 1 in a box; 1 dozen to a carton; weight per carton 12 lbs.

## No. 801
## DUMP TRUCK

NEW

METAL. Red cab and chassis, yellow dump with aluminum trim. Dump raises and lowers by using side lever. Black treaded wheels. Length 10 inches. Packed 1 in a box; 1 dozen to a carton; weight per carton 18 lbs.

## No. 802
## TRACTOR TRUCK

NEW

METAL. Yellow cab and flat bed truck with aluminum trim. Removable tractor. Black treaded wheels. Length 10¾ inches. Packed 1 in a box; 1 dozen to a carton; weight per carton 15 lbs.

## No. 483
## HELICOPTER

METAL. Yellow with transparent plastic bubble. Two revolving nickel plated rotor blades. Two black rubber wheels. Length 9¼ inches. Packed 1 in a box; 1 dozen to a carton; weight per carton 12 lbs.



## No. 851
## STOCK YARD TRUCK

NEW

METAL AND PLASTIC. Gree chassis, yellow high impac plastic body. Three pigs in cluded. When side of truck i opened and knob is turned pigs "walk" out of truck Length 10 inches. Packed in a box; 1 dozen to a carton weight per carton 16½ lbs.

## No. 497
## POULTRY TRUCK

METAL AND PLASTIC. Red fla bed truck. Complete wit three poultry crates with 1 chickens and ducks. Blac wheels. Length 10 inche Packed 1 in a box; 1 dozen t a carton; weight per carto 15 lbs.

## No. 498
## FISH HATCHERY

Fish "Swim"

METAL AND PLASTIC. Re chassis with aluminum trim ming. Transparent fish tan complete with "swimming fish. Fish net also supplie Black wheels. Length 1 inches. Packed 1 in a box; dozen to a carton; weight pe carton 14 lbs.

## No. 491
## Station Wagon
## ınd Boat Carrier

ETAL AND PLASTIC combina-on. Red station wagon with ellow boat trailer; red and hite plastic removable boat. lack wheels. Length 16 ıches. Packed 1 in a box; 1 ozen to a carton; weight per arton 17 lbs.

## lo. 495 NAVY
## IGHTER-BOMBER

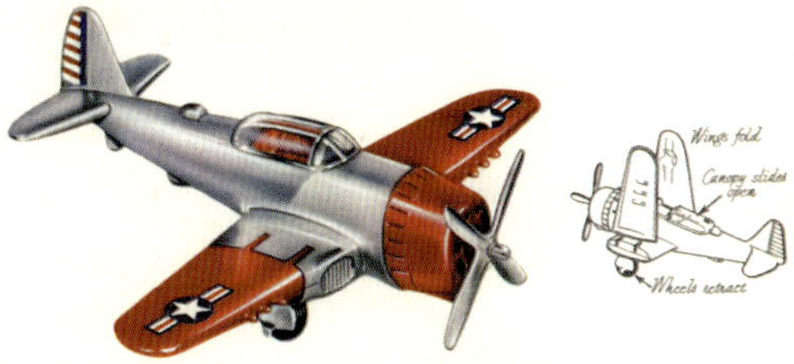


ETAL. Red wings and cowl, luminum body with red, hite and blue insignia. ockpit enclosed with trans-arent sliding bubble. Re-olving propeller, folding rings, retractable landing ear. Black wheels. Length 0 inches. Packed 1 in a box; dozen to a carton; weight er carton 18 lbs.

## No. 496
## TRACTOR

Front wheels steer

ETAL. Red with aluminum rimming. Realistic engine etails. Steering wheel oper-ates front wheels. Treaded lack tires. Length 9¼ inches. Packed 1 in a box; 1 dozen to carton; weight per carton 9 lbs.

## No. 499
## ROAD ROLLER

Steering lever act

ETAL. Orange with alumi-num trimming. Three large lack wooden rollers. Front ollers controlled by steering ever. Length 10½ inches. Packed 1 in a box; 1 dozen to carton; weight per carton 26 lbs.



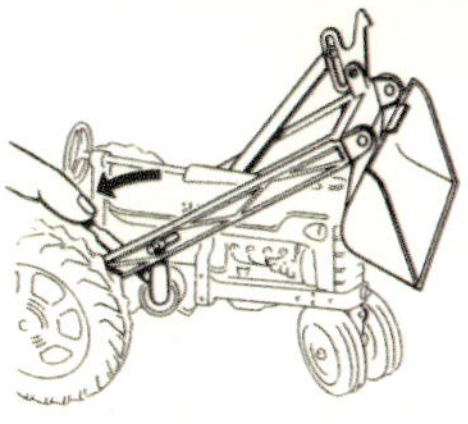
Pulling lever back dumps bucket

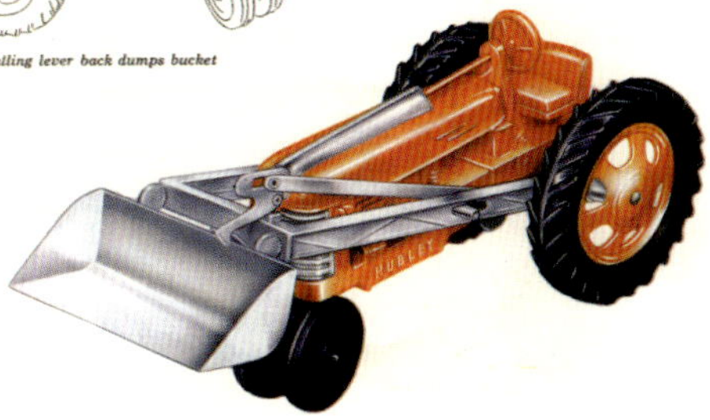

## No. 501
## TRACTOR LOADER

METAL. Orange with bright metal loader mechanism and steering wheel. Aluminum trimming. Realistic engine details. Steering wheel oper-ates front wheels. Side lever raises, lowers and dumps loader. Length 12¾ inches. Packed 1 in a box; ½ dozen to a carton; weight per carton 19 lbs.

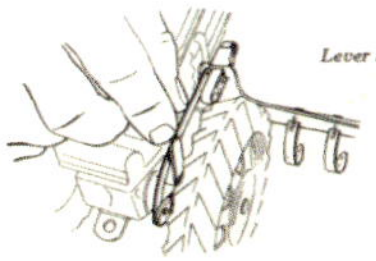
Lever raises, lowers cultivator blades

## No. 502
## TRACTOR with CULTIVATOR

METAL. Red tractor with bright metal cultivator and lowering mechanism. Alumi-num trim. Realistic engine details. Steering wheel oper-ates front wheels. Detachable cultivator rake. Side lever raises and lowers rake. Metal wheels with black, treaded tires. Length 9¼ inches. Packed 1 in a box; ½ dozen to a carton; weight per carton 17 lbs.



## No. 503
## ROAD SCRAPER

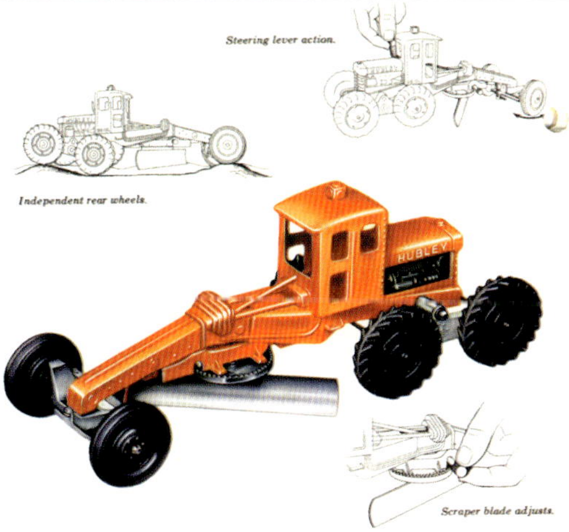

Steering lever action.

Independent rear wheels.

Scraper blade adjusts.

ETAL. Orange with nickel rimming. Movable scraper which can be locked in posi-ion by adjusting screw. Realistic motor details. Front wheels controlled by steering ever. Rear wheels mounted ndependently to roll over tones and obstacles. Length 2¾ inches. Packed 1 in a ox; ½ dozen to a carton; weight per carton 15 lbs.

## No. 505
## CAT LOADER

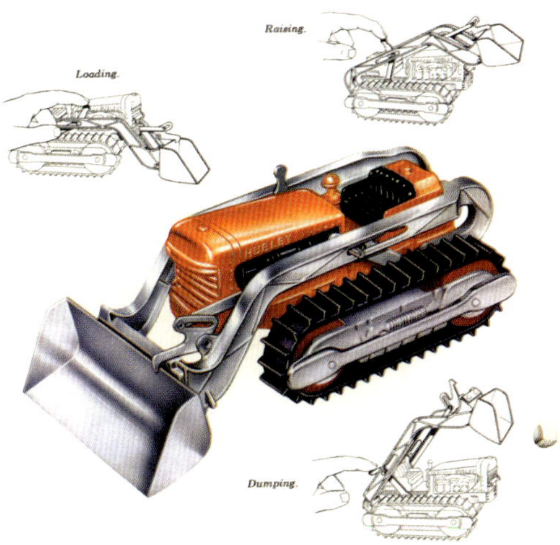
Loading.

Raising.

Dumping.

METAL. Orange with black realistic motor details. Alu-minum trimming and loader mechanism. Red wheels with realistic caterpillar tread. Loader operated by lever near driver's seat. Length 7¾ inches. Packed 1 in a box; ½ dozen to a carton; weight per carton 15 lbs.

AUTHORIZED Ford REPLICA

## No. 507
## FORD TRACTOR

METAL. Scale model of Ford 961 Powermaster Tractor. Tricycle type wheels. Red and grey with black rubber wheels. Realistic engine de-tails and three point hitch for accessories. Length 10½ inches. Packed 1 in a box; ½ dozen to a carton; weight per carton 20 lbs.

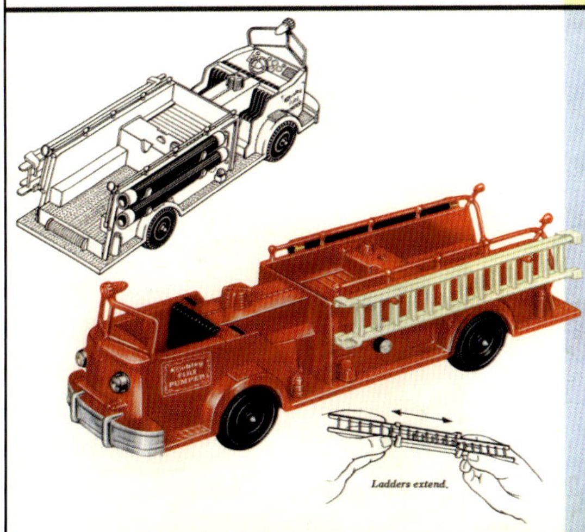
Ladders extend.

## No. 513
## FIRE PUMPER

METAL. Red with black and aluminum trimming. Black seat and lithographed instru-ment panel. Supplied with two pieces of black hose and extension ladder. Black wheels. Length 14¼ inches. Packed 1 in a box; ½ dozen to a carton; weight per carton 19 lbs.

## No. 520
## FIRE TRUCK

METAL. Red with cream seat and bright metal trim. Ladders elevate and revolve through 360° arc. Black wheels. Length 19 inches. Packed 1 in a box; ½ dozen to a carton; weight per carton 26 lbs.

## No. 525
## TRACTOR

METAL. Grey and red combination with finely detailed, realistic engine visible from both sides. Red seat, nickel plated steering wheel. Metal wheels with black treaded tires. "Tricycle" type front wheels operate through steering wheel. Length 12 inches. Packed 1 in a box; ½ dozen to a carton; weight per carton 29 lbs.



NEW

## No. 7
## FARM SET

SOFT, unbreakable, Polyethylene. Set consists of Milk Truck, Tractor, Pigs, Chickens and Ducks in bright colors. Packaged in attractive lithographed box. Packed 1 set in a box; 1 dozen to a carton; weight per carton 6 lbs.

NEW

## No. 15
## DEWLINE DEFENSE SET

SOFT, unbreakable Polyethylene. Set consists of Snow Cat, Rocket Launcher, and Bulldozer. Packed in attractive lithographed box. Packed 1 set in a box; 1 dozen to a carton; weight per carton 12 lbs.

NEW

## No. 14
## Farmer Brown's BARNYARD SET

HIGH IMPACT PLASTIC. Soft, unbreakable Polyethylene. Set consists of Farm Wagon, Cultipacker, Tractor, Milk Truck, Chickens, Ducks and two Pigs. Also a tray of 6 milk cans in bright colors. Packed in attractive lithographed box. Packed 1 set in a box, 1 dozen to a carton; weight per carton 16 lbs.



## No. 66
## AIR-SEA RESCUE SET

HIGH IMPACT PLASTIC. Set consists of Airplane, Helicopter, Duck, Boat and Blimp. Toys in red and white with silver and red Helicopter and Yellow Blimp. Assortment packaged in attractive lithographed box in full color. Packed 1 set in a box; ½ dozen sets to a carton; weight per carton 10 lbs.

NEW

## No. 31
## FARM SET

ALL METAL SET consists of Tractor, Truck, Spreader, Plow and Cultivator. Assorted colors. Attractively packaged in colorful lithographed box. Packed 1 set in a box; ½ dozen sets to a carton; weight per carton 20 lbs.



NEW

## No. 41
## FARM TRUCK COMBINATION

METAL AND PLASTIC SET consists of Poultry Truck, and Stock Yard Truck, complete with pigs, chickens and ducks. Attractively packaged in colorful lithographed box. Packed 1 set in a box; ½ dozen sets to a carton; weight per carton 18 lbs.

NEW

## No. 54
## AIR RACE SET

METAL. Set consists of 1 – #495 Airplane, 2 – #430 Airplanes and 2 – #751 Jet Planes in red, blue and silver combinations. Assortment packaged in attractive box resembling Pylon. Cut-out control tower and windsock included. Packed 1 set in a box; ½ dozen to a carton; weight per carton 26 lbs.

## No. 57
## FARM SET

AUTHORIZED *Ford* REPLICA

METAL. Set consists of one Ford Tractor, a three-bladed plow, a farm wagon and two crates of chickens and ducks. Attractive lithographed box in full color. Packed 1 set in a box; ¼ dozen to a carton; weight per carton 16 lbs.

## No. 90
## LARGE FARM SET

*Pushing lever forward raises cultivator.*

*Hitching to tractor.*

METAL. Set consists of #525 Tractor, Cultivator, Cultipacker and large Farm Wagon, all interlocking. Cultivator and Cultipacker can be individually attached to Tractor by means of hitch, which permits either to be raised or lowered for operation. Attractive corrugated box converts into play barn. Tractor and implements are red, grey and aluminum combination with black wheels. Packed 1 set in a box, ¼ dozen to a carton; weight per carton 25 lbs.



NEW

## No. 92
## Fire Department SET

METAL. Set consists of Fire Pumper, Fire Truck and Motorcycle in bright red with aluminum and nickel trimming. Beautiful lithographed box converts into a Fire Station and Flaming Warehouse as an added play feature. Packed 1 set in a box; ¼ dozen to a carton; weight per carton 30 lbs.

## No. 6980

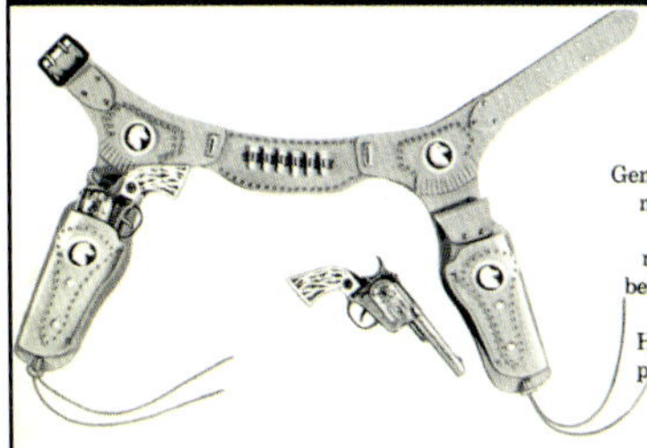

DOUBLE HOLSTER SET. Genuine leather in beautiful natural finish. Jewels and new Hubley cameo medallion. Large contour belt, adjustment bars and 6 bullets. Gunned with Hubley's No. 248 Marshal pistols with bone handles.

## No. 5981

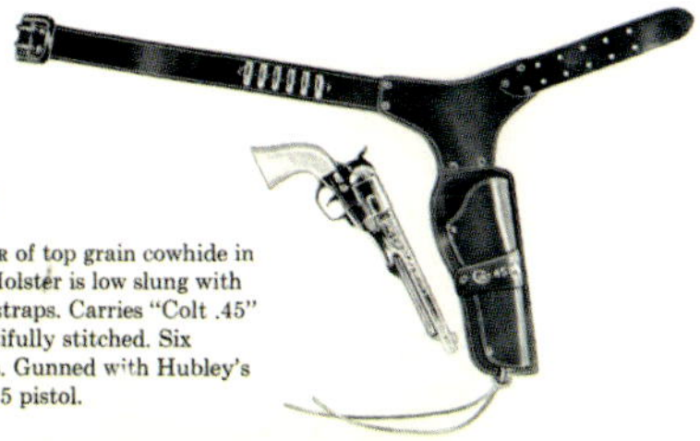

SINGLE HOLSTER of top grain cowhide in saddle finish. Holster is low slung with Western cross straps. Carries "Colt .45" identity. Beautifully stitched. Six realistic bullets. Gunned with Hubley's No. 281 Colt .45 pistol.

## HUBLEY OFFERS AN OUTSTANDING HOLSTER LINE

THE 1959 HUBLEY LINE offers buyers a wide range of holster design and superior leather finishes. Among the exclusives are such items as: The Miniature Colt Detective Special in the Chest Pack, the new Tubular Holster for the already famous Ric-O-Shay gun, the Wyatt Earp Series, the Colt .45 Series, and the new Remington Models. Many of the above items carry the outstanding injection molded medallion offered for the first time this year.

*Ask to see the full line!*



1959

## 1959 Hubley TOYS

| No. | NAME | PIECES IN BOX | CARTON PACKING | CARTON WEIGHT | CATALOG PAGE |
|---|---|---|---|---|---|
| 203 | Flip Special Rifle............(metal & polystyrene) .... | 1 | ½ doz. | 19 lbs. | [illegible] |
| 279 | Ric-O-Shay Repeater ........(metal) .............. | 1 | ½ doz. | 11 lbs. | [illegible] |
| 309 | Tractor ..................(polystyrene*) .......... | 12 | 3 doz. | 11 lbs. | 7 |
| 310 | Motorcycle ...............(polystyrene*) .......... | 12 | 3 doz. | 8 lbs. | 7 |
| 311 | Airplane .................(polystyrene*) .......... | 12 | 3 doz. | 5 lbs. | 7 |
| 316 | Road Scraper .............(polyethylene) .......... | 6 | 1 doz. | 4 lbs. | 7 |
| 338 | Helicopter ...............(polystyrene*) .......... | 6 | 1 doz. | 2 lbs. | 7 |
| 339 | Duck .....................(polystyrene*) .......... | 6 | 1 doz. | 2 lbs. | 7 |
| 340 | Blimp ....................(polystyrene*) .......... | 6 | 1 doz. | 4 lbs. | 7 |
| 360 | Milk Truck ...............(polyethylene) .......... | 1/bag | 1 doz. | 4 lbs. | 8 |
| 361 | Pig Truck ................(polyethylene) .......... | 1/bag | 1 doz. | 4 lbs. | 8 |
| 362 | Tractor Truck ............(polyethylene) .......... | 1/bag | 1 doz. | 4 lbs. | 8 |
| 363 | Chicken Truck ............(polyethylene) .......... | 1/bag | 1 doz. | 4 lbs. | 8 |
| 376 | Snow Cat .................(polyethylene) .......... | 1/bag | 1 doz. | 4 lbs. | 9 |
| 377 | Rocket Launcher ..........(polyethylene) .......... | 1/bag | 1 doz. | 4 lbs. | 9 |
| 378 | Bulldozer ................(polyethylene) .......... | 1/bag | 1 doz. | 4 lbs. | 9 |
| 430 | Airplane .................(metal) .............. | 6 | 1 doz. | 5 lbs. | 8 |
| 469 | Log Truck ................(metal) .............. | 1 | 1 doz. | 15 lbs. | 10 |
| 470 | Dump Truck ...............(metal) .............. | 1 | 1 doz. | 12 lbs. | 10 |
| 471 | Hook & Ladder ............(metal) .............. | 1 | 1 doz. | 13 lbs. | 11 |
| 472 | Tractor ..................(metal) .............. | 1 | 1 doz. | 14 lbs. | 11 |
| 476 | Station Wagon ............(metal) .............. | 1 | 1 doz. | 10 lbs. | 11 |
| 483 | Helicopter ...............(metal) .............. | 1 | 1 doz. | 12 lbs. | 12 |
| 491 | Sta. Wagon-Boat Carrier ......(metal, polystyrene*) ..... | 1 | 1 doz. | 17 lbs. | 14 |
| 495 | Navy Fighter-Bomber ........(metal) .............. | 1 | 1 doz. | 18 lbs. | 14 |
| 496 | Tractor ..................(metal) .............. | 1 | 1 doz. | 29 lbs. | 14 |
| 497 | Poultry Truck ............(metal, polystyrene*) ..... | 1 | 1 doz. | 15 lbs. | 13 |
| 498 | Fish Hatchery ............(metal, polystyrene*) ..... | 1 | 1 doz. | 14 lbs. | 13 |
| 499 | Road Roller ..............(metal) .............. | 1 | 1 doz. | 26 lbs. | 14 |
| 501 | Tractor Loader ...........(metal) .............. | 1 | ½ doz. | 19 lbs. | 15 |
| 502 | Tractor w/Cultivator .........(metal) .............. | 1 | ½ doz. | 17 lbs. | 15 |
| 503 | Road Scraper .............(metal) .............. | 1 | ½ doz. | 15 lbs. | 16 |
| 505 | Cat Loader ...............(metal) .............. | 1 | ½ doz. | 15 lbs. | 16 |
| 507 | Ford Tractor .............(metal) .............. | 1 | ½ doz. | 20 lbs. | 17 |
| 513 | Fire Pumper ..............(metal) .............. | 1 | ½ doz. | 19 lbs. | 17 |
| 520 | Fire Truck ...............(metal) .............. | 1 | ½ doz. | 26 lbs. | 18 |
| 525 | Tractor ..................(metal) .............. | 1 | ½ doz. | 29 lbs. | 18 |
| 601 | Fireboat .................(polystyrene*) .......... | 1 | 1 doz. | 7 lbs. | 6 |
| 650 | Color Camera .............(polystyrene*) .......... | 1 | 1 doz. | 9 lbs. | 6 |
| 652 | Howdy Pardner Auto. Hat.....(polystyrene**) .......... | 1 | 1 doz.-2 doz. | 6 lbs.-11 lbs. | 5 |
| 675 | Houseboat ................(polyethylene) .......... | 1 | ½ doz. | 10 lbs. | 5 |
| 690 | Battery Fighter Bomber ......(polystyrene*) .......... | 1 | ¼ doz. | 7 lbs. | 4 |
| 691 | Tic Toy Clock ............(polystyrene*) .......... | 1 | ¼ doz. | 10 lbs. | 4 |
| 751 | Jet Plane ................(metal) .............. | 1 | 1 doz. | 9 lbs. | 10 |
| 801 | Dump Truck ...............(metal) .............. | 1 | 1 doz. | 18 lbs. | 12 |
| 802 | Tractor Truck ............(metal) .............. | 1 | 1 doz. | 15 lbs. | 12 |
| 803 | Pipe Truck ...............(metal) .............. | 1 | 1 doz. | 12 lbs. | 12 |
| 851 | Stock Yard Truck ...........(metal, polystyrene*) ..... | 1 | 1 doz. | 16½ lbs. | 13 |
| 980 | Old Pal Horse ............(steel, polystyrene*) ...... | – | 1 ea. | 25 lbs. | 2 |
| | **BOXED ASSORTMENTS** | | | | |
| 7 | Farm Set .................(polyethylene) .......... | 1 set | 1 doz. | 6 lbs. | 19 |
| 14 | Barnyard Set .............(polyethylene, polystyrene*) | 1 set | 1 doz. | 16 lbs. | 19 |
| 15 | Dewline Defense Set ........(polyethylene) .......... | 1 set | 1 doz. | 12 lbs. | 19 |
| 31 | Farm Set .................(metal) .............. | 1 set | ½ doz. | 20 lbs. | 20 |
| 41 | Farm-Truck Combination .....(metal, polystyrene*) ..... | 1 set | ½ doz. | 18 lbs. | 21 |
| 54 | Air Race Set .............(metal) .............. | 1 set | ½ doz. | 26 lbs. | 21 |
| 57 | Farm Set .................(metal) .............. | 1 set | ¼ doz. | 16 lbs. | 22 |
| 66 | Air-Sea Rescue Set ..........(polystyrene*) .......... | 1 set | ½ doz. | 10 lbs. | 20 |
| 90 | Large Farm Set ...........(metal) .............. | 1 set | ¼ doz. | 25 lbs. | |
| 92 | Fire Dept. Set ...........(metal) .............. | 1 set | ¼ doz. | 30 lbs. | |

THE HUBLEY MANUFACTURING COMPANY, LANCASTER, PENNSYLVANIA, U. S. A.

*–HIGH IMPACT PLASTIC **–ULTRA HIGH IMPACT PLASTIC

HUBLEY CAP GUNS • HUBLEY GUN AND HOLSTER SETS • HUBLEY TOYS

PRINTED IN U.S. OF AMERICA ®

# 1960

# toys

## by Hubley

SCALE MODELS • METAL TOYS • PISTOLS & RIFLES • HOLSTER SET

1960

## No. 980
## OLD PAL WALKING HOBBY HORSE*

NEW, PATENTED hobby horse that actually walks. Slight rocking motion allows horse to be ridden almost anywhere. Horse can also be led. Heavy gauge steel and plastic. Beautiful enamel finish in contrasting colors. Length 36 inches; height 34 inches. Packed 1 in a corrugated carton; weight per carton 18 lbs.

*TRADEMARK

## No. 965
## TIC TOY CLOCK*

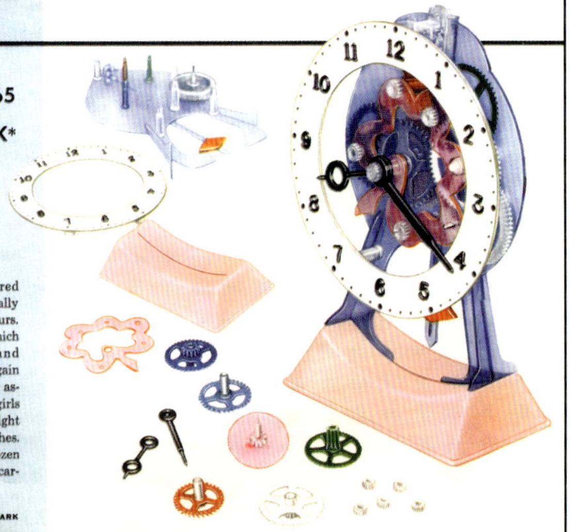

ATTRACTIVE, multi-colored plastic clock which actually runs as long as 14 hours. Spring driven, 25 parts which can be taken apart and quickly put together again through color-keyed gear assembly. For boys and girls 5 to 15 years of age. Height 11½ inches; width 8 inches. Packed 1 in a box; ¾ dozen to a carton; weight per carton 10 lbs.

*TRADEMARK



## No. 675
## HOUSEBOAT

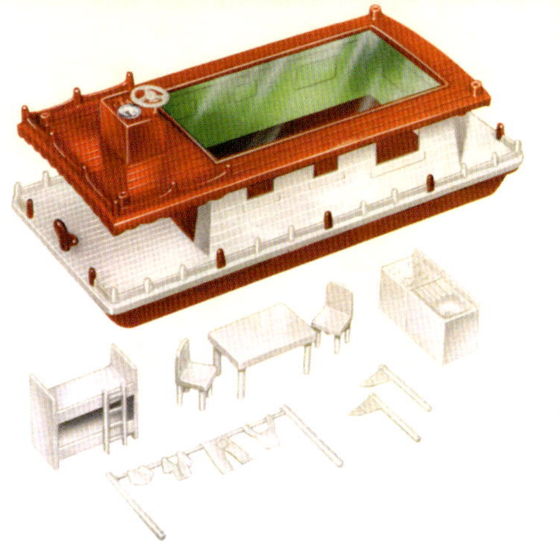

RED AND WHITE polyethylene houseboat. Complete with six pieces of removable furniture. Real compass on deck. Removable laundry lines. Floats and pulls. Clear plastic sun roof. Length 11 inches. Packed 1 in a box; ½ dozen to a carton; weight per carton 10 lbs.

## No. 601
## FIREBOAT

"SPRITZY"® the Mystery Water Shooting Fireboat is red and white high impact styrene with black stack. When diaphragm on bottom of boat is squeezed six times, boat pumps two streams of water by itself for approximately 40 seconds. Length 6¼ inches. Packed 1 in a box; 1 dozen to a carton; weight per carton 7 lbs.



1960

### No. 360 MILK TRUCK

SOFT, unbreakable polyethylene. Red, yellow combination. Complete with removable tray of six milk cans. Length 6 inches. Packed 1 in a poly bag; 1 dozen to a carton; weight per carton 4 lbs.

### No. 361 PIG TRUCK

SOFT, unbreakable polyethylene. Red and yellow truck; two brown removable pigs. Length 6 inches. Packed 1 in a poly bag; 1 dozen to a carton; weight per carton 4 lbs.

### No. 362 TRACTOR TRUCK

SOFT, unbreakable polyethylene. Color combinations of red and yellow. Removable tractor. Length 6 inches. Packed 1 in a poly bag; 1 dozen to a carton; weight per carton 4 lbs.

### No. 363 CHICKEN TRUCK

SOFT, unbreakable polyethylene. Red and yellow combination. Complete with crate of 3 ducks and chickens. Length 6 inches. Packed 1 in a poly bag; 1 dozen to a carton; weight per carton 4 lbs.

### No. 430 AIRPLANE

METAL. Assorted red and blue with aluminum wings. Folding wings, retractable landing gear. Black wheels. Length 6 inches. Packed 6 in a box; 1 dozen to a carton; weight per carton 5 lbs.

### No. 309 TRACTOR

HIGH IMPACT PLASTIC. Red, yellow and orange with aluminum trimming. Polyethylene wheels. Length 4¾ inches. Packed 12 in a box; 3 dozen to a carton; weight per carton 11 lbs.

### No. 310 MOTORCYCLE

HIGH IMPACT PLASTIC. Red or green motorcycle, black cop. Rubber wheels. Length 5 inches. Packed 12 in a box; 3 dozen to a carton; weight per carton 8 lbs.

### No. 311 AIRPLANE

HIGH IMPACT PLASTIC. Red and white colors. Retractable landing gear. Rubber wheels. Length 5 inches. Packed 12 in a box; 3 dozen to a carton; weight per carton 5 lbs.

### No. 340 BLIMP

HIGH IMPACT PLASTIC. Yellow with star insignia. Revolving propeller. Length 5¼ inches. Packed 6 in a box; 1 dozen to a carton; weight per carton 4 lbs.

### No. 338 HELICOPTER

HIGH IMPACT PLASTIC. Red and silver combination. Two rotor blades, revolving horizontally in the front and vertically on the tail. Length 5¼ inches. Packed 6 in a box; 1 dozen to a carton; weight per carton 2 lbs.

### No. 483 HELICOPTER

METAL. Yellow with transparent plastic bubble. Two revolving nickel plated rotor blades. Two black rubber wheels. Length 9¼ inches. Packed 1 in a box; 1 dozen to a carton; weight per carton 12 lbs.

## No. 751
## JET PLANE

METAL. Red and aluminum combination. Clear plastic bubble on cockpit. Folding wings and retractable landing gear. Black wheels. Length 7 inches; wingspread 6¼ inches. Packed 1 in a box; 1 dozen to a carton; weight per carton 9 lbs.

## No. 469
## LOG TRUCK

METAL. Orange with nickel trimming. Furnished with five 6-inch logs. Four black wheels. Length 10¾ inches. Packed 1 in a box; 1 dozen to a carton; weight per carton 15 lbs.

## No. 470
## DUMP TRUCK

METAL. Red cab and chassis; yellow dump body. Dump operated by side lever. Four black wheels. Length 9¼ inches. Packed 1 in a box; 1 dozen to a carton; weight per carton 12 lbs.

## No. 801
## DUMP TRUCK

METAL. Red cab and chassis, yellow dump with aluminum trim. Dump raises and lowers by using side lever. Black treaded wheels. Length 10 inches. Packed 1 in a box; 1 dozen to a carton; weight per carton 18 lbs.

Ladders mount in holes.

## No. 471
## HOOK AND LADDER

METAL. Red with nickel trim. Two white ladders. Black wheels. Length 11¼ inches. Packed 1 in a box; 1 dozen to a carton; weight per carton 13 lbs.

## No. 472
## TRACTOR

METAL. Red with aluminum trimming. Treaded rubber tires. Realistic engine details. Length 7¼ inches. Packed 1 in a box; 1 dozen to a carton; weight per carton 14 lbs.



1960

## No. 491
## Station Wagon and Boat Carrier

METAL AND PLASTIC combination. Red station wagon with yellow boat trailer; red and white plastic removable boat. Black wheels. Length 16 inches. Packed 1 in a box; 1 dozen to a carton; weight per carton 17 lbs.

## No. 495 NAVY FIGHTER-BOMBER

METAL. Red wings and cowl, aluminum body with red, white and blue insignia. Cockpit enclosed with transparent sliding bubble. Revolving propeller, folding wings, retractable landing gear. Black wheels. Length 10 inches. Packed 1 in a box; 1 dozen to a carton; weight per carton 18 lbs.

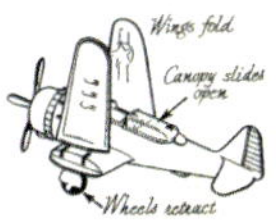


## No. 496
## TRACTOR

METAL. Red with aluminum trimming. Realistic engine details. Steering wheel operates front wheels. Treaded black tires. Length 9¼ inches. Packed 1 in a box; 1 dozen to a carton; weight per carton 29 lbs.

Front wheels steer

## No. 802
## TRACTOR TRUCK

METAL. Yellow cab and flat bed truck with aluminum trim. Removable tractor. Black treaded wheels. Length 10¼ inches. Packed 1 in a box; 1 dozen to a carton; weight per carton 15 lbs.

## No. 851
## STOCK YARD TRUCK

METAL AND PLASTIC. Green chassis, yellow high impact plastic body. Three pigs included. When side of truck is opened and knob is turned, pigs "walk" out of truck. Length 10 inches. Packed 1 in a box; 1 dozen to a carton; weight per carton 16½ lbs.

## No. 497
## POULTRY TRUCK

METAL AND PLASTIC. Red flat bed truck. Complete with three poultry crates with 15 chickens and ducks. Black wheels. Length 10 inches. Packed 1 in a box; 1 dozen to a carton; weight per carton 15 lbs.

Fish "Swim"

## No. 498
## FISH HATCHERY

METAL AND PLASTIC. Red chassis with aluminum trimming. Transparent fish tank complete with "swimming" fish. Fish net also supplied. Black wheels. Length 10 inches. Packed 1 in a box; 1 dozen to a carton; weight per carton 14 lbs.

## No. 503
## ROAD SCRAPER

METAL. Orange with nickel trimming. Movable scraper which can be locked in position by adjusting screw. Realistic motor details. Front wheels controlled by steering lever. Rear wheels mounted independently to roll over stones and obstacles. Length 12¾ inches. Packed 1 in a box; ½ dozen to a carton; weight per carton 15 lbs.

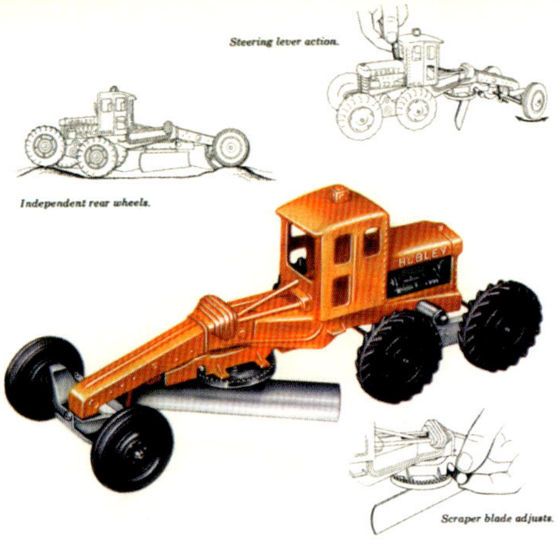


## No. 505
## FRONT END LOADER

METAL. Orange with black realistic motor details. Aluminum trimming and loader mechanism. Red wheels with realistic black rubber tread. Loader operated by lever near driver's seat. Length 7¾ inches. Packed 1 in a box; ½ dozen to a carton; weight per carton 15 lbs.

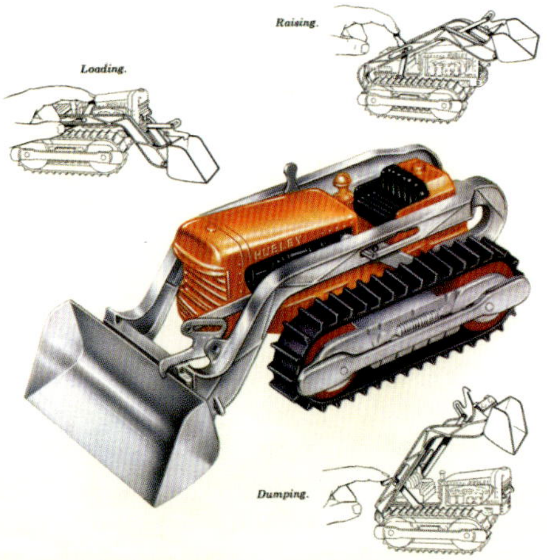


10

## No. 501
## TRACTOR LOADER

METAL. Orange with bright metal loader mechanism and steering wheel. Aluminum trimming. Realistic engine details. Steering wheel operates front wheels. Side lever raises, lowers and dumps loader. Length 12¾ inches. Packed 1 in a box; ½ dozen to a carton; weight per carton 19 lbs.

## No. 507
## FORD TRACTOR

METAL. Scale model of Ford 961 Powermaster Tractor. Tricycle type wheels. Red and grey with black rubber wheels. Realistic engine details and three point hitch for accessories. Length 10½ inches. Packed 1 in a box; ½ dozen to a carton; weight per carton 20 lbs.

### No. 758
### FORD SCRAPER BLADE

METAL. Attaches to back of No. 507 Ford Tractor. Made completely of stamped steel. Red with aluminum colored blade. Blade adjusts to different positions. Packed 1 in a box; 1 dozen to a carton; weight per carton 7 lbs.

### No. 757
### FORD POST HOLE DIGGER

METAL. Another accessory for the No. 507 Ford Tractor. Auger bores hole in ground for setting up posts. Red with nickel plated auger and handle. Packed 1 in a box; 1 dozen to a carton; weight per carton 6 lbs.

11

1960

## No. 520
## FIRE TRUCK

METAL. Red with cream seat and bright metal trim. Ladders elevate and revolve through 360° arc. Black wheels. Length 19 inches. Packed 1 in a box; ½ dozen to a carton; weight per carton 26 lbs.

## No. 525
## TRACTOR

METAL. Grey and red combination with finely detailed, realistic engine visible from both sides. Red seat, nickel plated steering wheel. Metal wheels with black treaded tires. "Tricycle" type front wheels operate through steering wheel. Length 12 inches. Packed 1 in a box; ½ dozen to a carton; weight per carton 29 lbs.

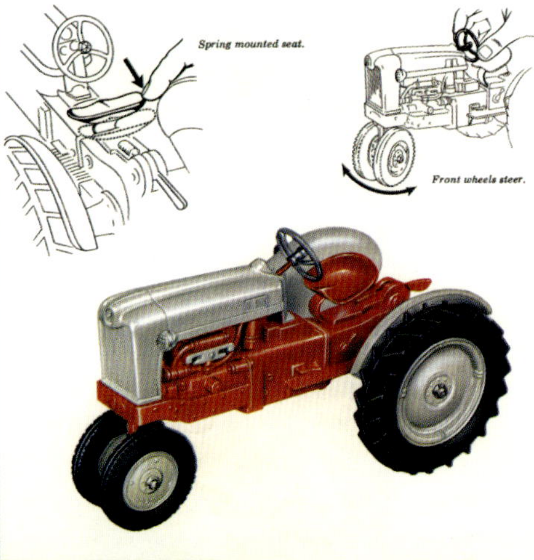


12

## No. 7
## FARM SET

SOFT, unbreakable, Polyethylene. Set consists of Milk Truck, Tractor, Pigs, Chickens and Ducks in bright colors. Packaged in attractive lithographed box. Packed 1 set in a box; 1 dozen to a carton; weight per carton 6 lbs.

## No. 31
## FARM SET

ALL METAL SET consists of Tractor, Truck, Spreader, Plow and Cultivator. Assorted colors. Attractively packaged in colorful lithographed box. Packed 1 set in a box; ½ dozen sets to a carton; weight per carton 20 lbs.

## No. 14
## Farmer Brown's BARNYARD SET

HIGH IMPACT PLASTIC. Soft, unbreakable Polyethylene. Set consists of Farm Wagon, Cultipacker, Tractor, Milk Truck, Chickens, Ducks and two Pigs. Also a tray of 6 milk cans in bright colors. Packed in attractive lithographed box. Packed 1 set in a box, 1 dozen to a carton; weight per carton 16 lbs.

13

## No. 57
## FARM SET

METAL. Set consists of one Ford Tractor, a three-bladed plow, a farm wagon and two crates of chickens and ducks. Attractive lithographed box in full color. Packed 1 set in a box; ¼ dozen to a carton; weight per carton 16 lbs.

AUTHORIZED Ford REPLICA

## No. 90
## LARGE FARM SET

*Pushing lever forward raises cultivator.*

*Hitching to tractor.*

METAL. Set consists of #525 Tractor, Cultivator, Cultipacker and large Farm Wagon, all interlocking. Cultivator and Cultipacker can be individually attached to Tractor by means of hitch, which permits either to be raised or lowered for operation. Attractive corrugated box converts into play barn. Tractor and implements are red, grey and aluminum combination with black wheels. Packed 1 set in a box, ¼ dozen to a carton; weight per carton 25 lbs.



## No. 68
## FARM SET

METAL. Set consists of one Ford Tractor, three bladed plow, farm wagon with two crates of ducks and chickens, Ford Scraper Blade and Ford Post Hole Digger.* Attractive box in full color sets up into farm yard. Packed 1 set in a box; ¼ dozen to a carton; weight per carton 20 lbs.

**All accessories may be attached to tractor hitch.*

## No. 6070

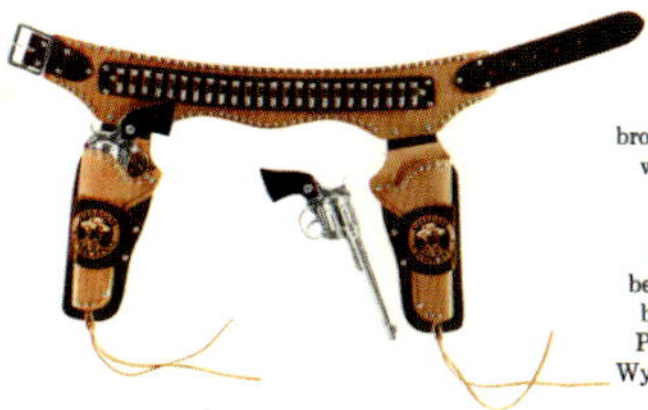

Genuine leather in rich brown and beige combination with Wyatt Earp insignia. Holster is three-piece, Western foldover, stand-away style. Large contour belt features 24 silver play bullets. Leg ties furnished. Packed with Hubley #247 Wyatt Earp Buntline pistols.

## No. 5081

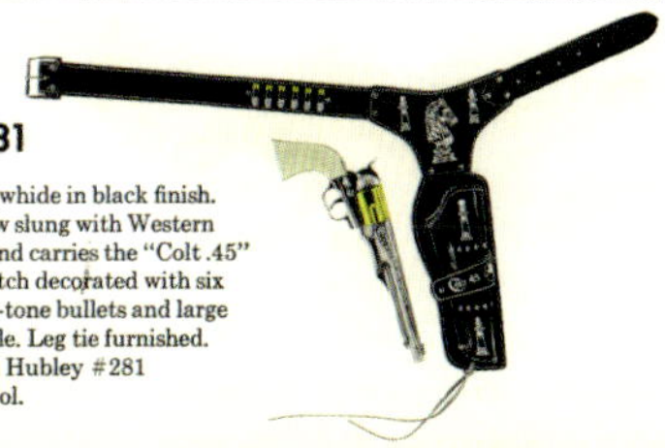

Top grain cowhide in black finish. Holster is low slung with Western cross strap and carries the "Colt .45" identity. Stitch decorated with six realistic two-tone bullets and large tongue buckle. Leg tie furnished. Packed with Hubley #281 Colt .45 pistol.

## HUBLEY OFFERS AN OUTSTANDING HOLSTER LINE

THE 1960 HUBLEY LINE offers buyers a wide range of holster design and superior leather finishes. Among the exclusives are such items as: The Tubular Holster for the already famous Ric-O-Shay gun, The Wyatt Earp Series, The Overland Trail Series, and The Colt .45 Series. Many of the above items carry the outstanding injection molded medallion.

*Ask to see the full line!*



# 1960 Hubley TOYS

| NO. | NAME | | CATALOG PAGE | CARTON PACKING | CARTON WEIGHT | SUGGESTED RETAIL PRICE |
|---|---|---|---|---|---|---|
| 309 | Tractor | (polystyrene) | 5 | 3 doz. | 11 lbs. | $ .29 |
| 310 | Motorcycle | (polystyrene) | 5 | 3 doz. | 8 lbs. | .29 |
| 311 | Airplane | (polystyrene) | 5 | 3 doz. | 5 lbs. | .29 |
| 338 | Helicopter | (polystyrene) | 5 | 1 doz. | 2 lbs. | .29 |
| 340 | Blimp | (polystyrene) | 5 | 1 doz. | 2 lbs. | .29 |
| 360 | Milk Truck | (polyethylene) | 4 | 1 doz. | 3 lbs. | .49 |
| 361 | Pig Truck | (polyethylene) | 4 | 1 doz. | 3 lbs. | .49 |
| 362 | Tractor Truck | (polyethylene) | 4 | 1 doz. | 4 lbs. | .49 |
| 363 | Chicken Truck | (polyethylene) | 4 | 1 doz. | 4 lbs. | .49 |
| 430 | Airplane | (metal) | 4 | 1 doz. | 5 lbs. | .49 |
| 469 | Log Truck | (metal) | 6 | 1 doz. | 15 lbs. | .98 |
| 470 | Dump Truck | (metal) | 6 | 1 doz. | 13 lbs. | .98 |
| 471 | Hook & Ladder | (metal) | 7 | 1 doz. | 13 lbs. | .98 |
| 472 | Tractor | (metal) | 7 | 1 doz. | 14 lbs. | .98 |
| 483 | Helicopter | (metal) | 5 | 1 doz. | 13 lbs. | 1.49 |
| 491 | Sta. Wagon-Boat Carrier | (metal, polystyrene) | 8 | 1 doz. | 17 lbs. | 1.98 |
| 495 | Navy Fighter-Bomber | (metal) | 8 | 1 doz. | 18 lbs. | 1.98 |
| 496 | Tractor | (metal) | 8 | 1 doz. | 29 lbs. | 1.98 |
| 497 | Poultry Truck | (metal, polystyrene) | 9 | 1 doz. | 15 lbs. | 1.98 |
| 498 | Fish Hatchery | (metal, polystyrene) | 9 | 1 doz. | 14 lbs. | 1.98 |
| 501 | Tractor Loader | (metal) | 11 | ½ doz. | 19 lbs. | 2.98 |
| 503 | Road Scraper | (metal) | 10 | ½ doz. | 15 lbs. | 2.98 |
| 505 | Front End Loader | (metal) | 10 | ½ doz. | 15 lbs. | 2.98 |
| 507 | Ford Tractor | (metal) | 11 | ½ doz. | 20 lbs. | 3.98 |
| 520 | Fire Truck | (metal) | 12 | ½ doz. | 26 lbs. | 4.98 |
| 525 | Tractor | (metal) | 12 | ½ doz. | 29 lbs. | 4.98 |
| 601 | Fireboat | (polystyrene) | 3 | 1 doz. | 7 lbs. | .98 |
| 675 | Houseboat | (polyethylene) | 3 | ½ doz. | 10 lbs. | 2.98 |
| 751 | Jet Plane | (metal) | 6 | 1 doz. | 9 lbs. | .98 |
| 757 | Ford Post Hole Digger | (metal) | 11 | 1 doz. | 6 lbs. | .98 |
| 758 | Ford Scraper Blade | (metal) | 11 | 1 doz. | 7 lbs. | .98 |
| 801 | Dump Truck | (metal) | 7 | 1 doz. | 16 lbs. | 1.49 |
| 802 | Tractor Truck | (metal) | 8 | 1 doz. | 16 lbs. | 1.49 |
| 851 | Stock Yard Truck | (metal, polystyrene) | 9 | 1 doz. | 15 lbs. | 1.98 |
| 965 | Tic Toy Clock | (polystyrene) | 2 | ¼ doz. | 10 lbs. | 5.98 |
| 980 | Old Pal Horse | (steel, polystyrene) | 2 | 1 ea. | 18 lbs. | 19.95 |
| | **BOXED ASSORTMENTS** | | | | | |
| 7 | Farm Set | (polyethylene) | 13 | 1 doz. | 7 lbs. | .98 |
| 14 | Barnyard Set | (polyethylene, polystyrene) | 13 | 1 doz. | 13 lbs. | 1.98 |
| 31 | Farm Set | (metal) | 13 | ½ doz. | 17 lbs. | 2.98 |
| 57 | Farm Set | (metal) | 14 | ¼ doz. | 16 lbs. | 5.98 |
| 68 | Farm Set | (metal) | 15 | ¼ doz. | 20 lbs. | 7.98 |
| 90 | Large Farm Set | (metal) | 14 | ¼ doz. | 24 lbs. | 9.98 |

THE HUBLEY MANUFACTURING CO., LANCASTER, PA. U. S. A.

SCALE MODELS • METAL TOYS • PISTOLS & RIFLES • HOLSTER SETS

Printed in U.S.A.

# 1961

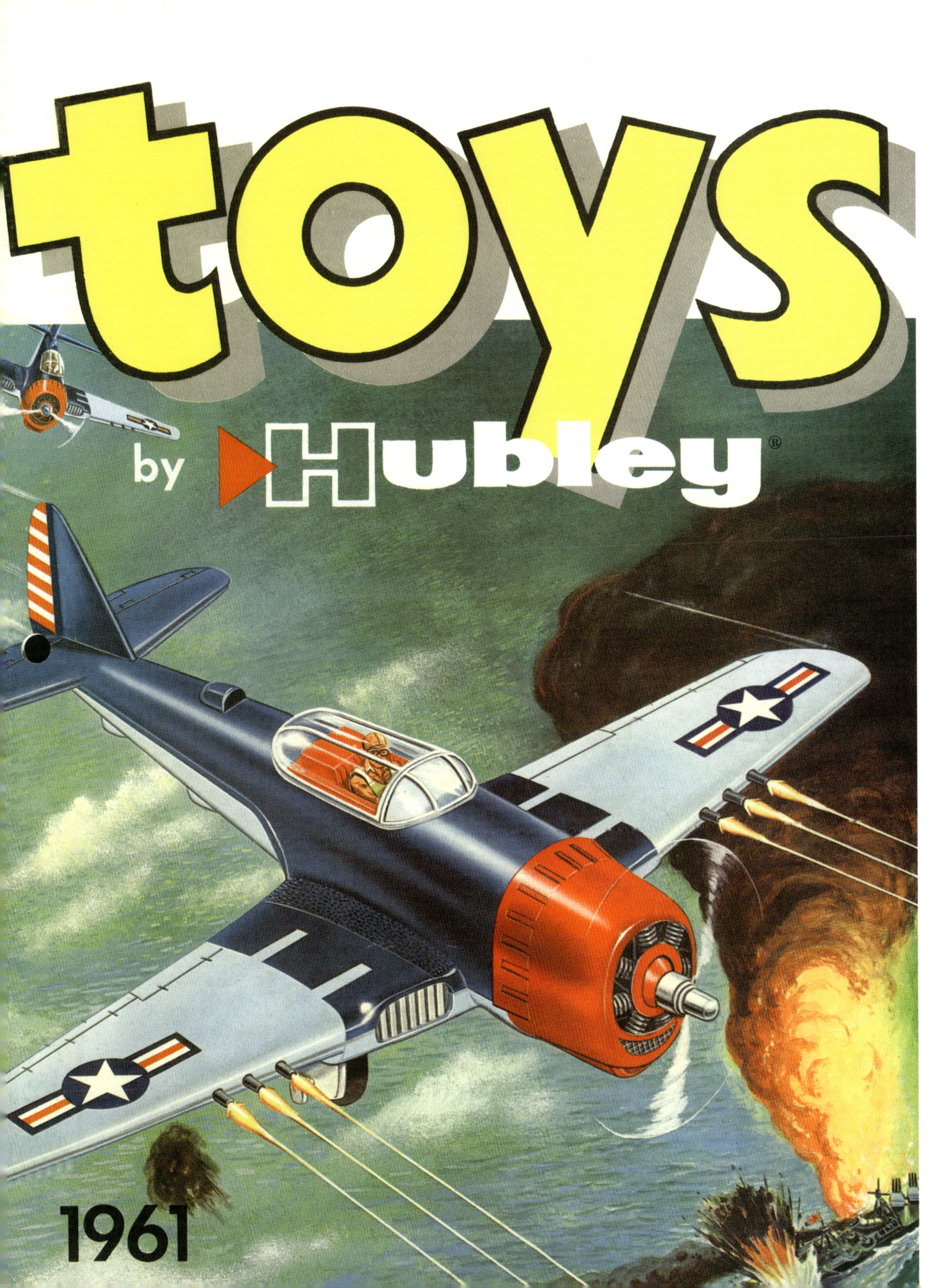
toys
by Hubley®
1961

**No. 309 TRACTOR**

HIGH IMPACT PLASTIC. Red, yellow and orange with aluminum trimming. Polyethylene wheels. Length 4¾ inches. Packed 12 in a box; 3 dozen to a carton; weight per carton 7 lbs.

**No. 310 MOTORCYCLE**

HIGH IMPACT PLASTIC. Red or green motorcycle, black cop. Rubber wheels. Length 5 inches. Packed 12 in a box; 3 dozen to a carton; weight per carton 8 lbs.

**No. 311 AIRPLANE**

HIGH IMPACT PLASTIC. Red and white colors. Retractable landing gear. Rubber wheels. Length 5 inches. Packed 12 in a box; 3 dozen to a carton; weight per carton 5 lbs.

**No. 338 HELICOPTER**

HIGH IMPACT PLASTIC. Red and silver combination. Two rotor blades, revolving horizontally in the front and vertically on the tail. Length 5¼ inches. Packed 6 in a box; 1 dozen to a carton; weight per carton 2 lbs.

**No. 965**

**TIC TOY CLOCK***

ATTRACTIVE, multi-colored plastic clock which actually runs as long as 14 hours. Spring driven, 25 parts which can be taken apart and quickly put together again through color-keyed gear assembly. For boys and girls 5 to 15 years of age. Height 11½ inches; width 8 inches. Packed 1 in a box; ¼ dozen to a carton; weight per carton 7 lbs.

*TRADEMARK



**No. 430 AIRPLANE**

METAL. Assorted red and blue with aluminum wings. Folding wings, retractable landing gear. Black wheels. Length 6 inches. Packed 6 in a box; 1 dozen to a carton; weight per carton 5 lbs.

**No. 467**
**NAVY FIGHTER**

METAL. Dark blue and light blue combination. Clear plastic bubble on cockpit. Folding wings and retractable landing gear. Black wheels. Length 6½ inches; wing span 8¾ inches. Packed 1 in a colorful box; 1 dozen to a carton; weight per carton 8 lbs.

**No. 469**

**LOG TRUCK**

METAL. Turquoise with nickel trimming. Furnished with five 6-inch logs. Four black wheels. Length 10¾ inches. Packed 1 in a box; 1 dozen to a carton; weight per carton 15 lbs.

**No. 470**

**DUMP TRUCK**

METAL. Red cab and chassis; yellow dump body. Dump operated by side lever. Four black wheels. Length 9¼ inches. Packed 1 in a box; 1 dozen to a carton; weight per carton 13 lbs.



1961

**No. 471**

**HOOK AND LADDER**

METAL. Red with nickel trim. Two white ladders. Black wheels. Length 11¼ inches. Packed 1 in a box; 1 dozen to a carton; weight per carton 13 lbs.

*Ladders mount in holes.*

**No. 472**

**TRACTOR**

METAL. Red with aluminum trimming. Treaded rubber tires. Realistic engine details. Length 7¼ inches. Packed 1 in a box; 1 dozen to a carton; weight per carton 16 lbs.

**No. 474**
**FARM TRACTOR AND WAGON**

METAL. All red with aluminum trimming. Treaded rubber tires. Realistic engine detail. Wagon attaches to tractor. Length 10¼ inches. Packed 1 in a colorful box with cutouts for added play value. 1 dozen to a carton; weight per carton 13 lbs.

**No. 751**

**JET PLANE**

METAL. Red and aluminum combination. Clear plastic bubble on cockpit. Folding wings and retractable landing gear. Black wheels. Length 7 inches; wingspread 6¼ inches. Packed 1 in a box; 1 dozen to a carton; weight per carton 8 lbs.

**No. 483 HELICOPTER**

METAL. Yellow with transparent plastic bubble. Two revolving nickel plated rotor blades. Two black rubber wheels. Length 9¼ inches. Packed 1 in a box; 1 dozen to a carton; weight per carton 13 lbs.

**No. 493**
**SCHOOL BUS**

METAL. Yellow with attractive red and black trimming. Black tires. Length 9½ inches. Individually packaged in colorful box with cutouts for added play value; 1 dozen to a carton; weight per carton 18 lbs.

**No. 494**
**BELL TELEPHONE TRUCK**

METAL. Bright red truck and trailer. Winch actually works. Telephone pole on trailer. Includes three digging tools. Length 17⅛ inches. Packed 1 in a colorful box; 1 dozen to a carton; weight per carton 22 lbs.

## No. 655 FORD FAIRLANE SEDAN & BOAT WITH TRAILER

METAL AND PLASTIC COMBINATION. Latest model Ford in red; yellow boat trailer; red and white plastic removable boat. Black wheels. Length 17½ inches. Packed 1 in a colorful box; 1 dozen to a carton; weight per carton 12 lbs.

## No. 495 NAVY FIGHTER-BOMBER

METAL. Dark blue top with light blue bottom and wings; red cowl. Cockpit enclosed with transparent sliding bubble. Revolving propeller, folding wings, retractable landing gear. Black wheels. Length 10 inches. Packed 1 in a box; 1 dozen to a carton; weight per carton 20 lbs.

## No. 496 TRACTOR

METAL. Red with aluminum trimming. Realistic engine details. Steering wheel operates front wheels. Treaded black tires. Length 9¼ inches. Packed 1 in a box; 1 dozen to a carton; weight per carton 29 lbs.

## No. 801 DUMP TRUCK

METAL. Red cab and chassis, yellow dump with aluminum trim. Dump raises and lowers by using side lever. Black treaded wheels. Length 10 inches. Packed 1 in a box; 1 dozen to a carton; weight per carton 16 lbs.

## No. 802 TRACTOR TRUCK

METAL. Turquoise cab and flat bed truck with aluminum trim. Removable tractor. Black treaded wheels. Length 10¼ inches. Packed 1 in a box; 1 dozen to a carton; weight per carton 16 lbs.

## No. 501 TRACTOR LOADER

METAL. Orange with bright metal loader mechanism and steering wheel. Aluminum trimming. Realistic engine details. Steering wheel operates front wheels. Side lever raises, lowers and dumps loader. Length 12¾ inches. Packed 1 in a box; ½ dozen to a carton; weight per carton 18 lbs.

## No. 503 ROAD SCRAPER

METAL. Orange with nickel trimming. Movable scraper which can be locked in position by adjusting screw. Realistic motor details. Front wheels controlled by steering lever. Rear wheels mounted independently to roll over stones and obstacles. Length 12¾ inches. Packed 1 in a box; ½ dozen to a carton; weight per carton 15 lbs.

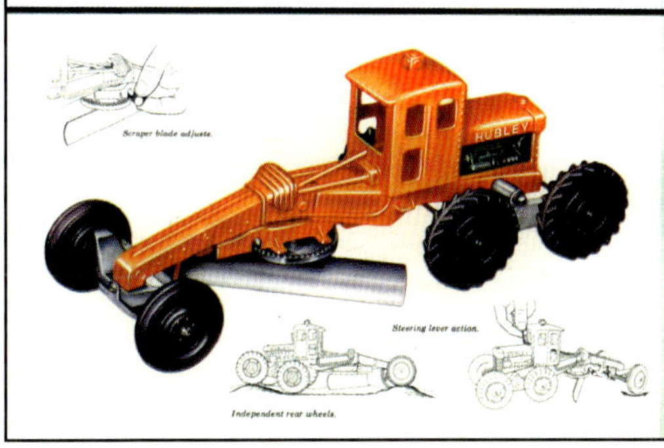




1961

## No. 505 FRONT END LOADER

METAL. Red with black realistic motor details and trimming. Yellow saddle, side arms and bucket. Red wheels with realistic black rubber tread. Loader operated by lever near driver's seat. Length 7¾ inches. Packed 1 in a box; ½ dozen to a carton; weight per carton 15 lbs.

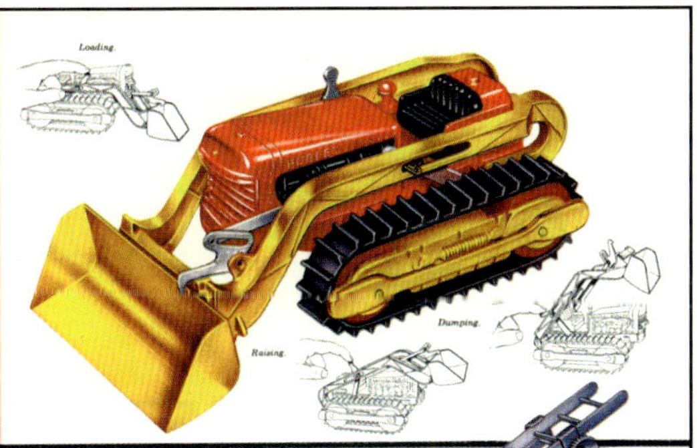


## No. 520 FIRE TRUCK

METAL. Red with cream seat and bright metal trim. Ladders elevate and revolve through 360° arc. Black wheels. Length 19 inches. Packed 1 in a box; ½ dozen to a carton; weight per carton 26 lbs.

## No. 525 TRACTOR

METAL. Grey and red combination with finely detailed, realistic engine visible from both sides. Red seat, nickel plated steering wheel. Metal wheels with black treaded tires. "Tricycle" type front wheels operate through steering wheel. Length 12 inches. Packed 1 in a box; ½ dozen to a carton; weight per carton 29 lbs.

## No. 507 FORD TRACTOR

METAL. Scale model of Ford 961 Powermaster Tractor. Tricycle type wheels. Red and grey with black rubber wheels. Realistic engine details and three point hitch for accessories. Length 10½ inches. Packed 1 in a box; ½ dozen to a carton; weight per carton 20 lbs.

### No. 758 FORD SCRAPER BLADE

METAL. Attaches to back of No. 507 Ford Tractor. Made completely of stamped steel. Red with aluminum colored blade. Blade adjusts to different positions. Packed 1 in a box; 1 dozen to a carton; weight per carton 6 lbs.

### No. 757 FORD POST HOLE DIGGER

METAL. Another accessory for the No. 507 Ford Tractor. Auger bores hole in ground for setting up posts. Red with nickel plated auger and handle. Packed 1 in a box; 1 dozen to a carton; weight per carton 4 lbs.

## No. 851 STOCK YARD TRUCK

METAL AND PLASTIC. Green chassis, yellow high impact plastic body. Three pigs included. When side of truck is opened and knob is turned, pigs "walk" out of truck. Length 10 inches. Packed 1 in a box; 1 dozen to a carton; weight per carton 15 lbs.

## No. 8
## FARM SET

METAL. Set consists of red tractor and wagon, yellow cultipacker, a pig, a crate of chickens and ducks. Attractive full color box sets up into barn. Packed 1 set in a box; one dozen to a carton; weight 17 lbs.

## No. 57
## FARM SET

METAL. Set consists of one Ford Tractor, a three-bladed plow, a farm wagon and two crates of chickens and ducks. Attractive lithographed box in full color. Packed 1 set in a box; ¼ dozen to a carton; weight per carton 16 lbs.

## No. 31
## FARM SET

ALL METAL SET consists of Tractor, Truck, Spreader, Plow and Cultivator. Assorted colors. Attractively packaged in colorful lithographed box. Packed 1 set in a box; ½ dozen sets to a carton; weight per carton 17 lbs.

10

*Pushing lever forward raises cultivator.*

*Hitching to tractor.*

## No. 90
## LARGE FARM SET

METAL. Set consists of #525 Tractor, Cultivator, Cultipacker and large Farm Wagon, all interlocking. Cultivator and Cultipacker can be individually attached to Tractor by means of hitch, which permits either to be raised or lowered for operation. Attractive corrugated box converts into play barn. Tractor and implements are red, grey and aluminum combination with black wheels. Packed 1 set in a box, ¼ dozen to a carton; weight per carton 25 lbs.

1

# 1961 Hubley TOYS

| | NAME | | CATALOG PAGE | CARTON PACKING | CARTON WEIGHT | SUGGESTED RETAIL PRIC |
|---|---|---|---|---|---|---|
| 9 | Tractor | (polystyrene) | 2 | 3 doz. | 7 lbs. | $ .29 |
| 0 | Motorcycle | (polystyrene) | 2 | 3 doz. | 8 lbs. | .29 |
| 1 | Airplane | (polystyrene) | 2 | 3 doz. | 5 lbs. | .29 |
| 3 | Helicopter | (polystyrene) | 2 | 1 doz. | 2 lbs. | .29 |
| 0 | Airplane | (metal) | 3 | 1 doz. | 5 lbs. | .49 |
| 7 | Navy Fighter | (metal) | 3 | 1 doz. | 8 lbs. | .98 |
| 9 | Log Truck | (metal) | 3 | 1 doz. | 15 lbs. | .98 |
| 0 | Dump Truck | (metal) | 3 | 1 doz. | 13 lbs. | .98 |
| 1 | Hook & Ladder | (metal) | 4 | 1 doz. | 13 lbs. | .98 |
| 2 | Tractor | (metal) | 4 | 1 doz. | 16 lbs. | .98 |
| 4 | Tractor & Wagon | (metal) | 4 | 1 doz. | 13 lbs. | .98 |
| 3 | Helicopter | (metal) | 5 | 1 doz. | 13 lbs. | 1.49 |
| 3 | School Bus | (metal) | 5 | 1 doz. | 18 lbs. | 1.98 |
| 4 | Bell Telephone Truck | (metal) | 5 | 1 doz. | 22 lbs. | 1.98 |
| 5 | Navy Fighter-Bomber | (metal) | 6 | 1 doz. | 20 lbs. | 1.98 |
| 6 | Tractor | (metal) | 6 | 1 doz. | 29 lbs. | 1.98 |
| 1 | Tractor Loader | (metal) | 7 | ½ doz. | 18 lbs. | 2.98 |
| 3 | Road Scraper | (metal) | 7 | ½ doz. | 15 lbs. | 2.98 |
| 5 | Front End Loader | (metal) | 8 | ½ doz. | 15 lbs. | 2.98 |
| 7 | Ford Tractor | (metal) | 9 | ½ doz. | 20 lbs. | 3.98 |
| 0 | Fire Truck | (metal) | 8 | ½ doz. | 26 lbs. | 4.98 |
| 5 | Tractor | (metal) | 8 | ½ doz. | 29 lbs. | 4.98 |
| 5 | Ford Sedan and Boat with Trailer | (metal, polystyrene) | 6 | 1 doz. | 12 lbs. | 1.98 |
| 1 | Jet Plane | (metal) | 5 | 1 doz. | 8 lbs. | .98 |
| 7 | Ford Post Hole Digger | (metal) | 9 | 1 doz. | 4 lbs. | .98 |
| 8 | Ford Scraper Blade | (metal) | 9 | 1 doz. | 6 lbs. | .98 |
| 1 | Dump Truck | (metal) | 6 | 1 doz. | 16 lbs. | 1.49 |
| 2 | Tractor Truck | (metal) | 7 | 1 doz. | 16 lbs. | 1.49 |
| 1 | Stock Yard Truck | (metal, polystyrene) | 9 | 1 doz. | 15 lbs. | 1.98 |
| 5 | Tic-Toy Clock | (polystyrene) | 2 | ¼ doz. | 7 lbs. | 5.98 |

## BOXED ASSORTMENTS

| | NAME | | CATALOG PAGE | CARTON PACKING | CARTON WEIGHT | SUGGESTED RETAIL PRIC |
|---|---|---|---|---|---|---|
| 8 | Farm Set | (metal) | 10 | 1 doz. | 17 lbs. | 1.98 |
| 1 | Farm Set | (metal) | 10 | ½ doz. | 17 lbs. | 2.98 |
| 7 | Farm Set | (metal) | 11 | ¼ doz. | 16 lbs. | 5.98 |
| 0 | Farm Set—Large | (metal) | 11 | ¼ doz. | 25 lbs. | 9.98 |

**THE HUBLEY MANUFACTURING CO., LANCASTER, PA. U.S.A.**

**SCALE MODELS • METAL TOYS • PISTOLS & RIFLES • HOLSTER SETS**

# 1962

# The 1962 line of GUNS HOLSTERS TOYS HOBBIES

## by Hubley®

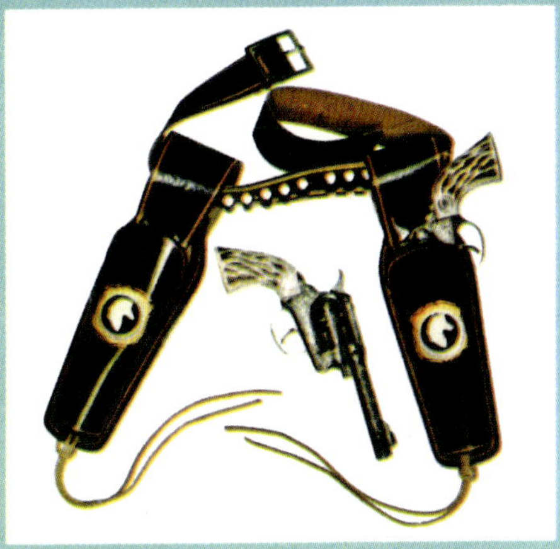

# Hubley® CAP GUNS—'62

*Exact replicas of famous guns make men feel like boys and boys feel like their television heroes . . . made of sturdy, die-cast metal or the finest high impact plastic . . . packaged and priced for quick turnover and steady, pleasing profit!*

## The Sure-Fire Dollar Line!

NEW

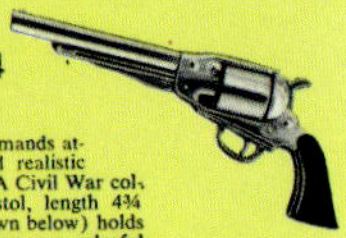

### 236 REMINGTON* .44 MINIATURE

Gleaming chrome finish commands attention, authentic detail and realistic smooth grip are convincers. A Civil War collector's item, single-shot pistol, length 4¾ in. Removable cylinder (shown below) holds 6 play bullets. Packed: 1 gun per colorful window box suitable for racking; 1 doz. guns per "quick-sell" counter display; 3 doz. guns per ctn.; wt. 7 lbs. Suggested retail $1.**

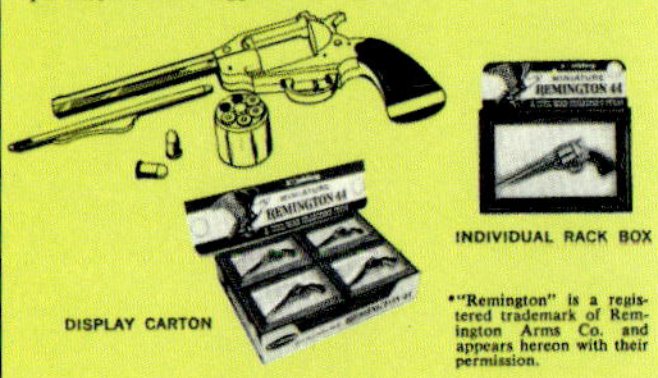

DISPLAY CARTON

INDIVIDUAL RACK BOX

*"Remington" is a registered trademark of Remington Arms Co. and appears hereon with their permission.

### 255R SNIPER

Brand new Western pistol with extra long barrel. Made of black, high impact plastic with realistic brown handles. 22 in. long. Single shot, automatic action. Individually packed on bright red and yellow card for racking or bins. 1 doz. cards per ctn. Wt. 9 lbs. Suggested retail $1.

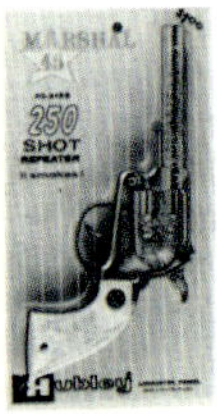


### 248S MARSHAL

Big Western 250 shot repeater, highly engraved with bright nickel finish. Simulated pearl handle bearing cameo steer head. Cylinder door slides open for easy loading. Length 9½ in. Individually skin packed on brightly colored card; packed 1 doz. per ctn.; wt. 10 lbs. Suggested retail $1.

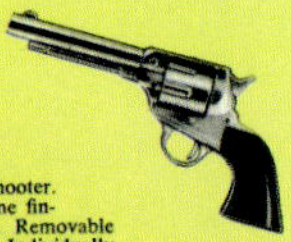

### 238 FRONTIER MINIATURE

Authentic single action six-shooter. Collectors want it. Bright chrome finish with realistic smooth grip. Removable cylinder holds 6 play bullets. Individually packed in window box, suitable for racking; 1 doz. guns per counter display; 3 doz. guns per ctn.; wt. 7 lbs. Suggested retail $1.

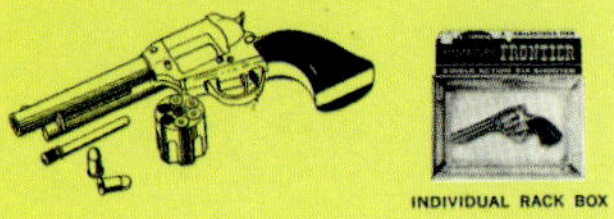

INDIVIDUAL RACK BOX

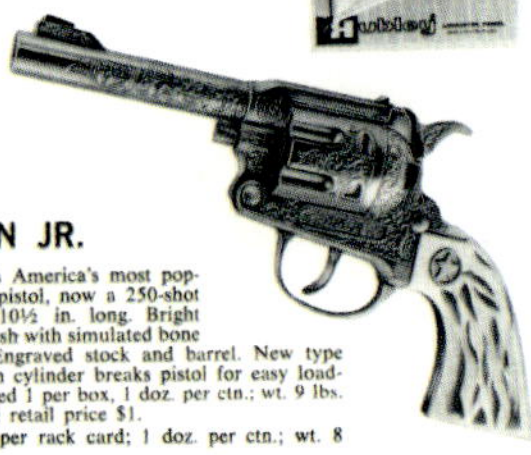

### 250 TEXAN JR.

For years America's most popular cap pistol, now a 250-shot repeater 10½ in. long. Bright nickel finish with simulated bone handle. Engraved stock and barrel. New type release on cylinder breaks pistol for easy loading. Packed 1 per box, 1 doz. per ctn.; wt. 9 lbs. Suggested retail price $1.

250R, 1 per rack card; 1 doz. per ctn.; wt. 8 lbs.

250S, Individually carded and skin packed; 1 doz. per ctn., wt. 8 lbs.

**All prices shown in this catalog are suggested retail.



## Pride and profit in every $1 sale!

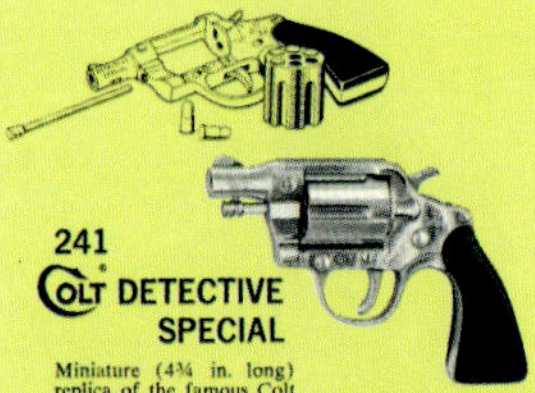

### 241 COLT® DETECTIVE SPECIAL

Miniature (4¾ in. long) replica of the famous Colt "Detective Special." Single shot. Removable cylinder loads with 6 play bullets furnished with the pistol. Bright chrome barrel and stock; black handles. 'Shipped in attractive counter display to sell for $1.

**Counter display:** 1 doz. Detective Specials in individual boxes with full acetate sleeve, suitable for racking. Plastic snap lid box with 6 bullets. One carton contains 3 display boxes (3 doz. guns); wt. per ctn. 11 lbs.

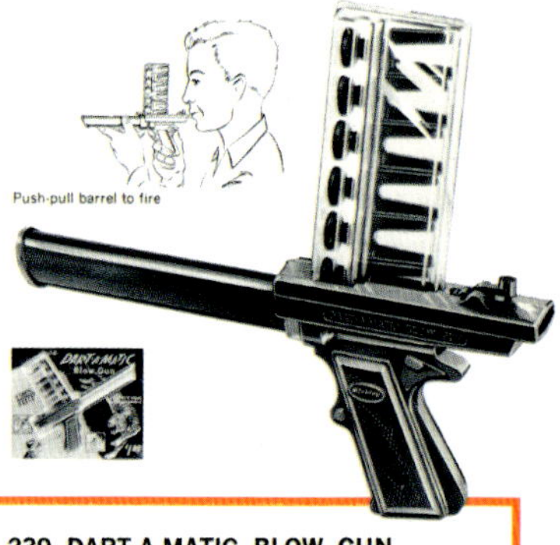

Push-pull barrel to fire

### 239 DART-A-MATIC BLOW GUN

Colorful gun with clear chamber fires 6 harmless darts (assorted colors) with suction cups. High impact plastic, length 9¾ in. Darts included. Packed 1 to a colorful "self-sell" stretch-pak* card; 1 doz. cards per ctn.; wt. 6 lbs. A fast-selling money-maker at $1 retail.

*Trade Mark of Impak Systems, Inc.

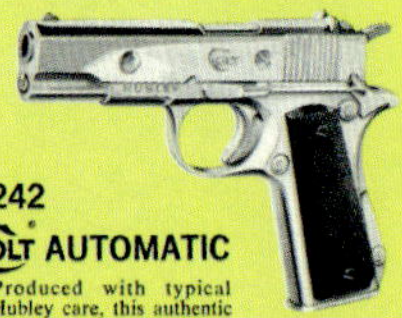

### 242 COLT® AUTOMATIC

Produced with typical Hubley care, this authentic miniature of the historically important Colt Automatic is in gleaming chrome with realistic knurled grips. Shoots single caps. Removable bullet clip, six play bullets. Length 5 in. Suggested retail $1.

Removable clip and 6 play bullets

Packed in individual box with full acetate sleeve, just right for racking. One doz. boxes per counter display; 3 displays (3 doz. guns) per ctn.; wt. per ctn. 10 lbs.

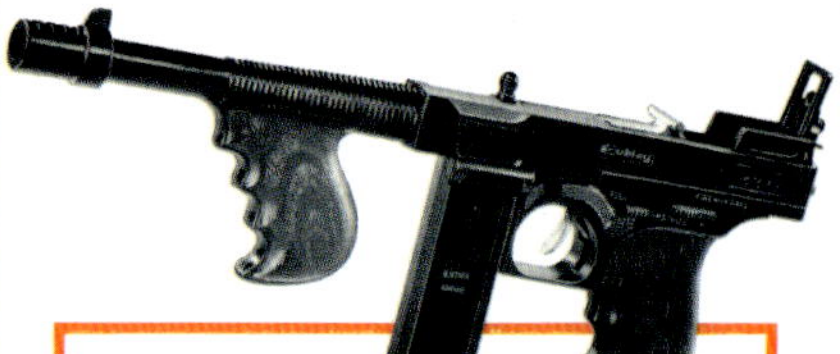

### 243 TINY TOMMY SUB-MACHINE GUN

Scale model of real-life Tommy-gun (10½ in. long) fires standard roll caps as fast as the triggerman can shoot. Made of high-impact plastic, authentically detailed, just like its big brother. Die-cast chamber pops up for easy loading. Rear sight folds down. Black with "walnut-grained" plastic hand grips. Retail price $1.

Packed in individual boxes with full acetate lid, 6 in each colorful counter display. Two displays (1 doz. guns) per ctn.; wt. 5 lbs.

243R—Individually packed on colorful "self-sell" card. One doz. per ctn.; wt. 4 lbs.

©Product mfgd. under license from and copyright 1958 by Colt Patent Firearms Mfg. Co., Inc.



1962

### 256 REMINGTON* .36

Authentic six-shooter with 6 take-apart cartridges which fire round caps. Shiny 9-in. replica of the notable "Remington .36." Bright chrome finish with smooth black handles. Easy-to-load revolving cylinder. Individually packed in mylar wrapped window box. 1 doz. per ctn.; wt. 10 lbs. Pleasing-profit retail price, $1.49.

*"Remington" is a registered trademark of Remington Arms Co. and appears hereon with their permission.

### 261 RIC-O-SHAY®* JR.

Whing! Whing! Whing! Real bullet whine with each pull of the trigger! Repeater, 10½ in. long. Engraved barrel and cylinder, with bright nickel finish. Cameo steer head on black grips. Hinged cylinder slides up for loading standard roll caps. Packed 1 per box, 1 doz. per ctn.; wt. 11 lbs. Demonstrate the bullet whine and sell 'em fast at $1.49.

*T.M. The Hubley Manufacturing Co. Patent No. 2,941,325

## Hubley Padlock Pistols for "Locked-in" Sales

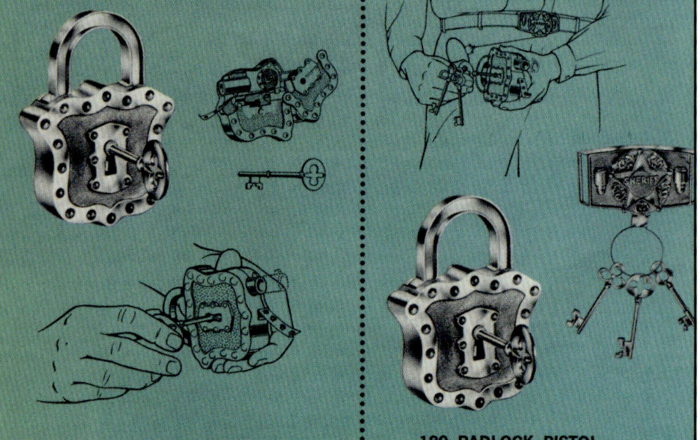

### 188 PADLOCK PISTOL

With a turn of the key, barrel of hidden pistol pops out and fires! Repeater action. Lock and key in polished nickel finish; 4½ in. long. Rear of engraved lock opens for easy loading of standard roll caps. Individually boxed and skin packed, 6 boxes per colorful counter display; 2 displays (1 doz. guns) per ctn.; wt. 12 lbs. Suggested retail, $1.98.

### 189 PADLOCK PISTOL AND KEY RING

Authentic "Sheriff" buckle doubles the play value of the Hubley Padlock Pistol. Three removable nickel keys on ring. All keys fire pistol. Spring pulley automatically returns ring and keys to buckle. Highly engraved chrome buckle with engraved brass star. Lock, keys and buckle skin-packed in display box; 1 doz. boxes per ctn.; wt. 17 lbs. Selling price $2.98.



# Hubley® GUNS for '62

**Target: Top Profits**

**Price: $2.98**

### 271 SUPER POP RIFLE

Deluxe pop gun loudly fires plastic cork and produces realistic bullet "whine." Length from yellow plastic cork to end of butt, 24½ in. Shock resistant plastic stock and front grip are walnut colored, highly embossed. Bright 3-color decal on butt. Highly detailed blue barrel and chamber. Chrome plated working parts. Three-step loading as illustrated. Individually boxed to sell at $2.98; ½ doz. per ctn.; wt. 9 lbs.

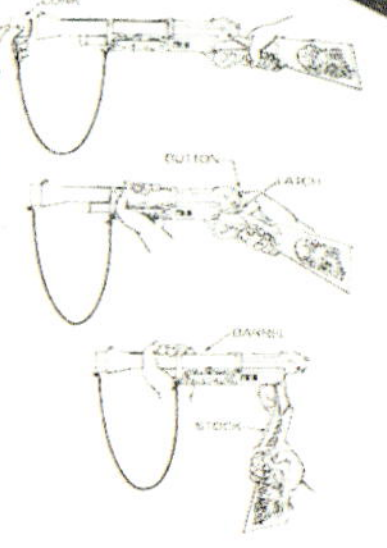

### 199 LAW ENFORCEMENT SET

Make new friends as you make money selling all this for $2.98: Tiny Tommy Machine Gun, Colt® Detective Special with shoulder holster, police badge and identification card. Invitingly skin packed in colorful open face display box; 1 doz. per ctn.; wt. 15 lbs. (Both guns described on page 3.)

# Hubley® CAP GUNS—'62

Cleverly packed in wood grained box with raised frame which permits counter demonstration of bullet whine. ½ doz. individual boxes per ctn.; wt. 12 lbs.

## 279 RIC-O-SHAY®

Real ricochet sound with each pull of the trigger! Big 50-shot repeater is 13 in. long. Decorated chrome plate barrel and chamber, smooth black grips. Revolving cylinder with six brass play bullets. Authentic side-action loading of standard roll caps. Proved popular and profitable, suggested retail $3.98.

*Trademark The Hubley Manufacturing Co. Patents 2,477,-033, 2,941,325. Other patents pending.

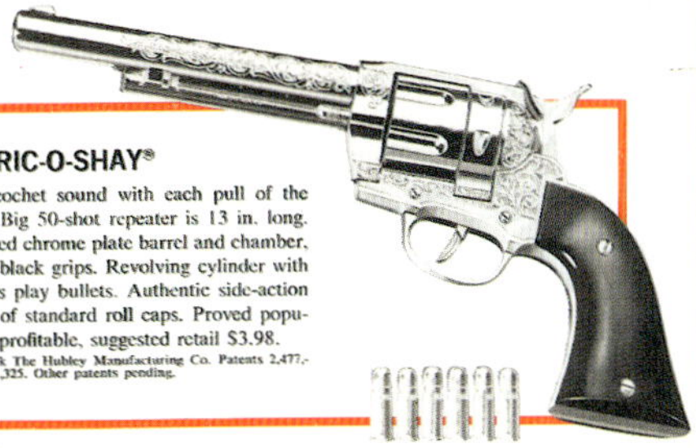

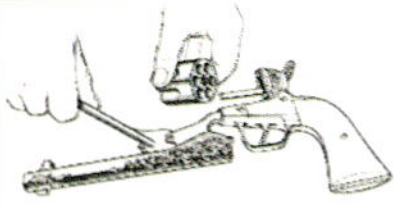

TO LOAD; Pull rammer down; swing barrel 180°; remove and load cylinder with pre-capped "cartridges"; replace cylinder; reposition barrel and rammer.

OR

Pull down latch to load chambers one at a time with take-apart "cartridges" using round caps.

## 281 COLT .45

Man-sized six-shooter with "cartridges" that fire round caps. Length 14⅜ in. Exact size and detailing of 1860 model used in Civil War. Decorated super chrome and gold finish; simulated bone grips. Individually boxed, ½ doz. per ctn.; wt. 14 lbs. Suggested retail $3.98.

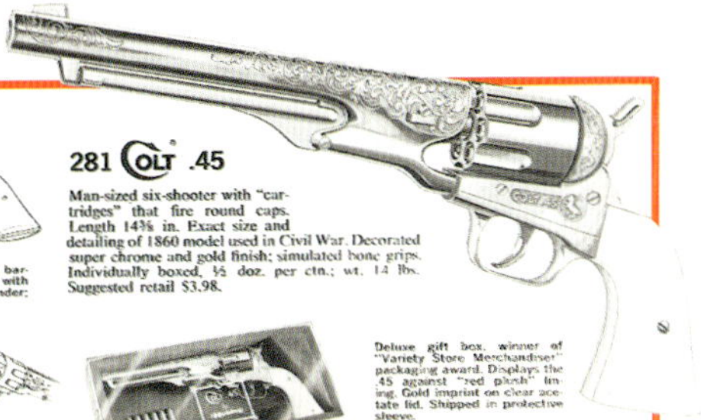

Deluxe gift box, winner of "Variety Store Merchandiser" packaging award. Displays the .45 against "red plush" lining. Gold imprint on clear acetate lid. Shipped in protective sleeve.



NEW

Loading chamber pops out automatically.

SNAP FIRE

PUMP FIRE

## 202 RING RIFLE

Handsome, new 250 shot repeating rifle, 32½ in. long. Special shock-resistant plastic butt and stock, walnut colored and richly embossed. Working parts nickel plated and beautifully decorated. Shoots standard roll caps. Packed individually; ½ doz. per ctn.; wt. 18 lbs. Retail price $3.98.

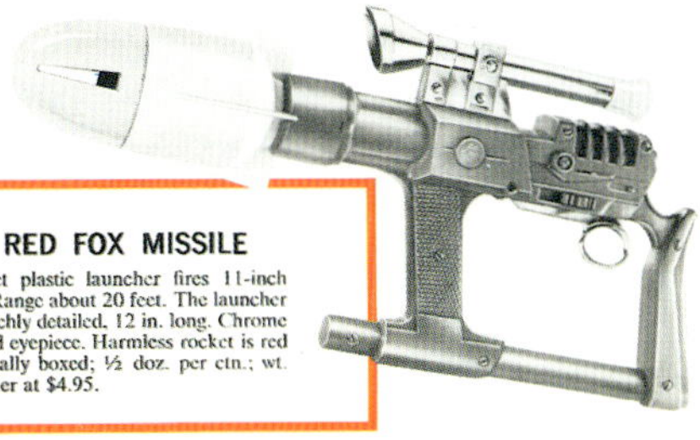

## 207 THE RED FOX MISSILE

Rugged high-impact plastic launcher fires 11-inch soft plastic rocket. Range about 20 feet. The launcher is gun metal gray, richly detailed, 12 in. long. Chrome plated sight with red eyepiece. Harmless rocket is red and white. Individually boxed; ½ doz. per ctn.; wt. 8 lbs. Popular retailer at $4.95.

## Other Fast-Selling Hubley Pistols . . from 25¢ to 69¢

### 211 PET

Low-priced beauty! Automatic action, single shot. Length 6½ in. Bright nickel finish with finely detailed cross-hatching on handle. Packed 12 in a box; 3 doz. per ctn.; wt. 8 lbs. Designed to ring up rapid-fire sales at 25c retail.

### 216 CHIEF

Single shot, automatic action. Bright nickel finish, 7⅝ in. long. Handle integral with richly decorated stock and barrel. Packed 12 in a box; 3 doz. per ctn.; wt. 10 lbs. Retail 49c.

Also 216R, Carded, suitable for racking; 1 doz. per ctn.; wt. 4 lbs.

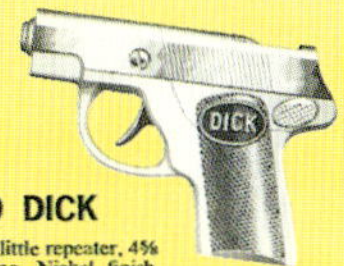

### 210 DICK

Shiny little repeater, 4⅝ in. long. Nickel finish. Rear part of barrel, left side, is hinged and slides open to load. Individually boxed; 3 doz. per ctn.; wt. 11 lbs. Retail 59c.

210R—One per rack card; 1 doz. per ctn.; wt. 4 lbs.

210S—Individual skin pack card; 1 doz. per ctn.; wt. 4 lbs.

### 218 RODEO

White simulated bone handles on a bright nickel pistol, 8¾ in. long. Engraved stock and barrel. Automatic action, single shot. Individually boxed, 3 doz. to a ctn.; wt. 17 lbs. Retail price 59c.

Also 218R, one pistol per rack card; 1 doz. per ctn.; wt. 6 lbs.

NEW

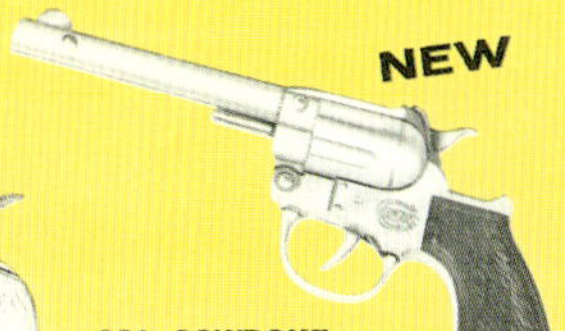

### 231 COWPOKE

Brand new Western repeater pistol, 8½ in. long. Bright nickel finish with brown woodgrain plastic grips. Barrel breaks for easy loading. Individually boxed; 3 doz. per ctn.; wt. 18 lbs. Retail price 69c.

231R, carded; 1 doz. per ctn.; wt. 6 lbs.

231S, skin packed on rack card; 1 doz. per ctn.; wt. 6 lbs.

### 234 HAWK

Automatic with repeater action, 5¾ in. long. Simulated mother of pearl handles add glamour to bright nickel finish and detailed engraving of barrel and stock. Section of barrel above handle is hinged and slides up for loading. Individually boxed; 3 doz. per ctn.; wt. 16 lbs. Suggested retail 69c.

234R, carded for racking; 1 doz. cards per ctn.; wt. 5 lbs.





## Volume Builders . . . Sell Them for 79¢ and 89¢

### 233S POCKET DERRINGER

Authentic short-barreled, large-caliber Derringer, 4 in. long. Bright chrome finish with white handles. Barrel breaks to load standard roll caps. Skin packed on pre-priced card. Packed 1 doz. cards per ctn.; wt. 5 lbs. Suggested retail 79c.

NEW

### 240 TROOPER

Brand new model to carry on the tradition of the long-popular Hubley Trooper. It's a 250-shot repeater, 5½ in. long, with bright nickel finish and black handles. Individually boxed; 3 doz. per ctn.; wt. 19 lbs. retail at 79c.

240R, carded for racking, and 240S, skin packed on colorful card; 1 doz. cards per ctn.; wt. 6 lbs. Same retail price, 79c.

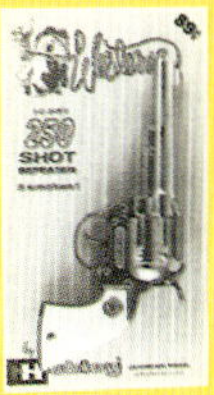


### 246S WESTERN

Western style 250-shot repeater, 8¾ in. long. Nickel plated with white bull's-head handle. Skin packed on colorful card. Packed 1 doz. cards per ctn.; wt. 10 lbs. Preprieed at 89¢.

## Full-View, Quick-Sell Display Assortments

### 182 Deluxe Pistol Assortment

Self-service assortment includes ½ doz. each of Nos. 210S Dick, 231S Cowpoke, 240S Trooper and 250S Texan, Jr. plus one extra 250S. All skin packed on brightly printed, pre-priced cards. Complete with sturdy, attractive space-saver wire display rack. Packed one assortment per ctn.; wt. 15 lbs.

### 183 Western Pistol Assortment

Pre-priced from 69c to $1, assortment contains ⅓ doz. each of Nos. 231S Cowpoke, 240S Trooper, 246S Western and 248S Marshal. All skin packed on gay colored cards. Complete with free wire display rack. Packed one assortment per ctn.; wt. 22 lbs.

### 181 WIRE DISPLAY RACK ONLY

Sturdy wire frame with four hooks, for best possible display in least possible space. Red and white Hubley banner across top adds to selling power of printed rack cards. Each hook holds ½ doz. carded pistols. Rack measures 22¾ in. wide, 16 in. high, 6¾ in. deep. Packed 1 per ctn.; net wt. 4 lbs.

### RACK CARDS

Combine your own choice of Hubley carded pistols with 181 Wire Display Rack. Create your own fast-selling assortment. Pistols are mounted on attractively designed, die-cut cards ready to hang.

The following guns are carded:

| | |
|---|---|
| 210R & S | 240R & S |
| 216R | 243R |
| 218R | 246S |
| 231R & S | 248S |
| 233S | 250R & S |
| 234R | |

# Hubley® TOYS—'62

*Low end toys of metal and plastic . . . plenty of value and built to last.*

## PLASTIC—29c

### 309 Tractor

Red, yellow or orange with aluminum trim. Polyethylene wheels. Length 4½ in. Packed 12 in a box; 3 doz. per ctn.; wt. 7 lbs. Suggested retail 29c.

### 310 Motorcycle

Red or green motorcycle, black rider. Rubber wheels. Length 5 in. Packed 12 in a box; 3 doz. per ctn.; wt. 8 lbs. Retail price 29c.

### 311 Airplane

Red and white. Insignia on wings with retractable landing gear. Rubber wheels. Length 5 in. Packed 12 in a box; 3 doz. per ctn.; wt. 5 lbs. Turnover fast at 29¢.

NEW

## METAL and only 39c

### 401 Continental Sedan

A 6-inch detailed die cast model of one of the finest cars on the American road, the Lincoln Continental. Blue with aluminum trim. Black treaded rubber tires. Individually skin packed on colorful card; 1 doz. cards per ctn.; wt. per ctn., 4 lbs. Retail 39¢.

### 402 Fire Engine

Cab-over-engine fire truck painted bright red, about 6 in. long. Aluminum trim. Black rubber tires. Individually skin packed on "self-seller" card; 1 doz. cards per ctn.; wt. 4 lbs. Retail price just 39c.

### 403 Falcon Pick-Up Truck

Turquoise blue 6-in. reproduction of Ford's stylish little truck. Black treaded tires. Aluminum brightwork. Individually skin packed; 1 doz. cards per ctn.; wt. 6 lbs. Retail price 39¢.

### 404 Ford 1934 Coupe

"They can have any color, as long as it's black," said Henry Ford, but a few years later the Model A came in tan, blue and green. Then Ford offered the speedy V-8 in this jade green. Individually skin packed; 1 doz. cards per ctn.; wt. 4 lbs. Retail price 39¢.

### 405 Corvair Station Wagon

Chevrolet's entry in the compact field is reproduced here in vivid red. About 6 in. long. Aluminum trim and black rubber tires. Individually skin packed; 1 doz. cards per ctn.; wt. 4 lbs. Retail only 39¢.

### 406 Gasoline Truck

Authentic die cast metal detail, painted orange with aluminum trim. 6 in. long. Black rubber tires. Individually skin packed; 1 doz. cards per ctn.; wt. 4 lbs. Retail price 39¢.

### No. 29 MIGHTY-METAL ASSORTMENT

Big business! Four each of all 6 Mighty-Metal Toys shown above, individually skin packed on brightly printed cards; total 2 doz.; shipping wt. 9 lbs. All toys 39¢ retail.

# Hubley® TOYS—'62

## MIGHTY-METAL™ Toys . . . Die Cast for Sharp Detail and Durability

### *Full-View, Factory-Fresh Packaging!*

The Mighty-Metal Toys shown on these two pages are electronically sealed in a plastic covering that fits the contour of the car, truck or airplane. It is called Stretch-Pak*. The bright colors and fine detailing of Mighty-Metal toys are fully visible through the pilfer-proof protective film. This three dimensional package has proven itself to be a big help to dealers with modern merchandising ideas.

### 429 LOG TRUCK

Sturdy die cast metal truck, 5¾ in. long, with three wooden logs. Orange with nickel plated trim. Six black rubber tires. Individual Stretch-Pak; 1 doz. to a ctn.; wt. per ctn. 5 lbs. Steady retail seller at 69¢.

### 430 AIRPLANE

Six-inch metal airplane, red or blue with shiny folding wings and retractable landing gear. Black wheels. Packed 6 in a box; 1 doz. to a ctn.; wt. 5 lbs. Sell fast at 49¢.

430S—Individual Stretch-Pak; 1 doz. to ctn.; wt. 6 lbs. Suggested retail 59¢.

### 431 DUMP TRUCK

Sturdy metal model with 6 treaded rubber tires, dump operated by center spring. Yellow cab and chassis, red dump bed. Shiny nickel plated grille and tail gate. Length 5½ in. Individual Stretch-Pak; 1 doz. cards per ctn.; wt. 5 lbs. Retail price 69¢.

### 432 M.G. SPORTS CAR

Graceful M.G. lines cast in long-lasting Mighty-Metal. Red body and seat with shiny nickel plated grille and windshield. Treaded rubber tires with spare on trunk lid. Length 5¾ in. Individual Stretch-Pak; 1 doz. to a ctn.; wt. 7 lbs. Retail price 69¢.

*Trade Mark by Impak Systems, Inc.
Mighty-Metal™ is a trade mark of Hubley Manufacturing Company

### 453 TOW TRUCK

Sells for 89¢ (like all the other fine trucks on this page). Red cab and chassis. Shiny nickel grille, side panels and tow arm. Black rubber tires. Length 7½ in. Individual Stretch-Pak; 1 doz. to a ctn.; wt. 8 pounds.

### 456 TRACTOR

Sturdy metal with realistically cast engine detail. Painted orange. Tires are just like real ones. Length 5½ in. Individual Stretch-Pak; 1 doz. to a ctn.; wt. 8 lbs. Retail price just 89¢.

### 458 DUMP TRUCK

Mighty-Metal cab and chassis are bright red with yellow dump bed. Nickel plated grille and tail gate. Side lever activates dump. Black rubber tires. Individual Stretch-Pak; 1 doz. to a ctn.; wt. 9 lbs. Attractive retail price 89¢.

### 459 LOG TRUCK

Rugged metal truck loaded with 5 wooden logs. Blue with nickel plated front end. Length 7¼ in. Black rubber tires. Individual Stretch-Pak; 1 doz to. a ctn.; wt. 8 lbs. Retail price 89¢.

### 460 STAKE TRUCK

Handsome metal truck to carry a big payload. Orange with nickel plated grille. Four black rubber tires. Length 7¼ in. Individual Stretch-Pak; 1 doz. to a ctn.; wt. 8 lbs. Retail price 89¢.

### 465 FIRE ENGINE

Snappy, sturdy red fire engine with sparkling nickel trim. 7½ in. long. Joined ladders extend to 9½ in. Treaded rubber tires. Individual Stretch-Pak; 1 doz. cards to a ctn.; wt. 8 lbs. Retail price 89¢.

### *ASSORTMENTS WITH DISPLAY RACKS*

***Open a year-round toy department!***

**No. 32** — Six Dozen Toys

Attractive wire display rack included with 1 doz. each of 453 Tow Truck, 456 Tractor, 458 Dump Truck, 459 Log Truck, 460 Stake Truck and 465 Fire Engine. Assortment wt. 54 lbs.

**No. 34** — Twelve Dozen Toys

Large wire display rack included with the following fast-selling Mighty-Metal toys: 2 doz. each of 456 Tractor and 460 Stake Truck; 1 doz. each of 453 Tow Truck, 458 Dump Truck, 459 Log Truck, 465 Fire Engine, 429 Log Truck, 430S Airplane, 431 Dump Truck, 432 M.G. Sports Car. Assortment wt. 110 lbs.

(see illus.)

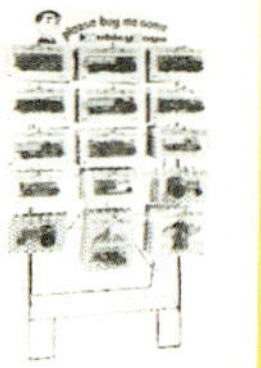





# Hubley® '62

### *A complete variety of $1 impulse toys*

The sharp, clean detail of die cast metal makes these tried and proven Hubley toys best sellers year after year. Long-lasting and always up to date in bright colors, they bring big volume and top-profit sales. All are attractively packaged, ready for the counter.

### 761 P-40 Fighter Plane

Hubley's latest winner – the authentic World War II combat airplane with Air Force insignia. Plane is 7½ in. long; wingspread 8 in. Red wings and silver fuselage, excellent detail. Shiny 3-bladed prop revolves. Individually skin packed; 1 doz. per ctn.; wt. 7 lbs. Retail price $1.00.

NEW

### 467 Navy Fighter

One of Hubley's most popular die cast metal models. Light and dark blue color combination. Clear plastic bubble over cockpit. Four-bladed prop, folding wings and retractable landing gear. Rubber tires. Length 6½ in.; wing span 8¾ in. Packed individually in colorful box; 1 doz. per ctn.; wt. 8 lbs. Retail $1.00.

### 469 Log Truck

This realistic timber-toter with five 6-inch wood logs is a staple, everyday seller because of its kid appeal. Die cast metal, handsome and durable. Blue with nickel trim. Four black wheels. Length 10¾ in. Packed 1 in a box; 1 doz. per ctn.; wt. 15 lbs. Retail $1.00.

### 470 Dump Truck

Big for the price—9¼ in. long with loads of play value! Red cab and chassis; yellow dump bed. Side lever operates dump. Black rubber tires. Individually packed in brightly printed box; 1 doz. per ctn.; wt. 13 lbs. Retail price $1.00.

### 471 Hook and Ladder

Fire engines always sell, and this is a great one! Red with nickel trim. Two white ladders that mount in holes of platform and can be fitted together. Length 11¼ in. Packed 1 in a box; 1 doz. per ctn.; wt. 13 lbs. Retail price $1.00.

### 472 Hubley Tractor

Your biggest bid for volume in the $1.00 retail class! Red with aluminum trimming. Realistic die cast engine detail. Black treaded tires. Length 7¼ in. Packed 1 in a box; 1 doz. per ctn.; wt. 16 lbs. A real value at $1.00.

### 474 Farm Tractor & Wagon

Die cast metal, painted red with aluminum trim. Utility wagon hitches to tractor. Plenty of eye appeal. Overall length 10¼ in. Packed 1 in a colorful box, with cutouts for added value; 1 doz. per ctn.; wt. 13 lbs. Retail $1.00.

# Hubley® TOYS–'62

## 6 ALL NEW skin-packed sets—$1.00

These skin-packed Mighty-Metal toys are fully displayed for eager eyes but safe from busy fingers. The tough, transparent plastic skin seals the toys to a brightly printed display card, pre-priced and easy to set up on rack or counter.

### 721
Garage Repairman

Set contains a Falcon Tow Truck, a '34 Ford Coupe (page 9) and battery, pliers, screwdriver and 2 car tires. Skin packed on the "self-sell" card as shown. One doz. to a ctn.; wt. 11 lbs. Retail price $1.

### 722
Where's the Fire?

Contains No. 402 Fire Engine and No. 405 Station Wagon (page 9) with 2 plastic ladders, bucket and plastic whistle. Completely skin packed on rack card. 1 doz. to a ctn.; wt. 9 lbs., retail price $1.

### 723
Gas 'er Up

Set consists of No. 401 Continental and No. 406 Gas Truck (page 9) with gas pump, pliers and screwdriver. Colorfully skin packed on pre-priced card, packed 1 doz. to a ctn., wt. 9 lbs., $1. retail.

### 26 ASSORTMENT

For modern merchandising with Mighty-Metal toys. Three each of Nos. 721, 722, 723 and 764. Packed 1 assortment per ctn.; wt. 10 lbs.

### 762
Farm Set

Complete set of No. 456 Tractor (page 11), cultipacker, chickens, pigs and ducks. Packed 1 doz to a ctn.; wt. 11 lbs. All skin packed on card to retail $1.

### 763
Highway and Skyway

Two best-sellers packaged together—No. 432 M.G. Sports Car and No. 430 Airplane. Both Mighty-Metal toys are described on page 10. Skin packed for protection and display 1 doz. to a ctn.; wt. 10 lbs. Retail price $1.

### 764
Speeders Beware!

Skin packing shows and sells both No. 310 Motorcycle (page 9) and No. 432 M.G. Sports Car (page 10). Plastic whistle included. Packed 1 doz. to a ctn.; wt. 9 lbs. Retail $1.

## THREE SALES CHAMPS at $1.49

### 483 HELICOPTER

Die cast metal Army model, 9¼ in. long. Yellow with clear plastic bubble and colorful decals. Two revolving nickel plated rotor blades that fold. Black rubber wheels. Individually boxed; 1 doz. per ctn.; wt. 13 lbs. Retail price $1.49.

### 801 DUMP TRUCK

Strong die cast metal. Red cab and chassis with aluminum trim. Yellow dump bed controlled by side lever. Black realistically treaded tires. Length 10 in. Individually boxed; 1 doz. per ctn.; wt. 16 lbs. Sell fast at retail for $1.49.

### 802 TRACTOR TRUCK

Two grand toys! Blue flat bed metal truck carries separate tractor. Black treaded tires on both vehicles. Truck length 10¼ in. The pair in one box; 1 doz. boxes per ctn.; wt. 16 lbs. Retail price $1.49.

NEW

### 881 P-38

Accurate die cast metal model of the famous World War II fighter. Red with authentic decal markings, 9 in. long, 13 in. wingspread. Two revolving propellers, retractable landing gear and nose wheel. Eye catching, durable, wonderful! Individually packed in display box carefully designed to sell the P-38 on sight. Ctn. contains 1 doz. boxes and weighs 20 lbs. A new sales leader at $1.98 retail.

# Hubley® TOYS–'62

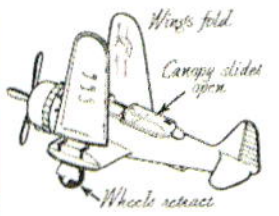


### 493 School Bus

Sturdy metal bus official school bus yellow with trim of aluminum, black and red. Black tires. Length 9½ in. Cutouts of driver and children included for realistic play. Individually packaged in colorful box; 1 doz. per ctn.; wt. 14 lbs. Retail price $1.98.

### 495 Navy Fighter-Bomber

Die cast metal. Dark blue top, light blue underside and wings. Red cowl, Air Force insignia. Clear plastic sliding bubble encloses cockpit. Revolving prop, folding wings, retractable landing gear. Length 10 in. Packed 1 in a box; 1 doz. per ctn.; wt. 20 lbs. Retail $1.98.

### 496 Tractor

Durable and accurately detailed in die cast metal. Bright red with aluminum trimming. Steering wheel turns front wheels. Large treaded black tires. Length 9¼ in. Individually boxed; 1 doz. per ctn.; wt. 29 lbs. Retail price $1.98.

### 655 Country Sedan and Boat with Trailer

Authentic scale model of 1962 Ford Country Sedan with yellow metal boat trailer and red and white plastic boat that actually floats. Overall length 17½ in. Individually packed in a colorful box; 1 doz. per ctn.; wt. 12 lbs. Retail price, complete, $1.98.

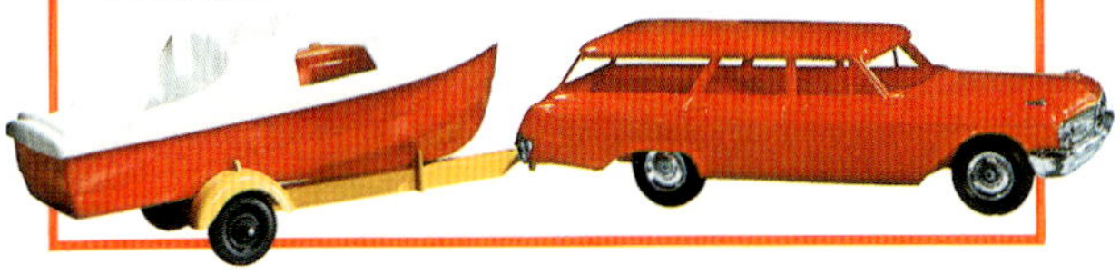



## Two NEW Mighty-Metal Toys with unlimited play value . . .

### 492 AUTO TRANSPORT

Strong, durable and workable metal car carrier with four plastic cars. Red trailer can be unhitched from cab to unload new cars. Special feature—metal ramp for loading and unloading. Overall length 14 in. Packed 1 in a colorful box; ½ doz. per ctn.; wt. 16 lbs. A bargain at $2.49 retail.

Packed in colorful NEW corrugated box complete with display base.

### 901 POWER SHOVEL

A BIG, new toy that really operates like the big shovel on major construction jobs. Almost 15 in. long, this durable metal cab and working boom are painted bright orange and black. Real rubber treads. Individually packed; ½ doz. per ctn.; wt. 18 lbs. Sure to win many friends at $2.98 retail.

Packed in colorful NEW corrugated box complete with display base.

SIDE LEVER OPERATES CRANE AND SCOOP

CAB ROTATES 360°

### THREE GREAT CONSTRUCTION TOYS

**$2.98 Retail**

**All new packaging**

#### 501 Tractor Loader

Realistic moving parts

True-to-life die cast tractor with aluminum loader mechanism and bucket. Tractor is orange, treaded tires are black. Steering wheel turns front wheels. Side lever raises and lowers loader and dumps bucket. Overall length 12¾ in. Individually packed in new display box; ½ doz. to a ctn.; wt. 15 lbs. Retail price $2.98.

#### 503 Road Grader

The best die cast grader on the market

Detailed die cast metal model, painted orange. Aluminum scraper blade adjusts. Steering lever controls front wheels. Independent rear wheels roll over rough terrain. Length 12¾ in. Individually packed in new display box; ½ doz. to a ctn.; wt. 15 lbs. Retail price $2.98.

#### 505 Front End Loader

A Hubley favorite for years!

Aluminum metal bucket scoops, raises, dumps. Realistic rubber treads roll back and forth. Accurate engine details contained in red tractor body. Loader operated by lever near driver's seat. Length 7¾ in. Individually packed in new display box; ½ doz. to a ctn.; wt. per ctn. 18 lbs. Retail price . . . for rapid turnover . . . $2.98.

NEW

AUTHORIZED Ford REPLICA

#### 508 FORD TRACTOR

Die cast scale model of new Ford Select-O-Speed Tractor. Red with gray trim. Spread wheels, black treaded rubber tires. Length 11 in. Actually steers. Authentic Ford decals on hood and fenders. Individually packed in new display box; ½ doz. to a ctn.; wt. 20 lbs. A big attraction at $3.98 retail.

Packed in colorful NEW corrugated box complete with display base.



## Hubley® TOYS–'62

NEW

#### 509 Ford 6000 Tractor

Authentic scale model of the new Ford 6000 Tractor reproduced in sturdy die-cast metal. Realistic engine details. Striking grey and red enamel. Nickel plated steering wheel operates "tricycle" type front wheels. Metal wheels with giant black treaded tires. Hitch for attaching accessories. Length 12 in. Packed 1 in a box; ½ doz. per ctn.: wt. 30 lbs. Suggested retail $4.98.

AUTHORIZED Ford REPLICA

Packed in colorful NEW corrugated box complete with display base.

ROCKS! ROLLS! RATTLES!

#### 952 The Official Mr. Magoo* Car

Mr. Magoo appears weekly on television all over the country, and his official car will be a fun toy in thousands of homes. It's a brightly colored metal action toy, 8½ in. long and 8¼ in. high. Battery operated. Crank controls backward and forward motion, while Mr. Magoo bounces up and down in his seat. Removable cloth top. Packed 1 in a bright "self-sell" box (batteries not included); 1 doz. per ctn.; wt. 20 lbs. Suggested retail price $4.98.

*Copyright 1961 U.P.A. Pictures, Inc.

#### 965 TIC-TOY® CLOCK

Family favorite! A complete sellout for three years, and millions of boys and girls are just becoming old enough to enjoy this classic toy. It actually runs as long as 14 hours on one winding. Spring driven. Color-keyed plastic parts are easy to assemble. Can be taken apart and put together repeatedly. For boys and girls 5 to 15 years of age. Height 11½ in.; width 8 in. Packed 1 per window box; ¼ doz. per ctn.; wt. 7 lbs. Retail price $5.95.





## Hubley® BOXED SETS–'62

***Durable and beautifully packaged for turnover and profit!***

NEW

#### No. 31 FARM SET

6 piece set with pick-up truck and orange tractor. Plow, spreader, cultipacker and wagon each attach to tractor. Colorful corrugated display box. Packed 1 set per box; ½ doz. sets per ctn.; wt. 17 lbs. Retail $2.98.

NEW

#### No. 42 AUTOMOTIVE SET

New 492 Auto Transport, M.G. car, tow truck and gasoline truck. All attractively assembled in colorful display box. One ctn. contains 6 boxes; ctn. wt. 30 lbs. Retail price $3.98.

NEW

#### No. 48 CONSTRUCTION SET

Brand new and beautiful! The set includes 801 Dump Truck, 505 Front End Loader and new metal flat bed trailer. The loader travels to the job site on the trailer! Each set packed in a colorful display box; ¼ doz. per ctn.; ctn. wt. 28 lbs. Retail price $4.98.

NEW

#### No. 43 MIGHTY-METAL ASSORTMENT

Realistic die cast metal trucks for all purposes—469 Log Truck, 470 Dump Truck, 471 Hook and Ladder, 474 Tractor with wagon. Complete set in a brightly printed window box for impulse purchase. One ctn. contains 6 boxes; ctn. wt. 35 lbs. Retail, per set, $3.98.

NEW

#### No. 49 AIRPORT SET

Brightly painted metal set consists of the P-38 and P-40 fighter planes, the 403 Pick-up Truck and the 402 Fire Engine for emergencies. Also includes 406 Gasoline Truck and 432 M.G. Packaged in big corrugated display box; ¼ doz. per ctn., ctn. wt. 30 lbs. Retail price per set $4.98.



#### No. 57 FARM SET

This perennial favorite contains the new 508 Ford tractor with wagon, plow and two crates of chickens and ducks. Full-color corrugated box provides barn and barnyard background. ¼ doz. per ctn., wt. 16 lbs. Retail, per set, $5.95.

NEW

#### No. 60 CONSTRUCTION SET

4 big metal toys to do a big building job. New Hubley 901 Power Shovel, 801 Dump Truck, tractor with large doughnut wheels and flat bed trailer. Packed complete in colorful display box; ¼ doz. per ctn.; ctn. wt. 18 lbs. Retail, per set, $7.95.

NEW

#### No. 69 ROAD BUILDING SET

Real buying value and play value in this giant set. Contains 503 Road Grader, the 505 Front End Loader, 801 Dump Truck and 901 Power Shovel. Complete set in a colorful display box; ¼ doz. per ctn.; wt. 22 lbs. Retail price, per set, $9.95.

NEW

#### No. 91 LARGE FARM SET

New model Ford 6000 tractor complete with plow, flat bed wagon and cultipacker (all of which can be hitched to tractor interchangeably). Packed in large corrugated display box; ¼ doz. per ctn.; ctn. wt. 25 lbs. Retail, $9.95.

## THE BEST NEW TOY FOR '62

Hubley® golferino™

### Tabletop Miniature Golf Course! Fun for All the Family!

GOLFERINO is a new, exciting game of skill—a complete 9-hole miniature golf course realistically molded in sturdy plastic, with bridges, tunnels and exciting hazards. Mom, Dad and the kids take turns pressing the control button to make the golfer swing his club and hit the ball. When the ball goes in the final hole, (No. 9), a bell rings and a gold-colored loving cup pops out of the ground! The plastic base, size 22¼ in. x 23½ in., can be placed on floor or table. Rules and scorecards furnished. It's a great game for one player or any number. Packed in this brightly printed box that tells its own sales story. Stock No. 995.

### Millions will see GOLFERINO on TV

To popularize the new game and spread the good news, Hubley will introduce it on television in selected key marketing areas this Fall and conduct a major publicity campaign across the nation throughout the year.

***Golferino!*** *The new game the entire family can enjoy!*





## THE BEST NEW ART-CRAFT FOR '62

*Exciting! Unique! Decorative!*

### Americana GOLDEN GALLERY SERIES by Hubley®

1001—Locomotive

1002—American Eagle

1003—Sailing Ship

Now anyone can have the thrill of making a beautiful picture with the rich appearance and characteristics of antique gold! The six pictures in the Golden Gallery series are constructed of pre-formed lustrous plastic parts, which may be antiqued with lampblack and mounted in keyed positions on a strong, stiff background board. Sturdy black frame (13½" x 19½") is included in kit. Simple instructions assure satisfying professional results. Each kit contains sheet of plastic parts, lampblack, cotton applicators and polishers, cement, background board and frame. Picture of each subject on cover of colorful box. Individually boxed; 6 per ctn.; wt. 14 lbs. Suggested retail price, $4.00.

1001—Locomotive
1002—American Eagle
1003—Sailing Ship
Also available:
1004—Floral Arrangement
1005—Antique Fire Engine
1006—Horse and Carriage



## Hubley® HOBBY LINE—'62

### Hubley Metal Car Kits—the kits of the future!

*Advertised in leading national magazines*

Metal car kits have become extremely popular among the most avid and enthusiastic model car builders. Young and old alike enjoy the screw driver assembly of these authentic scale models. Kits contain die cast body, chassis, running gear, steering mechanism, detailed engine parts, plastic seats and accessories, real rubber tires and decals for customizing. Complete instruction sheet including how to get real automotive paint job finish. These masterpieces are made of metal like the original cars, are extremely durable and will last for years. Exceptional attention to detail makes every Hubley Metal Kit a "must" for collectors.

#### 853K 1932 Ford Custom Roadster

Build your own Hot Rod in metal. A beautifully designed scale model over 7 inches long. Packed 1 doz. per ctn.; wt. 19 lbs. $2.98 retail.

#### 854K Model A Ford Roadster

One of the most popular cars of the late "twenties" and early "thirties." With removable top and rumble seat. Packed 1 doz. per ctn.; wt. 22 lbs. $2.98 retail.

#### 855K Model A Pick-Up Truck

Another famous Ford, the mate to the Roadster. Removable top and truck body. Packed 1 doz. per ctn.; wt. 22 lbs. $2.98 retail.

#### 856K Model A Phaeton

Four-door Ford with removable top. The Phaetons, used by police departments in the "twenties" have again been popularized by recent TV shows. Packed 1 doz. per ctn.; wt. 19 lbs. $2.98 retail.

853K

854K

855K

856K



#### 857K Model A Town Sedan

This beauty in the Model A series has complete metal body, side mounted spare tire, and luggage rack and trunk in rear. Individually cellophane wrapped, packed 1 doz. per ctn.; wt. 20 lbs. Retail price $2.98.

857K

#### 858K Model A Station Wagon

Marvelous detail! Wood-grain labels simulate side paneling. Additional rear seat and hinged tail gate. Individually cellophane wrapped; 1 doz. per ctn.; wt. 22 lbs. Retail price $3.49.

858K

NEW

#### 859K 1930 Packard Sport Phaeton

The largest, most complete metal model kit ever—more than 135 pieces in this 9½ in. model. Individual door handles, movable rear seat cowl (note color view above), pressure sensitive white walls and 6 open wire wheels! Side panel upholstery! Worm and sector gear steering! Under the removable hood are more than 14 detailed engine pieces. Individually cellophane wrapped; ½ doz. per ctn.; wt. 13 lbs. Retail price $4.98.

#### No. 142A Sensational Packard Display

Boost your sales with a colorful counter display, complete with a beautifully finished built-up model of the 1930 Packard Sport Phaeton. Offered with only ½ doz. Packard kits, wt. 15 lbs.

## *Customizing Kits, $1.49 and $1.69!* *Superbly Molded Scale Models!*

**(A) 163K—1962 Ford Country Sedan** NEW
(see illus.)
The latest station wagon model in the popular "Ford Family of Fine Cars." A must for all collectors.
Packed 1 doz. per shipping ctn.; wt. 10 lbs.
Suggested retail price $1.49.

**(B) 157K—Rolls-Royce Silver Cloud Sedan**
A beauty, 8½ in. long. Hood lifts to reveal famed Rolls-Royce engine and trunk with movable lid houses spare tire. (No customizing parts.)
Packed 1 doz. per ctn.; wt. 9 lbs.
Suggested retail price $1.69.

**(C) 151K—Triumph TR-3 Grand Touring**
Packed 1 doz. per ctn.; wt. 8 lbs.
Suggested retail price $1.49.

**(D) 152K—Mercedes-Benz 300SL Convertible**
Packed 1 doz. per ctn.; wt. 9 lbs.
Suggested retail price $1.49.

**(E) 159K—Renault Dauphine**
Packed 1 doz. per ctn.; wt. 8 lbs.
Suggested retail price $1.49.

**(F) 150K—Triumph TR-3 Convertible**
Packed 1 doz. per ctn.; wt. 8 lbs.
Suggested retail price $1.49.

**(G) 158K—Metropolitan Convertible**
Packed 1 doz. per ctn.; wt. 7 lbs.
Suggested retail price $1.49.

**(H) 153K—Mercedes-Benz 300 SL Hardtop**
Packed 1 doz. per ctn.; wt. 9 lbs.
Suggested retail price $1.49.

### INTERNATIONAL CAR KITS BY HUBLEY

Eight authentic 1/24 scale models.

Superbly molded in sturdy polystyrene. The cars are well known around the world and are prized by collectors and model builders who desire quality and attention to detail.

All kits come equipped with white sidewall tires, large decals and many chromed customizing parts in addition to the standard equipment.

# Hubley® HOLSTER SETS—'62

### *A Complete New Line . . . All New Window Box Packaging*

### *These Unbeatable Values*

## $1 genuine leather singles and doubles $1

**5210**—Genuine leather, tubular construction for left or right hand draw. Saddle color with black and ivory screening. Plastic Panther Medallion on pocket. Gun is #218 Rodeo. Individually packed in attractive window box, 2 doz. per ctn., wt. 16 lbs.

**5214**—Genuine leather, bright yellow screening on black. Pistol is #218 Rodeo. Packed individually in window box for easy display. 2 doz. boxes per ctn., wt. 20 lbs.

**5216**—MP Adventure Set—Genuine leather, white holster with black screening. Complete with #211 Pet Pistol, billy stick and whistle. Skin packed on attractive card suitable for racking. 1 doz. cards per ctn., wt. 5 lbs.

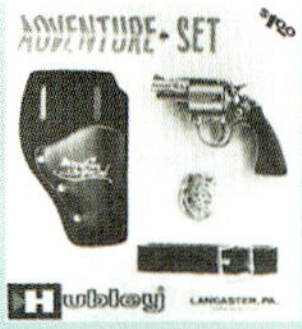


**5217**—Detective Special Adventure Set—Genuine leather holster, black with ivory screening. Includes nickel plated #241 Detective Special and "private eye's" whistle. Individually skin packed on card. 1 doz. per ctn., wt. 5 lbs.

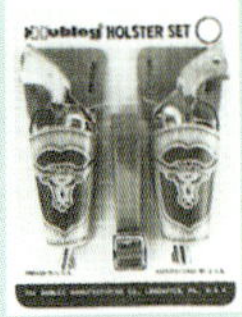


**6210**—Genuine leather, assorted colors—black with ivory screening, saddle with brown and buff with black. #211 Pet pistols. Skin packed on eye-catching card, 2 doz. per ctn., wt. 10 lbs.

**5218**—Marine Corps Adventure Set — Genuine leather holster, brown with ivory screening. Contains whistle and #242 Colt Automatic. Skin packed, 1 doz. cards per ctn., wt. 5 lbs.

**5219**—Western Adventure Set—Holster is genuine leather, brown with white screening. Belt has large trophy buckle. #218 Rodeo pistol. Individually skin packed on card, 1 doz. per ctn., wt. 10 lbs.

**6211**—Genuine leather, assorted colors—black, brown and saddle with white screening. #211 Pet pistols. Skin packed on card, 2 doz. cards per ctn., wt. 10 lbs.

**0110**—Spur Set—Genuine leather boot straps with shiny metal "Star" spurs. Assorted black and natural. Individually boxed pairs, 2 doz. per ctn., wt. 6 lbs.

**5200 Assortment**—Contains ½ doz. each Adventure Set series—Nos. 5216, 5217, 5218 and 5219. Packed one assortment per ctn., wt. 12 lbs.



1962

# Hubley® HOLSTER SETS—'62

## *5 Singles . . . . . . . . . . . . $2.00 each*

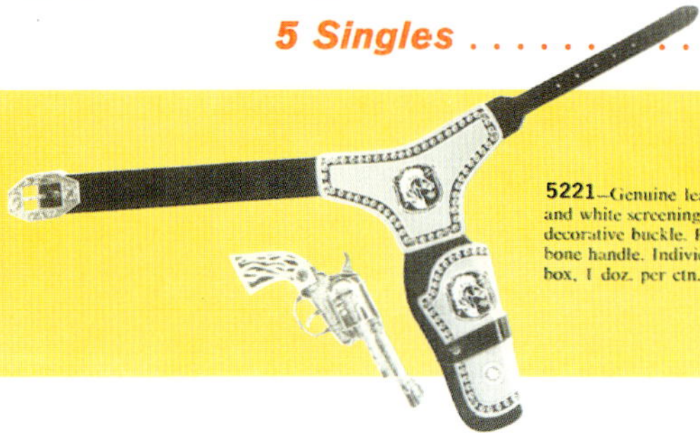

**5221**—Genuine leather, black and tan with black and white screening. Western cross strap on pocket, decorative buckle. Popular 250 Texan, Jr. gun with bone handle. Individually packaged in new window box, 1 doz. per ctn., wt. 13 lbs.

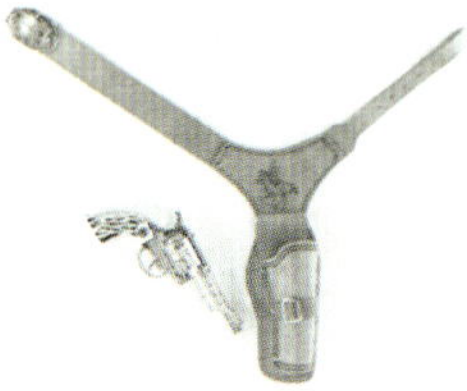

**5220**—Genuine leather, buff colored holster with brown screening. Has two piece Western foldover with cross strap and decorative buckle. Bone handled #250 Texan, Jr. pistol. This "authentic" Western holster is low slung for fast draw. Individually packed in window display box, 1 doz. per ctn., wt. 13 lbs.

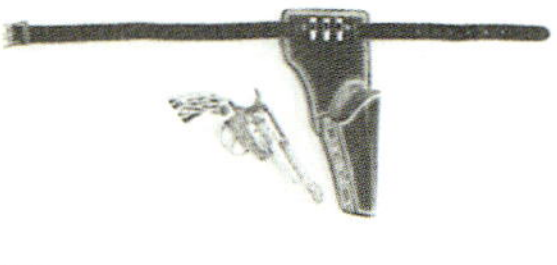

**5223**—Genuine leather, black with white screening on pocket and hanger. Three bullets and #250 Texan, Jr. pistol with bone handle. Packaged in new window box, 1 doz. boxes per ctn., wt. 13 lbs.

**5222**—Genuine leather, tubular design, assorted black and saddle colors with metal conchas and rope spot on pocket. Hubley Trophy buckle. 250 Texan, Jr. gun with bone handle. Skin packed individually on attractive card, 1 doz. per ctn., wt. 13 lbs.

**5229** Genuine leather black shoulder holster, richly embossed. Includes Trooper pistol. Skin packed on attractive card for easy display and fast selling, 1 doz. cards per ctn., wt. 12 lbs.



## *5 Doubles . . . . . . . . . $2.00 each*

**6221** Top grain leather, richly embossed Miniature holster. Natural color. Contains #211 Pet pistols. Neatly packaged in individual window box. 2 doz. boxes per ctn., wt. 10 lbs.

**6220** Genuine leather, assorted black and dark brown colors with shearling cross straps and conchas. Snap-on leather cuffs. #211 Pet guns. All pre-packaged in new window box. 2 doz. boxes per ctn., wt. 11 lbs.

**6223**—Genuine leather, tubular design, black with turquoise and ivory screening and embossed horsehead. Guns are top selling #218 Rodeos. Packaged in attractive window display box. 2 doz. per ctn., wt. 21 lbs.

**6224** Genuine leather holster. Color-black with yellow screening. Complete with #218 Rodeo pistols. Skin packed on colorful new self-selling card. 2 doz. cards per ctn., wt. 21 lbs.

**6113**—Genuine leather, tubular designed Miniature holster. Decorated with assorted color screening on black pocket. Includes cowboy lariat, bandana and keeper, and #211 Pet pistols. Individually skin packed on attractive card, 2 doz. cards per ctn., wt. 10 lbs.

# Hubley® HOLSTER SETS-'62

## 4 Doubles
## $3.00 each

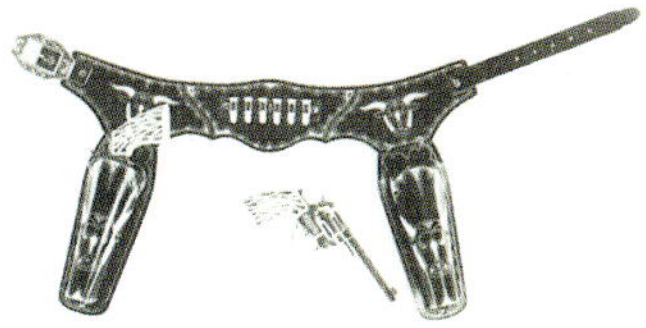

**6230**–Genuine leather tubular type holster. Black with red and white screening. Decorative buckle and six bullets. #232 Cowpoke guns with bone handles. Individually packed in window box, 1 doz. per ctn., wt. 22 lbs.

**6239**–Holster Set. 6230 skin packed on large colorful display card for racking. 1 doz. skin packed cards per ctn., wt. 22 lbs.

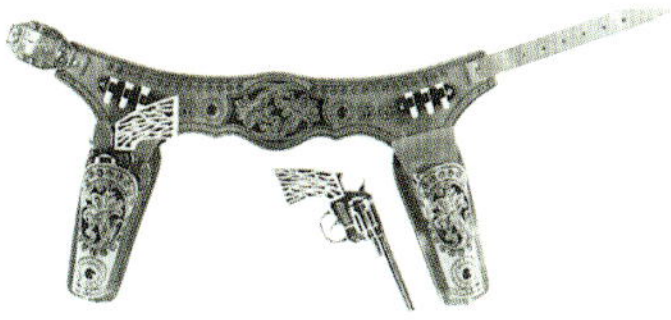

**6232**–Genuine leather tubular holster with stand-away pocket. Beige with black screening. Six bullets and #232 Cowpoke pistols with bone handles. Individually window boxed. 1 doz. boxes per ctn., wt. 22 lbs.

**6236** –Holster set 6232 skin packed on large colorful display card for racking. 1 doz. skin packed cards per ctn., wt. 22 lbs.

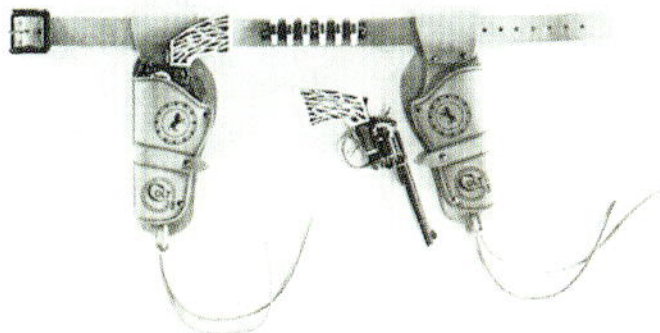

**6233**–Genuine leather, buff with brown screening. Large buckle. Western cross straps, six bullets. #232 Cowpoke pistols with bone handles. Leather tie strings. Individually packed in window box, 1 doz. per ctn., wt. 22 lbs.

**6231**–Top Grain leather. Natural color with richly embossed pockets, leather leg ties, and six bullets. #232 Cowpoke guns with bone handles. Individually window boxed, 1 doz. per ctn., wt. 22 lbs.

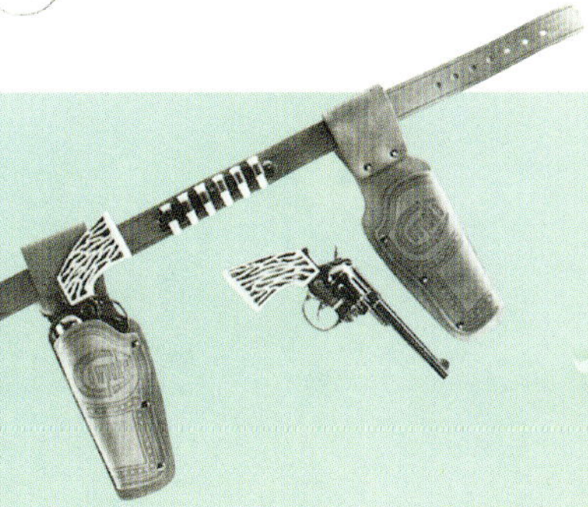



## 3 Singles
## $3.00 each

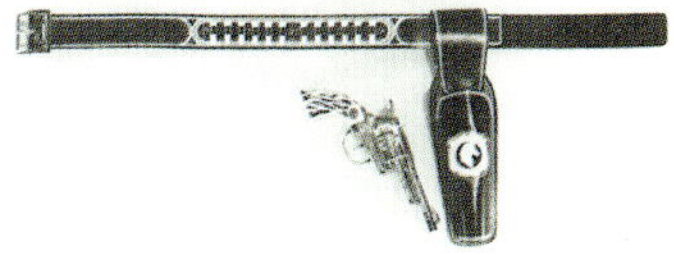

**5230**–Genuine leather holster, tubular construction for left or right hand draw, black with yellow and red screening. Beautiful plastic horsehead medallion on pocket, plus leather leg ties. Contains twelve bullets and #250 Texan, Jr. gun with bone handle. Individually boxed in "see through" window box, 1 doz. per ctn., wt. 18 lbs.

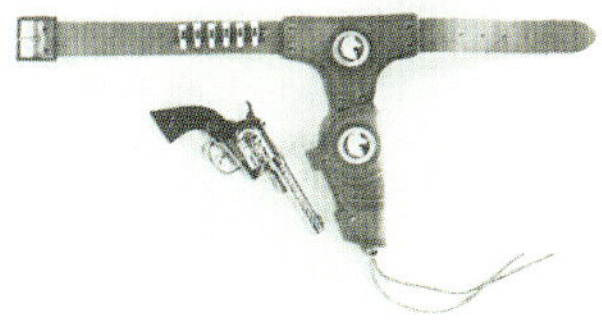

**5231**–Top grain leather, natural color holster with brown screening. Intricately tooled and embossed pocket with two horsehead medallions, leather leg tie, six bullets and #261 Ric-O-Shay Jr. gun. Large Western buckle on belt. Individually window boxed, 1 doz. per ctn., wt. 18 lbs.

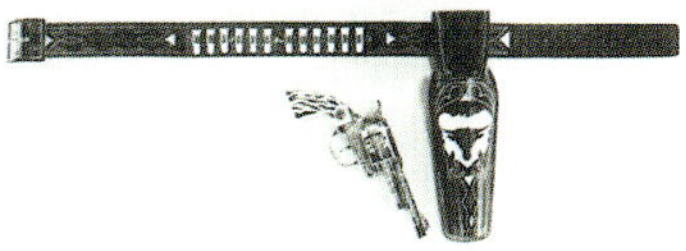

**5132**–Genuine leather, black with gay screening of orange, yellow and blue. Tubular designed with stand-away feature for fast draw. Twelve bullets, #250 Texan, Jr. gun with bone handle. Individually window boxed, 1 doz. per ctn., wt. 18 lbs.

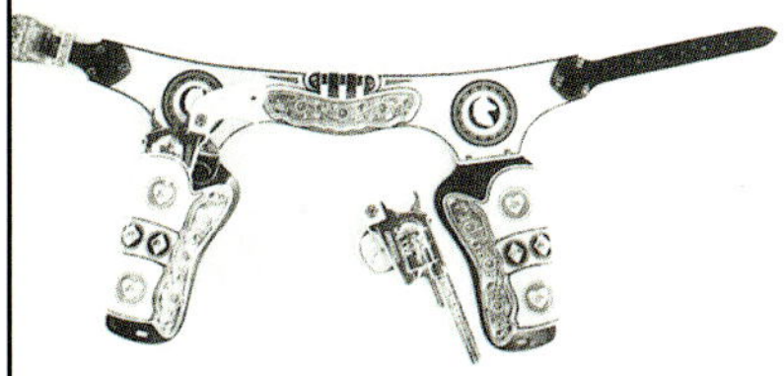

## 2 beauties
## $4.00 each

**6240**–Genuine leather, white and black with turquoise and black screening. Large trophy buckle, two horsehead medallions, and decorated with conchas and rope spots on pockets and belt. Leg ties and three bullets included. #248 Marshal guns. Individually boxed in window display box, 1 doz. per ctn., wt. 29 lbs.

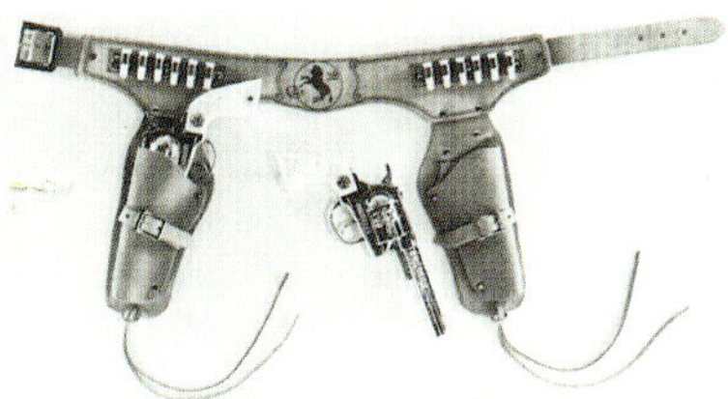

**6241**–Genuine leather, buff with brown screening. Western cross strap with buckle on pocket. Twelve bullets, leather leg ties and #248 Marshal guns. Individually window boxed, 1 doz. per ctn., wt. 29 lbs.

1962

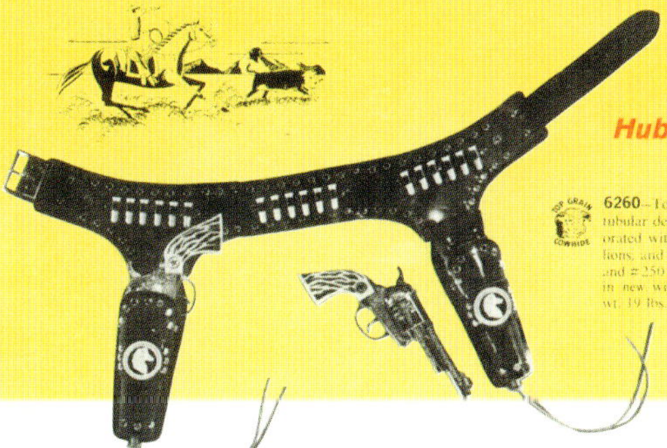

## Hubley's Finest . . .
## $6.00

**6260**–Top grain leather, saddle color, of tubular design with stand-away feature. Decorated with 54 spots, two horsehead medallions, and leather leg ties. Includes 18 bullets and #250 Texan, Jr. guns. Individually boxed in new window display box, ½ doz. per ctn., wt. 19 lbs.

## Many outstanding features...
## $5.00

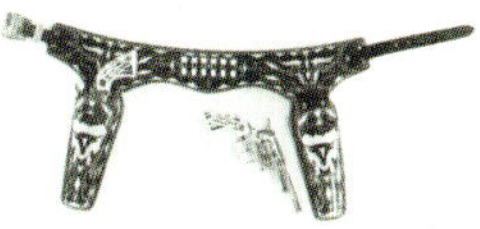

**6150**–Genuine leather, black with orange, blue, yellow and white screening. Tubular designed pocket with stand-away feature. Hubley Trophy buckle. Bone handled #250 Texan, Jr. guns and six bullets. Leather leg ties. Individually packed in new window display box, ½ doz. per ctn., wt. 18 lbs.

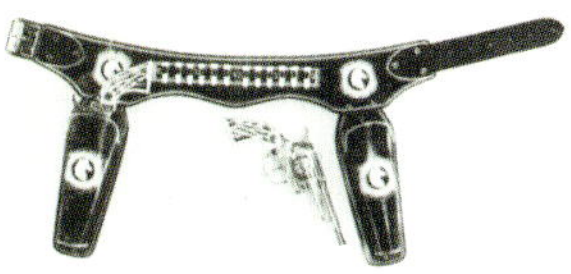

**6250**–Genuine leather, tubular designed holster. Black with yellow and red screening. Enhanced with four horsehead medallions and leather leg ties. Twelve bullets and #250 Texan, Jr. pistols with bone handles. Individually boxed in display box, ½ doz per ctn., wt. 18 lbs.

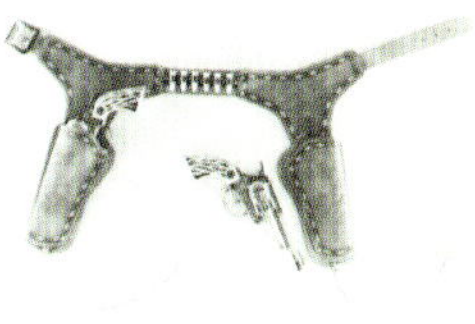

**6251**–Top grain natural leather, richly embossed and screened with large buckle. Six bullets and #250 Texan, Jr., guns with bone handles, leather leg ties. Packed individually in window display box, ½ doz. per ctn., wt. 19 lbs.

### Location of Hubley Offices and Representatives

**Home Office**
The Hubley Manufacturing Co.
110 Pitney Road
Lancaster, Pa.
EX 4-2691

**New England**
Mr. Gregory F. Kane
3 Maher Drive
Norwalk, Conn.
VI 7-5104

**Atlanta**
Mr. Edward V. Conrad
6910 Castleton Drive N.W.
Atlanta, Ga.
Blackburn 5-0681

**Chicago**
Mr. Robert L. Laughton
750 Monument Ave.
Barrington, Ill.
Dunkirk 1-1004

**Kansas City**
Mr. Richard S. Leedy
9716 Buena Vista
Overland Park, Kans.
Niagara 2-5250

**Houston**
Mr. Howard V. Campbell
2420 Washington Ave.
Houston, Texas
Capitol 4-2251 or Jackson 9-9480

**Rocky Mountain**
Leo A. Scherrer Co.
2840 W. 93rd St.
Seattle 7, Wash.
Sunset 3-2426

**California**
Mr. Harry H. Johnson, Jr.
11472 Gardenaire Lane
Garden Grove, Calif.
Lehigh 9-7629

**New York Office**
The Hubley Manufacturing Co.
Room 611 — 200 Fifth Ave.
New York 10, N. Y.
OR 5-9343
Mr. Donald A. Bolin
Mr. Gary Warren

## THE HUBLEY MANUFACTURING CO., LANCASTER, PA., USA

101-2-62

Printed in U.S.A.

# 1963

T V TOYS
GUNS
HOLSTERS
MIGHTY-METAL TOYS
CRAFTS
METAL CAR KITS
Hubley®
1963

## Network and Spot TV

Hubley's NEW

# ·RAZZ·MA·TAZZ·™ PLAYER PIANO

***The happy tinkling sound of the old-time music hall!***

***Helps kids acquire a sense of rhythm and it's fascinating to grownups, too!***

Play from the time you sit down at this piano and no mistakes either! Each time the keyboard is struck a different note plays; continued action produces a familiar tune. Sing along with RAZZ-MA-TAZZ!

Sturdy red plastic molded case and working parts insure many hours of play for little fingers. 14″ wide by 10½″ high, 6″ deep with see-through front to watch the key action. It's fascinating!

EASY-TO CHANGE ROLLS. Two sturdy molded plastic rolls furnished, each with 6 tunes, all familiar favorites. Roll is placed in the back of RAZZ-MA-TAZZ and is secured in spring holder. Snaps out quickly, easily. No paper to tear!

Packed in brightly printed box that tells the sales story.

**Plays these 12 tunes**

Lazy Mary
Sing a Song of Sixpence
Jack and Jill
Jolly Old St. Nicholas
Jingle Bells
Pop Goes the Weasel
Ring Around the Rosy
Twinkle, Twinkle Little Star
Old MacDonald
Merrily We Roll Along
London Bridge
Camp Town Races

**Network and Spot TV will sell these new items!**

**Powerful network and spot TV will carry the sales story of these items into millions of homes this Fall.**

*RAZZ-MA-TAZZ is a trademark of The Hubley Manufacturing Co.

## Behind these NEW ITEMS!



# JUNGLE HUNT™ by Hubley

## A FUN-GAME of SKILL for Hunters of all ages!

Let's go on a big game hunt for Lions, Tigers, Hippos, Rhinos, and Gorillas! Here's the Jungle in durable, molded plastic with animals that move in and out of the "bush country" and a Hunter whom you control with the pistol grip in front.

You start the timer (red dial, right front) and the animals appear one by one for you to "kill" by carefully aiming the gun and pulling the trigger. Sound easy? Well, it's not, because the beasts do not always appear in the same order and sometimes they start out, see the hunter, and return to the bush, where you can't shoot them. When you make the kill, the animal falls over.

25″ by 22″ by 8″ packed in brightly printed box which carries the whole story.

*JUNGLE HUNT is a trademark of the Hubley Manufacturing Co.

Length of game is determined by adjusting timer.

**No. 996 JUNGLE HUNT, the big game sport.**

3

1963

## A Success in '62 . . . still going strong

***Tabletop Golf is great fun for the whole family***

***Some luck, Some skill***

***Keep score***



Hubley

# golferino™

Here's golf realism in miniature, to play on a table. Great in gameroom, kids' room, living room. It's a complete 9 hole golf course, with bridges, tunnels, sand traps, and the regulation exciting hazards. Mr. Golferino is directed to hit the ball by turning the red knob and he hits the ball when the lever is pressed down. When the game is complete and the ball goes into the 9th hole a bell rings and a gold colored loving cup pops out of the ground. (left in illustration). Sturdy plastic, 22¼″ x 23½″, packed in brightly printed box. Rules and score cards furnished. Packed 3 to a shipping carton.

**GOLFERINO will be seen on network and spot television this Fall. The national publicity campaign will continue through 1963, to back up the TV and help your sales.**

*GOLFERINO is a trademark of The Hubley Manufacturing Co.

**No. 995 GOLFERINO, a game for the entire family**

# Hubley® 1963 Toys

***Low end toys in metal and plastic.***
***Sales builders for bin-ends and check-out counters.***

### PLASTIC

**309 Tractor**

Red, yellow or orange with aluminum trim. Polyethylene wheels. Length 4¾ in. Packed 12 in a box; 3 doz. per ctn.; wt. 7 lbs. Suggested list price 29¢.*

**310 Motorcycle**

Red or green motorcycle, black rider. Rubber wheels. Length 5 in. Packed 12 in a box; 3 doz. per ctn.; wt. 8 lbs. Suggested list price 29¢.

**311 Airplane**

Red and white. Insignia on wings with retractable landing gear. Rubber wheels. Length 5 in. Packed 12 in a box; 3 doz. per ctn.; wt. 5 lbs. Suggested list price 29¢.

*All list prices are furnished only for the identification of the products, and nothing in this catalogue should be regarded as an indication that the prices set forth are the usual retail prices. This material is sent to the retailer and/or distributor upon the express condition that it will not be used to represent usual selling prices."

### METAL

**401 Continental Sedan**

A 6 in. detailed die cast model of the Lincoln Continental. Blue with aluminum trim. Rubber tires. Individually bubble packed on colorful card; 1 doz. cards per ctn.; wt. 4 lbs. Suggested list price 39¢.

**402 Fire Engine**

6 in. red fire-pumper with aluminum trim. Rubber tires. Individually bubble packed on "self-seller" card; 1 doz. cards per ctn.; wt. 4 lbs. Suggested list price 39¢.

**403 Falcon Pick-Up Truck**

Turquoise reproduction of Ford's truck. Rubber tires. Aluminum bright work. Length 6 in. Individually bubble packed; 1 doz. cards per ctn.; wt. 6 lbs. Suggested list price 39¢.

**404 Ford 1934 Coupe**

Model B Ford V-8 in jade green. Rubber tires. Individually bubble packed; 1 doz. cards per ctn.; wt. 4 lbs. Suggested list price 39¢.

**405 Corvair Station Wagon**

Chevrolet's compact. About 6 in. long. Aluminum trim and rubber tires. Individually bubble packed; 1 doz. cards per ctn.; wt. 4 lbs. Suggested list price 39¢.

**406 Gasoline Truck**

Bright truck with aluminum trim. 6 in. long. Rubber tires. Individually bubble packed; 1 doz. cards per ctn.; wt. 4 lbs. Suggested list price 39¢.

**29 Mighty-Metal Assortment**

Four each of all 6 toys shown above. Individually skin packed on bright cards; total 2 doz.; shipping wt. 9 lbs. Suggested list price 39¢ each.

5

# Hubley 1963 Mighty-Metal Toys

***Durable die cast toys with amazing detail. Bright non-toxic paints and plenty of play features make these toys MOVE. Ready for display in colorful packages, they will increase volume and profits.***

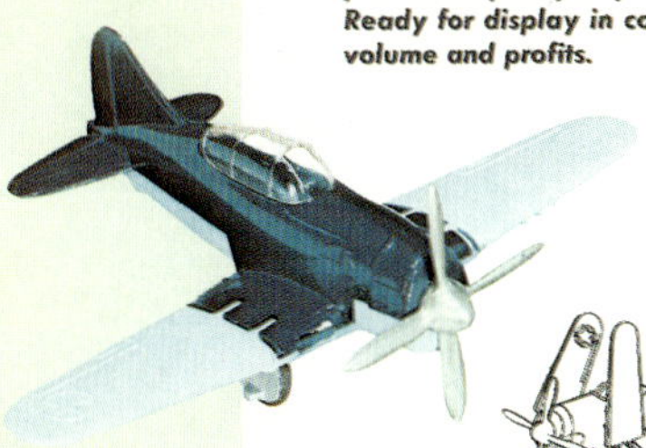

**467 Navy Fighter**

Hubley's popular airplane with plastic bubble over cockpit, rubber tires, folding wings, and retractable landing gear. Length 6½ in.; wing span 8¾ in. Packed individually in colorful box; 1 doz. per ctn.; wt. 8 lbs. Suggested list price $1.

**469 Log Truck**

The five 6 in. logs give this item real play appeal. Rubber tires. Length 10¾ in. Packed 1 in a box; 1 doz. per ctn.; wt. 15 lbs. Suggested list price $1.

**470 Dump Truck**

Side lever operated dump bed. 9¼ in. long. Rubber tires. Individually packed in brightly printed box. 1 doz. per ctn.; wt. 13 lbs. Suggested list price $1.

# Hubley 1963 Mighty-Metal Toys

**471 Hook and Ladder**

Kids love fire engines. Ladders connect and can be set up. Length 11¼ in. Rubber tires. Packed 1 in a box; 1 doz. to a carton. Wt. 13 lbs. Suggested list price $1.

**472 Tractor**

Realistic engine detail and heavy treaded tires make this an outstanding volume producer. Length 7¼ in. 1 in a box; 1 doz. per ctn.; wt. 16 lbs. Suggested list price $1.

**474 Farm Tractor and Wagon**

Detachable wagon. Realistic detail. Overall length 10¼ in. Packed in colorful box with cutouts for added play appeal. 1 doz. per ctn.; wt. 13 lbs. Suggested list price $1.

# Hubley 1963 Mighty-Metal Toy Sets

***These Mighty-Metal toys are brightly packaged on tamper-proof, sturdy, pre-priced cards for big volume in bin-end or rack sales. A "must" for the impulse sale.***

**721 Garage Set**

Set contains a Falcon Tow Truck, a '34 Ford Coupe, battery, pliers, screwdriver, and 2 car tires. Bubble packed. One doz. a ctn.; wt. 11 lbs. Suggested list price $1.

**722 Fire Engine Set**

Contains No. 402 Fire Engine, No. 405 Station Wagon, 2 plastic ladders, bucket, and plastic whistle. Bubble packed. 1 doz. to a ctn.; wt. 9 lbs. Suggested list price $1.

**723 Gas Station Set**

Consists of No. 401 Continental, No. 406 Gas Truck, gas pump, pliers, and screwdriver. Bubble packed. 1 doz. to a ctn., wt. 9 lbs. Suggested list price $1.

**762 Farm Set**

Set has No. 456 Tractor, cultipacker, chicken, pig, and duck. 1 doz. to a ctn.; wt. 11 lbs. Bubble packed. Suggested list price $1.

**763 Highway and Skyway Set**

No. 432 M. G. Sports Car and No. 430 Airplane. 1 doz. to a ctn.; wt. 10 lbs. Suggested list price $1.

**764 Traffic Control Set**

No. 310 Motorcycle, No. 432 M. G. Sports Car. Plastic whistle included. Bubble packed. 1 doz. to a ctn.; wt. 9 lbs. Suggested list price $1.

**#21 Assortment**

New set assortment. 3 each of the 721, 761, 765, and 766. Packed 1 assortment per ctn.; wt. 10 lbs.

**#22 Assortment**

New set assortment. 3 each of the 722, 723, 764, 767. Packed 1 assortment per ctn.; wt. 10 lbs.

**#38 Special Assortment**

12 each of Nos. 240S, 248S, 631O; 6 each of Nos. 5322, 721, 762; 9 each Nos. 765, 767 plus rack. Packed 1 assortment per ctn.; wt. 60 lbs.

## NEW Sets

**765 Continental and Racer Set**

Set has 401 Continental, Racer, and Trailer. Trailer holds racer and hooks to car. Bubble packed. 1 doz. to a ctn.; wt. 10 lbs. Suggested list price $1.

**766 Train Set**

Set contains engine and tender which hook together. Bubble packed. 1 doz. to a ctn.; wt. 6 lbs. Suggested list price $1.

**767 Cub and Racer Set**

Piper cub and racer. Bubble packed. 1 doz. to a ctn.; wt. 10 lbs. Suggested list price $1.

# Hubley 1963

**761 P-40 Plane**

World War II favorite. 7½ in. long with wingspread of 8 in. Rubber tires. Decals furnished. Individually bubble packed: 1 doz. per ctn.; wt. 7 lbs. Suggested list price $1.

**801 Dump Truck**

Dump body raises and lowers using side lever. Black treaded tires. Realistic detail. Length 10 in. Individually boxed; 1 doz. per ctn.; wt. 16 lbs. Suggested list price $1.49.

**Hubley® 1963** Mighty-Metal Toys

**483 Helicopter**

Clear plastic bubble, folding rotor blades, and rubber wheels, make this 9¼ in. helicopter a real sales winner. Individually boxed; 1 doz. per ctn.; wt. 13 lbs. Suggested list price $1.49.

**495 Navy Fighter-Bomber**

A sales leader for years. Retractable wheels, revolving prop, sliding plastic canopy, folding wings, rubber tires, and realistic detail. Length 10 in. Packed 1 per display box; 1 doz. per ctn.; wt. 20 lbs. Suggested list price $1.98.

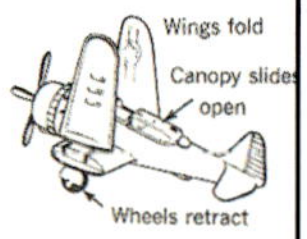

Front wheels steer.

**496 Tractor**

Detailed engine, actual steering, and heavy treaded rubber tires. Length 9¼ in. Individually boxed; 1 doz. per ctn.; wt. 29 lbs. Suggested list price $1.98.



**Hubley® 1963** Mighty-Metal Toys

**881 P-38**

Bright, realistic World War II fighter with lots of sales punch. Retractable rubber tires, props that spin, and accurate detail make this 9 in. beauty a sure winner. Packed in colorful display box. 1 doz. boxes to ctn. Weight 20 lbs. Suggested list price $1.98.

**501 Tractor Loader**

Steering wheel moves front wheels; side lever raises, lowers, and dumps the bucket; rubber tires with heavy treading. 12¾ in. long. Individually packed in colorful corrugated box. ½ doz. to ctn.; wt. 18 lbs. Suggested list price $2.98.

**492 Auto Transport**

Beautiful metal car transport with many play features. Four plastic cars can be loaded and unloaded on metal ramp. Trailer and cab detach. 14 in. long. Packed 1 in a colorful corrugated box with display base. 1 doz. per ctn.; wt. 29 lbs. Suggested list price $2.98.

1963

**Hubley® 1963** Mighty-Metal Toys

*True-to-life realism that kids go for!*

**503 Road Grader**

Independent front and rear suspension for rough terrain, adjustable blade, steering lever moves front wheels, and highly detailed white-walled tires. 12¾ in. long. Individually packed in colorful box. ½ doz. to a ctn.; wt. 15 lbs. Suggested list price $2.98.

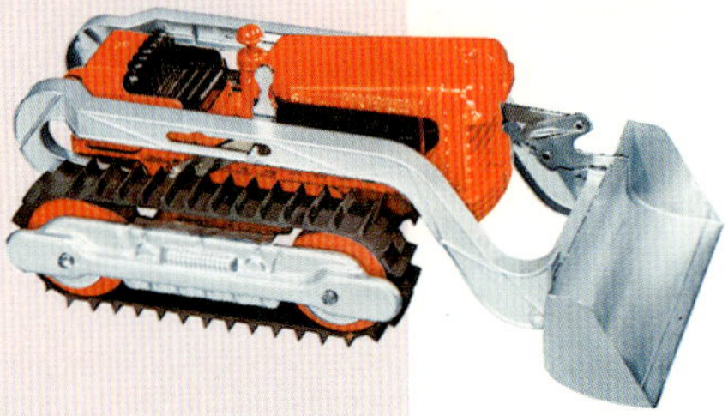

**505 Front End Loader**

Moves on rubber treads and has lever to raise, lower, and dump bucket. Realistic engine detail. 7¾ in. long. Individually packed in brightly colored box. ½ doz. per ctn.; wt. 18 lbs. Suggested list price $2.98.

**901 Power Shovel**

Scoops like its big brother. Cab rotates 360° and shovel rolls on rubber treads. 15 in. long. Individually packed in colorful corrugated box. ½ doz. per ctn.; wt. 18 lbs. Suggested list price $2.98.

**Hubley® 1963** Mighty-Metal Toys

*Farm Toys Exact in Detail*
*Good for Year Round Sales*

AUTHORIZED Ford REPLICA

NEW

**508 Ford 4000 Tractor**

Authentic scale model of the new Ford 4000 Tractor. Steering wheel actually moves front wheels. Heavy treaded rubber tires. Realistic detail including Ford decals. Length 11 in. Individually boxed; ½ doz. per ctn.; wt. 20 lbs. Suggested list price $3.98.

**509 Ford 6000 Tractor**

Authentic scale model of the Ford 6000 Tractor. This sturdy die cast model moves on deep treaded rubber tires and can actually be steered. Striking detail. Hitch for attaching accessories. Length 12 in. Packed 1 in a colorful corrugated display box. ½ doz. per ctn.; wt. 30 lbs. Suggested list price $5.98.

AUTHORIZED Ford REPLICA

# Hubley 1963 Mighty-Metal Toys

***A BRAND NEW LINE . . . of giant size, handsome construction toys, loaded with realism, play value, and best of all, durability.***

NEW

**882 Pickup Truck**
Sturdy pickup with realistic detailing. Deep treaded rubber white-wall tires. Hitch for attaching other Hubley items. 12 in. long. Individually packaged in colorful corrugated box. 1 doz. boxes per ctn.; wt. 30 lbs. Suggested list price $2.49.

NEW

**902 Dump Truck**
Heavy bodied dump with dual rear wheels and movable tailgate. Deep treaded rubber white-wall tires. Dump body operates from lever on side. 11 in. long. Individually packaged in colorful corrugated box. ½ doz. boxes per ctn.; wt. 20 lbs. Suggested list price $2.98.

NEW

**903 Bulldozer**
Adjustable scraper blade that raises and lowers. Moves on rubber treads. Careful detailing to look like real thing. 8¾ in. long. Individually packaged in colorful corrugated box. ½ doz. boxes per ctn.; wt. 15 lbs. Suggested list price $2.98.

4

# Hubley 1963 Mighty-Metal Toys

NEW

**926 Tow Truck**
Mighty-Metal at its best. Hook is operated by crank on right. Brake on left holds hook in place when towing. Deep tread rubber tires. 12 in. long. Individually packaged in colorful corrugated box. ½ doz. per ctn.; wt. 20 lbs. Suggested list price $3.69.

NEW

**927 Stake Truck with Trailer**
Careful detailing, sturdy construction, deep-tread rubber, white wall tires, and detachable trailer. Loaded with play features. 20½ in. long. Individually packaged in colorful corrugated box. ½ doz per ctn.; wt. 25 lbs. Suggested list price $3.98.

NEW

**953 Tractor with Trailer Dump**
Dump body has lever on side which automatically dumps contents by spring action. Dual wheels on trailer and truck. Deep tread rubber white wall tires. 16 in. long. Individually packaged in colorful corrugated box. ½ doz. per ctn.; wt. 24 lbs. Suggested list price $4.98.

# Hubley 1963 Mighty-Metal Toy

NEW

**966 Flat Bed with Shovel**
Truck, Flat bed Trailer, and Hubley's popular #901 Power Shovel. Deep tread rubber white wall tires. Shovel actually shovels and moves on rubber treads. 20 in. long. Individually boxed in colorful corrugated box. ¼ doz. per ctn.; wt. 16 lbs. Suggested list price $5.95.

**965 Tic-Toy Clock**
Colorful, bright and tremendously popular for 4 years. Actually runs as long as 14 hours, on one winding. Spring driven. Take apart and put together repeatedly using color-keyed parts and simple instruction sheet. For children 5 years and above. Height 11½ in. Width 8 in. Packed 1 per window box for easy counter display. ¼ doz. per ctn.; wt. 7 lbs. Suggested list price $5.95.

16

# Metal Toy Sets Hubley 1963

***Brightly packaged, popular sets for profit***

NEW

**16 Fighter Pilot Set**
Popular #761, #P-40 Plane, #242 Automatic pistol with genuine leather holster and belt. Brand new pilot wings and air award medal. Wings and medal have a clip for sweater or jacket. Packaged in colorful display box. 1 doz. boxes per ctn.; wt. 15 lbs. Suggested list price $1.98.

NEW

**19 Farm Set**
11 piece set including #456 tractor, plow, cultipacker, wagon, #403 Pick-up, chicken crate, 4 farm fowl, and pig. Colorfully packaged. ½ doz. boxes per ctn.; wt. 15 lbs. Suggested list price $2.98.

**48 Construction Set**
The set includes #801 Dump Truck, #505 Front End Loader and metal flat bed trailer. The loader travels to the job site on the trailer! Packed in a colorful display box; ¼ doz. per ctn.; ctn. wt. 16 lbs. Suggested list price $4.98.

17

# Hubley 1963 Metal Toy Sets

NEW

## 52 Aircraft Carrier Set

4 airplanes including #495 Fighter and 3 #430 planes. Hubley #242 Automatic pistol with leather holster and belt. New pilot wings and 2 hero medals. Wings and medals have clip for display on jacket or sweater. Packaged in colorful display box. ½ doz. per ctn.; wt. 25 lbs. Suggested list price $4.98.

## 57 Farm Set

This set contains the #508 Ford tractor with wagon, plow, and two crates of chickens and ducks. Full color corrugated box provides barn and barnyard background for extra play value. ¼ doz. per ctn.; wt. 16 lbs. Suggested list price $6.95

## 69 Road Building Set

Large items in a large set for large value. Contains #503 Road Grader; the #505 Front End Loader, #801 Dump Truck and #901 Power Shovel. Complete set in a colorful display box; ¼ doz. per ctn.; wt. 31 lbs. Suggested list price $9.95.

## 91 Large Farm Set

Authentic model of Ford 6000 tractor complete with plow, flat bed wagon and cultipacker (all hitch to tractor interchangeably). Packed in large corrugated display box; ¼ doz. per ctn.; wt. 25 lbs. Suggested list price $9.95.

# Hubley AMERICANA GOLDEN PICTURE KITS

Each kit consists of picture parts, background frame, cement and antiquing materials. Preformed deep dimension, plastic parts in lustrous golden finish are antiqued, cut out, assembled to keyed background and framed. 13½ x 19½" overall, with simple instructions to assure professional results. Picture of each subject on brightly printed window box. Individually packaged, six per carton, wt. 14 lbs. Suggested list price $3.98.

**#1020 Assortment**

1 each of the #1001, #1002, #1003, #1004, #1005, and #1006. Also 1 completed model for display. Wt. 16 lbs.

No. 1001 Locomotive

*Exciting and Unique!*

No. 1004 Floral Arrangement

No. 1002 American Eagle

*Beautify Den, Bedroom, Bar, Club*

No. 1005 Antique Fire Engine

No. 1003 Sailing Ship

*Fun for all ages*

No. 1006 Horse and Carriage

1963

# Hubley 1963 Metal Car Kits

**These classic metal models have become leaders in the model car field. Advertised in Boys' Life, Sports Illustrated, Mechanics Illustrated, Motor Trend, Car Craft, Sports Car Graphic, Hot Rod, and other consumer publications. Screwdriver assembly. Complete instructions furnished. Kits contain die cast body, chassis, running gear, steering mechanism, detailed engine parts, plastic seats and accessories, and rubber tires. Detail is exceptional. Finish with brush or spray paint.**

NEW

## 850K Model A Roadster

This classic has white walls and can be built with top up or down. Individually packed in cellophane wrapped, colorful box. 1 doz. per ctn.; wt. 22 lbs. Suggested list price $2.98.

## 855K Model A Pick-up Truck

Open truck bed adds play features to this detailed truck. Another Ford masterpiece with removable top. Individually packed in colorful box. 1 doz. per ctn.; wt. 22 lbs. Suggested list price $2.98.

## 856K Model A Phaeton

Removable top. This is a beautiful 4 door classic popularized by TV shows. Individually packed in cellophane wrapped, colorful box. 1 doz. per ctn.; wt. 19 lbs. Suggested list price $2.98.

## 857K Model A Town Sedan

One of the hard top models in the line. Complete metal body, luggage rack and trunk. Individually packaged in cellophane wrapped, colorful box. 1 doz. per ctn.; wt. 20 lbs. Suggested list price $2.98.

NEW

## 861K Model A Ford Coupe

Authentically detailed engine with real radiator hose and fan that turns. Movable rumble seat and white wall tires. Individually packaged in cellophane wrapped, colorful box. 1 doz. per ctn.; wt. 22 lbs. Suggested list price $2.98.



*Precision castings, easy assembly, authentic detail.*

# Hubley 1963

## 858K Model A Station Wagon

Rounding out the Model A collection is this classic. Woodgrain, 4 doors, luggage rack. Individually cellophane wrapped in colorful box. 1 doz. per ctn.; wt. 22 lbs. Suggested list price $3.49.

## 859K 1930 Packard Sport Phaeton

135 pieces. The finest detailing from bumper to bumper. Movable rear seat cowl, chromed mirrors, door handles, and accessories. White walls. 6 open spoke wheels. Individually cellophane wrapped in colorful box. ½ doz. per ctn.; wt. 13 lbs. Suggested list price $4.98.

NEW

## 860K 1930 Packard Roadster

White walls, chassis and motor detail are exact to the "nth"; fan that turns, real radiator hose, luggage rack, 6 spoked wheels, chrome accessories. Individually cellophane wrapped in colorful box. ½ doz. per ctn.; wt. 13 lbs. Suggested list price $4.98.

## 147A Packard Roadster Assortment

Colorful, counter display and beautifully finished built-up model offered with only ½ dozen Packard Roadster Kits. Weight 15 lbs.

NEW

## 862K 1932 Chevy Roadster

A wonderfully authentic model of this Classic Roadster. 6 rubber tires (white walls), chrome hood vents, door handles, headlights, cowl lights, and windshield frame. Individual chrome hub caps. Rumble seat. Luggage rack. Hood lifts off. Individually wrapped in cellophane wrapped colorful box. 1 doz. per ctn. 24 lbs. Suggested list price $3.49.

## 149A Chevy Roadster Assortment

More sales appeal with a 862K Chevy built-up and counter display. All yours with order for ½ doz. Chevy Roadster kits. Wt. 14 lbs. Nationally advertised.

*Nationally Advertised*

# Hubley® 1963

*The 1963 Hubley line of pistols and rifles is again loaded with typical Hubley qualities . . . sturdy die-cast metal or high-impact plastic construction . . . careful assembly . . . bright packages and cards . . . features to attract kids of all ages. These qualities mean sales and high turnover and they in turn mean PROFIT!*

### 211 Pet

Automatic action, single shot. Length 6½ inches. Bright nickel finish. Finely detailed cross-hatching on handle. Packed 12 in a box; 3 doz. to a carton. Wt. 8 lbs. Suggested list price 25¢.

### 216R Chief

Automatic action, single shot. Length 7⅝ inches. Bright nickel finish. Handle integral with engraved stock and barrel. Packed 1 per Rack Card; 1 doz. per carton. Wt. 4 lbs. Suggested list price 49¢.

### 210R Dick

Repeater. Length 4⅝ in. Bright nickel finish. Left handle slides open for easy loading. Packed 1 per Rack Card; 1 doz. per carton. Wt. 4 lbs. Suggested list price 59¢.

**210S:** 1 per bubble pack card; 1 doz. per carton, wt. 4 lbs. Suggested list price 59¢.

### 218R Rodeo

Automatic action, single shot. Length 8¾ inches. Bright nickel finish with engraved stock and barrel. White handles. Packed 1 per Rack Card; 1 doz. per carton. Wt. 6 lbs. Suggested list price 59¢.

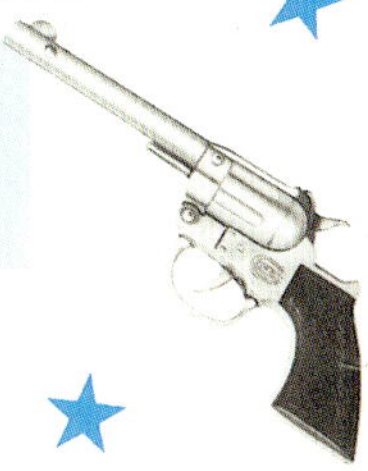

### 231R Cowpoke

Repeater. Length 8½ inches. Bright nickel finish with brown wood-grain plastic grips. Barrel breaks for easy loading. Individually carded; 1 doz. per ctn.; wt. 6 lbs. Suggested list price 69¢

**231S:** bubble packed on rack card; 1 doz. per carton; wt. 6 lbs.

### 234R Hawk

Repeater. Length 5¾ inches. Bright nickel finish with "mother of pearl" handles, finely detailed engraving. Portion of the barrel above handle left side is hinged, slides up to load caps. Packed 1 per Rack Card; 1 doz. per ctn. Wt. 6 lbs. Suggested list price 69¢.



Hubley® 1963

### 233S Pocket Derringer

Authentic short-barreled, large-caliber Derringer, 4 in. long. Bright chrome finish with white handles. Barrel breaks to load standard roll caps. Bubble packed on prepriced card. Packed 1 doz. card per ctn.; wt. 5 lbs. Suggested list price 79¢.

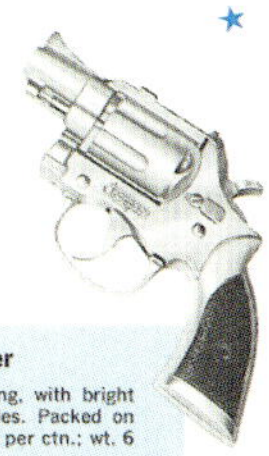

### 240R Trooper

250-Shot repeater, 5½ in. long, with bright nickel finish and black handles. Packed on card for racking; 1 doz. cards per ctn.; wt. 6 lbs. Suggested list price 79¢.

**240S:** 1 per bubble pack card; 1 doz. cards per ctn.; wt. 6 lbs. Suggested list price 79¢.

### 243 Tiny Tommy

Authentic scale model of real "Tommy" shoots standard roll caps as fast as you can pull the trigger. 10½ inches long. Of high-impact plastic, richly detailed just like its big brother. Die-cast chamber pops up for easy loading. Rear sight folds down. Black with wood grained hand grips. Suggested list price $1.

Packing: Individual boxes with full acetate lid, ½ doz. to colorful counter display. 2 displays, 12 guns, to carton. Wt. 5 lbs.

### 250R Texan Jr.

250 shot Repeater. Length 10½ in. Bright nickel finish with painted bullhead handles. Highly engraved stock and barrel. Breaks automatically for easy loading by pressing new type release on cylinder. Shoots smoke. Packed 1 per Rack Card; 1 doz. per carton. Wt. 8 lbs. Suggested list price $1.

**250S** with simulated bone handles; 1 per bubble pack card; 1 doz. per carton. wt. 8 lbs. Suggested list price $1.





Hubley® 1963

### 255R Sniper

Western pistol with extra long barrel. Made of black, high impact plastic with realistic grip. 22 in. long. Single shot, automatic action. Individually packed on bright red and yellow card for racking or bins. 1 doz. cards per ctn. Wt. 9 lbs. Suggested list price $1.

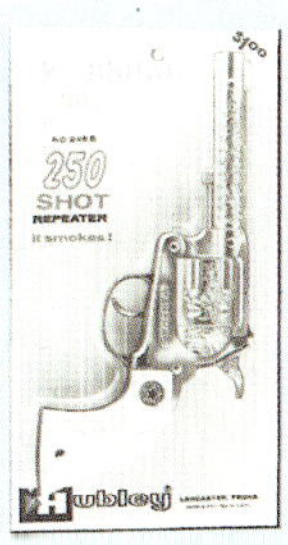


### 248S Marshal

Big western 250 shot repeater, highly engraved with bright nickel finish. Simulated pearl handle bearing cameo steer head. Cylinder door slides open for easy loading. Length 9½ in. Individually bubble packed on brightly colored card; packed 1 doz. per ctn.; wt. 10 lbs. Suggested list price $1.

NEW

### 262 Long Barrel Remington

Six shooter with cartridges. Bright nickel finish with black handles. Revolving cylinder loads with 6 take-apart "cartridges." Shoots round caps. Packed in an open counter display box. 1 doz. per ctn.; wt. 12 lbs. Suggested list price $1.69.

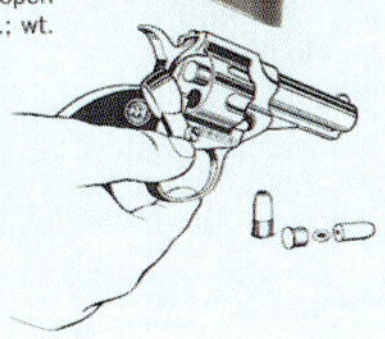

Pull down door behind cylinder to load.

Pre-loaded caps.



Hubley® 1963

## RACK CARDS

Bright, die-cut cards with a tamper-proof bubble make these items fast selling. Cards are pre-priced and punched, ready for hanging.

## RACK ASSORTMENTS

### 182 Deluxe Pistol Assortment

Self-service assortment includes ½ doz. each of Nos. 210S Dick, 231S Cowpoke, 240S Trooper and 250S Texan, Jr. plus one extra 250S. Complete with sturdy, attractive wire display rack. Packed one assortment per ctn.; wt. 15 lbs.

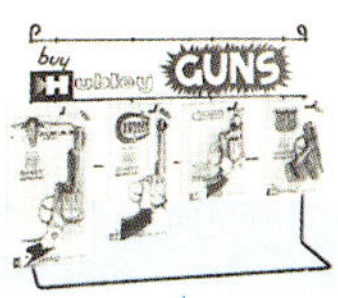


### 183 Western Pistol Assortment

Pre-priced from 69¢ to $1. assortment contains ¾ doz. each of Nos. 231S Cowpoke, 240S Trooper, 246S Western and 248S Marshal. Free wire display rack. Packed one assortment per ctn.; wt. 22 lbs.

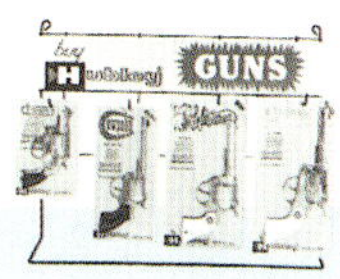


NEW

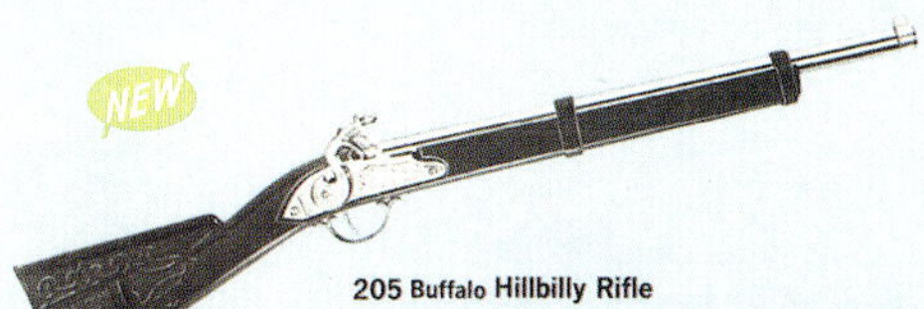

### 205 Buffalo Hillbilly Rifle

Walnut color plastic butt and hand grip. Metal portion has detailed engraving. Brightly plated barrel and front sight. Single shot flintlock operation. Length 25 inches. Individually packed on brightly colored card; one dozen per ctn. Weight 17 lbs. per carton. Suggested list price $1.98.

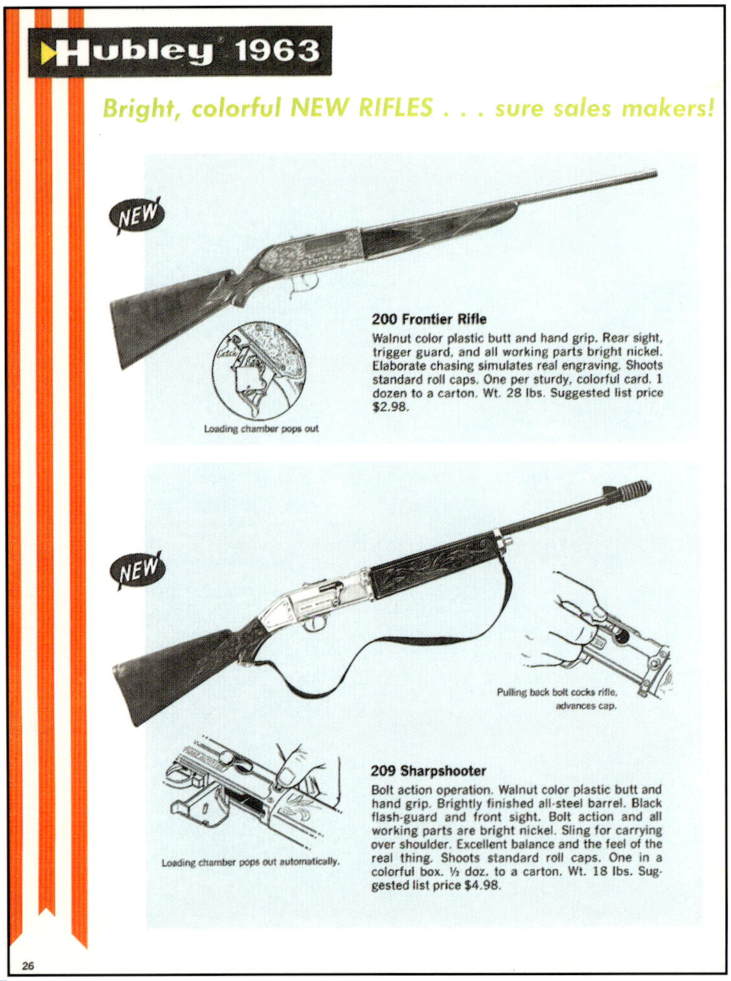

Hubley 1963

Bright, colorful NEW RIFLES . . . sure sales makers!

NEW

**200 Frontier Rifle**

Walnut color plastic butt and hand grip. Rear sight, trigger guard, and all working parts bright nickel. Elaborate chasing simulates real engraving. Shoots standard roll caps. One per sturdy, colorful card. 1 dozen to a carton. Wt. 28 lbs. Suggested list price $2.98.

Loading chamber pops out

NEW

Pulling back bolt cocks rifle, advances cap.

Loading chamber pops out automatically.

**209 Sharpshooter**

Bolt action operation. Walnut color plastic butt and hand grip. Brightly finished all-steel barrel. Black flash-guard and front sight. Bolt action and all working parts are bright nickel. Sling for carrying over shoulder. Excellent balance and the feel of the real thing. Shoots standard roll caps. One in a colorful box. ½ doz. to a carton. Wt. 18 lbs. Suggested list price $4.98.

26

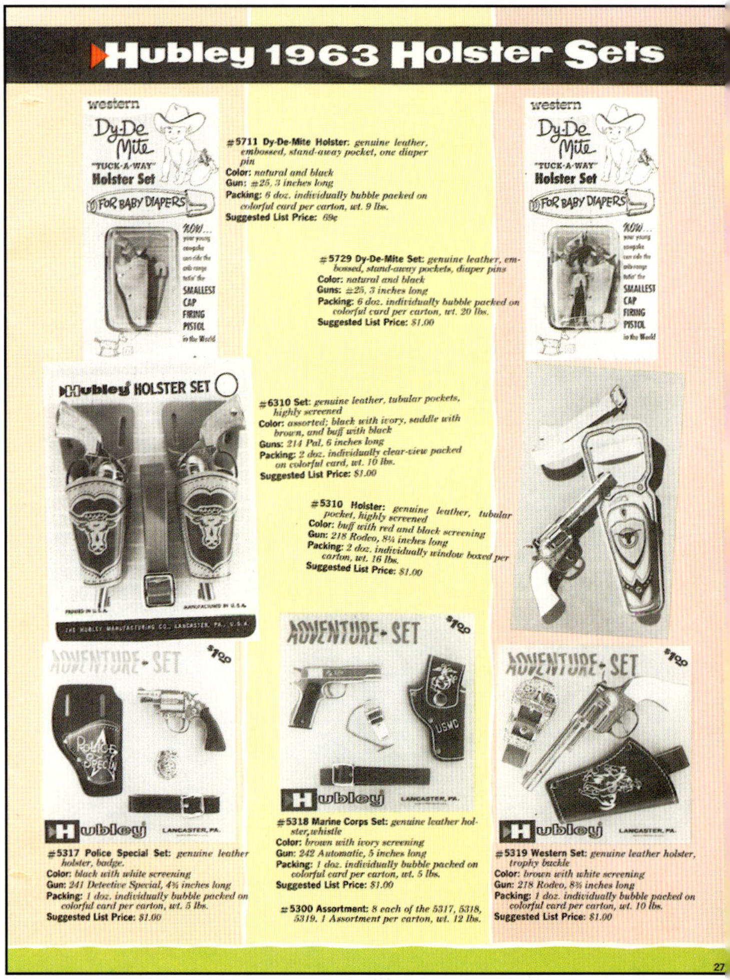

Hubley 1963 Holster Sets

**#5711 Dy-De-Mite Holster:** *genuine leather, embossed, stand-away pocket, one diaper pin*
**Color:** *natural and black*
**Gun:** *#25, 3 inches long*
**Packing:** *6 doz. individually bubble packed on colorful card per carton, wt. 9 lbs.*
**Suggested List Price:** *69¢*

**#5729 Dy-De-Mite Set:** *genuine leather, embossed, stand-away pockets, diaper pins*
**Color:** *natural and black*
**Guns:** *#25, 3 inches long*
**Packing:** *6 doz. individually bubble packed on colorful card per carton, wt. 20 lbs.*
**Suggested List Price:** *$1.00*

**#6310 Set:** *genuine leather, tubular pockets, highly screened*
**Color:** *assorted; black with ivory, saddle with brown, and buff with black*
**Guns:** *214 Pal, 6 inches long*
**Packing:** *2 doz. individually clear-view packed on colorful card, wt. 10 lbs.*
**Suggested List Price:** *$1.00*

**#5310 Holster:** *genuine leather, tubular pocket, highly screened*
**Color:** *buff with red and black screening*
**Gun:** *218 Rodeo, 8¼ inches long*
**Packing:** *2 doz. individually window boxed per carton, wt. 16 lbs.*
**Suggested List Price:** *$1.00*

**#5317 Police Special Set:** *genuine leather holster, badge.*
**Color:** *black with white screening*
**Gun:** *241 Detective Special, 4¾ inches long*
**Packing:** *1 doz. individually bubble packed on colorful card per carton, wt. 5 lbs.*
**Suggested List Price:** *$1.00*

**#5318 Marine Corps Set:** *genuine leather holster, whistle*
**Color:** *brown with ivory screening*
**Gun:** *242 Automatic, 5 inches long*
**Packing:** *1 doz. individually bubble packed on colorful card per carton, wt. 5 lbs.*
**Suggested List Price:** *$1.00*

**#5300 Assortment:** *8 each of the 5317, 5318, 5319. 1 Assortment per carton, wt. 12 lbs.*

**#5319 Western Set:** *genuine leather holster, trophy buckle*
**Color:** *brown with white screening*
**Gun:** *218 Rodeo, 8¾ inches long*
**Packing:** *1 doz. individually bubble packed on colorful card per carton, wt. 10 lbs.*
**Suggested List Price:** *$1.00*

27

1963

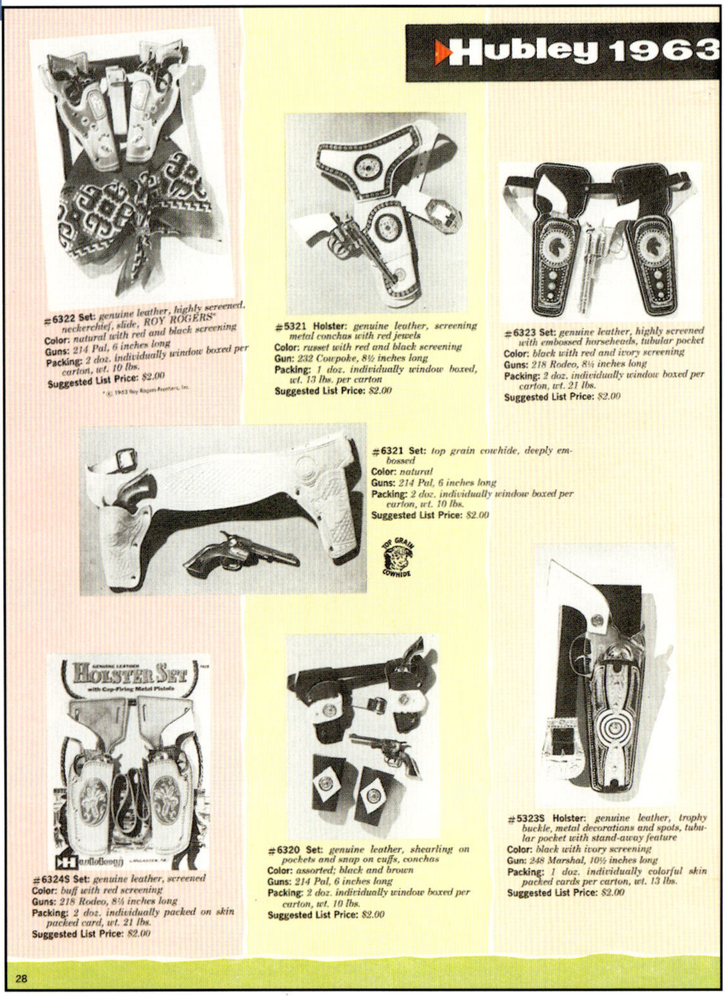

Hubley 1963

**#6322 Set:** *genuine leather, highly screened, neckerchief, slide, ROY ROGERS**
**Color:** *natural with red and black screening*
**Guns:** *214 Pal, 6 inches long*
**Packing:** *2 doz. individually window boxed per carton, wt. 10 lbs.*
**Suggested List Price:** *$2.00*
* © 1963 Roy Rogers-Frontiers, Inc.

**#5321 Holster:** *genuine leather, screening metal conchas with red jewels*
**Color:** *russet with red and black screening*
**Gun:** *232 Cowpoke, 8½ inches long*
**Packing:** *1 doz. individually window boxed, wt. 13 lbs. per carton*
**Suggested List Price:** *$2.00*

**#6323 Set:** *genuine leather, highly screened with embossed horseheads, tubular pocket*
**Color:** *black with red and ivory screening*
**Guns:** *218 Rodeo, 8¼ inches long*
**Packing:** *2 doz. individually window boxed per carton, wt. 21 lbs.*
**Suggested List Price:** *$2.00*

**#6321 Set:** *top grain cowhide, deeply embossed*
**Color:** *natural*
**Guns:** *214 Pal, 6 inches long*
**Packing:** *2 doz. individually window boxed per carton, wt. 10 lbs.*
**Suggested List Price:** *$2.00*

**#6324S Set:** *genuine leather, screened*
**Color:** *buff with red screening*
**Guns:** *218 Rodeo, 8¼ inches long*
**Packing:** *2 doz. individually packed on skin packed card, wt. 21 lbs.*
**Suggested List Price:** *$2.00*

**#6320 Set:** *genuine leather, shearling on pockets and snap on cuffs, conchas*
**Color:** *assorted; black and brown*
**Guns:** *214 Pal, 6 inches long*
**Packing:** *2 doz. individually window boxed per carton, wt. 10 lbs.*
**Suggested List Price:** *$2.00*

**#5323S Holster:** *genuine leather, trophy buckle, metal decorations and spots, tubular pocket with stand-away feature*
**Color:** *black with ivory screening*
**Gun:** *248 Marshal, 10½ inches long*
**Packing:** *1 doz. individually colorful skin packed cards per carton, wt. 13 lbs.*
**Suggested List Price:** *$2.00*

28

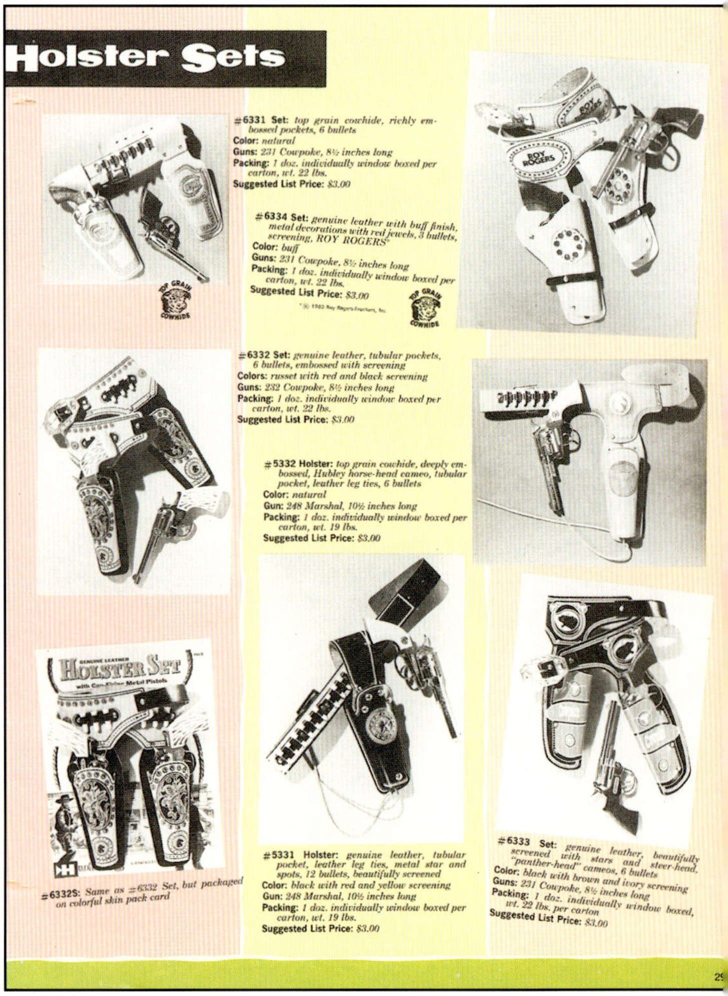

Holster Sets

**#6331 Set:** *top grain cowhide, richly embossed pockets, 6 bullets*
**Color:** *natural*
**Guns:** *231 Cowpoke, 8½ inches long*
**Packing:** *1 doz. individually window boxed per carton, wt. 22 lbs.*
**Suggested List Price:** *$3.00*

**#6334 Set:** *genuine leather with buff finish, metal decorations with red jewels, 3 bullets, screening, ROY ROGERS**
**Color:** *buff*
**Guns:** *231 Cowpoke, 8½ inches long*
**Packing:** *1 doz. individually window boxed per carton, wt. 22 lbs.*
**Suggested List Price:** *$3.00*
* © 1963 Roy Rogers-Frontiers, Inc.

**#6332 Set:** *genuine leather, tubular pockets, 6 bullets, embossed with screening*
**Colors:** *russet with red and black screening*
**Guns:** *232 Cowpoke, 8½ inches long*
**Packing:** *1 doz. individually window boxed per carton, wt. 22 lbs.*
**Suggested List Price:** *$3.00*

**#5332 Holster:** *top grain cowhide, deeply embossed, Hubley horse-head cameo, tubular pocket, leather leg ties, 6 bullets*
**Color:** *natural*
**Gun:** *248 Marshal, 10½ inches long*
**Packing:** *1 doz. individually window boxed per carton, wt. 19 lbs.*
**Suggested List Price:** *$3.00*

**#6332S:** *Same as #6332 Set, but packaged on colorful skin pack card*

**#5331 Holster:** *genuine leather, tubular pocket, leather leg ties, metal star and spots, 12 bullets, beautifully screened*
**Color:** *black with red and yellow screening*
**Gun:** *248 Marshal, 10½ inches long*
**Packing:** *1 doz. individually window boxed per carton, wt. 19 lbs.*
**Suggested List Price:** *$3.00*

**#6333 Set:** *genuine leather, beautifully screened with stars and steer-head, "panther-head" cameos, 6 bullets*
**Color:** *black with brown and ivory screening*
**Guns:** *231 Cowpoke, 8½ inches long*
**Packing:** *1 doz. individually window boxed, wt. 22 lbs. per carton*
**Suggested List Price:** *$3.00*

29

# Hubley 1963 Holster Sets

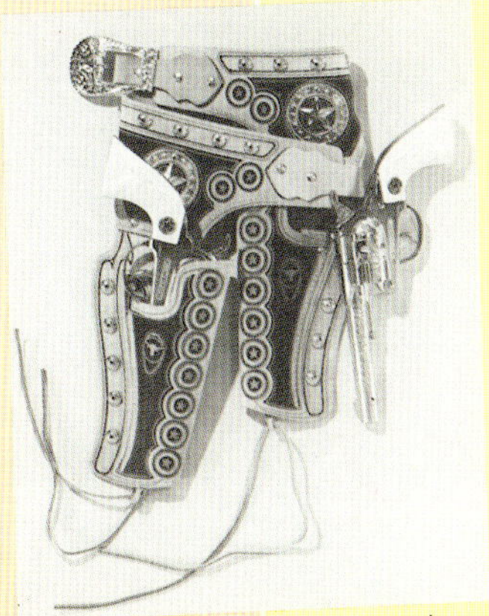

**#6342 Set:** *genuine leather, metal spots and stars, beautifully screened, trophy buckle, leather leg ties, 6 bullets*
**Colors:** *russet with red and black screening*
**Guns:** *248 Marshal, 10½ inches long*
**Packing:** *1 doz. individually window boxed per carton, wt. 29 lbs.*
**Suggested List Price:** *$4.00*

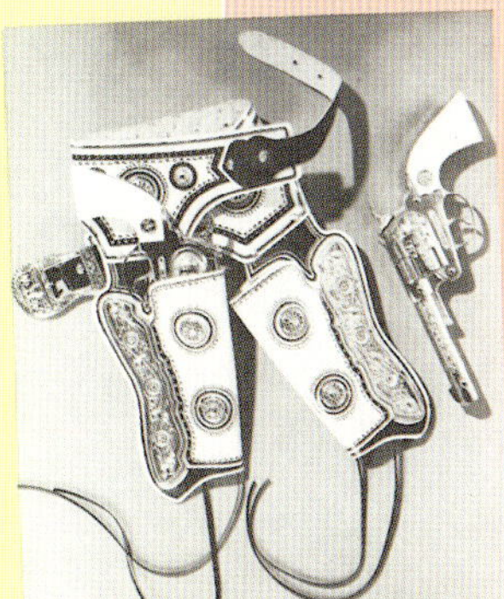

**#6340 Set:** *genuine leather, "Slim Jim" metal pocket trim, metal spots and conchas, trophy buckle, beautifully screened, 6 bullets, plastic leg ties*
**Color:** *white, black, and red*
**Guns:** *248 Marshal, 10½ inches long*
**Packing:** *1 doz. individually window boxed per carton, wt. 29 lbs.*
**Suggested List Price:** *$4.00*

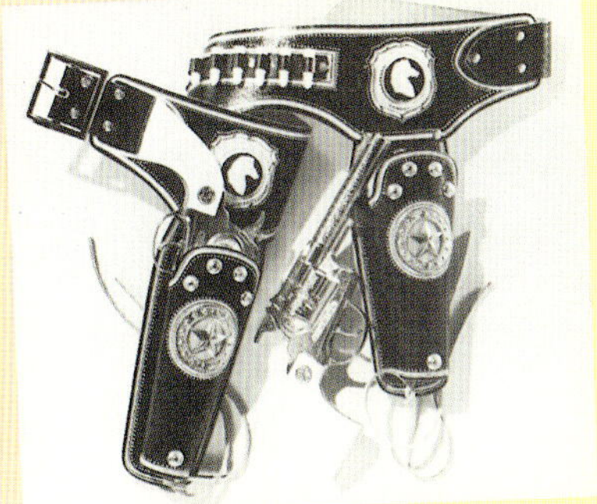

**#6351 Set:** *genuine leather, metal stars and spots, raised horseheads, leather leg ties, tubular pocket, 12 bullets*
**Colors:** *black with red and yellow screening*
**Guns:** *248 Marshal, 10½ inches long*
**Packing:** *½ doz. individually window boxed per carton, wt. 18 lbs.*
**Suggested List Price:** *$5.00*

**#6352 Set:** *genuine leather, metal spots, leather leg ties, pockets have cross straps with buckles, 6 bullets, trophy buckle, ROY ROGERS**
**Color:** *buff and brown with ivory screening*
**Guns:** *232 Cowpoke, 8½ inches long*
**Packing:** *½ doz. individually window boxed per carton, wt. 18 lbs.*
**Suggested List Price:** *$5.00*

* © 1963 Roy Rogers Frontiers, Inc.

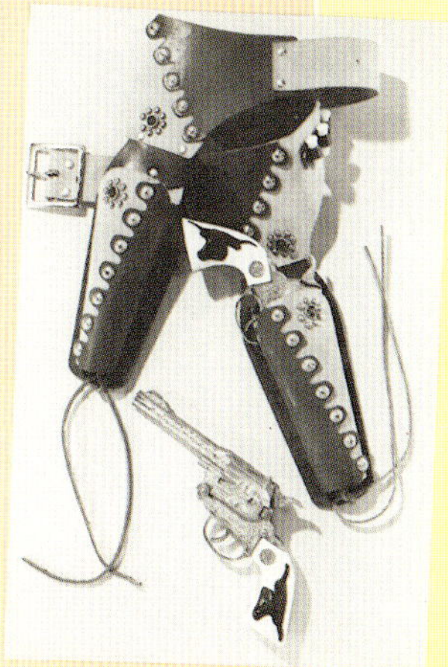

**#6361 Set:** *genuine cowhide, contour belt, metal spots and red jewels, 12 bullets, leather leg ties*
**Color:** *russet and brown*
**Guns:** *250 Texan Jr., 10½ inches long*
**Packing:** *½ doz. individually window boxed per carton, wt. 19 lbs.*
**Suggested List Price:** *$6.00*

TOP GRAIN COWHIDE

**#6354 Set:** *top grain cowhide, deeply embossed, tubular pockets with stand-away feature, 12 bullets, leather leg ties*
**Color:** *natural*
**Guns:** *248 Marshal, 10½ inches long*
**Packing:** *½ doz. individually window boxed, wt. 18 lbs.*
**Suggested List Price:** *$5.00*

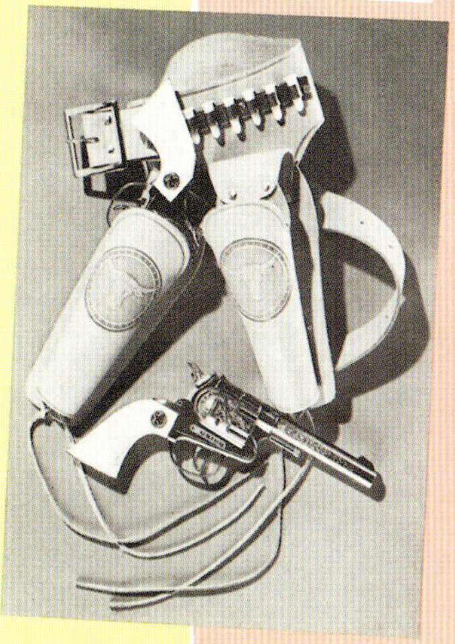



1963

# Hubley SALES TERRITORIES AND OFFICES

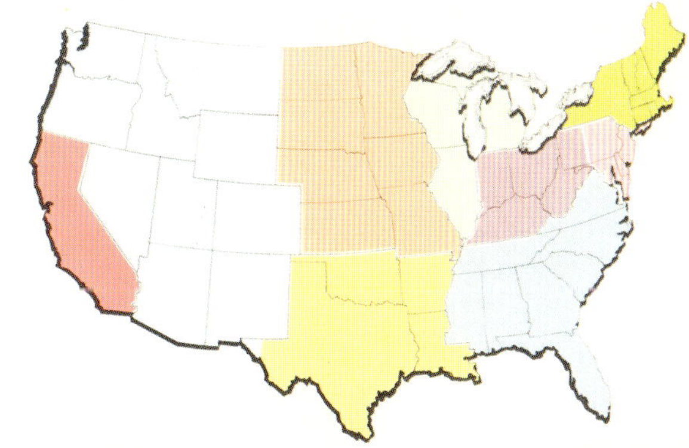

**New England**
Mr. Gregory F. Kane
3 Maher Drive
Norwalk, Conn.
203 VI 7-5104

**Cleveland**
Mr. George Antonelli
101 Union Avenue
Dover, Ohio
2-0906

**Houston**
Mr. Howard V. Campbell
2416 Washington Ave.
Houston, Texas
713 CA 4-2251 or 713 JA 9-9480

**New York Territory**
Mr. Gary Warren
35 Surrey Road
Clark, New Jersey
201-382-0108

**Chicago**
Mr. Robert L. Laughton
250 Monument Ave.
Barrington, Ill.
312 DU 1-1004

**Rocky Mountain**
Leo A. Scherrer Co.
2840 N. W. 93rd St.
Seattle 7, Wash.
206 SU 3-2426

**Atlanta**
Mr. Edward V. Conrad
6910 Castleton Drive N. W.
Atlanta, Ga.
404 BL 5-0681 or 404 875-7947

**Kansas City**
Mr. Richard S. Leedy
9716 Buena Vista
Leawood, Kans.
913 NI 2-5230

**California**
Mr. Harry H. Johnson, Jr.
11422 Gardenaire Lane
Garden Grove, Calif.
714 LE 9-7629

**HOME OFFICE:** The Hubley Manufacturing Co., 110 Pitney Road, Lancaster, Pa. • 717 394-2691
**NEW YORK OFFICE:** The Hubley Manufacturing Co., Suite 611-200 Fifth Ave., New York 10, N. Y. • 212 OR 5-9342 • Mr. Donald A. Bolin, Mr. Gary Warren
**CANADA:** Thompson Toy & Hobby Sales, 2nd Floor—200 Bay St., Toronto 1, Ont., Canada . 416 • 421-8321
**EXPORT:** Guiterman Co., Inc., 95 Broad Street, New York 4, N. Y. • 212 DI 4-1290

*Craftsmanship*

In a word, this defines the arts and skills you see in every Hubley Toy. FIRST, realistic detail is brought to life in miniature by our design staff. SECOND, our modelers make sure that every toy will "play" well and have continuing appeal. THIRD, our toolmakers make sure of a strength and durability that will stand up under the rough handling that toys get. FOURTH, attractive finishes and modern packaging are added to make a final package with maximum sales appeal. That's Craftsmanship!

Design with appeal, construction with strength, merchandising with impact, advertising with coverage . . . these things constitute our pledge to you.

**THE HUBLEY MANUFACTURING COMPANY, LANCASTER, PA., U.S.A.**

112-2-63

We reserve the right to make design and price changes without prior notice.

Printed in U. S. of America

# 1964

Hubley®
1964
TOYS
MIGHTY-
METAL
TOYS •
MIGHTY-METAL
TOYS • MIGHTY-METAL TOYS •
MIGHTY-METAL TOYS •
MIGHTY-METAL TOYS • MIGHTY-METAL
TOYS • MIGHTY-METAL TOYS • METAL CAR KITS • METAL
CAR KITS • METAL CAR KITS • METAL CAR KITS •
METAL CAR KITS • METAL CAR KITS • METAL CAR KITS •
GUNS • GUNS • GUNS • GUNS • GUNS •
GUNS • GUNS • GUNS • GUNS • GUNS • GUNS •
HOLSTERS • HOLSTERS • HOLSTERS • HOLSTERS •
HOLSTERS • HOLSTERS • HOLSTERS •

# LOW END TOYS IN METAL AND PLASTIC • SALES BUILDERS FOR BIN-ENDS AND CHECK-OUT COUNTERS

Hubley

**METAL** Suggested list price 39¢*

**1401 Continental Sedan** A 6 in. detailed die cast model of the Lincoln Continental. Blue with aluminum trim. Rubber tires. Individually bubble packed on colorful card; 1 doz. cards per ctn.; wt. 4 lbs.

**1402 Fire Engine** 6 in. red fire-pumper with aluminum trim. Rubber tires. Individually bubble packed on "self-seller" card; 1 doz. cards per ctn.; wt. 4 lbs.

**1403 Falcon Pick-Up Truck** Turquoise reproduction of Ford's truck. Rubber tires. Aluminum bright work. Length 6 in. Individually bubble packed; 1 doz. cards per ctn.; wt. 5 lbs.

**1404 Ford 1934 Coupe** Model B Ford V-8 in jade green. Rubber tires. Individually bubble packed; 1 doz. cards per ctn.; wt. 4 lbs.

**1405 Corvair Station Wagon** Chevrolet's compact. About 6 in. long. Aluminum trim and rubber tires. Individually bubble packed; 1 doz. cards per ctn.; wt. 4 lbs.

**1406 Gasoline Truck** Bright truck with aluminum trim. 6 in. long. Rubber tires. Individually bubble packed; 1 doz. cards per ctn.; wt. 4 lbs.

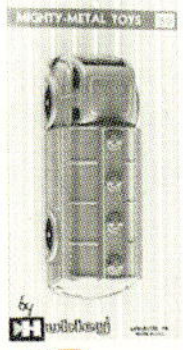


**1029 Mighty-Metal Assortment** Four each of all 6 toys shown above. Individually skin packed on bright cards; total 2 doz.; shipping wt. 9 lbs.

**PLASTIC** Suggested list price 29¢*

**1310 Motorcycle** Red or green motorcycle, black rider. Rubber wheels. Length 5 in. Packed 12 in a box; 3 doz. per ctn.; wt. 6 lbs.

**1311 Airplane** Red and white. Insignia on wings with retractable landing gear. Rubber wheels. Length 5 in. Packed 12 in a box; 4 doz. per ctn.; wt. 4 lbs.

**1309 Tractor** Red, yellow or orange with aluminum trim. Polyethylene wheels. Length 4¾ in. Packed 12 in a box; 3 doz. per ctn.; wt. 8 lbs.

*All list prices are furnished only for the identification of the products, and nothing in this catalogue should be regarded as an indication that the prices set forth are the usual retail prices. This material is sent to the retailer and/or distributor upon the express condition that it will not be used to represent usual selling prices.



# 1964 MIGHTY-METAL TOYS

**Durable die cast toys with amazing detail. Bright non-toxic paints and plenty of play features make these toys MOVE. Ready for display in colorful packages, they will increase volume and profits.**

**1467 Navy Fighter** Hubley's popular airplane with plastic bubble over cockpit, rubber tires, folding wings, and retractable landing gear. Length 6½ in.; wing span 8¾ in. Packed individually in colorful box; 1 doz. per ctn.; wt. 8 lbs. Suggested list price $1.00

**1469 Log Truck** The five 5 in. logs give this item real play appeal. Rubber tires. Length 10¾ in. Packed 1 in a box; 1 doz per ctn.; wt. 16 lbs. Suggested list price $1.00

**1470 Dump Truck** Side lever operated dump bed. 9¼ in. long. Rubber tires. Individually packed in brightly printed box. 1 doz. per ctn.; wt. 14 lbs. Suggested list price $1.00



1964

# MIGHTY-METAL TOYS

Hubley

**1471 Hook and Ladder** Kids love fire engines. Ladders connect and can be set up. Length 11¼ in. Rubber tires. Packed 1 in a box; 1 doz. per carton. wt. 13 lbs. Suggested list price $1.00

**1472 Tractor** Realistic engine detail and heavy treaded tires make this an outstanding volume producer. Length 7¼ in. 1 in a box; 1 doz. per ctn.; wt. 11 lbs. Suggested list price $1.00

**1474 Farm Tractor and Wagon** Detachable wagon. Realistic detail. Overall length 10¼ in. Packed in colorful box with cutouts for added play appeal. 1 doz. per ctn.; wt. 10 lbs. Suggested list price $1.00

**1721 Garage Set** Set contains a Falcon Tow Truck, a '34 Ford Coupe, battery, pliers, screwdriver, and 2 car tires. Bubble packed. One doz. to a ctn.; wt. 10 lbs. Suggested list $1.00

**1722 Fire Engine Set** Contains No. 1402 Fire Engine, No 1405 Station Wagon, 2 plastic ladders, bucket, and plastic whistle. Bubble packed. 1 doz. to a ctn.; wt. 9 lbs. Suggested list price $1.00

**1723 Gas Station Set** Consists of No. 1401 Continental, No. 1406 Gas Truck, gas pump, pliers, and screwdriver. Bubble packed. 1 doz. to a ctn.; wt. 9 lbs. Suggested list price $1.00

**1762 Farm Set** Set has No. 1456 Tractor, cultipacker, chicken, pig, and duck. 1 doz. to a ctn.; wt. 9 lbs. Bubble packed. Suggested list price $1.00

**1763 Highway and Skyway Set** No. 1432 M.G. Sports Car and No. 1430 Airplane. 1 doz. to a ctn.; wt. 10 lbs. Suggested list price $1.00



# 1964 MIGHTY-METAL TOY SETS

**1764 Traffic Control Set** No. 1310 Motorcycle, No. 1432 M. G. Sports Car. Plastic whistle included. Bubble packed. 1 doz. to a ctn.; wt. 8 lbs. Suggested list price $1.00

**1021 Assortment** New set assortment. 3 each of the 1721, 1761, 1765, and 1766. Packed 1 assortment per ctn.; wt. 10 lbs.

**1022 Assortment** New set assortment. 3 each of the 1722, 1723, 1764, 1767. Packed 1 assortment per ctn.; wt. 10 lbs.

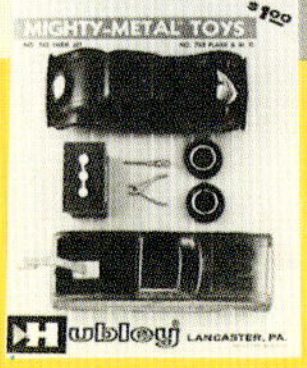


These Mighty-Metal toys are brightly packaged on tamper-proof, sturdy, pre-priced cards for big volume in bin-end or rack sales. A "must" for the impulse sale.

# MIGHTY-METAL TOY SETS

Hubley

1765

1766

1767

1768

1769

1770

1771

**1765 Continental and Racer Set** Set has 1401 Continental, Racer, and Trailer. Trailer holds racer and hooks to car. Bubble packed. 1 doz. to a ctn.; wt. 8 lbs. Suggested list price $1.00

**1766 Train Set** Set contains engine and tender which hook together. Bubble packed. 1 doz. to a ctn.; wt. 9 lbs. Suggested list price $1.00

**1767 Cub and Racer Set** Piper Cub and racer. Bubble packed. 1 doz. to a ctn.; wt. 6 lbs. Suggested list price $1.00

**1768 Jungle Patrol Set** A three piece set consisting of one No. 1338 plastic Helicopter, 7½ inches long; one No. 1433 metal Piper Cub Airplane, 8-inch wingspread; and one plastic medal. Pre-priced at $1.00. Skin packed on an 8½" x 13¾" 2-color card. Packed 1 dozen to a 6 lb. carton.



# 1964 MIGHTY-METAL TOYS

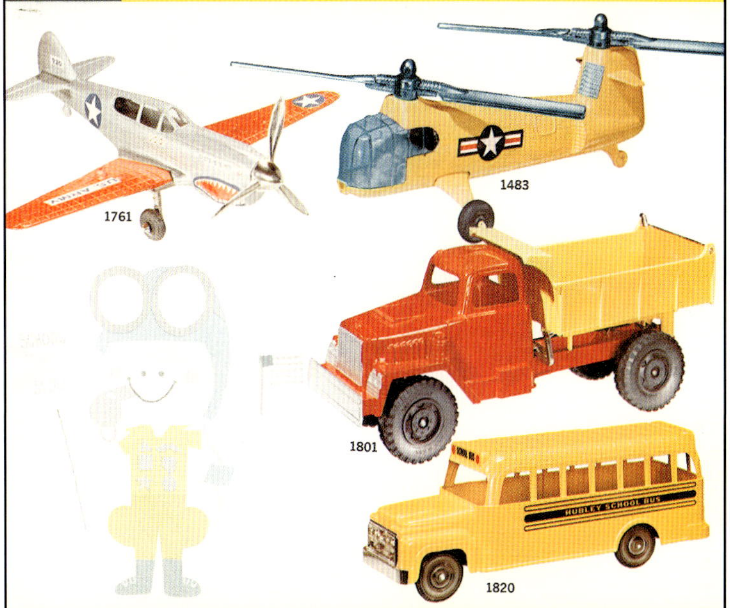

1761

1483

1801

1820

**1769 Army Engineers Bulldozer** Big for the price. Detailed Army Bulldozer with movable treads and dozer blade. Pre-priced at $1.00. Skin packed on an 8" x 10¼" 2-color card. Packed 1 dozen to a 15½ lb. shipping carton.

**1770 U. S. Air Patrol** Consists of one Piper Cub Airplane, one Airplane, 6-inch wingspread; and pilot's wings. Pre-priced at $1.00. Skin packed on an 8½" x 13¾" 2-color card. Packed 1 dozen to a 6½ lb. shipping carton.

**1771 Army Command Set** Consists of one Motorcycle, 5 inches long; one all metal Sedan, 6 inches long; and one whistle. Pre-priced at $1.00. Skin packed on an 8" x 10¼" 2-color card. Packed 1 dozen in a 7¼ lb. carton.

**1483 Helicopter** Clear plastic bubble, folding rotor blades and rubber wheels, make this 9¼ in. helicopter a real sales winner. Individually boxed; 1 doz. per ctn.; wt. 13 lbs. Suggested list price $1.49

**1761 P-40 Plane** World War II favorite. 7½ in. long with wingspread of 8 in. Rubber tires. Decals furnished. Individually bubble packed; 1 doz. per ctn.; wt. 8 lbs. Suggested list price $1.00

**1801 Dump Truck** Dump body raises and lowers using side lever. Black treaded tires. Realistic detail. Length 10 in. Individually boxed; 1 doz. per ctn.; wt. 17 lbs.
Suggested List Price $1.49

**1820 School Bus** Heavy duty die cast metal School Bus, painted school bus yellow with nickel, red and black trim and black tires. Length 9½ inches. Individually packaged in a colorful box. 1 doz. per ctn.; wt. 14 lbs.
Suggested List Price $1.69





Hubley

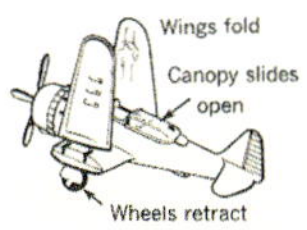


**1495 Navy Fighter Bomber** A sales leader for years. Retractable wheels, revolving prop, sliding plastic canopy, folding wings, rubber tires and realistic detail. Length 10 in. Packed 1 per display box; 1 doz. per ctn.; wt. 20 lbs. Suggested list price $1.98

Front wheels steer.

**1496 Tractor** Detailed engine, actual steering, and heavy treaded rubber tires. Length 9 ¼ in. Individually boxed; 1 doz. per ctn.; wt. 29 lbs. Suggested list $1.98

**1881 P-38** Bright, realistic World War II fighter with lots of sales punch. Retractable rubber tires, props that spin, and accurate detail make this 9 in. beauty a sure winner. Packed in colorful display box. 1 doz. boxes to ctn. Weight 20 lbs. Suggested list price $1.98



# 1964 MIGHTY-METAL TOYS

1492

1501

1503

**1492 Auto Transport** Beautiful metal car transport with many play features. Four plastic cars can be loaded and unloaded on metal ramp. Trailer and cab detach. 14 in. long. Packed 1 in a colorful corrugated box with display base. 1 doz. per ctn.; wt. 30 lbs. Suggested list price $2.98

**1501 Tractor Loader** Steering wheel moves front wheels; side lever raises, lowers, and dumps the bucket; rubber tires with heavy treading. 12¾ in. long. Individually packed in colorful corrugated box. ½ doz. to ctn.; wt. 19 lbs. Suggested list price $2.98

**1503 Road Grader** Independent front and rear suspension for rough terrain, adjustable blade, steering lever moves front wheels, and highly detailed white-walled tires. 12¾ in. long. Individually packed in colorful box ½ doz. to a ctn.; wt. 14 lbs. Suggested list price $2.98

## Hubley

# CONSTRUCTION AND FARM TOYS...

### exact in detail . . . good for year round sales

1901 Power Shovel

**1901 Power Shovel** Scoops like its big brother. Cab rotates 360° and shovel rolls on rubber treads. 15 in. long. Individually packed in colorful corrugated box ½ doz. per ctn.; wt. 19 lbs. Suggested list price $2.98

**1505 Front End Loader** Moves on rubber treads and has lever to raise, lower, and dump bucket. Realistic engine detail. 7¾ in. long. Individually packed in brightly colored box ½ doz. per ctn.; wt. 16 lbs. Suggested list price $2.98

**1903 Bulldozer** Adjustable scraper blade that raises and lowers. Moves on rubber treads. Careful detailing to look like real thing. 8¾ in. long. Individually packaged in colorful corrugated box ½ doz. boxes per ctn.; wt. 14 lbs. Suggested list price $2.98

**1508 Ford 4000 Tractor** Authentic scale model of the Ford 4000 Tractor. Steering wheel actually moves front wheels. Heavy treaded rubber tires. Realistic detail including Ford decals. Length 11 in. Individually boxed; ½ doz. per ctn.; wt. 21 lbs. Suggested list price $3.98

10

## 1964 MIGHTY-METAL TOYS

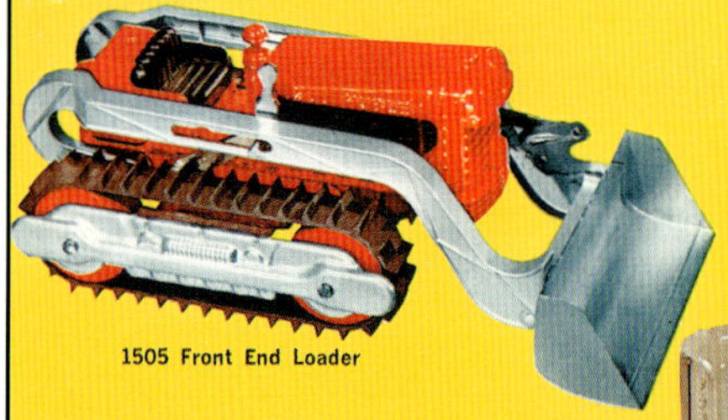

1505 Front End Loader

AUTHORIZED Ford REPLICA

1508 Ford 4000 Tractor

1903 Bulldozer

AUTHORIZED Ford REPLICA

**1509 Ford 6000 Tractor** Authentic scale model of the Ford 6000 Tractor. This sturdy die cast model moves on deep treaded rubber tires and can actually be steered. Striking detail. Hitch for attaching accessories. Length 12 in. Packed 1 in a colorful corrugated display box. ½ doz. per ctn.; wt. 31 lbs. Suggested list price $5.98

11

1964

## Hubley

1882

1902

1926

# A DURABLE LINE

**1882 Pickup Truck** Sturdy pickup with realistic detailing. Deep treaded white wall tires. Hitch for other Hubley items. 12 inches long. Individually packaged in colorful corrugated box. 1 doz. per carton; weight 28 pounds. Suggested list price $2.49

**1902 Dump Truck** Heavy Bodied dump with dual rear wheels and removable tailgate. Deep treaded white-wall tires. Dump body operates from lever on side. 11 inches long. Individually packaged in a colorful corrugated box. ½ doz. per carton; weight 15 lbs. Suggested list price $2.98

1927

12

## 1964 MIGHTY-METAL TOYS

1966

### • • of large size trucks of die cast metal that won't rust, loaded with realism, play value and best of all, durability.

**1926 Tow Truck** Mighty-Metal at its best. Hook is operated by crank on right. Brake on left holds hook in place when towing. Deep tread white-wall tires. 12 inches long. Individually packaged in colorful corrugated box. ½ doz. carton. wt. 17 lbs. Suggested list price $3.69

**1927 Stake Truck with Trailer** Careful detailing, sturdy construction, deep-tread white wall tires, and detachable trailer. Loaded with play features. 20½ inches long. Individually packaged in colorful corrugated box. ½ doz. per carton; Weight 22 pounds. Suggested list price $3.98

**1953 Tractor with Trailer Dump** Dump body has lever on side which automatically dumps contents by spring action. Dual wheels on trailer and truck. Deep treaded white side wall tires. 16 inches long. Individually packaged in colorful corrugated box. ½ doz. per carton; Weight 23 pounds. Suggested list price $4.98

**1966 Flat Bed with Shovel** Truck, Flat bed trailer and Hubley's popular 1901 Power Shovel. Deep Tread white side wall tires. Shovel actually shovels. Moves on rubber treads. 20 inches long. Individually packaged in colorful corrugated box. ¼ doz. per carton; Weight 16 pounds. Suggested list price $5.95

1953

13

# MIGHTY-METAL TOYS

Hubley

**1890 U. S. Army Carryall** A 12-inch long heavy duty die cast truck with a canvas cover over bed. Deep treaded tires. Color: Army green. Individually packaged in a colorful corrugated box. 1 dozen in a 30 lb. shipping carton. Suggested list price $2.69

**1929 Carpenters Truck** Heavy die cast metal truck with a clear plastic carpenter's tool box with 5 tools mounted on the back. The truck has deep treaded white sidewall tires, and is 12 inches long. Individually packed in a colorful corrugated box. Six pieces of lumber included. 1 dozen boxes per 41 lb. shipping carton. Suggested list price $3.98

1890 U. S. Army Carryall

1929 Carpenters Truck

**1928 Pile Driver** Heavy duty die cast metal truck with deep treaded white sidewall tires. Pile driver boom lowers over cab for traveling, raises for action. Pulling the string raises the weight, which is released at the top, driving one of the 6 wooden stakes furnished. Truck is 13 inches long in traveling position; 14½ inches high with boom up. Individually packed in a 2-color corrugated box. Packed 1 dozen in a 42 lb. shipping carton. Suggested list price $3.98



## 1964

**2829 Deluxe Pistol Assortment**
Self-service assortment includes ½ doz. each of Nos. 2102 Dick, 2312 Cowpoke, 2402 Trooper and 2502 Texan Jr., plus one extra 2502. Complete with sturdy, attractive wire display rack. Packed one assortment per ctn.; wt. 16 lbs.

**2189 Pistol and Caps Assortment**
One dozen each of the 2861, 2871, 2881, 2891 packed 1 assortment per ctn.; wt. 27 lbs.

**2861 Army***
4⅝ in. long, nickel finish, 50 shot repeater and box of roll caps.
1 doz. per ctn.; wgt. 6 lbs. Suggested Retail 69c.

**2871 Detective***
5½ in. long, nickel finish, 250 shot repeater and box of roll caps.
1 doz. per ctn.; wgt. 7 lbs. Suggested Retail 79c.

**2881 Western***
9½ in. long, nickel finish, 250 shot Western pistol and box of roll caps. 1 doz. per ctn.; wgt. 9 lbs. Suggested Retail $1.00.

**2891 Jungle Fighter***
10½ in. long, high impact plastic, 50 shot Tommy gun and box of roll caps. 1 doz. per ctn.; wgt. 5 lbs. Suggested Retail $1.00.

2861 2871 2881 2891

* Skin packed on 2-color card.

new

**1017 Farm Set** 11 piece set including tractor, plow, cultipacker, wagon, Pick-up, chicken crate, 4 farm fowl, and pig. Colorfully packaged. ½ doz. boxes per ctn.; wt. 15 lbs. Suggested List Price $2.98

new

**1055 Bomber And Fighter Escort** Set includes an authentic detailed B-25 Bomber with 11 inch wing spread and 2 Hellcat fighter planes 9½ inch wing spread. All are super detailed in unbreakable poly. Packaged in a bright colored display carton, shrink packed, one dozen in an 18 lb. shipping carton. Suggested List Price $2.30





# MIGHTY-METAL TOY SETS

Hubley

1048 Construction Set

1057 Farm Set

1069 Road Building Set

1091 Large Farm Set

**1048 Construction Set** The set includes 1801 Dump Truck 1505 Front End Loader and metal flat bed trailer. The loader travels to the job site on the trailer! Packed in a colorful display box; ¼ doz. per ctn.; wt. 16 lbs. Suggested list price $4.98

**1057 Farm Set** This set contains the 1508 Ford tractor with wagon, plow, and two crates of chickens and ducks. Full color corrugated box provides barn and barnyard background for extra play value. ¼ doz. per ctn.; wt. 16 lbs. Suggested list price $6.95

**1069 Road Building Set** Large items in a large set for large value. Contains 1503 Road Grader; the 1505 Front End, Loader, 1801 Dump Truck and 1901 Power Shovel. Complete set in a colorful display box; ¼ doz. per ctn.; wt. 30 lbs. Suggested list price $9.95

**1091 Large Farm Set** Authentic model of Ford 6000 tractor complete with plow, flat bed wagon and cuti-packer (all hitch to tractor interchangeable). Packed in large corrugated display box; ¼ doz. per ctn.; wt. 27 lbs Suggested list price $9.95



## 1964

# NEW METAL CAR KIT

# model SJ Duesenberg

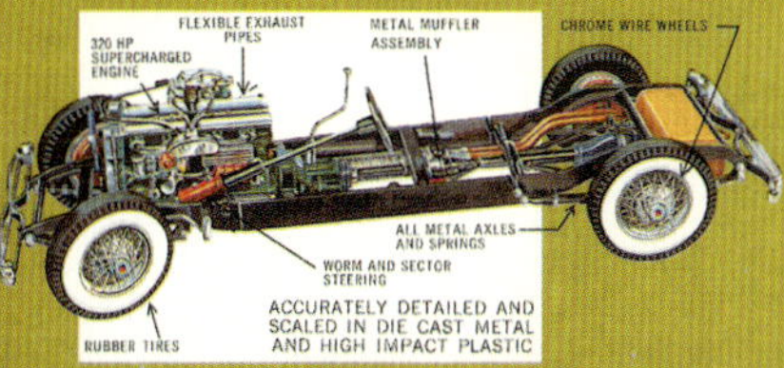


**4864 SJ Duesenberg Phaeton** One of the most desired classic cars. Model SJ Duesenberg, La Grande body, dual cowl Phaeton. Model is 12¼ inches long, 1/18" scale, made of die cast metal with chrome and plastic accessory parts; worm and sector steering; fold down windshield and movable rear cowl. Over 150 parts. Packaged in a 4-color over-wrapped box. Packed ½ dozen in a 21 lb. shipping carton. Suggested List Price $10.00

**4164 Duesenberg Assortment** Assortment consists of 6 metal kits and one built-up car in a 4-color display case. Car is covered with clear plastic to prevent pilferage and breakage.

- Beautifully and accurately detailed. Frame is sturdy die cast metal for durability; engine combines metal and metallized plastic for glamorous trim. Front wheels actually steer with worm and sector gears.

Hubley

4859 **Packard Sport Phaeton** 135 pieces. The finest detailing from bumper to bumper. Movable rear seat cowl, chromed mirrors, door handles, and accessories. White walls, 6 open spoke wheels. Individually cellophane wrapped in colorful box, ½ doz. per ctn.; wt. 13 lbs. Suggested list price $4.98

Hubley Metal Car Kits are the only car kits made of metal with plastic and metalized plastic accessories. Master car modelers prefer them because of their durability, detailing and authenticity. They are advertised in CAR CRAFT, MOTOR TREND, CAR MODEL and other consumer publications.

**4860 Packard Roadster** White walls, chassis and motor detail are exact to the "nth", fan that turns, real radiator hose, luggage rack, 6 spoked wheels, chrome accessories. Individually cellophane wrapped in colorful box. ½ doz. per ctn.; wt. 13 lbs. Suggested list price $4.98

**4858 Model A Station Wagon** Rounding out the Model A collection is this classic. Woodgrain, 4 doors, luggage rack. Individually cellophane wrapped in colorful box. 1 doz. per ctn.; wt. 22 lbs. Suggested list price $3.49

**4862 Chevy Roadster** A wonderfully authentic model of this Classic Roadster. 6 rubber tires (white walls), chrome hood vents, door handles, headlights, cowl lights, and windshield frame. Rumble seat. Luggage rack. Hood lifts off. Individually wrapped in cellophane wrapped colorful box. 1 doz. per ctn. 21 lbs. Suggested list price $3.49

new

**4863 Packard Dietrich** Another classic 1930 Packard, authentic in detail. 140 parts of die cast metal, plastic and metallized plastic accessories. Car actually steers by worm and sector gears. Individually cellophane wrapped 4-color box. Packed ½ dozen to 13 lb. shipping carton. Suggested list price $4.98



## 1964 METAL CAR KITS

Kit contains die cast body chassis, running gear, steering mechanism, engine block, plastic and metalized plastic accessories and parts. Detail is exceptional even to rubber tires. Easy screwdriver assembly with complete instructions. Finish with brush or spray paint.

**4850 Model A Roadster** This classic has white walls and can be built with top up or down. Individually packed in cellophane wrapped, colorful box. 1 doz. per ctn.; wt. 18 lbs. Suggested list price $2.98

**4857 Model A Town Sedan** One of the hard top models in the line. Complete metal body, luggage rack and trunk. Individually packaged in cellophane wrapped, colorful box. 1 doz. per ctn.; wt. 21 lbs. Suggested list price $2.98

**4856 Model A Phaeton** Removable top. This is a beautiful 4 door classic popularized by TV shows. Individually packed in cellophane wrapped, colorful box. 1 doz. per ctn.; wt. 18 lbs. Suggested list price $2.98

new

**4865 1932 Chevrolet Phaeton** A Chevrolet Phaeton metal model to go with the Chevy Roadster. Two side-mounted spare tires and wheels, die cast metal body, fenders, frame and motor block. Plastic and metallized plastic accessory parts. Hood lifts off to display a detailed engine. Individually cellophane wrapped 4-color box. Packed 1 dozen in a 20-lb shipping carton. Suggested list price $3.49

**4861 Model A Ford Coupe** Authentically detailed engine with real radiator hose and fan that turns. Movable rumble seat and white wall tires. Individually packaged in cellophane wrapped, colorful box. 1 doz. per ctn.; wt. 19 lbs. Suggested list price $2.98





Hubley

# NEW CONCEPT in DRAG RACING

# INSTANT TORQUE MOTOR !!!!

(NON-ELECTRIC)

**Two different body designs, a competition coupe and an altered Fiat coupe, have been scaled down from existing hot competition racers of different dragster classes. Cars can be run on a wire or conventional straight slot track. Both dragsters are the conventional 1/25 inch competition scale.**

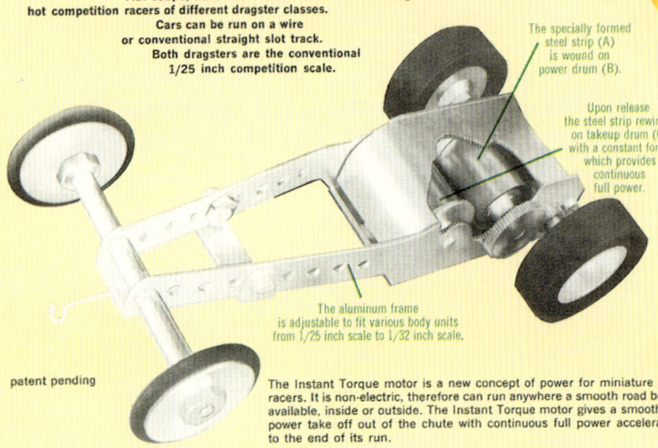


patent pending

The Instant Torque motor is a new concept of power for miniature drag racers. It is non-electric, therefore can run anywhere a smooth road bed is available, inside or outside. The Instant Torque motor gives a smooth full power take off out of the chute with continuous full power acceleration to the end of its run.

ADVANTAGES OF INSTANT TORQUE MOTOR **1. No batteries or electrical hookup 2. Full power out of the chute 3. Continuous acceleration for full run 4. Simple design—fewer parts 5. Will out-perform standard production electric cars.**

A sturdy platform has a turntable disc for easy winding of the Instant Torque motor. Platform also has guide wire and track attachments.

A plastic strip is threaded on to the guide wire. When the car completes the run the strip folds bringing the car to a safe stop.



## 1964 DRAGSTER RACE SETS

## COMBINATIONS AND ITEMS AVAILABLE

**4507 DRAGSTER RACE SET** Consists of 2 unassembled competition coupes 1/25 scale in different colors, dual track, guide wires and track holding platform with winder. Packaged in a four-color box. 3 per shipping carton.
Suggested List Price $18.00

**4506 DRAGSTER RACE SET** Consists of 2 unassembled altered Fiat Coupes, 1/25 scale in different colors, dual track, guide wires and track holding platform with winder. Packaged in a four-color box. 3 per shipping carton.
Suggested List Price $18.00

**4505 COMPETITION COUPE KIT** Consists of one unassembled competition coupe complete with body, frame, tires, wheels and Instant Torque motor. Packaged in a four-color box. 1 doz. to a shipping carton.
Suggested List Price $5.00

**4504 ALTERED FIAT COUPE KIT** Consists of one unassembled altered Fiat coupe complete with body, frame, tires, wheels and Instant Torque motor. Packaged in a four-color box. 1 doz. per shipping carton.
Suggested List Price $5.00

**4503 "INSTANT TORQUE" Motorized Chassis** Consists of unassembled frame, Instant Torque motor drive, wheels, tires, gears, and axles. Packaged in a colorful box. 1 doz. to a shipping carton.
Suggested List Price $4.00

**4501 ALTERED FIAT COUPE BODY** One altered Fiat body 1/25 scale and Decals included. Packaged in a colorful box. 1 doz. to a shipping carton.
Suggested List Price $0.89

**4502 COMPETITION COUPE BODY** One competition coupe body, engine. Decals included. Packaged in a colorful box. 1 doz. to a shipping carton.
Suggested List price $1.29

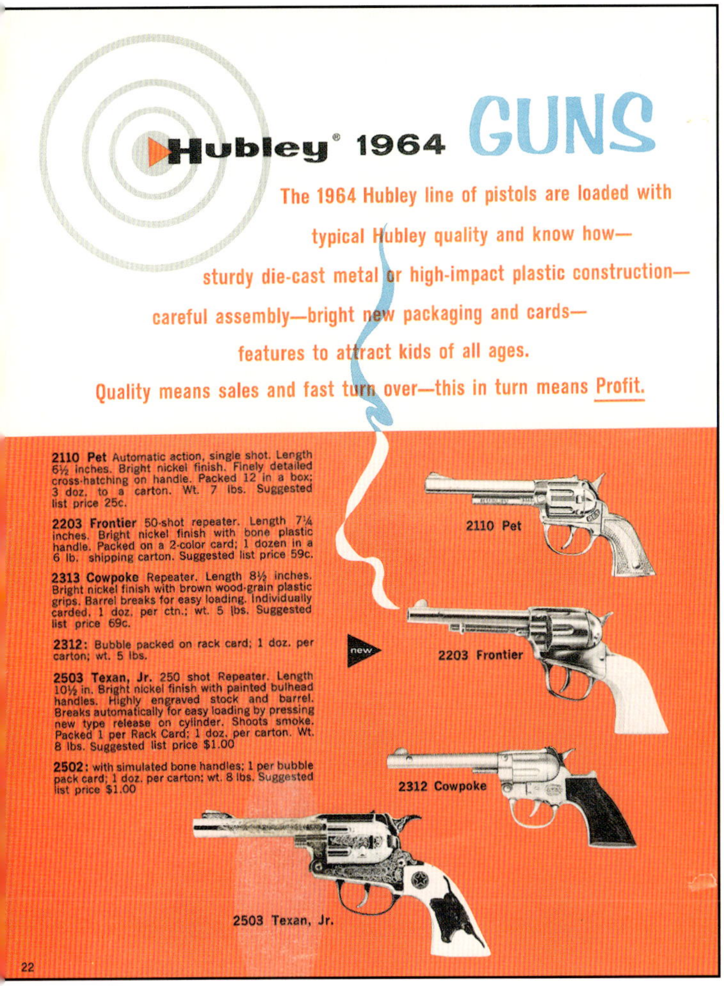

Hubley® 1964 GUNS

The 1964 Hubley line of pistols are loaded with typical Hubley quality and know how—sturdy die-cast metal or high-impact plastic construction—careful assembly—bright new packaging and cards—features to attract kids of all ages.

Quality means sales and fast turn over—this in turn means Profit.

**2110 Pet** Automatic action, single shot. Length 6½ inches. Bright nickel finish. Finely detailed cross-hatching on handle. Packed 12 in a box; 3 doz. to a carton. Wt. 7 lbs. Suggested list price 25c.

**2203 Frontier** 50-shot repeater. Length 7¼ inches. Bright nickel finish with bone plastic handle. Packed on a 2-color card; 1 dozen in a 6 lb. shipping carton. Suggested list price 59c.

**2313 Cowpoke** Repeater. Length 8½ inches. Bright nickel finish with brown wood-grain plastic grips. Barrel breaks for easy loading. Individually carded. 1 doz. per ctn.; wt. 5 lbs. Suggested list price 69c.

**2312:** Bubble packed on rack card; 1 doz. per carton; wt. 5 lbs.

**2503 Texan, Jr.** 250 shot Repeater. Length 10½ in. Bright nickel finish with painted bulhead handles. Highly engraved stock and barrel. Breaks automatically for easy loading by pressing new type release on cylinder. Shoots smoke. Packed 1 per Rack Card; 1 doz. per carton. Wt. 8 lbs. Suggested list price $1.00

**2502:** with simulated bone handles; 1 per bubble pack card; 1 doz. per carton; wt. 8 lbs. Suggested list price $1.00

2110 Pet

new

2203 Frontier

2312 Cowpoke

2503 Texan, Jr.

22

2153 Li'l Cowpoke

new

**2153 Li'l Cowpoke** Automatic action, single shot. Length 6¾ inches. Bright nickel finish. Bone handle with engraved barrel. Packaged on a 2-color card; 1 dozen in a 4 lb. shipping carton. Suggested list price 49c.

**2103 Dick** Repeater. Length 4⅝ in. Bright nickel finish. Left handle slides open for easy loading. Packed 1 per Rack Card; 1 doz. per carton. Wt. 4 lbs. Suggested list price 59c.

**2102:** 1 per bubble pack card; 1 doz. per carton, wt. 4 lbs. Suggested list price 59c.

**2343 Hawk** Repeater. Length 5¾ inches. Bright nickel finish with "mother of pearl" handles, finely detailed engraving. Portion of the barrel above handle left side is hinged, slides up to load caps. Packed 1 per Rack Card; 1 doz. per ctn. Wt. 5 lbs. Suggested list price 69c.

**2403 Trooper** 250-Shot repeater. 5½ in. long, with bright nickel finish and black handles. Packed on card for racking; 1 doz. cards per ctn.; wt. 6 lbs. Suggested list price 79c.

**2402:** 1 per bubble pack card; 1 doz. cards per ctn.; wt. 6 lbs. Suggested list price 79c.

**2511 .45 Automatic** A 50-shot cap repeater. Length 7⅛ inches. Bright nickel and engraved finish. Packaged on a 2-color card; 1 dozen in a 8 lb. shipping carton. Suggested list price $1.00.

**2482 Marshal** Big western 250-shot repeater, highly engraved with bright nickel finish. Simulated pearl handle bearing cameo steer head. Cylinder door slides open for easy loading. Length 9½ in. Individually bubble packed on brightly colored card; packed 1 doz. per ctn.; wt. 9 lbs. Suggested list price $1.00



2102 Dick

**2553 Sniper** Western pistol with extra long barrel. Made of black, high impact plastic with realistic grip. 22 in. long. Single shot, automatic action. Individually packed on bright red and yellow card for racking or bins. 1 doz. cards per ctn. Wt. 7 lbs. Suggested list price $1.00

2343 Hawk

2511 .45 Automatic

2402 Trooper

23

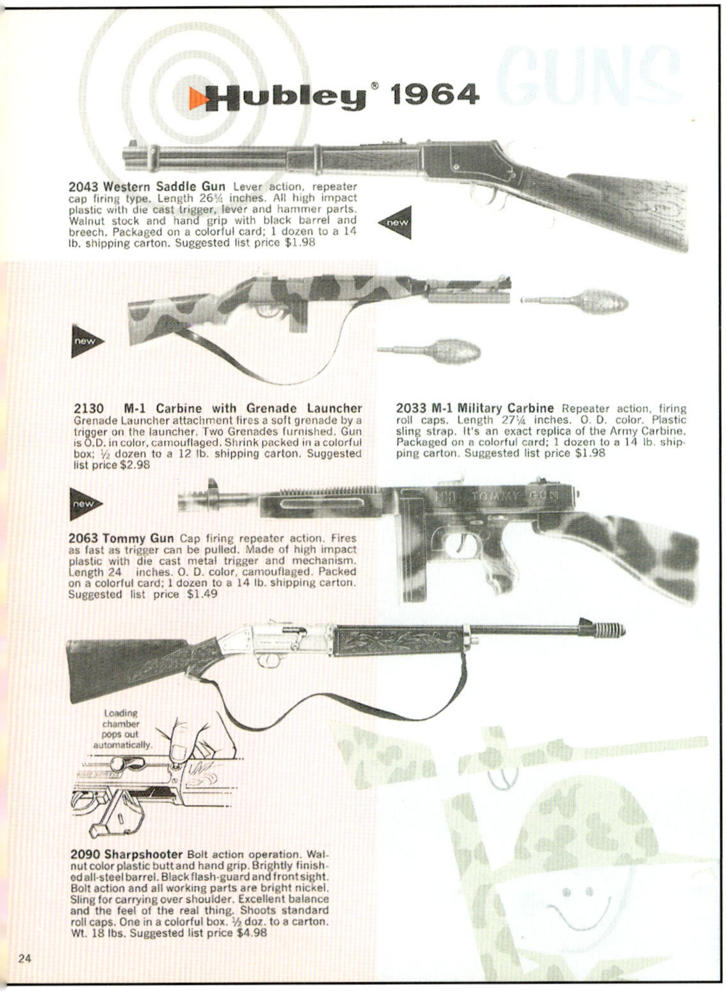

Hubley® 1964 GUNS

**2043 Western Saddle Gun** Lever action, repeater cap firing type. Length 26½ inches. All high impact plastic with die cast trigger, lever and hammer parts. Walnut stock and hand grip with black barrel and breech. Packaged on a colorful card; 1 dozen to a 14 lb. shipping carton. Suggested list price $1.98

new

new

**2130 M-1 Carbine with Grenade Launcher** Grenade Launcher attachment fires a soft grenade by a trigger on the launcher. Two Grenades furnished. Gun is O.D. in color, camouflaged. Shrink packed in a colorful box; ½ dozen to a 12 lb. shipping carton. Suggested list price $2.98

**2033 M-1 Military Carbine** Repeater action, firing roll caps. Length 27¼ inches. O. D. color. Plastic sling strap. It's an exact replica of the Army Carbine. Packaged on a colorful card; 1 dozen to a 14 lb. shipping carton. Suggested list price $1.98

new

**2063 Tommy Gun** Cap firing repeater action. Fires as fast as trigger can be pulled. Made of high impact plastic with die cast metal trigger and mechanism. Length 24 inches. O. D. color, camouflaged. Packed on a colorful card; 1 dozen to a 14 lb. shipping carton. Suggested list price $1.49

Loading chamber pops out automatically.

**2090 Sharpshooter** Bolt action operation. Walnut color plastic butt and hand grip. Brightly finished all-steel barrel. Black flash-guard and front sight. Bolt action and all working parts are bright nickel. Sling for carrying over shoulder. Excellent balance and the feel of the real thing. Shoots standard roll caps. One in a colorful box. ½ doz. to a carton. Wt. 18 lbs. Suggested list price $4.98

24

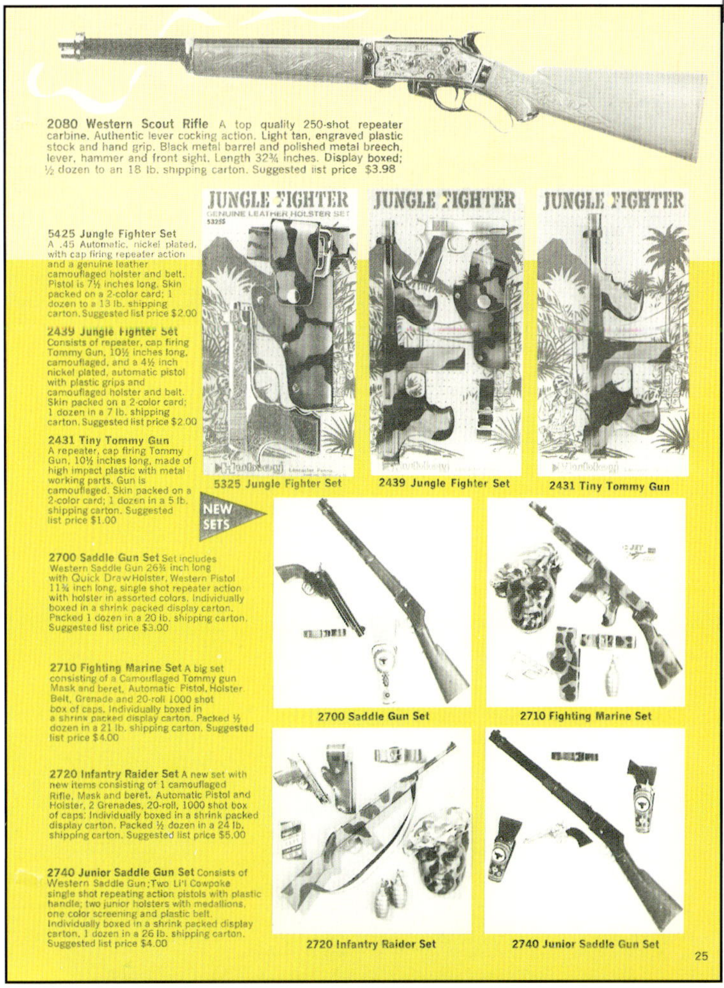

**2080 Western Scout Rifle** A top quality 250-shot repeater carbine. Authentic lever cocking action. Light tan, engraved plastic stock and hand grip. Black metal barrel and polished metal breech, lever, hammer and front sight. Length 32¾ inches. Display boxed; ½ dozen to an 18 lb. shipping carton. Suggested list price $3.98

**5425 Jungle Fighter Set** A .45 Automatic, nickel plated, with cap firing repeater action and a genuine leather camouflaged holster and belt. Pistol is 7½ inches long. Skin packed on a 2-color card; 1 dozen to a 13 lb. shipping carton. Suggested list price $2.00

**2439 Jungle Fighter Set** Consists of repeater, cap firing Tommy Gun, 10½ inches long, camouflaged, and a 4½ inch nickel plated, automatic pistol with plastic grips and camouflaged holster and belt. Skin packed on a 2-color card; 1 dozen in a 7 lb. shipping carton. Suggested list price $2.00

**2431 Tiny Tommy Gun** A repeater, cap firing Tommy Gun, 10½ inches long, made of high impact plastic with metal working parts. Gun is camouflaged. Skin packed on a 2-color card; 1 dozen in a 5 lb. shipping carton. Suggested list price $1.00



5325 Jungle Fighter Set

2439 Jungle Fighter Set

2431 Tiny Tommy Gun

NEW SETS

**2700 Saddle Gun Set** Set includes Western Saddle Gun 26½ inch long with Quick Draw Holster, Western Pistol 11¾ inch long, single shot repeater action with holster in assorted colors. Individually boxed in a shrink packed display carton. Packed 1 dozen in a 20 lb. shipping carton. Suggested list price $3.00

**2710 Fighting Marine Set** A big set consisting of a Camouflaged Tommy gun Mask and beret, Automatic Pistol, Holster Belt, Grenade and 20-roll 1000 shot box of caps. Individually boxed in a shrink packed display carton. Packed ½ dozen in a 21 lb. shipping carton. Suggested list price $4.00

**2720 Infantry Raider Set** A new set with new items consisting of 1 camouflaged Rifle, Mask and beret, Automatic Pistol and Holster, 2 Grenades, 20-roll, 1000 shot box of caps; Individually boxed in a shrink packed display carton. Packed ½ dozen in a 24 lb. shipping carton. Suggested list price $5.00

**2740 Junior Saddle Gun Set** Consists of Western Saddle Gun; Two Li'l Cowpoke single shot repeating action pistols with plastic handle; two junior holsters with medallions, one color screening and plastic belt. Individually boxed in a shrink packed display carton. 1 dozen in a 26 lb. shipping carton. Suggested list price $4.00

2700 Saddle Gun Set

2710 Fighting Marine Set

2720 Infantry Raider Set

2740 Junior Saddle Gun Set

25

# Hubley® 1964

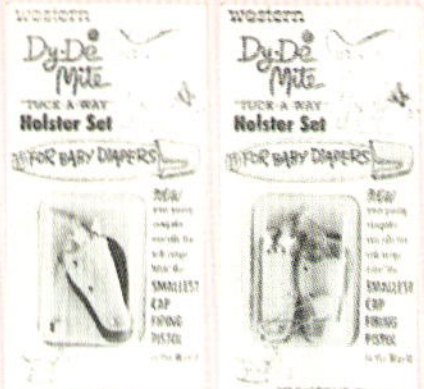

5711 5729

**5711 Dy-De-Mite Holster** Genuine leather, embossed, stand-away pocket, one diaper pin
**Color:** Natural and black
**Gun:** #2014, 3 inches long.
**Packing:** 6 doz. individually bubble packed on colorful card per carton, wt. 9 lbs.
Suggested list price 69c.

**5729 Dy-De-Mite Set** Genuine leather, embossed, stand-away pockets, diaper pins.
**Color:** natural and black.
**Guns:** #2014, 3 inches long.
**Packing:** 6 doz. individually bubble packed on colorful card per carton, wt. 20 lbs.
Suggested list price $1.00

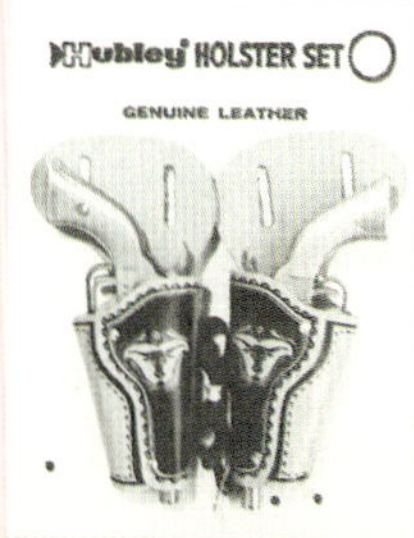

6410

**6410 Set** Genuine leather, tubular pockets with sweep back hanger highly screened.
**Color:** Assorted Colors
**Guns:** #2144 Pal Single Shot pistol
**Packing:** 2 doz. individually skin packed on colorful card, wt. 10 lbs.
Suggested list price. $1.00

**5411 Holster** A beau ful 2 color screened holster with sweep back hanger and belt.
**Color:** Assorted colors.
**Gun:** No. 2204 50 Shot side action repeater.
**Packing:** 2 doz. individually packed in a window box carton, wt. 15 lbs. Suggested list price $1.00

**5417 Police Special Set** Genuine leather holster, badge.
**Color:** black with white screening.
**Gun:** 2414 Detective Special, 4¾ inches.
**Packing:** 1 doz. individually bubble packed on colorful card per carton, wt. 5 lbs.
Suggested list price: $1.00

**5418 Marine Corps Set** Genuine leather holster, whistle.
**Color:** brown with ivory screening.
**Gun:** 2424 Automatic, 5 inches long.
**Packing:** 1 doz. individually bubble packed on colorful card per carton, wt. 5 lbs.
Suggested List Price $1.00

**5400 Assortment** 8 each of the 5417, 5418, 5419. 1 Assortment per carton, wt. 12 lbs.

**5419 Western Set** leather holster.
**Color:** brown with white screening
**Gun:** 2154 Lil Cowpoke, 6¾" long.
**Packing:** 1 doz. individually packed on colorful card per carton, wt. 10 lbs.
Suggested list price. $1.00

**6422 Double Holster Set** Top grain leather double holsters, with embossed pocket and leather belt. Three 2 piece brass bullets on clip.
**Color:** Natural leather color
**Guns:** 2154 nickel plated with black handles, Single shot, repeating action,.
**Packing:** Packed in a display box, shrink packed. 2 dozen in a 12 lb. carton. Suggested list price $2.00

**5421 Single Holster Set** Genuine leather holster decorated with concha, jewel and 1 color screening.
**Color:** Two-toned brown
**Gun:** 2534 nickel plated with white handles, 250 repeater.
**Packing:** Individually boxed in an open display box shrink packed; 1 dozen in a 13 lb. carton. Suggested list price $2.00

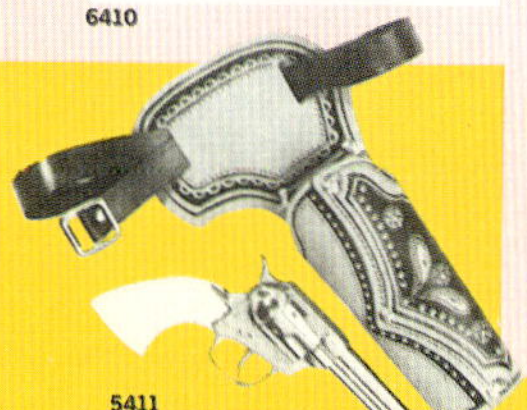
5411

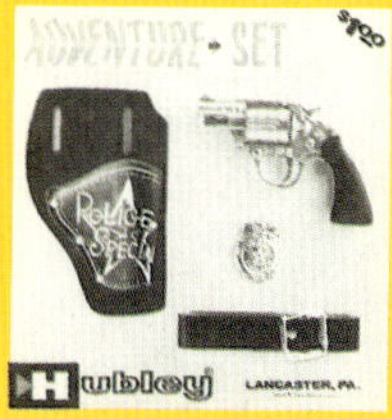

5417

5418

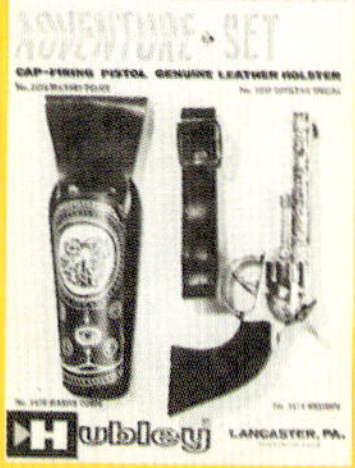

5419



## HOLSTER SETS

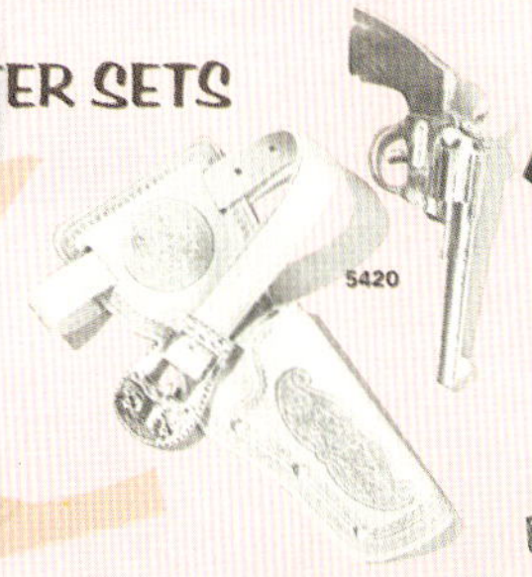
5420

6425

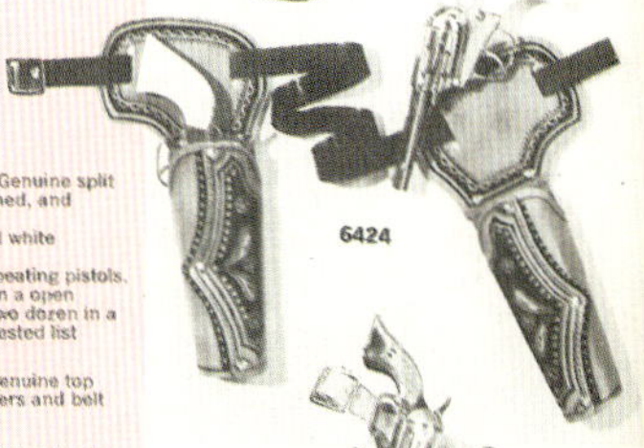
6424

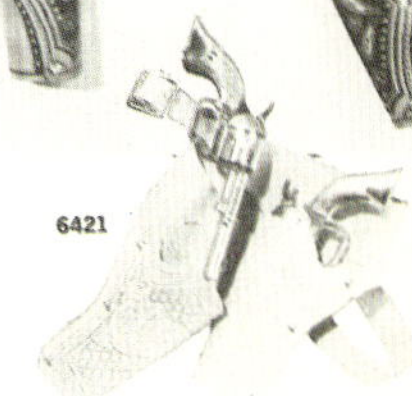
6421

TOT SIZE

**6423 Double Holster Set** Genuine split leather holsters highly screened.
**Color:** Natural with 2 tone screening
**Guns:** Two 2204 fifty shot repeater pistols.
**Packing:** Individually boxed in an open display box shrink packed, 2 dozen in a 21 lb. shipping carton. Suggested list price $2.00

**6421 Double Holster and Belt Set** Top grain cowhide, deeply embossed.
**Color:** Natural
**Guns:** Two 2144 Pal single shot pistols 6 inches long.
**Packing:** Individually boxed in an open display box shrink packed, 2 dozen in a 10 lb. carton. Suggested list price $2.00

**6424 Double Holster Set, Tubular Pockets** with sweep back hangers and plastic belt.
**Colors:** Assorted colors with 2 color screening
**Guns:** Two 2204—50 shot repeating pistols
**Packing:** Individually boxed in an open display box shrink packed. Two dozen in a 21 lb. shipping carton. Suggested list price $2.00

**6425 Double Holster Set** Genuine split leather holsters highly screened, and plastic belt.
**Color:** Natural with black and white screening.
**Guns:** Two 2204—50 shot repeating pistols.
**Packing:** Individually boxed in a open display box shrink packed. Two dozen in a 21 lb. shipping carton. Suggested list price $2.00

**5420 Single Holster Set** Genuine top grain embossed leather holsters and belt with trophy buckle.
**Color:** Natural
**Guns:** No. 2314 50 Shot repeater, break action, brown handles.
**Packing:** Individually boxed in an open display carton shrink packed. One dozen in a 13 lb. shipping carton. Suggested list price $2.00

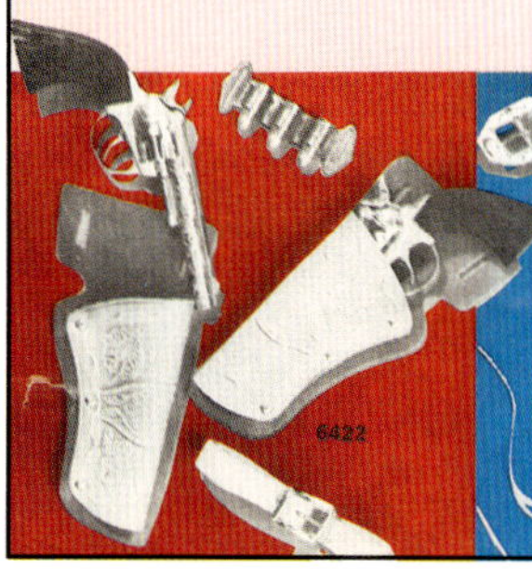
6422

5421

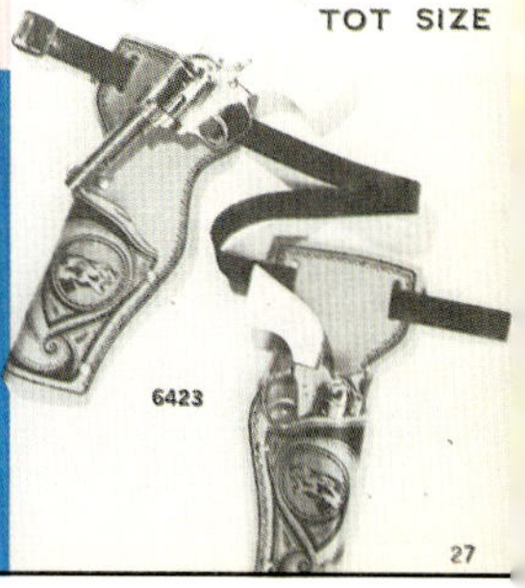
6423



# Hubley® 1964

5422

6420

**5422 Single Holster Set** Tubular holster, large hanger, highly screened with concha and jewel. Belt with trophy buckle.
**Color:** Natural with 2 color screening.
**Guns:** No. 2534 with white handles, 250-shot repeater.
**Packing:** Skin packed in a colorful card. One dozen in a 13 lb. shipping carton. Suggested list price $2.00

**6420 Set** Genuine leather, shearling on pockets and snap-on cuffs, conchas
**Color:** Assorted; black and brown
**Guns:** 2144 Pal, 6 inches long.
**Packing:** 2 doz. individually window boxed per carton, wt. 10 lbs. Suggested list price $2.00

**6431 Double Holster Set** Top grain leather Holsters with richly embossed pockets, 6 bullets.
**Color:** Natural
**Guns:** Two 2314 pistols 8½" long.
**Packing:** Individually boxed in an open display carton, shrink packed; 1 doz. in a 22 lb. carton.
Suggested list price $3.00

**5431 Single Holster Set** Top grain leather two piece pocket, stand-away hanger, 3 bullets, cross strap with trophy buckle.
**Color:** Natural
**Gun:** 2354—50 shot break action repeater with bone handle.
**Packing:** Individually boxed in an open display box shrink packed. One doz. per 19 lbs. shipping carton. Suggested list price $3.00

**6430 Double Holster Set** Genuine leather holster with tubular pockets, highly screened, full belt, 6 white bullets, leg ties.
**Color:** White tube black hangers and belt with 2 color screening.
**Guns:** 2354—50 shot break action repeater
**Packing:** Individually boxed with open display carton, shrink packed. One doz. in a 22 lb. shipping carton.
Suggested list price $3.00

**5432 SINGLE HOLSTER SET**
Genuine leather holster, 2 metal conchas with jewels, 6 silver bullets.
**Color:** 2 color screening on black
**Gun:** No. 2504 pistol,
**Packing:** Individually boxed in a shrink packed display carton
1 dozen in a 19 lb. shipping carton
Suggested list price $3.00.

**6432 DOUBLE HOLSTER SET**
Genuine leather with fringe, 6 white bullets
**Color:** highly screened in 3 colors
**Guns:** Two No. 2325 pistols,
**Packing:** Individually boxed in a shrink packed display box.
1 dozen in a 22 lb. shipping carton.
Suggested list price $3.00.

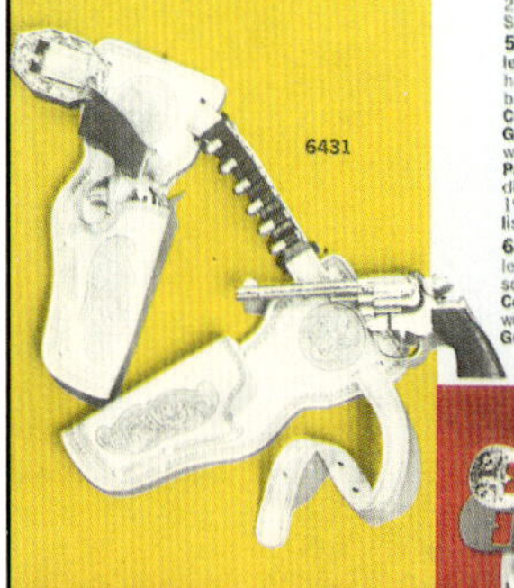
6431

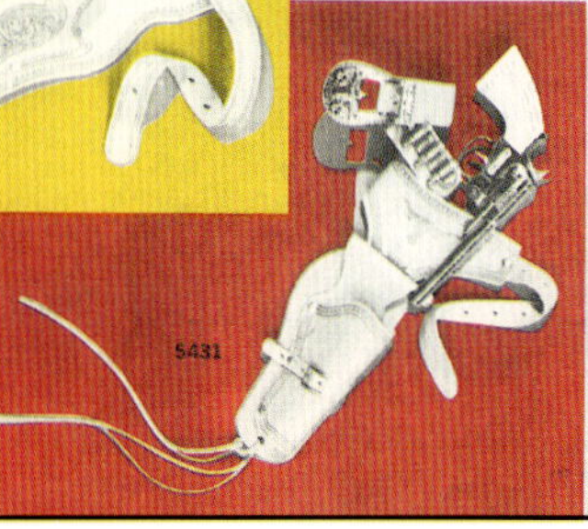
5431

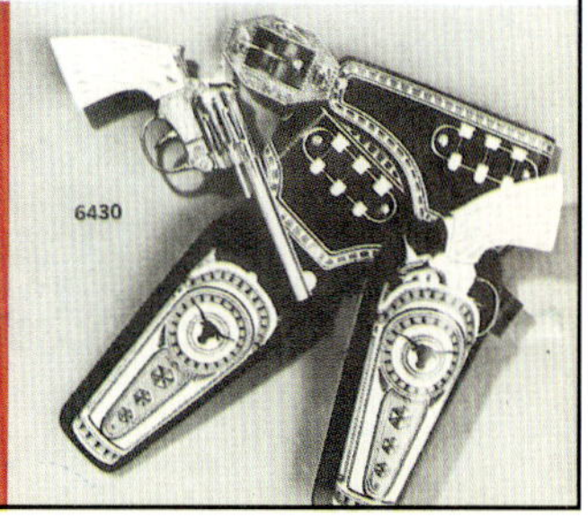
6430



## HOLSTER SETS

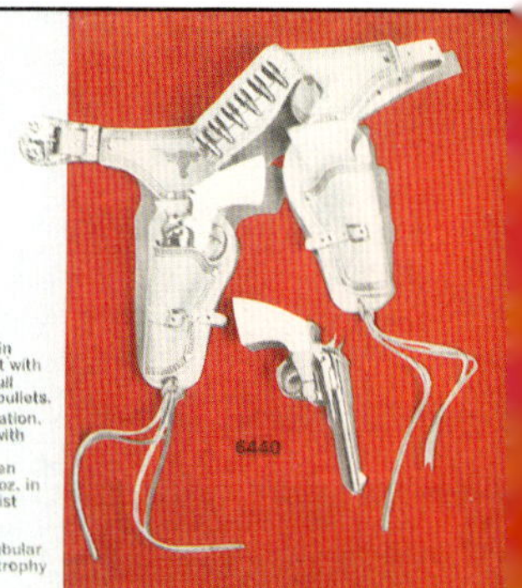
6440

**6440 Double Holster Set** Top grain cowhide holsters and belt, full pocket with cross straps and buckles, leg ties, full belt with trophy buckle and 6 silver bullets.
**Color:** Natural with silk screen decoration.
**Guns:** Two 2325—50 shot repeater with break action.
**Packing:** Individually boxed in an open display carton, shrink packed. One doz. in a 22 lb. shipping carton. Suggested list price $4.00

**6441 Double Holster Set** Large tubular holster full belt 4 conchas, 4 jewels, trophy buckle and 6 silver bullets.
**Color:** Black silk screen in tan.
**Guns:** 2504—250 shot repeater with white handle black decorated.
**Packing:** Individually boxed in an open display carton, shrink packed. One doz. in a 36 lbs. shipping carton. Suggested List price $4.00

**6442 Double Holster Set** Genuine leather, large holster, full belt, two steer head medallions, 6 silver bullets.
**Color:** 2 color silk screen on black.
**Guns:** Two 2504—250 shot repeater pistol.
**Packing:** Individually boxed in an open display carton, shrink packed. One doz. in a 29 lbs. shipping carton. Suggested list price $4.00

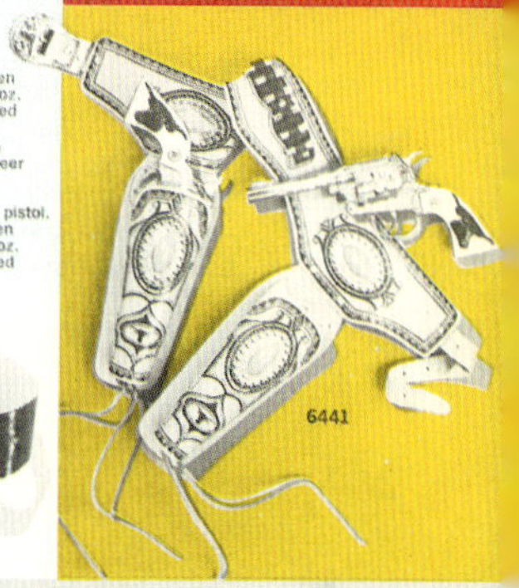
6441

5432

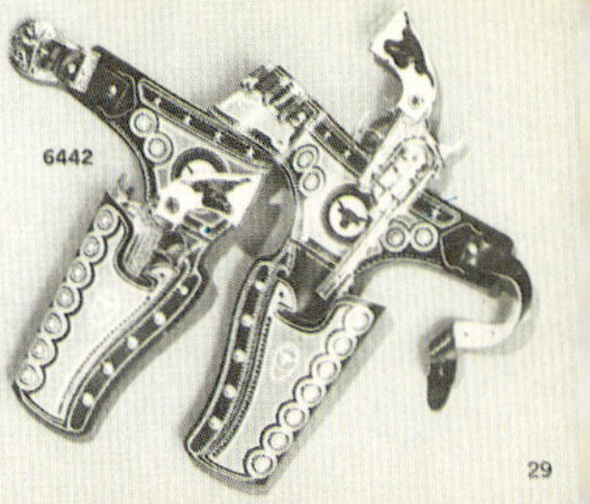
6442

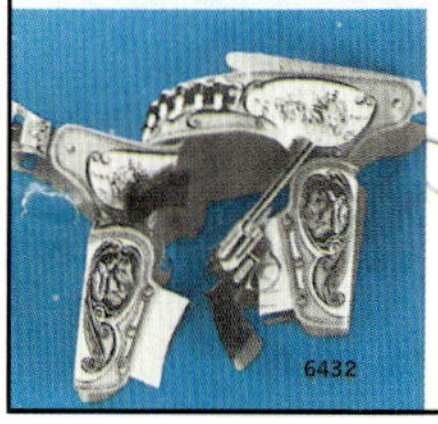
6432

1964

# Hubley® 1964 HOLSTER SETS

**No. 6452 DOUBLE HOLSTER SET**
Genuine leather, 2 conchas, with jewels, leather leg ties, pockets have cross straps, 6 silver bullets.
**Color:** Screened cream on black
**Guns:** No. 2504 pistols, 250 shot repeater
**Packing:** Individually boxed in a shrink pack display box.
½ dozen in an 18 lb. shipping carton.
Suggested list price $5.00

**No. 6451 DOUBLE HOLSTER SET**
Genuine leather holsters, 4 metal conchas, red jewels, 12 silver bullets.
**Color:** 2 color screenings on black tubular pockets
**Guns:** Two No. 2504 pistols, 250 shot repeater, white handles with black steer heads.
**Packing:** Individually boxed in a shrink packed display box
½ dozen per 18 lb. shipping carton
Suggested list price $5.00

**6450 Double Holster Set** Top grain cowhide, deep embossed tubular stand-away holsters and full belt, leg ties, 6 silver bullets.
**Color:** Natural color with colored decoration.
**Guns:** Two 2504—250 shot repeating pistol with white and black plastic handle.
**Packing:** Individually boxed in an open display carton, shrink packed. ½ doz. in a 18 lbs. shipping carton. Suggested list price $5.00

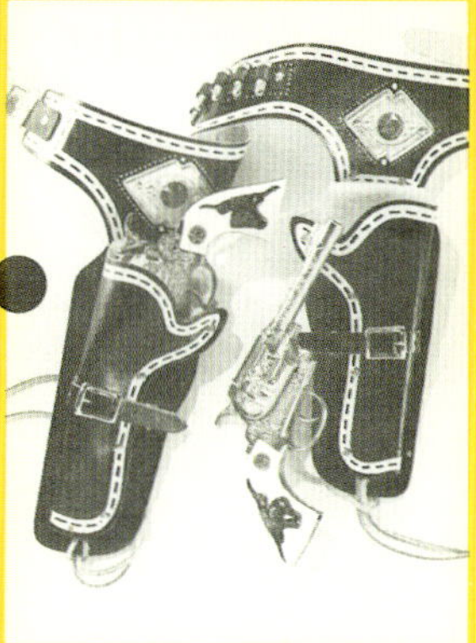
6452

6451

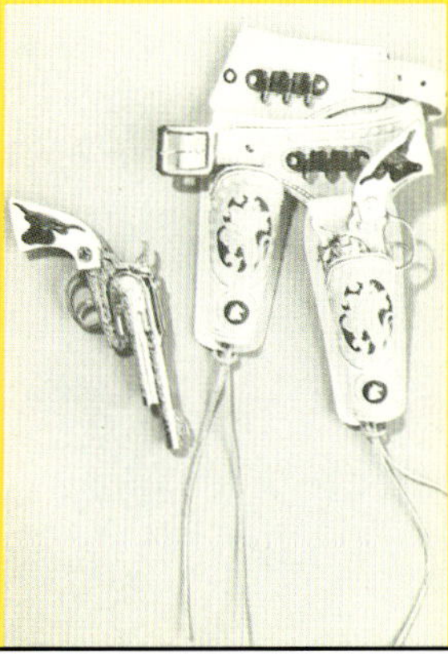
6450

30

# Hubley® golferino™

**9950 Golferino** An exciting golf game anyone can play. Some luck, some skill makes the winner. Turning the knob lines up the golfer, pressing the lever swings the club. When the 9th is holed out, a loving cup pops up. Golferino is made of sturdy plastic, 22¼ x 23½. It is non-electric. Packaged in a bright printed box with rules and score card furnished. Packed 3 to a 25 lb. shipping carton.
Suggested List Price $12.95

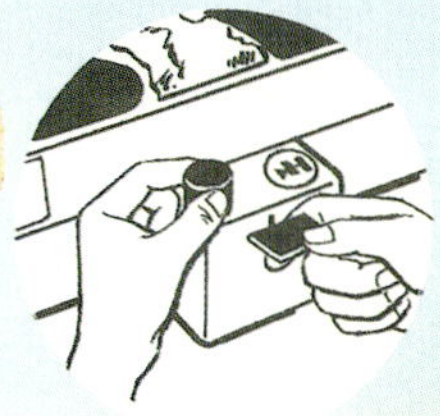

## TIC-TOY CLOCK

**9650 Tic Toy Clock** A very colorful, actual working clock, tremendously popular with 4-year olds and up. Runs as long as 14 hours on one winding. The older child can take it apart and re-assemble by following the color keyed parts and simple instructions. Clock is 11½ inches high, 8 inches wide. Packaged in a colorful display box. Packed ¼ dozen in a 6-lb shipping carton.
Suggested list price $5.95

31

## TO BETTER SERVE YOU
## Hubley SALES TERRITORIES AND OFFICES

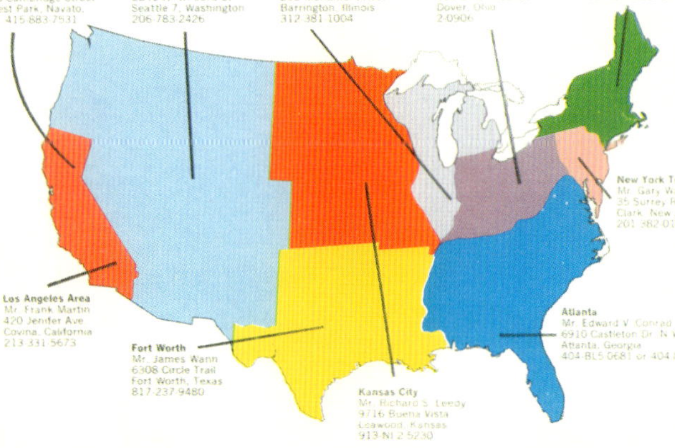


**HOME OFFICE:** The Hubley Manufacturing Co., 110 Pitney Road, Lancaster, Pa., Phone 717-394-2691
**NEW YORK OFFICE:** The Hubley Manufacturing Co., Suite 611—200 Fifth Ave., New York 10, N.Y., 212-OR 5-9343
Mr. Donald Bolin, N.Y. office manager
**CANADA:** Thompson Toy & Hobby Sales, 2nd Floor—200 Bay Street, Toronto 1, Ontario, Canada 416-421-8321
**EXPORT:** Guiterman Co., Inc., 95 Broad Street, New York 4, N.Y. 212 Di 4-1290

## 70th YEAR OF QUALITY TOYS

Hubley has been producing quality toys since 1894. Many oldsters remember the cast iron trucks, circus wagons, fire engines and kitchen ranges of those early years. Many have watched the progression from cast iron toys to die cast metal and plastic.

To stay in business this long proves the long time quality and acceptance of Hubley toys. We are proud of our accomplishments, length of service to children of several generations. We pledge our future to the continuation of durable toys with play value.

**THE HUBLEY MANUFACTURING COMPANY**
LANCASTER, PA. U.S.A.

134-2-64 We reserve the right to make design and price changes without prior notice. Printed in the United States of America

# 1965

Hubley

1965

toys

THE HUBLEY MANUFACTURING COMPANY, LANCASTER, PENNSYLVANIA

No. 1490 Dump Truck
7½ inches long

No. 1491 Log Truck
8 inches long

No. 1493 Rescue Truck
8¼ inches long

## *An Exciting New $1.00 Truck Line*

Up to the minute styling gives this new cab-over-engine truck line a realistic detailed appearance. Chassis and cabs are diecast, backs are sturdy polyethylene plastic. Wheels have black tires, white centers. A new protective see-through package will stimulate sales.

**No. 1034 ASSORTMENT** (Consists of 4 each of the following 3 items.) No. 1490 Dump Truck, No. 1491 Log Truck, No. 1493 Rescue Truck.

| No. | Pack | Wt. | Retail Each |
|---|---|---|---|
| 1490 | 1 doz | 10 lbs | $1.00 |
| 1491 | 1 doz | 16 lbs | 1.00 |
| 1493 | 1 doz | 12 lbs | 1.00 |
| 1034 Asst | 1 doz | 14 lbs | 1.00 |

# MIGHTY METAL TOYS

## *Three New Models of the Famous Jeeps—at $1.00*

Brilliant modern colors and striking detail on these vehicles will make them stand out on the counter. Rugged diecast metal bodies, combined with tough plastic seats and accessories make these big 7-inch Jeeps a top buy. New tamper-proof, see-through packages offer eye-catching impact.

**No. 1028 ASSORTMENT** (Consists of 4 each of the following 3 items.) No. 1710 Civilian Jeep, No. 1711 Jeep Wrecker, No. 1712 Jeep Surfer.

| No. | Pack | Wt. | Retail Each |
|---|---|---|---|
| 1710 | 1 doz | 7 lbs | $1.00 |
| 1711 | 1 doz | 7 lbs | 1.00 |
| 1712 | 1 doz | 7 lbs | 1.00 |
| 1028 Asst | 1 doz | 7 lbs | 1.00 |

No. 1710 Civilian Jeep
Removable top—Folding windshield

No. 1711 Jeep Wrecker
Folding windshield—Wrecker crane

No. 1712 Jeep Surfer
Surf board, Fishing rod accessories



1965

No. 1467 Navy Fighter Plane
6¼ inches long, 8¾ inch wing span

No. 1472 Tractor
7¼ inches long

No. 1474 Tractor and Wagon
10¼ inches long

## *Sales Proven Staple Items—$1.00 Range*

Year after year these items have had high appeal to the younger set. They are small enough for little fingers, realistic enough to stimulate imaginative play. Made of unbreakable diecast metal. Low priced. Visually packed for volume sales.

| No. | Pack | Wt. | Retail Each |
|---|---|---|---|
| 1467 | 1 doz | 8 lbs | $1.00 |
| 1472 | 1 doz | 10 lbs | 1.00 |
| 1474 | 1 doz | 10 lbs | 1.00 |



# MIGHTY METAL TOYS

## *Hubley Carded Toy Sets*

## *18 Sets—3 Assortments—Prepriced at $1.00*

Popular toy combinations that excite the child's imagination. Boost your sales in bin, counter and rack areas. Colorful, eye catching display cards assure fast stock turn-over. Tamper-proof packaging allows customer handling.

**No. 1061 ASSORTMENT** (Consists of 2 each of the following 6 items.) No. 1713 All Purpose Jeep, No. 1754 Traffic Set, No. 1755 Fire Fighting Set, No. 1756 Airport Set, No. 1757 Road Service Set, No. 1759 Gas Station Set.

| No. | Pack | Wt. | Retail Each |
|---|---|---|---|
| 1713 | 1 doz | 6 lbs | $1.00 |
| 1754 | 1 doz | 8 lbs | 1.00 |
| 1755 | 1 doz | 9 lbs | 1.00 |
| 1756 | 1 doz | 7 lbs | 1.00 |
| 1757 | 1 doz | 9 lbs | 1.00 |
| 1759 | 1 doz | 7 lbs | 1.00 |
| 1061 Asst | 1 doz | 8 lbs | 1.00 |

No. 1713 All Purpose Jeep

No. 1754 Traffic Set

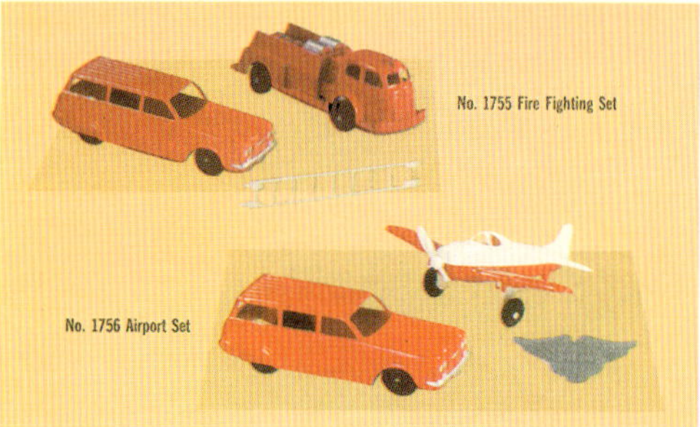
No. 1755 Fire Fighting Set

No. 1756 Airport Set

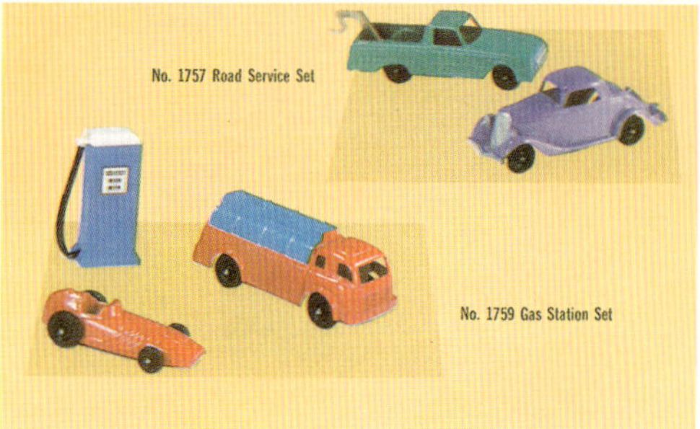
No. 1757 Road Service Set

No. 1759 Gas Station Set

No. 1758 Midget Racer Set

No. 1760 Farm Set

No. 1765 Racer Transport Set

No. 1766 Train Set

No. 1767 Air and Track Set

No. 1772 Bulldozer

A big variety of rugged diecast toys in each assortment. All of them have proven staple year around sales records. Sturdy, tamper-proof packaging allows customer handling.

**No. 1062 ASSORTMENT** (Consists of 2 each of the following 6 items.) No. 1758 Midget Racer Set, No. 1760 Farm Set, No. 1765 Racer Transport Set, No. 1766 Train Set, No. 1767 Air and Track Set, No. 1772 Bulldozer.

| No. | Pack | Wt. | Retail Each |
|---|---|---|---|
| 1758 | 1 doz | 9 lbs | $1.00 |
| 1760 | 1 doz | 9 lbs | 1.00 |
| 1765 | 1 doz | 8 lbs | 1.00 |
| 1766 | 1 doz | 9 lbs | 1.00 |
| 1767 | 1 doz | 6 lbs | 1.00 |
| 1772 | 1 doz | 8 lbs | 1.00 |
| 1062 Asst | 1 doz | 8 lbs | 1.00 |



# MIGHTY METAL TOYS

## *Hubley Carded Toy Sets*

Supply your customers with fresh items all year long by stocking the 3 assortments—different items in each assortment. Built-in child appeal in each set.

**No. 1063 ASSORTMENT** (Consists of 2 each of the following 6 items.) No. 1714 G. I. Jeep, No. 1761 P-40 Fighter Plane, No. 1768 Jungle Patrol Set, No. 1769 Army Engineers Bulldozer, No. 1770 U. S. Air Patrol Set, No. 1771 Army Command Set.

| No. | Pack | Wt. | Retail Each |
|---|---|---|---|
| 1714 | 1 doz | 6 lbs | $1.00 |
| 1761 | 1 doz | 8 lbs | 1.00 |
| 1768 | 1 doz | 6 lbs | 1.00 |
| 1769 | 1 doz | 8 lbs | 1.00 |
| 1770 | 1 doz | 7 lbs | 1.00 |
| 1771 | 1 doz | 8 lbs | 1.00 |
| 1063 Asst | 1 doz | 8 lbs | 1.00 |

No. 1714 G. I. Jeep

No. 1761 P-40 Fighter Plane

No. 1768 Jungle Patrol Set

No. 1769 Army Engineers Bulldozer

No. 1770 U. S. Air Patrol Set

No. 1771 Army Command Set



1965

No. 1801 Dump Truck
Dump body raises and lowers with side lever.

No. 1820 School Bus
Made of heavy duty diecast metal.

No. 1483 Helicopter
Roto blades fold. Clear plastic canopy.

## *3 Metal Toys with Proven Sales Appeal*

These long time favorite toys of the younger set are made of rust proof diecast metal, painted with brilliant colors. They are 9 to 10 inches long, packaged in see-through boxes for sales impact. Top quality, staple toys in the $1.50 price range.

| No. | Pack | Wt. | Retail Each |
|---|---|---|---|
| 1483 | 1 doz | 13 lbs | $1.49 |
| 1801 | 1 doz | 17 lbs | 1.49 |
| 1820 | 1 doz | 13 lbs | 1.69 |



# MIGHTY METAL TOYS

## *A New Hot Truck Line—at $1.98*

Modern, realistic, cab-over-engine, tractor-trailer trucks that feature unbreakable diecast metal cabs and chassis, and tough plastic trailers. Hubley trucks will last and last with many hours of play value assured. Packaged in self-selling see-through boxes.

| No. | Pack | Wt. | Retail Each |
|---|---|---|---|
| 1511 | 1 doz | 10 lbs | $1.98 |
| 1513 | 1 doz | 10 lbs | 1.98 |
| 1514 | 1 doz | 9 lbs | 1.98 |
| 1515 | 1 doz | 11 lbs | 1.98 |

**SPECIAL TRUCK ASST.**

NO. 1071

Consists of ¼ Doz. ea. of 1511, 1513, 1516, 1517.

Pack 1 Doz.

Assortment Wt. 12 lbs.

No. 1511 Auto Transport Truck
13 inches long

No. 1513 Cattle Truck
11½ inches long

No. 1514 Tanker Truck
12 inches long

No. 1515 Lumber Truck
12 inches long

No. 1520 Tractor
9¼ inches long

No. 1517 Jeep with Speedboat
15 inches long

No. 1516 Dump Truck with Bulldozer
14 inches long

Realistic vehicles and combination with kid appeal, combine unbreakabl diecast metal with tough plastic. Au thentic detailing throughout is high lighted with brilliant colors. Colorful tamper-proof, see-through packagin stimulates impulse sales.

| No. | Pack | Wt. | Retail Each |
|---|---|---|---|
| 1516 | 1 doz | 15 lbs | $1.98 |
| 1517 | 1 doz | 10 lbs | 1.98 |
| 1520 | 1 doz | 10 lbs | 1.98 |



# MIGHTY METAL TOYS

## *Sales Proven Favorites—$2.00 Range*

Kids like the realistic detail, bright colors, big size of these diecast metal toys. Realistic detail—right down to the rivets on the wings—white side-walls on the truck. Year after year sales records prove their continued appeal.

| No. | Pack | Wt. | Retail Each |
|---|---|---|---|
| 1882 | 1 doz | 28 lbs | $1.98 |
| 1495 | 1 doz | 20 lbs | 1.98 |
| 1881 | 1 doz | 20 lbs | 1.98 |

No. 1882 Pick-up Truck
12 inches long, deep tread white wall tires.

No. 1495 Fighter Bomber Airplane
10 inches long, folding wings and landing gear. New see-through packaging.

No. 1881 P-38 Fighter Plane
9 inches long, foldup landing gear. New see-through packaging.



1965

No. 1502 Tractor Loader
12¼ inches long, scoop loads, lifts and dumps.

No. 1503 Road Grader
12¾ inches long, independent wheel suspension, scraper blade adjusts, front wheels steer.

No. 1504 Tractor with Stake Trailer
18½ inches long, trailer unhitches, tractor steers.

| No. | Pack | Wt. | Retail Each |
|---|---|---|---|
| 1502 | ½ doz | 19 lbs | $2.98 |
| 1503 | ½ doz | 14 lbs | 2.98 |
| 1504 | ½ doz | 20 lbs | 2.98 |



# MIGHTY METAL TOYS

## *Heavy Duty, Life-Like Action Toys at $3.00*

Haul, scrape and load dirt with these non-rusting diecast metal toys. Action-a-plenty for the future earth moving engineer. Bright colors, big size and colorful packaging gives these toys built-in sales appeal.

| No. | Pack | Wt. | Retail Each |
|---|---|---|---|
| 1901 | ½ doz | 19 lbs | $2.98 |
| 1902 | ½ doz | 15 lbs | 2.98 |
| 1903 | ½ doz | 14 lbs | 2.98 |
| 1505 | ½ doz | 16 lbs | 2.98 |

No. 1901 Power Shovel
15 inches long, scoop operates by side lever, cab rotates, rolls on rubber treads.

No. 1902 Dump Truck
11 inches long, dump body raises by side lever, tail gate swings open, dual rear wheels.

No. 1903 Bulldozer
8¾ inches long, rolls on rubber tracks, adjustable dozer blade.

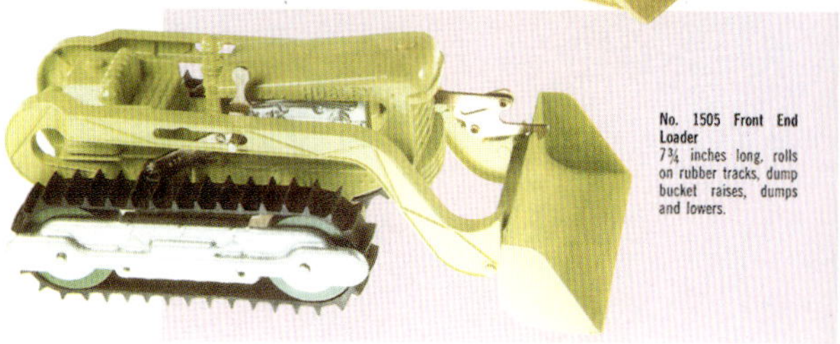

No. 1505 Front End Loader
7¾ inches long, rolls on rubber tracks, dump bucket raises, dumps and lowers.

No. 1506 Tractor
11 inches long, front wheels steer, super detailed engine, rubber tires.

## *Big Size—Big Value in Metal Vehicles*

A durable line of non-rusting, diecast metal trucks and tractors, loaded with realism and play value. These toys are designed for hard indoor or outdoor play. Bright colors and rugged appearance command attention at the counter.

| No. | Pack | Wt. | Retail Each |
|---|---|---|---|
| 1506 | ½ doz | 21 lbs | $3.98 |
| 1926 | ½ doz | 17 lbs | 3.69 |
| 1927 | ½ doz | 17 lbs | 3.98 |

No. 1926 Tow Truck
12 inches long, all metal including crane. Hook is crank operated.

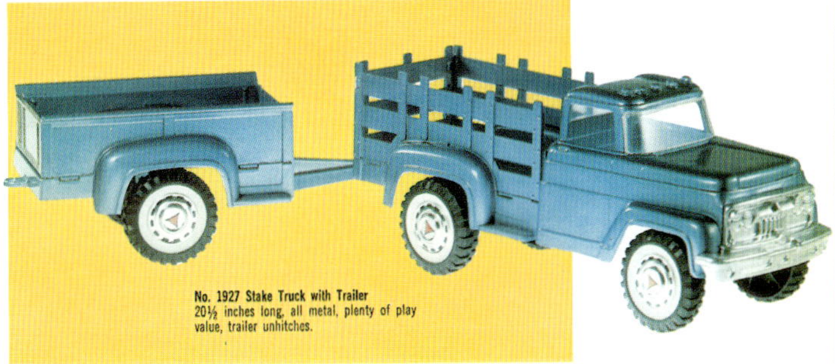

No. 1927 Stake Truck with Trailer
20½ inches long, all metal, plenty of play value, trailer unhitches.



# MIGHTY METAL TOYS

No. 1929 Carpenter's Truck
12 inches long, heavy diecast metal truck, clear plastic tool box with 5 Carpenter's tools and 5 pieces of wood.

No. 1509 Ford 6000 Tractor
12 inches long, authentically detailed Ford styling. Model steers, has deep tractor tread tires.

No. 1928 Pile Driver Truck
13 inches long in travelling position, 14½ inches high with boom up. Weight lifts, drops automatically at the top. Stakes included.

| No. | Pack | Wt. | Retail Each |
|---|---|---|---|
| 1929 | ½ doz | 19 lbs | $3.98 |
| 1509 | ½ doz | 31 lbs | 4.98 |
| 1928 | ½ doz | 21 lbs | 3.98 |

NEW

No. 1014 Airport Set
Consists of 2 metal piper cubs, 8" span, gas truck, crash truck, airport limousine, gas pump. Packed in full-view box.

NEW

No. 1017 Farm Set
11 piece set with lots of play value consists of 3 all metal implements that attach to a 5¼ inch long tractor. 6 inch pick up truck, 6 plastic animals.

NEW

No. 1044 Transportation Set
Consists of 13 inch car-carrier with two cars, tank truck, jeep wrecker and gas pump.

NEW

No. 1047 Builders Set
Set includes a jeep, 7 inches long; 12 inch tractor-trailer with load of lumber; dump truck with bulldozer and trailer.



# MIGHTY METAL TOYS

## *Outstanding Boxed Sets—$2.00 to $10.00 Price Range*

A play-packed combination of well known Hubley Toys make up boxed sets of outstanding value, in a variety of price categories. Six colorful and fast selling gift sets for year-round gift giving.

| No. | Pack | Wt. | Retail Each |
|---|---|---|---|
| 1014 | 1 doz | 20 lbs | $1.98 |
| 1017 | ½ doz | 15 lbs | 2.98 |
| 1044 | ¼ doz | 8 lbs | 4.98 |
| 1047 | ¼ doz | 9 lbs | 4.98 |
| 1049 | ¼ doz | 8 lbs | 3.98 |
| 1069 | ¼ doz | 30 lbs | 9.95 |
| 1091 | ¼ doz | 27 lbs | 8.95 |

NEW

No. 1049 Rancher Set
Set includes tractor with detachable wagon, 10¼ inches long; cultipacker and plow; 11½ inch cattle truck, and farm animals.

No. 1069 Road Building Set
A sturdily built all metal set which includes a 15 inch power shovel; 13 inch road grader; 10 inch dump truck; 10½ inch front end loader.

No. 1091 Deluxe Farm Set
All metal set consisting of large Ford tractor, 11 inches long; farm wagon with a 5 x 11 inch bed; cultivator and plow. All implements hitch to the tractor.

# HUBLEY GOLFERINO

No. 9950 Golferino

An exciting golf game for players of all ages. It takes some skill, some luck to be a winner. Turning the knob lines up the little golfer, pressing the lever swings the club. When the 9th is holed out, a loving cup pops up. Golferino is made of sturdy plastic, 22¼" x 23½". It is non-electric. Packaged in a brightly colored box with rules and score card.

| No. | Pack | Wt. |
|---|---|---|
| 9950 | ¼ | 25 lbs |

# HUBLEY PLASTIC TOYS

No. 1311 Airplane

No. 1310 Motorcycle

No. 1309 Tractor

Just the toys for that extra sales volume at bin ends and check out counters. Bulk packed, 12 to an inner carton, for ease in handling. The toys are approximately 5 inches long, in bright colors and made of tough high impact plastic—a long standing record of volume sales. The best buy is assortment 1008.

**No. 1008 ASSORTMENT** (Consists of 24 each of the following three items.) No. 1309 Tractor, No. 1310 Motorcycle, No. 1311 Airplane.

| No. | Pack | Wt. | Retail Each |
|---|---|---|---|
| 1309 | 3 doz | 6 lbs | 29¢ |
| 1310 | 3 doz | 6 lbs | 29¢ |
| 1311 | 3 doz | 5 lbs | 29¢ |
| 1008 Asst | 6 doz | 11½ lbs | 29¢ |



## *Diecast Metal Vehicles—Big for the Price—at 39¢*

Vehicles are 6 inches long, painted and decorated in bright colors. Individually skin packed on colorful cards. A perfect assortment for bin ends, check out counters and racks. They create plus business with a minimum of space and effort.

**ASSORTMENT 1029** (Consists of 4 each of the following items.) No. 1401, No. 1402, No. 1403, No. 1404, No. 1405, No. 1406.

| No. | Pack | Wt. | Retail Each |
|---|---|---|---|
| 1401 | 1 doz | 4 lbs | 39¢ |
| 1402 | 1 doz | 4 lbs | 39¢ |
| 1403 | 1 doz | 5 lbs | 39¢ |
| 1404 | 1 doz | 4 lbs | 39¢ |
| 1405 | 1 doz | 4 lbs | 39¢ |
| 1406 | 1 doz | 4 lbs | 39¢ |
| 1029 Asst | 2 doz | 8 lbs | 39¢ |

No. 1401 Continental Sedan

No. 1402 Fire Engine

No. 1403 Falcon Pick-up Truck

No. 1404 1934 Ford Coupe

No. 1405 Corvair Station Wagon

No. 1406 Gas Truck

## *4 Great New Trucks—Visually Packed—at 79¢*

Vehicles combine unbreakable diecast metal cabs and chassis with tough plastic backs. They are 6½ to 9½ inches long, in brilliant colors, and bubble packed on colorful cards.

**1031 ASSORTMENT** (Consists of 3 each of the following items.) No. 1458, No. 1459, No. 1460, No. 1461.

| No. | Pack | Wt. | Retail Each |
|---|---|---|---|
| 1458 | 1 doz | 7 lbs | 79¢ |
| 1459 | 1 doz | 8 lbs | 79¢ |
| 1460 | 1 doz | 7 lbs | 79¢ |
| 1461 | 1 doz | 7 lbs | 79¢ |
| 1031 Asst | 1 doz | 7 lbs | 79¢ |

No. 1458 Dump Truck

No. 1459 Log Truck

No. 1460 Motor Express

No. 1461 Gas Truck



1965

NEW

## *No. 4868 SJ Duesenberg Town Car*

The luxury car of the 1930's has been duplicated in diecast metal 1/18th scale, 12¼ inches long. Detailed parts are in chrome and hi-impact plastic—steers by worm and sector gears—hood lifts off to display highly detailed engine—over 150 parts. Easy screwdriver assembly.

| No. | Pack | Wt. | Retail Each |
|---|---|---|---|
| 4868 | ½ doz | 20 lbs | $9.95 |

## *No. 4864 SJ Duesenberg Phaeton*

The dual cowl, sweep panel Phaeton, body by LaGrande is one of the most talked about classic cars. This superb 1/18th scale model, 12¼ inches long consists of 150 parts made of diecast metal with plastic chrome trim. Flexible exhaust pipes, worm and sector steering, rubber tires, detailed engine, frame and running gear intrigue the model builder.

| No. | Pack | Wt. | Retail Each |
|---|---|---|---|
| 4864 | ½ doz | 21 lbs | $9.95 |

No. 4863 Packard Dietrich

No. 4859 Packard Sport Phaeton

No. 4860 Packard Roadster

## *The Elegant 1930 Packards*

In 1930 Packard was considered the car for the discerning buyer. Today these authentic reproductions of famous Packard stylings are appreciated by model builders and collectors alike. Each Model has over 140 diecast metal and chromed plastic parts. The Models are 1/22nd scale, 9½ inches long. Front wheels steer by worm and sector gears. Hoods lift off to display the famous straight 8 engine.

| No. | Pack | Wt. | Retail Each |
|---|---|---|---|
| 4859 | ½ doz | 13 lbs | 4.98 |
| 4860 | ½ doz | 13 lbs | 4.98 |
| 4863 | ½ doz | 12 lbs | 4.98 |

# METAL CAR KITS

No. 4865 Chevrolet Phaeton

No. 4869 Chevrolet Coupe

No. 4862 Chevrolet Roadster

## *3 Snappy 1932 Chevrolets*

To compete with the depression and popularity of the Model A, Chevrolet introduced this snappy looking, low priced car in 1932.

These reproductions are 1/20th scale, 8 inches long with over 75 diecast metal and chromed plastic parts. The hoods lift off to show the detailed engine. Front wheels steer.

| No. | Pack | Wt. | Retail Each |
|---|---|---|---|
| 4869 | 1 doz | 21 lbs | $3.00 |
| 4865 | 1 doz | 21 lbs | 3.49 |
| 4862 | 1 doz | 21 lbs | 3.49 |

# METAL CAR KITS

## *The Ever-Famous Model A Ford*

These eye-catching models have captured the charm of the most popular car of the 1930's. There are over 35 parts in the Model A Ford Kits. Most of the parts are diecast metal with high impact plastic accessory parts. The models are 1/20th scale, 7½ inches long. Front wheels actually steer, hoods lift off to show the famous four-cylinder engine.

| No. | Pack | Wt. | Retail Each |
|---|---|---|---|
| 4850 | 1 doz | 18 lbs | $2.98 |
| 4855 | 1 doz | 19 lbs | 2.98 |
| 4856 | 1 doz | 18 lbs | 2.98 |
| 4857 | 1 doz | 21 lbs | 2.98 |
| 4858 | 1 doz | 22 lbs | 3.49 |
| 4861 | 1 doz | 19 lbs | 2.98 |
| 4866 | 1 doz | 20 lbs | 2.98 |

No. 4866 Ford Victoria

No. 4850 Ford Roadster

No. 4855 Ford Pick-up

No. 4858 Model A Station Wagon

No. 4856 Ford Phaeton

No. 4857 Ford Town Sedan

No. 4861 Ford Coupe

22

see the complete line of **GUNS** and **HOLSTERS** for **1965**

New Pistols
New Rifles
New Holsters
New Sets
New Packaging

**Ask your Hubley salesman for the new Gun & Holster Catalog.**

All list prices are furnished only for the identification of the products, and nothing in this catalog should be regarded as an indication that the prices set forth are the usual retail prices. This material is sent to the retailer and/or distributor upon the express condition that it will not be used to represent usual selling prices.

23



TO BETTER SERVE YOU

## Hubley SALES TERRITORIES AND OFFICES

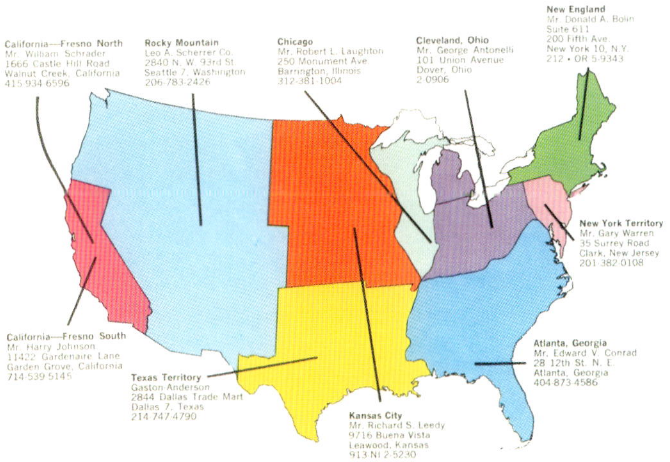


**HOME OFFICE:** The Hubley Manufacturing Co., 110 Pitney Road, Lancaster, Pa., Phone 717-394-2691

**NEW YORK OFFICE:** The Hubley Manufacturing Co., Suite 611—200 Fifth Ave., New York 10, N.Y., 212-OR 5-9343
Mr. Donald Bolin, N.Y. office manager

**CANADA:** Thompson Toy & Hobby Sales, 2nd Floor—200 Bay Street, Toronto 1, Ontario, Canada 416-421-8321

**EXPORT:** Guiterman Co., Inc., 95 Broad Street, New York 4, N.Y. 212-DI 4-1290

### 71st YEAR OF QUALITY TOYS

Hubley has been producing quality toys since 1894. Many oldsters remember the cast iron trucks, circus wagons, fire engines and kitchen ranges of those early years. Many have watched the progression from cast iron toys to die cast metal and plastic.

To stay in business this long proves the long time quality and acceptance of Hubley toys. We are proud of our accomplishments, length of service to children of several generations. We pledge our future to the continuation of durable toys with play value.

**THE HUBLEY MANUFACTURING COMPANY**

LANCASTER, PA. U.S.A.

152-1-65 We reserve the right to make design and price changes without prior notice. Printed in the United States of America

# VALUE GUIDE

Although this book is intended to illustrate the exemplary catalogs issued by Hubley in the immediate postwar period and until they were acquired by Gabriel Industries, values are provided herein because they seem to always be of interest to collectors. The values are presented in price ranges from average condition to optimal condition as described below. More detailed values for vehicular toys with distinctions involving details such as colors, accessories, design variations and the like can be found in *Hubley Toy Vehicles: 1946-1965*.

Listed in this section is the Model Number and Model name for each item appearing in the Hubley factory catalogs illustrated earlier in this book. The toys are grouped by type as follows:

AUTOMOBILES
TRUCKS
MOTORCYCLES
CONSTRUCTION
FARM
AIRCRAFT
SETS
KITS
GUNS & WESTERN
MISCELLANEOUS

In some instances Hubley changed the Model Name with no change to the toy, but retained the same Model Number. The different model names are shown for the Model Number with the value(s) presented on the last line in the group. In other instances when Hubley discontinued a toy, they reused the Model Number for a different toy. In the value listings herein, such changes can be identified by the different Model Name associated with the reused Model Number. In other instances the toy itself changed, but the Model Name and Number did not. In the listings that follow, a catalog year is presented in parentheses to make that distinction. Examples of this use of the year are:

- (1959) - refers to the specific catalog year, 1959 for example
- (<1959) - refers to toys appearing in years prior to the specified year
- (>1959) - refers to toys appearing in catalogs after the specified year

Given the above, the listing for one **505 LOG TRUCK** is supplemented by *(1952)* to indicate the truck shown in the 1952 catalog. A **460 STAKE TRUCK** is supplemented with *(<1954)* to indicate that truck as shown in catalogs prior to 1954. A **497 POULTRY TRUCK** is supplemented with *(>1958)* to indicate that truck as it appears in catalogs after 1958.

Hubley used model number suffixes for differing purposes. A "K" suffix was used to denote a kit. That suffix is included as a part of the applicable model numbers in the value guide listings that follow. The company also used "R" and "S" as suffixes to denote packaging differences. These suffixes are not included in the listings that follow.

The values provided are given in dollar ranges for most toys. The lower amount represents a toy in **Average Condition**. Examples in lesser condition have negligible value except for parts or as candidates for restoration. The higher amount is for the toy in **Optimal Condition**. Note tha only the optimal condition value is given for:

- shrink-wrapped sets and they must be unopened
- kits and they must be unbuilt (and not started) and in their origina packaging
- other miscellaneous toys that include accessory items

A Hubley toy in **Average Condition** is one that has:

- for metal toys at least 60% of the original paint or virtually 100% fo a repaint of professional quality using the correct colors
- on plastic toys several instances of surface abrasions such as scratches and heavy rubs
- no sign of repair
- no damage, including breaks or cracks
- no severe wear or usage
- no broken or missing parts or accessories that are not replaceable
- moderate, if any, warping of plastic parts

A toy in **Optimal Condition** is a candidate for the best of collections and is in a condition that is extremely difficult to locate. Such a toy shoulc have:

- for metal toys virtually all of its original paint (about 98%) with nc touch-ups or repainting
- no sign of repair
- no missing parts or accessories
- no replacement parts or accessories unless they are new-old-stock as original to the toy
- no damage
- virtually no sign of wear or use
- no warping of plastic parts

Original packaging is becoming an increasingly significant factor ir establishing values. Following are percentages to add to the toy's value based on the presence and condition of the original packaging:

**Original box.** For the original box add 40% for closed sided boxes and 25% for open-sided boxes. Hubley toys were typically issued ir attractive but very fragile boxes. They did not age well and tore easily, especially the end and tuck flaps when opened and closed too frequently. The box must match the model name and numbe of the toy and be of commensurate condition with the toy to justify this premium. Add proportionately lesser amounts for boxes in lesse condition than the toy.

**Box liner.** Deduct 15% if the liner for a boxed set is missing.

**Shrink wrapped.** Add 25% if still on the card and unopened.

## AUTOMOBILES

305 FIRE CHIEF CAR - *$10 to $45*
308 TAXI CAB - *$15 to $55*
325 RACER - *$15 to $65*
401 CONTINENTAL SEDAN - *$10 to $35*
404 FORD 1934 COUPE
1934 FORD COUPE - *$10 to $35*
405 CORVAIR STATION WAGON - *$10 to $35*
432 SPORT CAR
M.G. SPORTS CAR - *$25 to $85*
452 DELUXE SEDAN - *$45 to $100*
455 SPORT CAR
JAGUAR - *$50 to $85*
456 RACER - *(<1948) $40 to $115*
456 RACER - *(1950) $30 to $95*
457 RACER - *$35 to $125*
458 CONVERTIBLE - *$50 to $115*
459 TAXI CAB - *$50 to $115*
465 CONVERTIBLE - *$55 to $125*
475 THUNDERBIRD - *$60 to $ 90*
476 STATION WAGON - *$35 to $100*
476 AMBULANCE - *$35 to $100*
485 SPORT CAR
M.G. - *$85 to $195*
486 DELUXE SPORT CAR
THUNDERBIRD - *$65 to $165*
491 STATION WAGON AND BOAT CARRIER - *$65 to $150*
509 CUSTOM SPORT CAR
CORVETTE - *$250 to $550*
655 FORD FAIRLANE SEDAN & BOAT TRAILER - *$85 to $185*
952 THE OFFICIAL MR. MAGOO CAR - *$100 to $285*
1401 CONTINENTAL SEDAN (See 401)
1404 FORD 1934 COUPE (See 404)
1405 CORVAIR STATION WAGON (See 405)

## TRUCKS

306 FIRE ENGINE - *$10 to $25*
307 HOOK AND LADDER - *$12 to $30*
317 REPAIR TRUCK - *$15 to $35*
318 LOG TRUCK - *$10 to $25*
319 GAS TRUCK - *$12 to $35*
320 DUMP TRUCK - *$10 to $35*
321 TOW TRUCK - *$12 to $35*
322 DUMP TRUCK - *$20 to $45*
322 HOOK & LADDER - *$12 to $45*
323 WRECKER
TOW TRUCK - *$20 to $65*
324 FIRE TRUCK
HOOK AND LADDER - *$20 to $65*
327 TELEPHONE TRUCK - *$25 to $80*
329 GAS TRUCK - *$20 to $65*
330 MOTOR EXPRESS - *$20 to $65*
331 DIESEL DUMP TRUCK - *$30 to $75*
332 DIESEL TOW TRUCK
DIESEL WRECKER - *$35 to $80*
333 DIESEL HOOK & LADDER - *$35 to $80*
334 DIESEL TELEPHONE TRUCK - *$40 to $90*
335 DIESEL GAS TRUCK - *$35 to $80*
336 DIESEL MOTOR EXPRESS - *$35 to $80*
350 HOOK AND LADDER - *$65 to $160*
351 LOG TRUCK - *$50 to $140*
351 LUMBER TRUCK - *$75 to $150*
352 MOTOR EXPRESS - *$50 to $115*
353 MOTOR TRANSPORT
AUTO TRANSPORT - *$85 to $150*
355 HOOK AND LADDER - *$75 to $150*
356 LOG TRUCK - *$45 to $100*
357 CATTLE TRUCK - *$50 to $115*
358 HUBLEY TANKER - *$75 to $150*
359 MILK TANKER - *$95 to $235*
360 MILK TRUCK - *$10 to $25*
361 PIG TRUCK - *$10 to $25*
362 TRACTOR TRUCK - *$10 to $25*
363 CHICKEN TRUCK - *$12 to $30*
376 SNOW CAT - *$15 to $35*
377 ROCKET LAUNCHER -*$15 to $35*
402 FIRE ENGINE - *$15 to $40*
403 FALCON PICK-UP TRUCK - *$15 to $45*
406 GASOLINE TRUCK - *$10 to $25*
429 LOG TRUCK - *$25 to $65*
431 DUMP TRUCK - *$25 to $65*
452 STAKE TRUCK - *$30 to $95*
453 FIRE ENGINE - *$60 to $145*
453 TOW TRUCK - *$30 to $100*
454 HOOK AND LADDER - *$55 to $160*
454 LOG TRUCK - *$25 to $85*
458 DUMP TRUCK - *$60 to $140*
459 LOG TRUCK - *$55 to $130*
460 STAKE TRUCK - *(<1954) $30 to $95*
STAKE TRUCK - (>1956) *$65 to $150*
461 PICK-UP TRUCK - *$35 to $100*
462 TOW TRUCK - *$35 to $100*
463 HOOK AND LADDER - *$35 to $100*
464 FIRE ENGINE - *$30 to $85*
465 HOOK & LADDER
FIRE ENGINE - *$35 to $100*
466 AIR COMPRESSOR - *$30 to $100*
468 HOOK & LADDER - *$65 to $150*
469 LOG TRUCK - *(<1956) $55 to $145*
LOG TRUCK - *(>1957) $50 to $125*
470 STAKE TRUCK - *$85 to $200*
470 LUMBER TRUCK - *$55 to $165*
470 DUMP TRUCK - *$35 to $200*
471 LUMBER TRUCK - *$85 to $200*
471 DUMP TRUCK - *$60 to $145*
471 HOOK & LADDER - *$50 to $135*
472 HOOK & LADDER - *$95 to $185*
473 HOOK & LADDER - *$85 to $200*
474 TOW TRUCK - *$75 to $150*
475 DUMP TRUCK - *$45 to $135*

476 DUMP TRUCK - *$75 to $150*
477 CEMENT MIXER - *$85 to $185*
477 STAKE TRUCK - *$65 to $175*
478 BELL TELEPHONE TRUCK
TELEPHONE TRUCK - *$115 to $225*
478 DUMP TRUCK - *$75 to $175*
479 LOG TRUCK - *$65 to $165*
482 TELEPHONE TRUCK
BELL TELEPHONE TRUCK - *$95 to $175*
482 TOW TRUCK - *$100 to $185*
483 CEMENT MIXER - *$100 to $185*
484 TELEPHONE TRUCK - *$125 to $235*
485 PIPE TRUCK. - *$115 to $235*
487 CEMENT MIXER - *$110 to $195*
489 GRAIN TRUCK - *$110 to $200*
491 SHOVEL TRUCK - *$110 to $225*
492 AUTO TRANSPORT
TRANSPORT - *$135 to $265*
493 LUMBER TRUCK
LOG TRUCK - *$110 to $195*
494 SHOVEL TRUCK - *$100 to $200*
494 BELL TELEPHONE TRUCK - *$130 to $250*
497 POULTRY TRUCK - *(<1959) $100 to $200*
POULTRY TRUCK - *(>1958) $85 to $175*
498 FISH HATCHERY - *$95 to $185*
500 TRACTOR TRAILER TRUCK - *$150 to $375*
501 AUTO TRANSPORT - *$175 to $385*
502 LUMBER TRUCK - *$110 to $315*
503 STAKE TRUCK - *$140 to $300*
504 TELEPHONE TRUCK - *(1952) $150 to $300*
TELEPHONE TRUCK
TELEPHONE TRUCK (METAL)
TELEPHONE TRUCK - *(>1952) $120 to $285*
505 LOG TRUCK - *(1952) $100 to $300*
505 LOG TRUCK - *(>1952) $100 to $265*
506 CARRYALL - *$125 to $300*
507 MOTOR EXPRESS - *$115 to $275*
508 DUMP TRUCK - *$120 to $285*
510 LOG TRUCK - *$125 to $325*
511 CARRYALL - *$150 to $375*
512 DUMP TRUCK - *$135 to $350*
513 FIRE PUMPER - *$350 to $850*
520 FIRE TRUCK - *$135 to $335*
521 AUTO TRANSPORT - *$175 to $385*
522 AIR FORCE BOMBER TRANSPORTER - *$115 to $300*
801 DUMP TRUCK - *$20 to $85*
802 TRACTOR TRUCK - *$25 to $90*
803 PIPE TRUCK - *$30 to $100*
851 STOCK YARD TRUCK - *$100 to $200*
882 PICK-UP TRUCK - *$50 to $125*
902 DUMP TRUCK - *$55 to $135*
926 TOW TRUCK - *$60 to $150*
927 STAKE TRUCK WITH TRAILER - *$60 to $150*
953 TRACTOR WITH TRAILER DUMP - *$80 to $175*
966 FLAT BED WITH SHOVEL - *$100 to $195*
1402 FIRE ENGINE (See 402)
1403 FALCON PICK-UP TRUCK (See 403)
1406 GASOLENE TRUCK (See 406)
1458 DUMP TRUCK - *$10 to $30*
1953 TRACTOR WITH TRAILER DUMP (See 953)
1459 LOG TRUCK - *$5 to $25*
1460 MOTOR EXPRESS - *$10 to $35*
1461 GAS TRUCK - *$10 to $35*
1470 DUMP TRUCK (See 470)
1471 HOOK & LADDER (See 471)
1490 DUMP TRUCK - *$20 to $65*
1491 LOG TRUCK - *$20 to $65*
1492 TRANSPORT (DIESEL) (See 492)
1493 RESCUE TRUCK - *$25 to $75*
1511 AUTO TRANSPORT TRUCK - *$45 to $135*
1513 CATTLE TRUCK - *$20 to $65*
1514 TANKER TRUCK - *$25 to $85*
1515 LUMBER TRUCK - *$20 to $75*
1516 DUMP TRUCK WITH BULLDOZER - *$45 to $145*
1517 JEEP WITH SPEEDBOAT - *$40 to $100*
1710 CIVILIAN JEEP - *$25 to $75*
1711 JEEP WRECKER - *$20 to $65*
1712 JEEP SURFER - *$20 to $65*
1713 ALL PURPOSE JEEP - *$10 to $40*
1714 G.I. JEEP - *$15 to $25*
1801 DUMP TRUCK (See 801)
1882 PICK-UP TRUCK (See 882)
1890 U.S. ARMY CARRYALL. - *$65 to $165*
1902 DUMP TRUCK (See 902)
1926 TOW TRUCK (See 926)
1927 STAKE TRUCK WITH TRAILER (See 927)
1928 PILE DRIVER - *$125 to $250*
1929 CARPENTERS TRUCK - *$100 to $250*
1966 FLAT BED WITH SHOVEL (See 966)

## CONSTRUCTION

315 ROAD ROLLER - *$10 to $30*
316 ROAD SCRAPER - *$10 to $35*
354 EARTH MOVER - *$25 to $75*
378 BULLDOZER - *$7 to 25*
480 ROAD ROLLER - *$25 to $75*
481 ROAD SCRAPER - *$25 to $75*
488 POWER SHOVEL - *$35 to $85*
499 ROAD ROLLER - *$45 to $100*
503 ROAD GRADER
ROAD SCRAPER - *$35 to $85*
505 CAT LOADER
FRONT END LOADER - *$50 to $115*
514 CAT LOG TRUCK - *$65 to $150*
901 POWER SHOVEL - *$50 to $115*
903 BULLDOZER - *$35 to $85*
1503 ROAD GRADER (See 503)
1505 FRONT END LOADER (See 505)
1769 ARMY ENGINEERS BULLDOZER - *$20 to $60*
1772 BULLDOZER - *$25 to $65*
1901 POWER SHOVEL (See 901)
1903 BULLDOZER (See 903)

## MOTORCYCLES

10 MOTORCYCLE - *$15 to$ 65*
79 MOTORCYCLE - *$275 to $450*
84 MOTORCYCLE - *$275 to $600*

## FARM

25 TRACTOR - *$15 to $50*
309 TRACTOR - *$7 to $25*
328 TRACTOR - *$18 to $45*
337 TRACTOR - *$15 to $40*
451 TRACTOR - *$15 to $45*
456 TRACTOR - *$15 to $40*
472 TRACTOR - *(<1954) $30 to $85*
472 TRACTOR
HUBLEY TRACTOR - *(>1956) $15 to $50*
473 TRACTOR - *(<1952) $40 to $100*
473 TRACTOR
HUBLEY JR. TRACTOR - *(>1953) $15 to $50*
474 FARM TRACTOR AND WAGON. - *$30 to $60*
475 TRACTOR - *$25 to $75*
490 TRACTOR - *$25 to $85*
496 TRACTOR - *$25 to $75*
500 TRACTOR-LOADER - *$50 to $125*
501 TRACTOR LOADER - *$45 to $100*
502 TRACTOR WITH CULTIVATOR - *$65 to $150*
507 FORD TRACTOR - *$85 to $350*
508 FORD TRACTOR - *$115 to $265*
508 FORD 4000 TRACTOR - *$100 to $225*
509 FORD 6000 TRACTOR. - *$100 to $235*
525 TRACTOR - *$75 to $215*
757 FORD POST HOLE DIGGER - *$125 to $200*
758 FORD SCRAPER BLADE - *$135 to $215*
1472 TRACTOR (See 472)
1474 FARM TRACTOR AND WAGON (See 474)
1496 TRACTOR (See 496)
1501 TRACTOR LOADER (See 501)
1502 TRACTOR LOADER - *$35 to $85*
1504 TRACTOR WITH STAKE TRAILER - *$35 to $85*
1506 TRACTOR - *$65 to $135*
1508 FORD 4000 TRACTOR (See 508)
1509 FORD 6000 TRACTOR (See 509)
1520 TRACTOR - *$25 to $65*

## AIRCRAFT

311 AIRPLANE - *$10 to $35*
326 ATTACK BOMBER
AIRPLANE (2 ENGINE) - *$25 to $85*
338 HELICOPTER - *$10 to $30*
340 BLIMP - *$10 to $30*
430 AIRPLANE JET - *$20 to $50*
441 U.S. ARMY PLANE - *$20 to $65*
455 U.S. ARMY PLANE - *$45 to $115*
467 NAVY PLANE
NAVY FIGHTER - *$30 to $85*
483 HELICOPTER - *$35 to $115*
495 NAVY FIGHTER BOMBER - *$50 to $125*
690 BATTERY POWERED FIGHTER BOMBER PLANE - *$30 to $85*
751 JET PLANE - *$35 to $100*
761 P-40 FIGHTER PLANE
P-40 PLANE
P-40 FIGHTER PLANE - *$25 to $75*
881 P-38 - *$100 to $235*
1467 NAVY FIGHTER (See 467)
1483 HELICOPTER (See 483)
1495 NAVY FIGHTER BOMBER (See 495)
1761 P-40 PLANE (See 761)
1881 P-38 (See 881)

## SETS

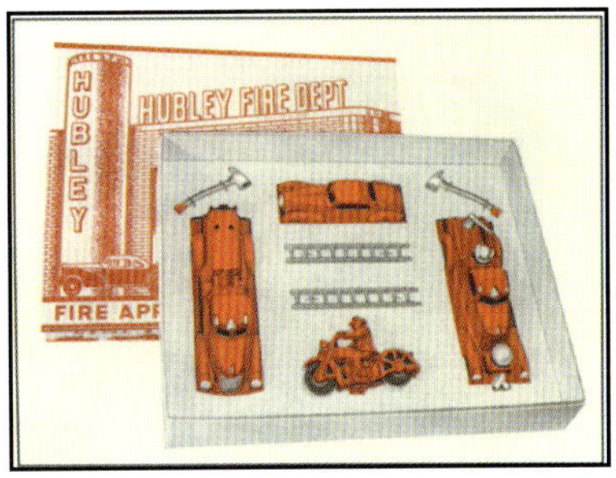


3 FIRE DEPARTMENT SET - *$75 to $285*
4 FARM SET
FARM SET (PLASTIC) - *$50 to $140*
5 FARM SET (METAL) - *$60 to $145*
6 FARM SET (METAL)
FARM SET - *$65 to $140*
7 FARM SET - *$40 to $95*
8 FARM SET - *$75 to $135*
10 TAXI CAB SET - *$300 to $700*
10 ASSORTMENT (METAL) - *$115 to $335*
11 ASSORTMENT (METAL) - *$160 to $440*
12 BOXED ASSORTMENT (METAL) - *$160 to $440*
14 FARMER BROWN'S BARNYARD SET - *$85 to $165*
15 MIDGET RACER SET - *$150 to $475*
15 DEWLINE DEFENSE SET - *$60 to $160*
16 FIGHTER PILOT SET - *$95 to $235*
19 FARM SET - *$100 to $250*
20 MIDGET RACER SET - *$200 to $725*
25 BIG 3 ASSORTMENT - *$210 to $550*

25 ASSORTMENT (PLASTIC) - *$110 to $380*

30 FIRE DEPARTMENT - *(1948) $400 to $1000*

FIRE DEPARTMENT - *(>1948) $235 to $635*

31 FARM SET - *(<1962) $175 to $400*

31 FARM SET - *(1962) $85 to $215*

35 FIRE DEPARTMENT - *$160 to $425*

40 TRUCK ASSORTMENT - *$225 to $600*

40 ASSORTMENT (METAL) - *$200 to $565*

41 FARM TRUCK COMBINATION - *$295 to $600*

42 AUTOMOTIVE SET - *$275 to $625*

43 MIGHTY-METAL ASSORTMENT - *$235 to $600*

45 ASSORTMENT (METAL) - *$240 to $585*

46 ASSORTMENT (METAL) - *$235 to $585*

48 CONSTRUCTION SET - *$125 to $350*

49 AIRPORT SET - *$275 to $825*

50 FARM SET - *(<1951) $125 to $285*

FARM SET - *(>1950) $115 to $270*

50 FARM SET (METAL) - *$115 to $275*

52 AIRCRAFT CARRIER SET - *$225 to $775*

53 FIGHTER-BOMBER SQUADRON (METAL) - *$215 to $535*

54 AIR RACE SET - *$265 to $675*

55 HIGHWAY SET - *$80 to $225*

55 ASSORTMENT (METAL) - *$265 to $660*

56 ARMY-AIR COMBAT SET - *$265 to $700*

57 FARM SET - *(<1962) $240 to $825*

FARM SET - *(>1961) $285 to $750*

60 ROAD BUILDING SET

ROAD BUILDING SET (PLASTIC)

ROAD BUILDING SET - *$85 to $250*

60 CONSTRUCTION SET - *$165 to $300*

65 LIFT THE HOOD TOY SET - *$125 to $295*

65 BOXED ASSORTMENT - *$95 to $285*

65 ASSORTMENT - *$100 to $225*

66 AIR-SEA RESCUE SET - *$100 to $265*

68 FARM SET - *$365 to $925*

69 ROAD BUILDING SET - *$225 to $550*

70 ASSORTMENT (PLASTIC) - *$335 to $800*

71 ARMY ENGINEERS SET - *$375 to $900*

75 ROAD BUILDING SET (METAL) - *$400 to $875*

76 ROAD BUILDING SET (METAL) - *$500 to $1165*

80 NAVY AIRFIELD SET - *$350 to $975*

85 DELUXE ASSORTMENT (METAL) - *$250 to $675*

86 DELUXE ASSORTMENT (METAL) - *$500 to $1300*

87 SUPER HIGHWAY TRUCK FLEET (METAL) - *$500 to $1350*

90 FARM SET (METAL)

LARGE FARM SET - *$225 to $625*

91 LARGE FARM SET - *$300 to $750*

92 FIRE DEPARTMENT SET - *$1000 to $2300*

325 FIRE DEPARTMENT - *$145 to $385*

326 TAXI CAB SET - *$150 to $550*

327 AUTO SET - *$80 to $235*

721 GARAGE REPAIRMAN

GARAGE SET - *$185*

722 WHERE'S THE FIRE?

FIRE ENGINE SET - *$150*

723 GAS'ER UP

GAS STATION SET - *$165*

762 FARM SET - *$150*

763 HIGHWAY AND SKYWAY - *$165*

764 SPEEDERS BEWARE!

TRAFFIC CONTROL SET - *$185*

765 CONTINENTAL AND RACER SET - *$165*

766 TRAIN SET - *$115*

767 CUB AND RACER SET - *$185*

1014 AIRPORT SET - *$200 to $500*

1017 FARM SET - *$100 to $250*

1044 TRANSPORTATION SET - *$150 to $450*

1047 BUILDERS SET - *$135 to $435*

1048 CONSTRUCTION SET (See 48)

1049 RANCHER SET - *$95 to $235*

1055 BOMBER AND FIGHTER ESCORT - *$150 to $425*

1057 FARM SET (See 57, >1960)

1069 ROAD BUILDING SET (See 69)

1091 LARGE FARM SET (See 91)

DELUXE FARM SET (See 91)

1754 TRAFFIC SET - *$165*

1755 FIRE FIGHTING SET - *$150*

1756 AIRPORT SET- *$165*

1757 ROAD SERVICE SET - *$150*

1758 MIDGET RACER SET - *$150*

1759 GAS STATION SET - *$165*

1760 FARM SET - *$85*

1762 FARM SET (See 762)

1763 HIGHWAY AND SKYWAY (See 763)

1765 CONTINENTAL AND RACER SET (See 765)

1766 TRAIN SET (See 766)

1767 AIR AND TRACK SET (See 767)

1768 JUNGLE PATROL SET - *$200*

1770 U.S. AIR PATROL

U.S. AIR PATROL SET - *$200*

1771 ARMY COMMAND SET - *$150*

1917 FARM SET (See 17)

1091 LARGE FARM SET (See 91)

## KITS

150K TRIUMPH TR-3 CONVERTIBLE - *$100*

151K TRIUMPH TR-3 GRAND TOURING - *$100*

152K MERCEDES-BENZ 300SL CONVERTIBLE - *$50*

153K MERCEDES-BENZ 300SL HARDTOP- *$50*

157K ROLLS-ROYCE SILVER CLOUD SEDAN - *$75*

158K METROPOLITAN CONVERTIBLE - *$150*

159K RENAULT DAUPHINE - *$60*

163K 1962 FORD COUNTRY SEDAN - *$85*

850K MODEL A ROADSTER (Same as 854K)

FORD ROADSTER MODEL A - *$50*

853K 1932 FORD CUSTOM ROADSTER - *$235*

854K MODEL A FORD ROADSTER (Same as 850K) - *$50*

855K MODEL A PICK-UP TRUCK - *$50*

856K MODEL A PHAETON

FORD PHAETON MODEL A - *$50*

857K MODEL A TOWN SEDAN

FORD TOWN SEDAN MODEL A - *$50*

858K MODEL A STATION WAGON - *$60*

859K 1930 PACKARD SPORT PHAETON

PACKARD SPORT PHAETON - *$85*

60K 1930 PACKARD ROADSTER

PACKARD ROADSTER - *$85*

61K MODEL A FORD COUPE

FORD COUPE MODEL A - *$50*

62K 1932 CHEVY ROADSTER

CHEVY ROADSTER

932 CHEVROLET ROADSTER - *$80*

501 ALTERED FIAT COUPE BODY - *$20*

502 COMPETITION COUPE BODY - *$20*

503 "INSTANT TORQUE" MOTORIZED CHASSIS - *$50*

504 ALTERED FIAT COUPE KIT - *$165*

505 COMPETITION COUPE KIT - *$165*

506 DRAGSTER RACE SET- *$800*

507 DRAGSTER RACE SET - *$800*

850 MODEL A FORD ROADSTER (See 850K)

855 FORD PICK-UP MODEL A (See 855K)

856 MODEL A PHAETON (See 856K)

857 MODEL A TOWN SEDAN (See 857K)

858 MODEL A STATION WAGON (See 858K)

859 PACKARD SPORT PHAETON (See 859K)

860 PACKARD ROADSTER (See 860K)

861 MODEL A FORD COUPE (See 861K)

862 CHEVY ROADSTER (See 862K)

863 PACKARD DIETRICH 1930 - *$85*

864 SJ DUESENBERG PHAETON - *$95*

865 1932 CHEVROLET PHAETON - *$75*

866 FORD VICTORIA MODEL A - *$65*

868 SJ DUESENBERG TOWN CAR - *$95*

869 1932 CHEVROLET COUPE - *$75*

## GUNS & WESTERN

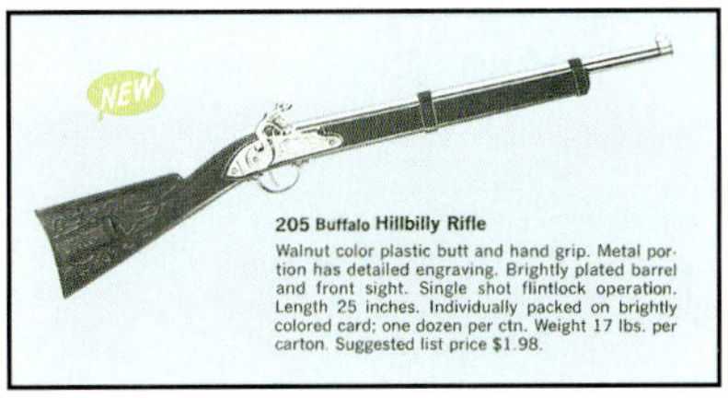


110 SPUR SET - *$45 to $85*

177 CARTRIDGE CLIP - *$35*

178 CLIP - *$85*

188 PADLOCK PISTOL - *$65 to $115*

189 PADLOCK PISTOL AND KEY RING - *$85 to $150*

199 LAW ENFORCEMENT SET - *$185*

200 FRONTIER RIFLE - *$75 to $225*

202 RING RIFLE - *$65 to $200*

203 FLIP SPECIAL RIFLE - THE RIFLEMAN - *$165 to $425*

205 BUFFALO HILLBILLY RIFLE - *$65 to $200*

207 RED FOX MISSILE - *$95*

209 SHARPSHOOTER - *$55 to $235*

210 DICK - *$15 to $30*

211 PET - *$10 to $25*

216 CHIEF - *$25 to $55*

218 RODEO - *$15 to $40*

231 COWPOKE - *$20 to $50*

234 HAWK- *$35 to $70*

233 DERRINGER - *$35 to $70*

236 REMINGTON .44 MINIATURE - *$15 to $45*

238 FRONTIER MINIATURE - *$10 to $35*

239 DART-A-MATIC BLOW GUN - *$30*

240 TROOPER - *$25 to $55*

241 COLT DETECTIVE SPECIAL - *$15 to $45*

242 COLT AUTOMATIC - *$15 to $45*

243 TINY TOMMY SUB-MACHINE GUN

TINY TOMMY- *$8 to $35*

246 WESTERN - *$40 to $85*

248 MARSHALL - *$35 to $85*

250 TEXAN, JR. - *$45 to $95*

255 SNIPER - *$40 to $95*

256 REMINGTON .36 - *$65 to $185*

261 RIC-O-SHAY JR. - *$65 to $135*

262 LONG BARREL REMINGTON - *$75 to $175*

271 SUPER POP RIFLE - *$30 to $85*

278 COLT .38 SIX SHOOTER - *$85 to $265*

279 RIC-O-SHAY - *$65 to $185*

281 COLT .45

COLT .45 SIX SHOOTER - *$75 to $225*

652 AUTOGRAPH HAT - *$15 to $50*

980 OLD PAL WALKING HOBBY HORSE - *$65 to $215*

2033 M-1 MILITARY CARBINE - *$75 to $175*

2043 WESTERN SADDLE GUN - *$75 to $195*

2063 TOMMY GUN - *$50 to $150*

2080 WESTERN SCOUT RIFLE - *$85 to $250*

2090 SHARPSHOOTER (See 209)

2102 DICK (See 210)

2103 DICK (See 210)

2110 PET (See 211)

2130 M-1 CARBINE WITH GRENADE LAUNCHER - *$85 to $215*

2153 LI'L COWPOKE - *$15 to $40*

2203 FRONTIER - *$20 to $65*

2312 COWPOKE (See 231)

2313 COWPOKE (See 231)

2343 HAWK (See 234)

2402 TROOPER (See 240)

2403 TROOPER (See 240)

2431 TINY TOMMY GUN - *$15 to $60*

2439 JUNGLE FIGHTER SET - *$100*

2482 MARSHALL (See 248)

2502 TEXAN, JR. (See 250)

2503 TEXAN, JR. (See 250)

2511 .45 AUTOMATIC - *$40 to $85*

2503 TEXAN, JR. (See 250) - *$25 to $55*

2553 SNIPER (See 255)

2700 SADDLE GUN SET - *$300*

2710 FIGHTING MARINE SET - *$325*

2720 INFANTRY RAIDER SET - *$375*

2740 JUNIOR SADDLE SET - *$335*

2861 ARMY (See 210)

2871 DETECTIVE (See 240)

2881 WESTERN (See 248S)

2891 JUNGLE FIGHTER (See 243)

5081 COLT .45 SET - *$375*

5132 HOLSTER SET - SINGLE - *$200*

5210 HOLSTER SET - *$90*

5214 HOLSTER SET - *$90*

5216 MP ADVENTURE SET - *$95*

5217 DETECTIVE SPECIAL ADVENTURE SET - *$90*

5218 MARINE CORPS ADVENTURE SET - *$95*

5219 WESTERN ADVENTURE SET - *$90*

5220 HOLSTER SET - SINGLE - *$165*

5221 HOLSTER SET - SINGLE - *$165*

5222 HOLSTER SET - SINGLE - *$165*

5223 HOLSTER SET - SINGLE - *$175*

5229 ADVENTURE SET - SINGLE - *$125*

5230 HOLSTER SET - SINGLE - *$200*

5231 HOLSTER SET - SINGLE - *$235*
5425 JUNGLE FIGHTER SET - *$225*
5310 HOLSTER SET - *$90*
5317 POLICE SPECIAL SET (See 5217)
5318 MARINE CORPS SET (See 5218)
5319 WESTERN SET (See 5219)
5321 HOLSTER SET - *$175*
5323 HOLSTER SET - *$175*
5331 HOLSTER SET - *$195*
5332 HOLSTER SET - *$195*
5411 HOLSTER SET - *$165*
5417 POLICE SPECIAL SET (See 5217)
5418 MARINE CORPS SET (See 5218)
5419 WESTERN SET - *$100*
5420 SINGLE HOLSTER SET - *$185*
5421 SINGLE HOLSTER SET - *$185*
5422 SINGLE HOLSTER SET - *$185*
5425 JUNGLE FIGHTER SET - *$200*
5431 SINGLE HOLSTER SET - *$200*
5432 SINGLE HOLSTER SET - *$235*
5711 DY-DE-MITE HOLSTER - *$65*
5729 DY-DE-MITE SET - *$135*
5981 SINGLE HOLSTER SET - COLT .45 - *$365*
6055 DOUBLE HOLSTER SET - *$185*
6070 WYATT EARP BUNTLINE SET - *$625*
6087 DOUBLE HOLSTER SET - *$585*
6113 HOLSTER SET - DOUBLE - *$200*
6150 HOLSTER SET - DOUBLE - *$325*
6210 HOLSTER SET - *$150*
6211 HOLSTER SET - *$150*
6220 HOLSTER SET - DOUBLE - *$185*
6221 HOLSTER SET - DOUBLE - *$165*
6223 HOLSTER SET - DOUBLE - *$175*
6224 HOLSTER SET - DOUBLE - *$165*
6230 HOLSTER SET - DOUBLE - *$225*
6231 HOLSTER SET - DOUBLE - *$225*
6232 HOLSTER SET - DOUBLE - *$225*
6233 HOLSTER SET - DOUBLE - *$235*
6236 HOLSTER SET - DOUBLE (See 6232)
6239 HOLSTER SET - DOUBLE (See 6230)
6240 HOLSTER SET - DOUBLE - *$295*
6241 HOLSTER SET - DOUBLE - *$295*
6250 HOLSTER SET - DOUBLE - *$325*
6251 HOLSTER SET - DOUBLE - *$335*
6260 HOLSTER SET - DOUBLE - *$365*
6310 SET (See 6210)
6320 SET - *$185*
6321 SET - *$175*
6322 SET - ROY ROGERS - *$235*
6323 SET - *$200*
6324 SET - *$185*
6331 SET - *$215*
6332 SET - *$215*
6333 SET - *$215*
6334 SET- ROY ROGERS - *$295*
6340 SET - *$300*
6342 SET - *$300*
6351 SET - *$335*
6352 SET - ROY ROGERS - *$350*
6354 SET - *$335*
6361 SET - *$385*
6410 SET - *$165*
6420 SET - *$200*
6421 DOUBLE HOLSTER AND BELT SET - *$175*
6422 DOUBLE HOLSTER SET - *$185*
6423 DOUBLE HOLSTER SET - *$185*
6424 DOUBLE HOLSTER SET - *$185*
6425 DOUBLE HOLSTER SET - *$185*
6430 DOUBLE HOLSTER SET - *$250*
6431 DOUBLE HOLSTER SET - *$235*
6432 DOUBLE HOLSTER SET - *$225*
6440 DOUBLE HOLSTER SET - *$250*
6441 DOUBLE HOLSTER SET - *$300*
6442 DOUBLE HOLSTER SET - *$300*
6450 DOUBLE HOLSTER SET - *$335*
6451 DOUBLE HOLSTER SET - *$335*
6452 DOUBLE HOLSTER SET - *$335*
6980 DOUBLE HOLSTER SET - *$235*

## MISCELLANEOUS

100 SCOTTY- *$15 to $65*
105 MARY'S LAMB - *$15 to $65*
110 PANDA - *$20 to $70*
115 ELEPHANT - *$20 to $70*
120 DUCKY-WUCKY - *$30 to $85*
125 ALPHABET LETTERS - *$25*
339 DUCK - *$10 to $25*
493 SCHOOL BUS - *$30 to $85*
601 FIREBOAT - *$10 to $25*
650 COLOR CAMERA - *$65*
675 HOUSEBOAT - *$12 to $35*
818 MAMMY BANK - *$65 to $135*
820 KITTY BANK - *$35 to $85*
818 FIDO BANK - *$35 to $85*
944 RAZZ-MA-TAZZ - *$45 to $125*
965 TIC TOY CLOCK - *$85*
995 GOLFERINO - *$35 to $115*
996 JUNGLE HUNT - *$35 to $125*
1001 LOCOMOTIVE - *$25*
1002 AMERICAN EAGLE - *$25*
1003 SAILING SHIP - *$25*
1004 FLORAL ARRANGEMENT - *$25*
1005 ANTIQUE FIRE ENGINE - *$25*
1006 HORSE AND CARRIAGE - *$25*
1820 SCHOOL BUS (See 493)
9950 GOLERINO (See 995)